DAYTRIPS
—FROM—
NEW YORK

—100—

One Day Adventures From the Metropolitan Area

Edited by
Earl Steinbicker

I love David and we're gonna do lots of fun things together. love, Heather

HASTINGS HOUSE
MAMARONECK, NEW YORK

We are always grateful for comments from readers, which are extremely useful in preparing future editions of this or other books in the series. Please write directly to the editor, Earl Steinbicker, % Hastings House, 141 Halstead Avenue, Mamaroneck, NY 10543; or FAX (914) 835-1037. Thank you.

Contents

Introduction

Some twenty-odd years ago, a fresh new kind of guidebook for the New York Metropolitan Area made its first appearance. Lida Newberry's *One-Day Adventures by Car*, with its unique format that organized myriad attractions into easy daytrips, soon became a classic and was updated several times during the author's lifetime and later by Joy Johannessen.

Now, with changing times and conditions but always with the same spirit of adventure and discovery, that book has been born again as a part of the growing "Daytrip" series of guides published by Hastings House. Specially-drawn maps have been added along with photos, a few destinations replaced with more relevant ones, and the practical information of course brought up to date.

The sites covered lie mainly within a 100-mile radius of New York City, though there are some extended trips of up to 150 miles away. The territory is divided into seven adjoining areas beginning south along the Atlantic Coast and forming an arc encompassing much of New Jersey, parts of eastern Pennsylvania, the Catskills and Hudson River Valley of New York State, western Connecticut, a sliver of Massachusetts, and, finally, virtually all of Long Island.

All of the trips begin with a list of highlights and an approximate distance measured from central Manhattan, followed by a "For the Driver" section with detailed driving instructions. When appropriate, a "Public Transportation" section appears after this. Most of the trips include several attractions and list each separately, with information on opening times, fees, and facilities in italics, followed by a full description of the site. A few of the longer trips are arranged as pleasure drives, with various points of interest along the way highlighted in **bold type** along with capsule descriptions incorporated into the driving instructions.

CHOOSING DESTINATIONS:

With a hundred trips to choose from, and usually several attractions for each trip, deciding which are the most enjoyable for you and yours might be problematic. You could, of course, read through the whole book and mark the most appealing spots, but there's an easier way to at least start. Just turn to the index beginning on page 316 and scan it, looking out for the special-interest categories set in **BOLD FACE** type. These will immediately lead you to choices under such headings as Art Museums, Restored Historic Villages, Revolutionary War Sites, Amusement Parks, Children's Activities, Railfan Excursions, and many others.

The elements of one trip can often be combined with another to create a custom itinerary, using the book maps as a rough guide and a good road map for the final routing.

Some of the trips, listed in the index as **SCENIC DRIVES.** are just that—they are primarily designed for the pure pleasure of driving, with just enough attractions along the way to keep things lively. These are especially enjoyable if you are blessed with a car that's fun to drive, and doubly so during the fall foliage season.

In a few cases, there are more attractions than can be appreciated during a single day, so you'll have to pick and choose—being careful not to overdo it. There will always be another day.

GETTING THERE:

The driving directions given in the "For the Driver" section of each trip assume that you're leaving from New York City. Chances are, however, that you live elsewhere in the tri-state metropolitan area, so you'll need to modify the route a bit. These directions become more specific as you get closer to the destination, and are then valid regardless of the starting point.

The **maps** scattered throughout the book show you approximately where the sites are, and which main roads lead to them. You'll still need a good, up-to-date road map. An excellent choice for a single-sheet map that covers nearly all (but not the most distant) of the destinations is the *New York 75-Mile-Radius Map* published by Hagstrom. Rand McNally's spiral-bound *Northeastern U.S. Road Atlas* is superb and easy to use, although a bit expensive. The free maps distributed by state tourist offices vary greatly in quality, so if the one they give you isn't clear enough, head for your bookstore and look over their selection.

All **distances** given in this book are measured from Columbus Circle (near the center of Manhattan), if for no other reason than that they had to be measured from *somewhere*. You probably don't live there, so you'll have to make a simple adjustment.

PUBLIC TRANSPORTATION:

For those who *do* live in the center of Manhattan and may not have a car, a section on public transportation has been added for those specific trips where the sites can *easily* be reached by *convenient* trains or buses without too much walking. These are: A-6 (Point Pleasant Beach, NJ), A-9 (Atlantic City), A-10 (New Brunswick), A-11 (Princeton), A-12 (Flemington, NJ), A-18 (Philadelphia), B-2 (Newark), B-13 (Paterson), D-2 (Tarrytown NY), D-3 (White Plains), E-9 (Hartford, CT), F-6 (Norwalk), and F-10 (New Haven). A true public transit fanatic will find ways of getting *anywhere* by train or bus, of course, but for most people the best solution is to rent a car.

HOURS, FEES, AND FACILITIES:

The italicized material following the name, address, and telephone number of each site gives information on opening dates, hours, admission fees (including senior citizens' and children's rates), facilities, and other useful information such as special events, pet policies, wheelchair access, etc. All of this is subject to change without notice and will undoubtedly do so during the life of this edition. If the reason for taking any of the trips is to see a specific site, be sure to call ahead to verify this information. And also be sure to take enough money with you to allow for increasing prices.

WHEN TO GO:

Many of the sites are open only during certain seasons, or have reduced opening times during their off-season, while museums and some other attractions are usually closed at least one day a week. This information is noted in the italicized heading for each site description, but it's still wise to call ahead. When making any trip into the great outdoors, be sure to dress appropriately and be prepared for changing weather conditions. In some cases you should bring along some insect repellent and/or sun block lotion. Comfortable walking shoes always make a trip more enjoyable.

HANDICAPPED TRAVELERS:

A special effort has been made to include information on wheelchair facilities and other features designed to increase a site's accessibility to all visitors. This information appears at the end of the italicized material for each entry.

A site described as "fully wheelchair-accessible" has reserved or unproblematic parking, at least one wide entrance, ramps and/or elevators, and specially equipped restrooms; "wheelchair-accessible" means that the site has wide doors and ramps designed for wheelchairs or that it is naturally barrier-free; "manageable for wheelchairs" means that hills, rough spots, low steps, or other impediments are negotiable. If a site "will accommodate wheelchairs," it has no special facilities and is difficult or impossible to manage unaided, but the staff will assist you and show you as much of the site as possible; in these cases it is advisable to call in advance.

GROUP TRAVEL:

If you're planning a group outing, *always* call ahead. Most sites require advance reservations and offer special discounts for groups, often at a substantial savings over the regular admission fee. Some sites will open specially or remain open beyond their scheduled hours to accommodate groups; some have tours, demonstrations, lectures, film showings, etc., available only to groups; and some have facilities for rental to groups.

ADDITIONAL INFORMATION:

The addresses and phone numbers of local and regional tourist offices are given in the text whenever appropriate. These are usually your best source for specific information and current brochures. On a wider scale, state tourist offices offer free "vacation planning kits," maps, and brochures that you might find useful. You can contact them at:

Connecticut Division of Tourism
865 Brook St., Rocky Hill CT 06067-3405
Phone 800-CT-BOUND *or* 203-258-4289

Massachusetts Division of Tourism
100 Cambridge St., Boston MA 02202
Phone 800-632-8038 *or* 617-727-3201

New Jersey Division of Travel & Tourism
CN 826, Trenton NJ 08625
Phone 800-JERSEY-7 *or* 609-292-2470

New York State Division of Tourism
One Commerce Plaza, Albany NY 12245
Phone 800-CALL-NYS *or* 518-474-4116

Pennsylvania Bureau of Travel Marketing
453 Forum Bldg., Harrisburg PA 17120
Phone 800-VISIT-PA *or* 717-787-5453

Area A

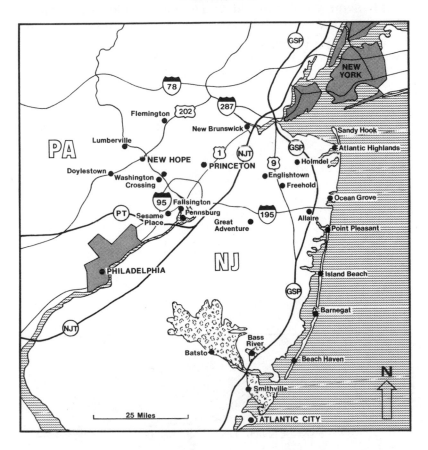

NEW JERSEY SHORELINE and COLONIAL TRAILS

These first trips unlock a treasure chest that lies close to New York City in New Jersey. Nature has been lavish with this shoreline, providing over 120 miles of white ocean sand, rolling breakers, and fresh unpolluted air. Sandy Hook, Long Beach Island, and Atlantic City are along the route. Seaside amusement parks, marine museums, wildlife refuges, and pine barrens beckon. Turning inland, you follow historic trails that lead to Revolutionary battlefields and white mansions preserved from Colonial days. Eventually, you can cross the Delaware River into beautiful Bucks County in southeastern Pennsylvania, and then continue on to the heart of historic Philadelphia.

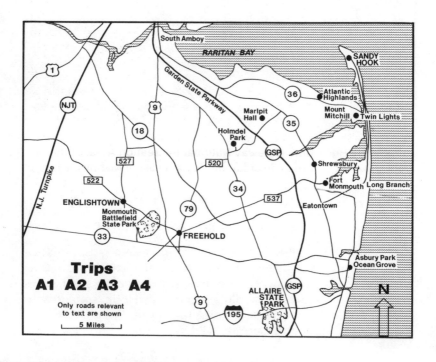

Trip A-1
Sandy Beach and Highlands
at New York's Doorstep

- MOUNT MITCHILL
- TWIN LIGHTS HISTORIC SITE
- SANDY HOOK

DISTANCE: The farthest point, Sandy Hook, is about 50 miles from Columbus Circle.

FOR THE DRIVER: Take the **Garden State Parkway** south to Exit 117 and pick up **NJ-36** southeast through Keansburg, passing signs for **Keansburg Amusement Park** (908-495-1400), a place for family fun. A few miles later, exit at the sign to Atlantic Highlands Business District. At Mount Ave. (Borough Hall and police station on corner) turn right and go uphill to Prospect Ave. and the **Atlantic Highlands Historical Society Museum,** on right. To reach Mount Mitchill County Park, go back down hill to the road you came into town on and continue toward the municipal harbor. Just before the harbor, turn right on Ocean Blvd. and go about 1½ miles to the top of **Mount Mitchill** and park.

Continue on Ocean Blvd. and rejoin NJ-36 southeast to Highlands. Just before Highlands Bridge, turn right on Portland Rd. and take an immediate right onto Highland Ave. Proceed uphill to **Twin Lights** entrance, on left. Access road is steep and narrow, so be careful.

Go back to NJ-36, turn right, cross Highlands Bridge, and turn left into **Sandy Hook Unit, Gateway National Recreation Area.** At the entrance to Sandy Hook, you are about 5 miles east of Marlpit Hall, one of the sites on Trip A-3.

MOUNT MITCHILL, Atlantic Highlands, NJ. The highest point along the Atlantic Coast from Maine to Florida (263 feet) offers views of distant New York, Sandy Hook, and the Atlantic Highlands Municipal Harbor. Mount Mitchill County Park is a nice place to stop and picnic while enjoying the sights. The **Atlantic Highlands Historical Society,** 27 Prospect Ave., Atlantic Highlands, NJ 07716 (908-291-1861), maintains a museum and library *(open Sundays 1–4 from Memorial Day to Labor Day, free, wheelchair-accessible)* in a restored 20-room Victorian mansion on the slope of Mount Mitchill.

TWIN LIGHTS STATE HISTORIC SITE, Lighthouse Rd., Highlands, NJ 07732 (908-872-1814). *Grounds open daily all year 9–dusk; museum open Wed.–Sun. 10–5; closed Thanksgiving, Christmas, New Year's. Dona-tion. Self-guided tour, picnic facilities. Leashed pets only. Partially wheelchair-accessible.*

Twin Lights, on the Navesink Highlands, has been the site of a lighthouse since 1756. The present structure was built in 1862 and be-came America's first electrically powered lighthouse in 1898. The next year Guglielmo Marconi conducted the first practical demonstration of wireless telegraphy by transmitting the America's Cup race results from Twin Lights to the *New York Herald* newspaper, some 15 miles away. The museum chronicles these and other significant chapters in the history of American seafaring; in addition to a working replica of Marconi's wireless, there are specimens of Jersey-built boats, a light-house lens exhibit, and the one remaining station of the old U.S. Life Saving Service, which merged with the Revenue Cutter Service in 1915 to become the U.S. Coast Guard. From the twin towers of the light-house you can enjoy a panoramic view of the Atlantic and New York Harbor.

SANDY HOOK UNIT, Gateway National Recreation Area, P.O. Box 530, Highlands, NJ 07732 (908-872-0155). *Grounds open daily all year 7–dusk; visitor center daily 8:30–5, reduced hours in winter. Admission: Me-morial Day to Labor Day $4 per car on weekdays, $5 on weekends and holidays, free other times of year. Ranger-led and self-guided tours; swimming during season in lifeguard areas only; picnicking; fishing by permit; hiking and nature trails; refreshments; restrooms. Leashed pets in some areas. Partially wheelchair-accessible.*

Gateway National Recreation Area was created by Congress in 1972 as one of the nation's first major urban park areas. It opened in 1974 under the management of the National Park Service, which has spear-headed a vigorous effort to preserve the area and reverse the environ-mental degradation that has taken place over the centuries since the Algonquin Indians roamed these shores. It consist of four units: the Jamaica Bay, Breezy Point, and Staten Island units in New York, and Sandy Hook in New Jersey. Together they serve as a refuge in the heart of the megalopolis for many species of flora and fauna, includ-ing *Homo sapiens.*

The Sandy Hook Unit extends over an arm of land that has had strategic importance in the defense of New York Harbor since Colo-nial times. At the Spermaceti Cove Visitor Center there are exhibits describing the natural and cultural history of Sandy Hook, aquariums with local marine life, and a 14-minute slide program shown on re-quest. From the Sandy Hook Museum in Fort Hancock's guardhouse and jail you can take guided tours through the fort and the great gun emplacements. You can also visit the Sandy Hook Proving Ground, where U.S. Army weapons were tested from 1876 to 1920. Sandy Hook boasts the oldest operating lighthouse (1764) in the U.S., and the peninsula's fragile sand dunes shelter a great variety of plant and animal life. The famed holly forest is a perennial attraction; over 300 species of birds have been sighted in the area, including the endangered osprey.

Sandy Hook is still under development, and the National Park Service is continually experimenting with new programs. It is wise to check hours and scheduling in advance if you are interested in a particular attraction or activity. Millions of people visit the park each year; you may want to plan your trip for spring, fall, or winter, when it is less crowded.

Trip A-2
To a Restored Village and a Religious Retreat

- **ALLAIRE STATE PARK**
- **OCEAN GROVE**

DISTANCE: Allaire is about 65 miles from Columbus Circle; from Allaire to Ocean Grove about 10 miles.

FOR THE DRIVER: Take the **Garden State Parkway** south to Exit 98 and pick up **I-195** west toward Trenton, or take the **New Jersey Turnpike** south to Exit 7A and pick up **I-195** east. From I-195 take Exit 31B, Allaire State Park, making a right at the first traffic light onto **Rte. 524,** then follow signs into park.

Return to the **Garden State Parkway** and go north to Exit 100. Pick up **NJ-33** east and take it about 4 miles to Ocean Grove.

ALLAIRE STATE PARK, P.O. Box 220, Farmingdale, NJ 07727 (908-938-2371). *Open daily all year, late Oct. to mid-March 8–4:30, mid-March to Memorial Day 8–6, Memorial Day to 1st week of Sept. 8–8, 2nd week of Sept. to last week of Oct. 8–6. Parking fee (Memorial Day to Labor Day only): cars $4 weekdays, $5 weekends and holidays; motor-*

cycles $2. Picnic facilities, boating, nature center, fishing, riding and hiking trails, campsites, snack bar with hot meals. Leashed pets only in park, no pets in campsites. Most facilities not wheelchair-accessible.

In 1941 the family of newspaperman Arthur Brisbane deeded 1,200 acres of land to the people of New Jersey for use as a "historical center and forest park reservation." Since then the park has grown to cover some 3,000 acres of the New Jersey coastal plain. Its attractions include:

Historic Allaire Village, Allaire, NJ 07727 (908-938-2253). *Buildings open Wed. through Sun.; May through Labor Day, weekends in Sept. and Oct., call for other times. Special events throughout the year. Building program ticket $2 adults, $1 children 5 through 17. Buildings not wheelchair-accessible.* In the late 1700s Allaire was the site of a furnace and forge where iron was smelted from the "bog ore" produced by decaying vegetation. In 1822 James P. Allaire purchased the ironworks to supply his foundry in New York City and built a bustling industrial community of over 400 people. With the discovery of higher-grade Pennsylvania ore and the increasing use of coal, Allaire declined, and the ironworks shut down in 1848. Today, the village has been beautifully restored; and you can visit a furnace, a carpenter's shop, a blacksmith's, a bakery, a general store, and other original buildings where staff dressed in the work clothes of the 1830s demonstrate the old trades. This is a fascinating experience for young and old alike.

Pine Creek Railroad, Allaire State Park (908-938-5524). *Operates daily in July and Aug.; weekends and holidays mid-Apr. through June and Sept. through mid-Oct. Fare $1.50 per person. Not wheelchair-accessible. All Aboard!* for a trip back in time on New Jersey's only live-steam narrow-guage railroad. You'll ride in antique cars pulled by a coal-burning locomotive of the kind that was used to push back the frontiers of the American West. Adjacent to the station is an open work area where many old locomotives and cars are being painstakingly restored by volunteers.

OCEAN GROVE. *Tourist season Memorial Day to weekend after Labor Day. Beach fees (per person): adults $4.50 weekdays, children under 12 free. Beach picnics (fires by permit), swimming, fishing, boardwalk activities. No pets on beaches. Boardwalks wheelchair-accessible. For further information contact the Ocean Grove Camp Meeting Association, 54 Pitman Ave., Ocean Grove, NJ 07756 (908-775-0035).*

This attractive small town, noted for its Victorian architecture, serves as a setting for religious and cultural programs, Bible meetings, evan-

The Pine Creek Railroad at Historic Allaire

gelical talks, recitals. A National and State Historic Site, it was founded in 1869 for Methodist camp meetings. The **Ocean Grove Auditorium,** built in 1894, seats 6,500 persons and is the focal point of the town. Preachers and evangelists use its big stage on Sundays, while famous entertainers and musicians perform on Saturday evenings. The **Centennial Cottage,** an authentic Ocean Grove seashore vacation home, has been completely restored to its 1870s appearance and is operated as a period museum. *(Corner of Central Ave. and McClintock St. Open July and Aug., daily except Sun., 10–noon and 2–4. Adults $1, children 25¢.)*

Trip A-3
To the Heart of
Historic Monmouth County

- MARLPIT HALL
- SHREWSBURY
- FORT MONMOUTH
- FREEHOLD
- HOLMDEL PARK and LONGSTREET FARM

DISTANCE: About 45 miles from Columbus Circle to the first stop, Marlpit Hall. From there, the loop to the last stop adds another 40 miles.

FOR THE DRIVER: Take the **Garden State Parkway** south to Exit 114, then go east (left) on Red Hill Rd. until it ends at Kings Hwy. Turn left and go about a mile to **Marlpit Hall,** on right.

From Marlpit Hall turn left and go east on Kings Hwy. to the junction with **NJ-35.** Turn right on 35 and go south about 5 miles to **Shrewsbury.** At Sycamore Ave., on the left, is the Old Christ Church. On right is the Allen House.

Continue south on NJ-35 briefly to the junction with **Rte. 537.** Turn left (east) to west gate of **Fort Monmouth.** Enter and go down Ave. of Memories about 2 miles to a sign for the Communications Museum.

Go back to the junction of NJ-35 and Rte. 537. Proceed west on 537 about 10 miles to **Freehold.** The road merges with **NJ-79** to become Main St. Continue on this to Court St. and turn right to the Monmouth County Historical Association at number 70 Court St., across from the Battle Monument.

Go back to Main St. and follow it west to the Covenhoven House at number 150, just before the junction with US-9.

From Covenhoven House, turn right on Main St. and go back into town to the junction with NJ-79. Follow 79 north about 6 miles to **Rte. 520** and turn right (east) to the junction with **NJ-34.** Turn left (north) on 34 and go about ½ mile to first right, Roberts Rd. Take this about 1½ miles, bearing left onto Longstreet Rd. and the entrance to **Holmdel Park** and Longstreet Farm.

Return to Roberts Rd. and turn left, then right onto Crawfords Corner Rd. At Red Hill Rd. turn left to Exit 114 of the Garden State Parkway.

You now turn inland to explore the natural, historical, and cultural attractions of nearby Monmouth County. For further information, contact the Monmouth County Department of Public Information and Tourism, 27 East Main St., Freehold, NJ 07728 (908-431-7476).

MARLPIT HALL, 137 Kings Highway, Middletown, NJ 07748 (908-462-1466). *Open Apr. through Oct.; Tues., Thurs., Sun. 1–4, and Sat. 10–4. Adults $2, seniors $1.50, children $1. First floor manageable for wheelchairs.*

Begun in 1685 by James Grover, Jr. as a one-room Dutch cottage, Marlpit was enlarged in the English style about 1740 by Tory merchant John Taylor. A rare example of its type, it is today maintained as a museum by the Monmouth County Historical Association. The period furnishings reflect its ownership from 1685 through 1820, with five rooms providing the time line.

SHREWSBURY has two Colonial structures of considerable historic interest, both of which can be visited.

Old Christ Church, 380 Sycamore Ave., Shrewsbury, NJ 07702 (908-741-2220). Built in 1769 to serve a congregation founded in 1702, this is the only church in the U.S. that retains its original gilt crown (signifying royal beginnings) atop its spire. Inside, there is a copy of the rare "Vinegar Bible," so-called for the misspellings it contains (vinegar instead of vineyard, etc.). You can see a portion of the communion service given to the congregation by Queen Anne in 1708, and the parish's royal charter of 1738. It is said that a member of this church also belonged to Captain Kidd's pirate crew.

Allen House, Sycamore Ave. at NJ-35, Shrewsbury, NJ 07702 (908-462-1466). *(Open Apr. through Dec.; Tues., Thurs., Sun. 1–4; Sat. 10–4. Adults $2, seniors $1.50, children $1).* Displaying both Dutch and English influences, this early-18th-century house was used as a tavern during the Revolutionary period. Now restored, it has two rooms furnished as a tavern of that time, and other rooms that are used for changing historical exhibitions and special programs.

FORT MONMOUTH, long associated with military communications, is open to the public who come to see the:

U.S. Army Communications-Electronics Museum, Kaplan Hall, Bldg. 275, Fort Monmouth, NJ 07703 (908-532-2445). *Open all year Mon.–Thurs., noon–4, closed federal holidays. Free. Wheelchair-accessible.*

Here you can learn what a big role communications play in military campaigns, an aspect of warfare rarely seen by the civilian. You'll view apparatus of all kinds, from the signal flags of the Civil War to the latest state-of-the-art electronics technology.

FREEHOLD, the seat of Monmouth County, was founded in 1715 and is close to the spot where George Washington and his army defeated the British under General Clinton at the Battle of Monmouth on June 28, 1778. Among the places of historic interest are:

Monmouth County Historical Association Museum and Library, 70 Court St., Freehold, NJ 07728 (908-462-1466). *Museum open all year Tues.–Sat. 10–4, Sun. 1–4; library open all year Wed.–Sat. 10–4. Adults $2, seniors $1.50, children $1. Difficult for wheelchairs.* Founded in 1898, the Historical Association is dedicated to preserving Monmouth County's heritage. Its headquarters, a beautiful three-story Georgian structure built in 1931, is the setting for one of the country's best regional museums. Fine examples of period furnishings and Americana are well displayed. The floor devoted to "attic artifacts" is especially popular with kids. The library is primarily for research and includes a genealogical and historical reference section. In addition to the museum, the association maintains four historic buildings in Monmouth County (Marlpit Hall, Covenhoven House, Allen House, Holmes-Hendrickson House).

Covenhoven House, 150 West Main St., Freehold, NJ 07728 (908-462-1466). *Open May through Oct.; Tues., Thurs., Sun. 1–4; Sat. 10–4. Adults $2, seniors $1.50, children $1. First floor wheelchair-accessible.* Maintained by the Monmouth County Historical Association, this Georgian house was built in the mid-18th century by William A. Covenhoven, a successful local farmer, and is furnished according to a 1790 inventory of his estate. In 1778, just before the Battle of Monmouth, the house served as headquarters for British General Sir Henry Clinton.

HOLMDEL PARK and LONGSTREET FARM, Longstreet Rd., Holmdel, NJ 07733 (park 908-946-2669, farm 908-946-3758). *Park open every day, 8–dusk, free. Pets must be on leashes. Farm open daily 10–4; from Memorial Day to Labor Day 10–5. Farmhouse open weekends and holidays Apr.–Nov., noon–4. No smoking on farm, do not feed or touch animals. Admission free.*

Holmdel Park, with its arboretum, hiking and fitness trails, picnic and play areas, ponds and streams, is an ideal place to end your day of exploring Monmouth County. Its star attraction, the **Longstreet Farm,** is worth the journey in itself. This authentic working farm has been restored to its 1890s condition and is manned by park employees and volunteers in period costume. You can enjoy a rare slice of our agricultural heritage as you visit the farmhouse of 1775, the many out-buildings, the crop fields, and of course the animals. Phone ahead for information about special activities that are held throughout the year. Another nearby feature, on Longstreet Road just north of the park entrance, is the **Holmes-Hendrickson House** of 1754. This Dutch-style house contains fine examples of mid-18th-century furnishings along with displays of home crafts and early farm life. *Open May through Oct.; Tues., Thurs., Sun. 1–4; Sat. 10–4. Nominal admission charge). (908-462-1466).*

Trip A-4
To the Great Flea Market

- ENGLISHTOWN AUCTION SALES

DISTANCE: About 45 miles from Columbus Circle.

FOR THE DRIVER: Take the **New Jersey Turnpike** south to Exit 9, New Brunswick, then **NJ-18** east about 4½ miles to **Rte. 527** (English-town-Old Bridge Rd.). Turn right and go south about 8 miles to Englishtown, following signs for the auction. *Or,* take the **Garden State Parkway** south to Exit 123, follow **US-9** south for 7 miles to Texas Rd., turn right and go 2½ miles to Englishtown-Old Bridge Rd. Turn left here and go about 3 miles to Englishtown.

Englishtown is only about 5 miles from **Freehold.** If your flea market tolerance doesn't extend to a full day, you can easily combine this trip with parts of Trip A-3 or visit **Raceway Park** (908-446-6331; taped message 908-446-6370), home of the National Hot Rod Association Summer Nationals, on Pension Rd. off Rte. 527 just north of the auction.

For a different route home and possibly an ocean dip after the dust of the battlefield, go south a few miles on Rte. 527 to the junction with NJ-33, then take 33 east about 20 miles past **Monmouth Battlefield State Park** to **Asbury Park.**

ENGLISHTOWN AUCTION SALES, 90 Wilson Ave., Englishtown, NJ 07726 (908-446-9644). *Open all year Sat. 7–5, Sun. 9–5; also open 9–5 Mon. of Memorial Day and Labor Day weekends, Fri. after Thanksgiving, Fri. before Christmas; if phoning, call Fri.–Mon. 9–4. Free entry. Wheelchair-accessible parking and restrooms.*

The mileage to Englishtown may look incongruous for a trip to a kind of glorified rummage sale, but not so to the avid hunter of bargains and unusual collectibles. To tens of thousands of these, coming from as far away as upper New England, the Midwest, and the Deep South, this 50-acre flea market with 700 vendors is a shopper's paradise. Described by the *New York Times* as "a glorious heap, with infinite possibilities," Englishtown Auction Sales was begun in 1929 by Steve and Katie Sobechko on land where the Battle of Monmouth once raged. It has survived two devastating fires and is still operated by the Sobechko family in the person of grandson Steve.

As you roam the streets and buildings, you can exchange your cash for evening dresses, army boots, cut-rate games, kitchen tables, ice cream molds, an elephant (so the story goes), and other treasures in untold categories. Concession stands dispense home-baked delicacies and foods of all kinds, and there are mountains of New Jersey produce. Arrive early to avoid parking problems and get a jump on the bargains.

Trip A-5
A Safari in the Pine Barrens

- **SIX FLAGS GREAT ADVENTURE**

DISTANCE: About 70 miles from Columbus Circle.

FOR THE DRIVER: Take the **New Jersey Turnpike** south to Exit 7A, then **I-195** east about 12 miles to Exit 16, Mount Holly-Freehold, and follow signs to Great Adventure, about 3 miles southwest on **Rte. 537.** *Or* take the **Garden State Parkway** south to Exit 98, pick up **I-195** west about 15 miles to Exit 16, and proceed as above.

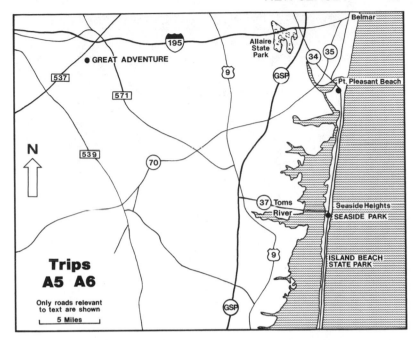

Belmar

195

Allaire
State
Park

GREAT ADVENTURE

537

9

34 35

GSP

Pt. Pleasant Beach

571

N

539

70

37 Toms
River

Seaside Heights
SEASIDE PARK

9

ISLAND BEACH
STATE PARK

**Trips
A5 A6**

Only roads relevant
to text are shown

5 Miles

GSP

SIX FLAGS GREAT ADVENTURE, P.O. Box 120, Jackson, NJ 08527 (908-928-1821). *Operating schedule varies each year; check in advance. Basic season is late Mar. through Oct.: Mar. to late Apr. and Labor Day to late Sept. 10–8 weekends, and occasional weekdays; May–June 10–6 or 8 most weeekdays, 10–10 weekends; July to late Aug. 10–10 weekdays, 10–10 or 11 weekends; late Aug. to Labor Day 10–8 weekdays, 10–10 weekends; Oct. 10–6 weekends and occasional weekdays. Safari open 9–5, weather permitting, on days when park is open. Combination ticket (theme park and safari) Adults $27.82, seniors 55+ $13.91, children 54" and under $18.19; theme park only costs $2.14 less; safari only $9.63; parking $5 per car. No pets in park; free kennels (owner provides food). No picnics in park, but picnic area adjoins parking lot; numerous restaurants and snack bars. Rental strollers and free wheelchairs available at Guest Relations. Ramps to buildings and to all shows except Arena; restrooms adapted for wheelchairs; plenty of benches and shade, level walks.*

Great Adventure, opened in 1974 on 1,500 acres of Pine Barrens, is really two parks—a drive-through safari and a theme park. Since every year brings new attractions and improvements, it is an annual affair for many visitors. The **Safari** park is a maze of auto roads through 350 acres of simulated wilderness habitats harboring Siberian tigers, rhi-

Riding along the Adventure Rivers
(Photo courtesy of Six Flags Great Adventure)

noceroses, giraffes, European brown bears, kangaroos, llamas, bison, elk, and about 60 other exotic species from all over the world. Three lanes provide stopping areas on either side; for those who don't want to drive, the park operates a safari bus ($2 per person). The animals take noontime siestas and are best viewed early or late in the day.

The **Theme Park** is alive with clowns, dancing dolphins, and rides galore, including roller coasters, runaway trains, flying waves, two flume rides, and the thrilling **Great American Scream Machine** where guests speed at nearly 70 mph through seven loops. A new addition is the 15-acre **Adventure Rivers,** 12 aquatic raft rides through exciting waterways representing the most exotic rivers of the world. A familiar rabbit and his friends entertain in **Bugs Bunny Land,** where even the smallest fry get into the act. There's an elaborate 19th century carousel, and a 15-story ferris wheel in constant motion. You can shop at international bazaars and eat in an oversized Conestoga wagon, an emporium shaped like an ice cream sundae, a filigreed gazebo, or outdoors at an umbrella-shaded table.

Trip A-6
Sea Breezes and
Sparkling Beaches

- POINT PLEASANT BEACH
- SEASIDE HEIGHTS AND SEASIDE PARK
- ISLAND BEACH STATE PARK
- TOMS RIVER

DISTANCE: From Columbus Circle to Point Pleasant Beach, about 70 miles; to Seaside Heights, about 80 miles.

FOR THE DRIVER: Take the **Garden State Parkway** south to Exit 98 and pick up **NJ-34** southeast to the junction with **NJ-35.** Continue southeast on 35 into Point Pleasant Beach. From here go south on 35 about 10 miles to Seaside Heights and Seaside Park. Entrance to Island Beach State Park is just south of Seaside Park as you go through town on Central Ave.

Return to Seaside Heights and take **NJ-37** west to Toms River. Just beyond this you can get on the Garden State Parkway for the drive home, or you might want to head north on **US-9** as far as Lakewood, then a mile east on **NJ-88** to **Ocean County Park** (908-370-7360). Once a Rockefeller estate and arboretum of some 300 acres, the park offers swimming, boating, playgrounds, picnicking, and other activities. You can get back on the GSP at Exit 90.

PUBLIC TRANSPORTATION: Point Pleasant Beach is served by New Jersey Transit commuter trains on the North Jersey Coast Line, operating frequently from New York's Pennsylvania Station, Newark, and other points. All other destinations on this trip really require a private car.

This excursion takes you to three attractive beach areas, each with its own personality. You might prefer to select just one of them and spend most of the day there. Toms River, on the return route, has a good historical museum and some nearby parks that are worth a visit.

27

POINT PLEASANT BEACH. *Beach season Memorial Day to Labor Day. Boardwalk beach fees: adults $5 weekends and holidays, $4 weekdays; less for seniors and children, and for nonboardwalk beaches (fees vary). Swimming, deep-sea fishing, boat rentals, waterskiing, rides, amusements, boardwalk activities, special events. No pets on beaches. Boardwalk wheelchair-accessible. For further information contact Point Pleasant Beach Chamber of Commerce, 517A Arnold Ave., Point Pleasant Beach, NJ 08742 (908-899-2424).*

This Atlantic Ocean bungalow colony has 2 miles of white sandy beaches and a bustling boardwalk lined with arcades, rides, stores, and restaurants. The town is home port to a fleet of commercial fishing vessels, but folks out for pleasure rather than business will find plenty of action in these waters, either on their own or in numerous fishing tournaments throughout the season. The Walsh Off-Shore Grand Prix, one of the major powerboat races in the United States, attracts large crowds every July, and in September the Seafood Festival offers delicacies from the deep as well as an art show. Moonlight sailing is popular and provides good views of the Thursday night fireworks in summer.

SEASIDE HEIGHTS and SEASIDE PARK. *Tourist season late May to mid-Sept. Beach fee: adults $4 weekdays, $5 weekends and holidays; children under 12 free. Some free parking on west side of town. Swimming, fishing, crabbing, surfboat rental, water skiing, jet skiing. Free entry to amusement park, fees per activity. No pets on beach. Beach has ramp for wheelchairs. For further information, contact Seaside Heights Visitor Information, P.O. Box 38, Seaside Heights, NJ 08751 (908-793-9100), and Seaside Park Borough Hall, Seaside Park, NJ 08752 (908-793-0234).*

Fun and games for the whole family here on this beautiful 3-mile beachfront and mile-long boardwalk amusement park crammed with some of the best rides, wheels of chance, snack bars, restaurants, and shops to be found along the Jersey shore. The Ferris wheel offers great views of it all. In late May Father Neptune opens the beaches for the season, and there are special events all summer, including fireworks on July 4th and every Wednesday night. There's an annual Mardi Gras celebration the weekend after Labor Day.

ISLAND BEACH STATE PARK, PO Box 37, Seaside Park, NJ 08752 (908-793-0506). *Open daily all year, daylight hours; summer hours 8–8. Parking fee: Memorial Day to Labor Day $5 per car weekends and holidays, $4 weekdays; cars off-season and motorcycles all season $4; all vehicles an additional $1 at southern end of park from Memorial Day to Labor Day. Guided nature tours, swimming, surf fishing (24 hours a*

The beach at Seaside Park

day by permit), picnicking and barbecuing (no facilities provided), surfing, beach strolling, scuba diving, beach buggies (for fishing only, by permit): all permitted in designated areas only. Life guards, bathhouses, storage lockers, snack bars from mid-June through Labor Day. No pets in swimming areas, leashed pets only elsewhere. Some facilities wheelchair-accessible.

One of the few remaining natural barrier beaches and by far the best along the Jersey shore, this narrow 10-mile strip of land is a lovely spot to picnic and enjoy the sights and sounds of the ocean. Two nature areas offer acres of dunes dotted with holly clumps and briar thickets, and there's a recreation area for more active pursuits along with a self-guided nature trail. The southern tip of the park is just a stone's throw from Barnegat Light on Long Beach Island (Trip A-7). Please remember that the dunes and beach grass are crucial to the island's fragile ecology; walk and drive only in designated areas.

TOMS RIVER, back on the mainland, makes a convenient stop before returning to the Garden State Parkway. Rich in memories of the Revolutionary War, this small old town is home to the **Ocean County Museum** which features, among other things, displays on the dirigibles that once operated from nearby Lakehurst Naval Air Station until the famous *Hindenburg* disaster occurred there in 1937. *26 Hadley Ave., Toms River, NJ 08753 (908-341-1880). Open Tues. through Thurs., 1–3, and Sat. 10–noon. Admission $1.*

Also nearby is the **Cattus Island Park** with its scenic bay views, abundant bird life, nature center, and 14 miles of hiking trails. *1170 Cattus Island Blvd. (via Fischer Blvd. off NJ-37, follow signs), Toms River, NJ 08753 (908-270-6960).*

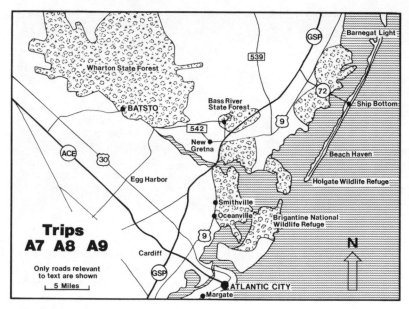

Trip A-7
A Day-Long Marine Drive

- **LONG BEACH ISLAND**
- **BARNEGAT LIGHTHOUSE**
- **BEACH HAVEN**
- **HOLGATE WILDLIFE REFUGE**

DISTANCE: From Columbus Circle to the center of Long Beach Island is about 110 miles.

FOR THE DRIVER: Take the **Garden State Parkway** south to Exit 63, then **NJ-72** east to Ship Bottom at the center of **Long Beach Island.** Turn left (north) onto Long Beach Blvd., the main road that runs the length of the island, and follow it about 8 miles to **Barnegat Light** at the northern tip.

Return on the same road past Ship Bottom and continue south to **Beach Haven,** then on to **Holgate** and the Wildlife Refuge at the southern tip of the island.

Barnegat Lighthouse

Homebound, you must return to Ship Bottom in order to get back to the mainland, where you continue west on NJ-72 to the Garden State Parkway.

This is a fairly long drive from New York, but it does offer a chance to get away from the crowds and explore an 18-mile-long barrier isle that features New Jersey's most picturesque lighthouse, several quiet villages reminiscent of Cape Cod, a small but highly enjoyable amusement park, and (from September through March only) a national wildlife refuge for birds. For further information, contact the Southern Ocean County Chamber of Commerce, 265 West 9th St., Ship Bottom, NJ 08008 (609-494-7211).

BARNEGAT LIGHTHOUSE STATE PARK, Box 167, Barnegat Light, NJ 08006 (609-494-2016). *Park open daily all year from dawn to dusk; lighthouse daily in season, weekends off-season, 10–4:30. Lighthouse fee $1. Beach, changing facilities, fishing, picnic tables, snack bar nearby.*
    Located at the northern tip of the island, this small, 31-acre state park features "Old Barney," a classic red-and-white lighthouse from the mid-19th century. You can climb all 217 steps of its spiral staircase for a spectacular view, or just admire the scene from sea level. The

waters around here were always dangerous, with many a sailing ship breaking up on the shoals when their captains hugged the coast too closely. Legend has it that pirates, including Captain Kidd (1645-1701), practiced their trade here; as did the notorious scavengers who lured boats into shallow waters with deceptive lights on shore—and then robbed them. To reduce the carnage, the first lighthouse on this site was built in 1834. The present structure was completed in 1858 by General George Meade of Civil War fame. Its light served as a beacon until being extinguished in 1944. The open seas off Barnegat are still rough, making them popular with surfers. Note that the beach is presently closed for dredging.

Just a few blocks south of the lighthouse is an old one-room schoolhouse that now houses the **Barnegat Light Museum,** where artifacts of local history are displayed along with Old Barney's original Fresnel lens. *Central Ave. at 5th St., Barnegat Light, NJ 08006, 609-494-3407. Open daily in summer, 2–5; by appointment at other times. Donation.*

BEACH HAVEN, reached after driving south through affluent beachfront villages (with some surprisingly modern architecture) for about 15 miles, is the only really commercialized town on the island. Its **historic district** has a number of well-restored Victorian buildings, and there are some excellent **shopping areas** along Bay Avenue between 3rd and 9th streets. For most visitors, however, the main attraction is **Fantasy Island,** an unusually good family-oriented amusement park that also offers a "medieval" miniature golf course and a casino arcade for adults. *320 West 7th St. at Bay Ave., Beach Haven, NJ 08008, 609-492-4000. Open daily.* Use of the **beach** requires a tag, obtainable at the beach entrance.

HOLGATE WILDLIFE REFUGE, a part of the Edwin B. Forsythe National Wildlife Refuge, occupies the southern tip of the island. It is only open to the public from approximately September through March, depending on the nesting preferences of the birds. At other times it is closed in order to preserve an essential wetlands habitat for certain rare species such as the piping plover. When it is open, it can only be explored on foot unless you have a suitable four-wheel-drive vehicle and follow strict regulations. Still, this is a wonderful place to momentarily escape civilization. Ironically, parts of it also offer a great view of the Atlantic City skyline. For further information and use fees, contact the Edwin B. Forsythe National Wildlife Refuge, P.O. Box 72, Great Creek Road, Oceanville, NJ 08231 (609-652-1665).

Trip A-8
More Adventures
in the Pine Barrens

- BASS RIVER STATE FOREST
- BATSTO HISTORIC VILLAGE
- TOWNE OF HISTORIC SMITHVILLE
- BRIGANTINE NATIONAL WILDLIFE REFUGE

DISTANCE: From Columbus Circle to Bass River is about 120 miles.

FOR THE DRIVER: Take the **Garden State Parkway** south to Exit 52 for New Gretna. Turn right off the ramp and go ¼ mile to a sign for **Bass River State Forest.** Turn right here and go about one mile to the park entrance on the left.

Continuing to Batsto, follow signs from Bass River via back roads and Leektown, or return to the Parkway junction and go past it for about one mile to **US-9.** Go south about a mile on 9, through New Gretna, to **Route 542.** Turn right here and go about 12 miles to **Batsto.**

Return to the junction of 542 and US-9 in New Gretna. Go south on 9, shortly rejoining the Parkway, then take Exit 48 and continue south on 9 to **Smithville.**

From Smithville continue south about a mile and a half on US-9 to Oceanville. Watch for a sign on the left, just before the post office, to the **Wildlife Refuge.**

Plunging deeply into the heart of New Jersey's famous Pine Barrens, this one-day excursion combines history with natural splendor. Why not bring along a picnic basket and enjoy lunch in the woods?

BASS RIVER STATE FOREST, PO Box 118, New Gretna, NJ 08224 (609-296-1114). *Open daily all year, daylight hours. Parking fee Memorial Day to Labor Day $3 per car weekdays, $4 weekends and holidays; otherwise free. Swimming, bathhouse, picnic area and grills at beach, boating, canoe rentals, fishing, hiking and riding trails, camping, playground, nature area. No pets on beach, leashed pets only elsewhere. Wheelchair-accessible restrooms and beach at Lake Absegami. Brochure with map available at entrance.*

This large and beautiful 18,208-acre forest has good facilities and a lovely lake, Absegami, which makes a perfect spot for a swim or a picnic lunch. Horses may be rented just outside the park.

BATSTO HISTORIC VILLAGE, RD4, Hammonton, NJ 08037 (609-561-3262). *Grounds open daily all year except Thanksgiving, Christmas, and New Years Day; 10–6 from Memorial Day to Labor Day, 11–5 at other times. Parking fee weekends and holidays from Memorial Day to Labor Day $5 per car, otherwise free. Free self-guided walking tour and nature trail, guided mansion tour $2 adults, $1 children under 12. Visitor center and restrooms wheelchair-accessible; otherwise difficult for wheelchairs.*

Located near abundant bog-iron deposits, the historic village of Batsto played an important role in the industrial development of the region. Its ironworks were such a vital source of cannons and other weapons during the Revolutionary War that its workers were exempted from military service. During the mid-19th century it turned to the manufacture of glass after the iron deposits were exhausted; and later to lumbering and cranberry farming. From a population of nearly a thousand at its peak, the village declined severely toward the end of the century, later becoming part of the vast Wharton Estate that was sold to the State of New Jersey in 1954 as a nature preserve.

Many of the original buildings survived, and others have been restored. The **Batsto Mansion** with its Victorian tower, the perfect picture of a haunted house, may be visited on 45-minute guided tours that begin at the Visitors Center. While there, you can also pick up a free map for a self-guided exploration of the entire village, which includes the village store, gristmill, blacksmith's shop, barns, workers' homes, and other attractions. Many of these are open to the public and often have craftsmen in period costumes demonstrating the old trades.

Batsto Village lies at the southern edge of the **Wharton State Forest** (609-561-3262), an 108,000-acre tract of Pine Barrens offering picnicking, primitive camping, hiking, swimming, fishing, canoeing, and some winter sports. Just beyond the village is the **Batsto Nature Area** with over 130 species of plants and many small animals.

TOWNE OF HISTORIC SMITHVILLE, Smithville, NJ 08201 (609-652-7775). *Open daily all year; shop hours vary with season. No admission fee, ample free parking. Annual Mayfest, Oktoberfest, tree-lighting ceremony, and other special events. Cobbled walk with curb, no wheelchair access to most buildings.*

The original Smithville Inn was established in 1787, and that era provides the flavor of the town reconstructed around it for your shop-

The gristmill at Batsto

ping and dining pleasure. Over 30 restored buildings are open for business, including several restaurants, antique shops, craft shops, and boutiques. The Smithville Train offers seasonal rides through town, and there are pony rides, a horse-drawn carriage, and other such amusements.

BRIGANTINE NATIONAL WILDLIFE REFUGE, P.O. Box 72, Great Creek Road, Oceanville, NJ 08231 (609-652-1665). *Open all year, daylight hours, weather permitting; office hours 8–4 weekdays. Admission $3 per car. Pets must be kept on short leash. Interpretive nature trails, self-guided auto tour, fishing, crabbing. Insect repellent recommended mid-May through Sept.*

Brigantine, established in 1939, is part of the Edwin B. Forsythe National Wildlife Refuge, over 36,000 acres of coastal wetlands vital to the protection of waterfowl and their habitat. The eight-mile **auto tour** includes 14 stops and takes over an hour to complete. Over 250 species of birds have been sighted here and at the refuge's Holgate unit on Long Beach Island (Trip A-7), including the endangered peregrine falcon, piping plover, least tern, and the black skimmer. The spring and fall migrations are spectacular (write or call in advance for a calendar of wildlife events); the birds nest in Canada, winter in Florida, and regularly pass through here via the Atlantic Flyway. Besides these transients, over 150,000 waterfowl winter here. And all this with the high-rise skyline of swinging Atlantic City as a backdrop across the bay!

NOYES MUSEUM, Lily Lake Road, Oceanville, NJ 08231 (609-652-8848). *Open Wed. through Sat. 11–4 and Sun. noon–4. Adults $2, seniors $1, children 50¢. Wheelchair-accessible.*

Located near the entrance of the Brigantine Wildlife Refuge (above), this pleasantly modern museum in a gorgeous setting presents an eclectic mixture of contemporary art, New Jersey folk art, and duck decoys.

Trip A-9
A Day in
"The World's Playground"

- ATLANTIC CITY

DISTANCE: About 135 miles from Columbus Circle.

FOR THE DRIVER: Take the **Garden State Parkway** south to Exit 38, then the **Atlantic City Expressway** east directly to Atlantic City. Casino parking lots are usually free if you at least visit their gambling halls.

PUBLIC TRANSPORTATION: Atlantic City is well served by **Amtrak** trains from New York and other points, usually via Philadelphia. Phone 1-800-USA-RAIL for schedules. Both New Jersey Transit and Greyhound/Trailways provide frequent, fast express **bus** service from New York's Port Authority bus terminal and other locations. Numerous bus operators throughout the region offer inexpensive one-day bus trips to specific casinos; you can use these to visit the city in general.

Casino gambling is Atlantic City's major (and nearly only) drawing card, with its gaming halls offering the greatest concentration of glitz and glitter this side of Las Vegas. Within its casinos you'll find a total world of escapist fantasy, while on the outside this aging resort has clearly seen better days.

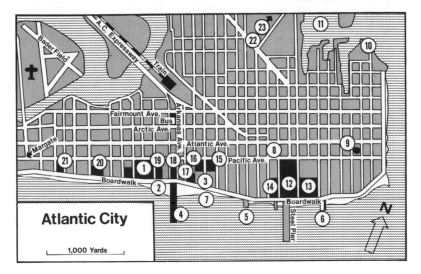

Atlantic City

1,000 Yards

Atlantic City does have a few other attractions, to be sure. These, along with the casinos, are numbered here and on the map. The **Convention Center** (1) was built in 1929, seats some 22,000, has the world's largest pipe organ, and hosts the annual **Miss America Pageant** early each September. The famous **Boardwalk** (2) next to the beach was first erected in 1870 to reduce the amount of sand carried by visitors' feet into hotel lobbies. In 1890 this was rebuilt into something resembling the present structure, about 60 feet wide by five miles long. The traditional way to experience the boardwalk is to ride in one of the attendant-pushed **rolling wicker chairs** that have been used here since 1884, but be sure to settle on a price first lest you be fleeced.

Along the Boardwalk you will soon come to the original **Park Place** (3) of "Monopoly" fame, which is decorated with a statue of the game's inventor. In fact, street names all over town remind you that this most popular of board games was based on the acquisition of wealth through Atlantic City real estate.

Jutting out from the Boardwalk are several piers that date from earlier times. The westernmost of these, built in 1906 and once known as the Million Dollar Pier after its cost, has been reworked to resemble an ocean liner (more or less), and now houses a snazzy indoor mall called **The Shops on Ocean One** (4). Besides some 150 boutiques and specialty stores, it features an amusement area and over 25 places to eat anything from a hot dog to a luxury meal. The upper outdoor decks offer a nice, free view of the ocean and skyline.

Farther along, the **Central Pier** (5), begun in 1884, has shops and a small amusement area that operates in the summer. The Steeplechase and Steel piers, both dating from the turn of the century, are at present unused and awaiting development. At the eastern end, the city-owned **Garden Pier** (6) is a bit dilapidated but may bounce back to life if and when its art museum reopens.

The **beach** (7) has much to recommend it, especially as it's free and open to all. While there are no public bath houses for changing, there are several free public rest rooms along the boardwalk. Life guards are on duty throughout the summer. Even if you don't go in the water, this is a fine beach for sunbathing or just frolicking in the sand.

Gordon's Alley (8), between Pacific and Atlantic avenues by North Carolina Avenue, was New Jersey's first pedestrian mall and houses a number of quality shops. Not far from it is the attractive **Absecon Lighthouse** (9) of 1857, which is not presently open to the public. **Gardner's Basin** (10), on the Inlet side of the island, has a small collection of historic boats, a popular restaurant, and an honest nautical atmosphere that contrasts sharply with the casinos' glitter. Close to this is the **Farley State Marina** (11), a modern sheltered harbor with a wide range of facilities.

Casino hotels are, of course, the lifeblood of Atlantic City and the lure that brings tens of thousands of visitors there daily. Among them, the most utterly fantastic is the **Trump Taj Mahal** (12), which has to be seen to be believed. Surely one of the most expensive buildings on Earth, it is also New Jersey's tallest. Its ludicrous façade facing the Boardwalk is like a scene out of a 1930s Hollywood adventure epic set in an imagined Orient. Inside, it gets even better, so be sure to pop in for a peep. The **Showboat** (13), practically next door, is less outrageous but still worth a visit.

Stroll west on the Boardwalk to Atlantic City's first casino hotel, now known as **Merv Griffin's Resorts** (14). Passing rows of fast-food places and souvenir shops brings you to the **Sands** (15) and **Claridge** (16) casino hotels, both set back from Park Place and reached from the Boardwalk by a people mover. Next to this due is **Bally's Park Place** (17), noted for its monumental escalator connecting the casino and dining levels.

At the corner of Arkansas Avenue, just across the Boardwalk from the Ocean One pier (4), a larger-than-life statue of Augustus Caesar lets you know that you've arrived at **Caesars Atlantic City** (18), one of the glitziest casino hotels in town. Be sure to explore its grandiose interior to gain a new understanding of the word decadence.

Trump Plaza (19), by contrast, is almost tasteful and caters to a high-rolling clientele with its mix of luxury suites, superb cuisine, and ice-cold elegance.

Passing the Convention Center (1), the next casino is **TropWorld** (20), where Atlantic City's past is echoed at the **Tivoli Pier** indoor

The Trump Taj Mahal

amusement park. All sorts of rides, including a miniature Ferris wheel, are offered here along with games and strolling entertainers. One single admission price takes you back in time to the Boardwalk of the 1930s.

The last casino on the Boardwalk, **Bally's Grand** (21), is among the smallest in town but by no means the least glitzy. Atlantic City has two other casino hotels, both out by the Absecon Inlet. More relaxed and tasteful than the Boardwalk establishments, these are **Harrah's Marina** (22) and the **Trump Castle** (23).

NEARBY ATTRACTIONS: Should you tire of Atlantic City, there are several other sights nearby that can easily be reached by car. The closest, just south of town on Atlantic Avenue, is **Lucy the Margate Elephant,** a six-story, 90-ton pachyderm made of wood and tin. This National Historic Landmark was built in 1881 as a real estate promotion, then operated as a tourist attraction into the early 1960s. Facing demolition, the sadly deteriorated Lucy was donated to the City of Margate and rescued by the Save Lucy Committee, a volunteer civic group that began restoring her in 1973. Today, you can tour this Victorian architectural folly, beginning at the hind legs and climbing up the spiral staircase to Lucy's "howdah" for a nice view of the surrounding seascape. *(609-823-6473) 9200 Atlantic Ave., Margate, NJ 08402. Open daily 10–8:30 from mid-June to Labor Day, and weekends 10–4:30 in spring and fall. Adults $2, children $1.*

Heading north on US-9 soon brings you to **Oceanville** and the **Towne of Historic Smithville,** both of which are described on Trip A-8. Alternatively, you can drive about 16 miles northwest along US-30 to Egg Harbor, where you'll find the **Renault Winery,** located about two miles to the right on Bremen Avenue. Established in 1864, this is the oldest vineyard in the land. It survived Prohibition by cleverly producing a legal, popular "medicinal tonic" that was actually 22% alcohol! Highly enjoyable **tours** of the premises are offered, ending with wine tastings. There are three restaurants with appropriate wine dishes, a gift shop, and a museum. *(609-965-2111) Open daily except Thanksgiving, Christmas, and New Years Day; Mon.–Sat 10–5, Sun. noon–5, last tour at 4:15; admission $1, children free.*

Small children will enjoy a visit to **Storybook Land,** where they can play in fairytale structures, pet the animals, and ride in a miniature train. *(609-641-7847) 1671 Black Horse Pike, Cardiff NJ 08232, 10 miles west of Atlantic City via US-322. Open daily 10–5 from mid-June to early September; off-season on Thurs. and Fri. 10–3 and weekends 11–5. Admission $7.95, infants under 1 are free.*

For **additional information** about Atlantic City and its environs, contact the Greater Atlantic City Convention and Visitors Bureau, 2314 Pacific Avenue, Atlantic City NJ 08401; or phone 609-348-7130. In season, they have information booths in the Convention Center and the Ocean One pier.

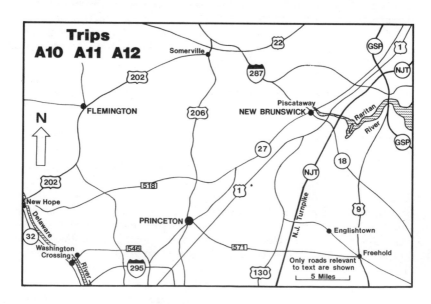

Trip A-10
In and Around New Brunswick

- RUTGERS UNIVERSITY
- MIDDLESEX COUNTY MUSEUM
- EAST JERSEY OLDE TOWNE
- BUCCLEUCH MANSION

DISTANCE: About 40 miles from Columbus Circle.

FOR THE DRIVER: Take the **New Jersey Turnpike** south to Exit 9, then **NJ-18** northwest into New Brunswick. Just beyond the railroad station, bear right and then left onto College Ave., bordering the **Rutgers University** campus. To the right is the **Geology Museum** and, just beyond Hamilton St., the **Zimmerli Art Museum.**

Cross the Raritan River via the bridge at the foot of nearby Albany St. Immediately over the water, turn sharply left onto River Rd. Continue to the second stoplight, turn right, and take the first left into the parking lot for the **Middlesex County Museum.**

Continue on River Rd. for about a mile to another stoplight and turn left into **East Jersey Olde Towne,** on the left in Johnson Park.

Return on River Rd. about a mile to the Landing Lane bridge, cross it, and turn left on Easton Ave. to Buccleuch Park and the **Buccleuch Mansion.**

Continue southeast on Easton Ave. Just beyond the train station it merges with **NJ-18,** which takes you southeast back to the Turnpike.

PUBLIC TRANSPORTATION: New Jersey Transit commuter trains leave Pennsylvania Station in New York at least hourly for the 45-minute ride to New Brunswick, making stops at Newark and other towns en route. For details, call 201-460-8444. You can visit all of the sites on this trip by foot if you don't mind walking a few miles.

You are now in the heart of Middlesex County, land of the Lenni Lenape Indians, Thomas Edison, and Joyce Kilmer, among others. The county has a rich Colonial and Revolutionary legacy and boasts an eclectic assortment of historical milestones, including the invention of the lightbulb and phonograph, the first printing press in New Jersey, the first medical society in the New World, the first snuff factory

41

in the United States, the first canned food in the world (possibly the universe!), the first U.S. black man to vote, the first intercollegiate football game, and the first U.S.-made harmonicas. For further information, contact the New Brunswick Chamber of Commerce, 123 Church St., New Brunswick, NJ 08901 (908-545-4800).

RUTGERS UNIVERSITY, Van Nest Hall, New Brunswick, NJ 08903 (information 908-932-1766, campus tours 908-932-7799). *Most of campus is wheelchair-accessible.*

Rutgers, the State University, was chartered in 1766 as Queens College and opened its doors in 1771. Today it serves a student population of over 47,000. Its libraries, art galleries, and museums are open to the public free of charge, and there are several theaters offering a varied program of plays and concerts. Of special interest are the:

Rutgers Geology Museum. *Geology Hall, Queens Campus (908-932-7243). Open Sept.–June, Mon. 1–4, Tues.–Fri. 9–12; call for summer hours. Free.* A mastodon, dinosaurs, other interesting animal relics, Egyptian mummies, fossils, minerals, Indian artifacts, and the geology of New Jersey can all be seen in this fascinating museum of natural history.

Jane Voorhees Zimmerli Art Museum. *Hamilton and George St., Queens Campus (908-932-7237). Open Mon.–Tues. and Thurs.–Fri. 10–4:30, Sat.–Sun. noon–5; closed Aug., holidays, and Sat. in summer. Free.* This university art museum is noted for its fine permanent collection of works by American artists, other paintings, graphics, book illustrations, and a recently-acquired collection of Soviet art—one of the most outstanding of its type in the world.

MIDDLESEX COUNTY MUSEUM, 1225 River Rd., Piscataway, NY 08854 (908-745-4177). *Open all year Tues.–Sun. 1–4; closed Mon. and holidays; may be closed during installation of exhibits (call in advance). Free. Can accommodate wheelchairs, call in advance.*

Administered as a museum by the Middlesex County Cultural and Heritage Commission, the Cornelius Low House was built in 1741 and is considered one of the finest examples of Georgian manor house in the United States. The museum offers changing cultural, historical, and scientific exhibits and sponsors an ambitious program of workshops, concerts, and special events.

EAST JERSEY OLDE TOWN, 1050 River Rd. at Hoes Lane, Piscataway, NJ 08854 (908-463-9077). *Grounds open all year daily during daylight hours, gift shop Mon.–Fri. 10–3, other buildings at special times (call for current schedule). Partially manageable for wheelchairs.*

This restored 18th-century village grew out of a successful campaign to save New Brunswick's historic Indian Queen Tavern (1686) from demolition. Under the leadership of Dr. Joseph H. Kler, East Jersey Olde Towne went on to mount similar rescue operations for other buildings threatened by the march of progress. All but two of the 20 buildings are original (Three Mile Run Church and the barracks are replicas), and most were dismantled stone by stone from threatened sites to be reassembled here on the banks of the Raritan. In addition to the tavern, the village includes a farmhouse (c. 1748), a schoolhouse (c. 1760), and several homes and outbuildings. For an authentic glimpse of rural Colonial life, it's hard to beat this model of painstaking preservation and restoration.

BUCCLEUCH MANSION, Buccleuch Park, Easton Ave., New Brunswick, NJ 08903 (908-745-5094). *Open late May through Oct., Sun. 2–4; closed holidays. Donations accepted. Not wheelchair-accessible.*

The floorboards of this lovely Georgian house of 1739 still bear the saber and spur marks left by the Enniskillen Guards of Northern Ireland, quartered there during the Revolutionary War. The rooms are filled with 18th- and 19th-century antiques, ranging from Queen Anne to Victorian, and—yes—George Washington did sleep here, after the British left.

Trip A-11
The Halls of Ivy

- **PRINCETON UNIVERSITY**
- **PRINCETON TOWN**

DISTANCE: About 55 miles from Columbus Circle.

FOR THE DRIVER: Take the **New Jersey Turnpike** south to Exit 9, then turn right towards New Brunswick on **NJ-18** and shortly pick up **US-1** south. Follow this to the Princeton exit, turning right on Rte. 571 (Washington Rd.) into town. Park as close to Nassau St. (NJ-27) as possible; there are several lots just north of this.

PUBLIC TRANSPORTATION: New Jersey Transit trains leave Pennsylvania Station in New York city at least hourly for the 70-minute ride to Princeton, making stops at Newark and other towns en route. Take any train marked for Trenton and change at **Princeton Junction** to a shuttle train that goes directly to the station on campus, within walking distance of the sights. Bargain round-trip tickets are available. Call 201-460-8444 for more details.

Founded in 1696 by Quakers who called it "Prince's Town," Princeton is one of the most pleasant towns anywhere for casual strolling. Its streets are lined with well-preserved 18th- and 19th-century houses recalling a major battle of the Revolutionary War, the brief times when this was the nation's capital, and the many famous people who lived here over the years. Its major attraction is, of course, the University, which can easily take hours to explore.

PRINCETON UNIVERSITY, Princeton, NJ 08544 (609-452-3603). *Orange Key Guide Service conducts free campus tours lasting about 1 hour. They depart from the rear of Maclean House (1), to the right of the main gates of the University (see map); Mon.–Sat. at 10, 11, 1:30, and 3:30; Sun. at 1:30 and 3:30. Groups should make advance reservations. No tours on Sat. afternoons during home football games, or on Christmas or New Year's. Summer hours may vary, check first. Most of the campus is wheelchair-accessible.*

Tours, led by undergraduates, include visits to Nassau Hall, the University Chapel, and Prospect Gardens. You can also take self-guided tours, first stopping at the **Tour Office** (1) for a map and guide pamphlets. Among the attractions are:

Nassau Hall (2). *Usually open on Sun.–Fri. afternoons until 5, and on Sat. 9–5.* Built in 1756 and twice rebuilt after fires, this was the original home of what was then called the College of New Jersey. The college was founded in 1746 under a royal charter from King George II and first located in Elizabeth, then in Newark. In 1756 it moved to Princeton when the town offered £1,000 and a tract of land, but it did not officially adopt its present name until 1896. In addition to housing the entire college at that time, Nassau Hall also served as a barracks for both Continental and British troops during the Revolution, as a meeting place for the first legislature of the State of New Jersey, and as the capitol of the United States from June through November of 1783. It was named in honor of King William III of the House of Orange-Nassau, which also explains Princeton's colors. The Faculty Room, which you may visit, contains Charles Willson Peale's famous painting of *Washington at the Battle of Princeton* along with portraits of King George II, King William III, and those of a number of illustrous graduates including presidents James Madison and Woodrow Wilson.

University Chapel (3) was completed in 1928 to replace an earlier one that had burned down. Services are held in a variety of faiths,

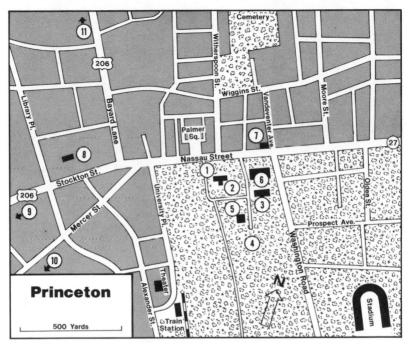

Princeton

500 Yards

including Protestant, Catholic, Orthodox, and Jewish. Modeled after the chapel of King's College in Cambridge, England, it has four great stained-glass windows representing Love, Truth, Endurance, and Hope. Among the figures depicted are John Witherspoon, the University's sixth president and the only clergyman to sign the Declaration of Independence.

Prospect Garden (4) surrounds the Florentine-style Prospect House, a mansion of 1849 that became the residence of the University's presidents in 1878 and is now a dining and social facility for the faculty. After its garden was demolished by a rampaging football crowd in 1904, Princeton's then-president Woodrow Wilson had an iron fence erected to enclose the five acres, and Mrs. Wilson laid out the flower garden in approximately its present form. It contains a vast array of trees, bushes, plants, and flowers; from common domestic varieties to the most exotic. Some of the trees predate the house, and at least one example of each variety is labeled with its botanical and common name.

The Art Museum (5), McCormick Hall (609-258-3787). *Open Tues.– Sat. 10–5, Sun. 1–5, closed Mon. and major holidays. Free.* Picasso's 1971 sculpture, *Head of a Woman,* stands in front of this modern museum building. Inside, the absolutely first-rate collections range

Nassau Hall

all the way from Egyptian, Greek, and Roman antiquities to contemporary American painting and sculpture. Between these are medieval works of art including a stained-glass window from Chartres, Renaissance paintings, Oriental art, some major works of the French Impressionists, and fine photography. If you like art, you'll love this museum.

The Putnam Sculptures, a collection of some 22 modern sculptures, is scattered all over the campus, both indoors and out. It includes works by Calder, Epstein, Lipchitz, Moore, Nevelson, Noguchi, Picasso, and Segal among other 20th-century masters.

Firestone Library (6), the home of more than four million books, is the central research library for the University. Its holdings are especially rich in material relating to the American Revolution. You might want to visit its Exhibition Gallery, to the right of the main entrance.

PRINCETON TOWN, whose historic core lies just north of the campus, has a number of attractions of its own, including:

Bainbridge House (7), 158 Nassau St., Princeton, NJ 08542 (609-921-6748). *Open daily June–Aug., daily except Mon. the rest of the year, noon–4. Closed Thanksgiving, Christmas, New Year's, and weekdays in Jan.–Feb. Donation.* Built in 1766, this was the birthplace of Commodore William "Old Ironsides" Bainbridge, who commanded the

USS *Constitution* during the War of 1812. Now the headquarters of the **Princeton Historical Society,** the house features restored 18th-century period rooms and special exhibitions. Maps and other information for self-guided tours of the town are available here.

Morven (8), 55 Stockton St., Princeton, NJ 08542 (609-292-5421). *Open by appointment.* Once the home of Richard Stockton, a signer of the Declaration of Independence, this brick house of 1755 reportedly served as headquarters for British General Cornwallis in 1777, was visited by Washington, and from 1953 until 1981 was the official residence of New Jersey's governors. The present governor lives down the road at **Drumthwacket** (9), a restored 1835 mansion that may sometimes be visited (609-924-3044).

Thomas Clarke House (10), 500 Mercer St., Princeton, NJ 08542 (609-921-0074). *Usually open Wed.–Sun., call first.* Located in the 85-acre **Princeton Battlefield State Park,** about a mile southwest of town on Mercer St., this Quaker farmhouse of 1770 is furnished as it would have been during the Revolutionary War.

Rockingham (11), Route 518 and River Rd., Rocky Hill, NJ 08553 (609-921-8835). Five miles north of Princeton via US-206 (Bayard Lane). *Currently under restoration, call for hours. Also known as the Berrien Mansion. Not wheelchair-accessible.* While waiting for the signing of the peace treaty with England, the Continental Congress convened at Princeton. General Washington was invited to attend and made his headquarters at nearby Rockingham, using the Blue Room as his study. Here, in November 1783, he wrote his "Fairwell Address to the Armies." You can visit his study and step out as he must have on the balcony, but you won't see the same terrain he saw, for the restored building has been moved from its original site.

Trip A-12
Finding Outlets and
History in Flemington

- HISTORIC FLEMINGTON
- FACTORY OUTLETS IN TOWN
- LIBERTY VILLAGE and TURNTABLE JUNCTION
- BLACK RIVER & WESTERN RAILROAD
- FLEMINGTON FAIR AND SPEEDWAY

DISTANCE: About 65 miles from Columbus Circle.

FOR THE DRIVER: Take the **New Jersey Turnpike** south to Exit 14, Newark Airport, then **I-78** west to Exit 30. Head south on **I-287** to Exit 13, then take **US-202** south to Flemington. In town, at the traffic light just before the Flemington Mall, turn right to Main St., just ahead. Turn right on Main, crossing railroad tracks, and park on a side street or in a lot.

Come back down Main St. to Church St. and turn right to **Liberty Village.** The **Black River and Western Railroad** Station is by the main Liberty Village parking lot.

To reach the fairgrounds, go back through town on Church St. to **NJ-31** and drive north about 1½ miles.

PUBLIC TRANSPORTATION; There is direct bus service from the Port Authority Bus Terminal in New York City to Flemington. Phone 212-564-8484 for current schedules. All of the attractions except the fair are within walking distance.

Bargains, fun, and a strong sense of America's past go together in Flemington, New Jersey's factory outlet town *par excellence.* First settled in 1756 by Samuel Fleming on land originally owned by William Penn, this friendly small town has a remarkably well-preserved core with historic buildings dating as far back as the mid-18th century. In fact, some 60% of its structures are on the National Register of Historic Places. In the late 1800s Flemington became a center for the production of fine pottery and glassware, as it still is, and a hub of railroad activity with some 54 trains a day by 1889. Today, its lovely old center

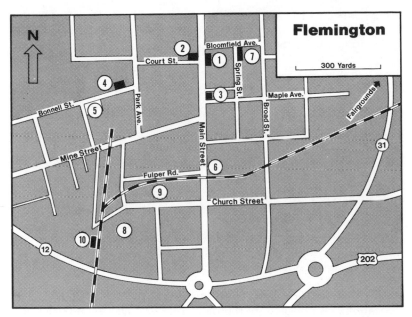

is surrounded by a formidable array of factory outlets, shops, and restaurants. The railroad still runs on steam; only now it carries tourists and shoppers out for a few hours of nostalgic fun. For further information contact the Hunterdon County Chamber of Commerce Visitors Information Center, 76 Main St., Flemington, NJ 08822 (908-782-5955).

HISTORIC FLEMINGTON is centered on Main St., where the Visitors Information Center is located in the imposing **Union Hotel** (1) of 1877, a 4-story brick structure with a mansard roof and gingerbread porches. Many famous media people stayed there during the notorious 1935 "Trial of the Century" that took place across the street in the **Hunterdon County Courthouse** (2), a Greek Revival building of 1828. It was here that Bruno Hauptmann was convicted and sentenced to death for the kidnapping and murder of Charles Lindbergh Jr., the infant son of the pioneer aviator. Memorabilia of the trial is displayed in the center hall.

Nearby, at 114 Main St., is the **Doric House** (3), a Greek Revival structure dating from 1846. Built as a home, it has been restored and is now occupied by the Hunterdon County Historical Society. Visits may be made by appointment, phone 908-782-1091. Turn right on Mine St. and right again on Park Ave. A left on Bonnell St. takes you past **Fleming's Castle** (4) at number 5, a simple Colonial home that must have seemed like a palace in those primitive days. Built in 1756 by the town's founder as an inn, it is the oldest house in Flemington and has been preserved by the Daughters of the American Revolution. For an appointment to see the interior, phone 908-782-4655. Across the street, between numbers 56 and 60, is the small **Case Cemetery** (5), where the area's first settlers are buried along with their friend, Indian Chief Tuccamirgan.

FACTORY OUTLETS IN TOWN tend to be located up and down Main St. and along the nearby side streets. Large color-coded directories with maps will guide you to more than 120 stores. Some of the most famous of these are in the **Flemington Cut Glass Complex** (6) beginning at Main and Church streets. The first and largest factory outlet in the U.S. for crystal and glass, this series of stores also offers a wide assortment of cookware, gifts, home decorations, and fixtures. Another pioneer in this kind of retailing is the **Flemington Fur Company** (7) on Spring St., a block east of the Union Hotel, which has been serving customers from all over the country since 1921.

LIBERTY VILLAGE (8) and **TURNTABLE JUNCTION** (9) are two adjacent shopping "villages" of reproduction Colonial-style buildings attractively arranged around open commons. Located 2 blocks west of Main St. on either side of Church St., they contain some 80 factory outlet shops featuring all kinds of famous-brand merchandise at discount prices, a dinner theater, cafés, restaurants, and a branch office of the New Jersey Tourist Information Center (908-788-5729). *Like the shops in town, those in Liberty Village and Turntable Junction are open every day except Easter, Thanksgiving, Christmas, and New Year's; usually from 10–5:30; and are largely wheelchair-accessible.*

BLACK RIVER & WESTERN RAILROAD (10), P.O. Box 200, Ringoes, NJ 08551 (908-782-9600). *Trains operate from mid-April through Nov. for 1½-hour round trip from Flemington to Ringoes; daily July–Aug., weekends and holidays Apr.–June, Sept.–Nov. Adults $5, children 4– 12 $2.50. Restored 1854 station, snack bar, picnic area at Ringoes. Sunday trips May through Oct. from Ringoes to Lambertville on the Delaware River. Special events throughout the year. Will accommodate wheelchairs.*

You can ride in coaches, some built in 1875, with oil-burning lamps, potbelly stoves, plush seats—all in perfect condition. This is a working passenger and freight standard-gauge steam-and-diesel railroad, not a miniature, and its colorful rolling stock attracts railroad buffs from all over. But you don't have to be a railfan to get a thrill out of the ride through the historic countryside.

FLEMINGTON FAIR and SPEEDWAY, P.O. Box 293, Flemington, NJ 08822 (908-782-2413). *Fair opens Tues. before Labor Day and runs through Labor Day. Speedway open Apr. through Oct. for Sat. night races. For flea market times call 908-782-7326.*

This annual event is a treat for all, and an especially good opportunity to show the youngsters what a typical small country fair is like. The speedway is located on the fairgrounds. Flea markets are held at other times throughout the year.

Trip A-13
Journeys in Bucks County, Pennsylvania

- NEW HOPE
- LUMBERVILLE
- PEDDLER'S VILLAGE

DISTANCE. About 65 miles from Columbus Circle.

FOR THE DRIVER: Take the **New Jersey Turnpike** south to Exit 14, Newark Airport, then **I-78** west to Exit 30. Head south on **I-287** to Exit 13, then take **US-202** south toward Flemington. Continue south on 202 across Delaware River and pick up **PA-32** south for about a mile, which becomes Main St. in **New Hope.** Metered parking is available on the side streets, and there are several commercial parking lots.

To reach **Lumberville,** turn north on **PA-32** along the river for about 6 miles. Return to New Hope on the same road.

Peddler's Village is about 4 miles west of New Hope. Take Bridge St., which become **PA-179** and soon merges with **US-202.**

Bucks County, founded in 1682 by William Penn, is a large and historically important area. You really need more than a day to do it justice, so more of the county is explored on Trips A-14 through A-17. For further information, contact the Bucks County Tourist Commission, P.O. Box 912, Doylestown, PA 18901 (215-345-4552).

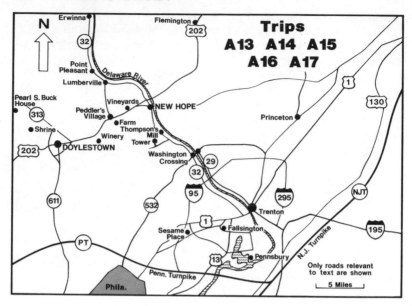

NEW HOPE began to flourish in the 1720s as a ferry town. It was known as Coryell's Ferry during the Revolutionary War, when the local people aided the Continental Army. The mills operated by Benjamin Parry in the late 18th century and the opening of the Delaware Canal in 1834 made the town a bustling commercial center for a time. In the early 1900s New Hope attracted many noted painters, and its reputation as an artists' colony was enhanced by the opening in 1939 of the Bucks County Playhouse. Annual New Hope events include the Auto Show in August, the Showcase of the Arts in September, and the Antique Show in November. For further information, contact the New Hope Information Center, S. Main & Mechanic Sts., New Hope, PA 18938 (215-862-5880).

   Parry Mansion, S. Main & W. Ferry Sts., New Hope, PA 18938 (215-862-5652). *Open May through Oct., Fri.–Sun. 1–5. Donation $4 per person, seniors $3. Not wheelchair-accessible.* This house was purchased by the New Hope Historical Society in 1966 from the descendants of Benjamin Parry, a wealthy lumbermill owner who built it in 1784. It has been restored to reflect the changes in interior decoration over time. You can see whitewash yield to wallpaper, candles to oil lamps, and the craze for Victoriana to more severe modern tastes.

   Mule Barge, New Hope Barge Co., PO box 164, New Hope, PA 18938 (215-862-2842). *Operates April through mid-Nov., weather permitting. Departures daily May through Oct. 15 at 11:30, 1, 2, 3, 4:30,*

The Mule Barge
(Photo courtesy of New Hope Information Center)

and 6; on Wed., Sat., Sun. in April at 1, 2, 4, and 4:30; on Wed., Sat., Sun. from mid-Oct. to mid-Nov. at 11:30, 1, 2, 3, and 4:30; open all holidays during season. Adults $6.95, over 65 $6.50, students with ID $5.50, children under 12 $4.25; free parking. Call for schedule and prices on evening dining barge (summer only). Barge is wheelchair-accessible. Here's a chance for a quiet, relaxing, hour-long ride on the historic Delaware Canal through New Hope and the surrounding countryside. During most of the season a barge musician and historian are aboard to entertain and inform you. Bring your camera, forget your problems, enjoy the ride.

New Hope & Ivyland Rail Road, 36 West Bridge St., New Hope, PA 18938 (215-862-2332). Operates daily mid-May through Oct.; weekends only from mid-March to mid-May, Nov., and Dec.; trains run hourly Mon. through Sat. 10–6, Sun. noon–6. Fares: Adults $6.50, seniors $5, children (3–11) $3.25. Will accommodate wheelchairs. This 9-mile, 50-minute narrated round trip by vintage steam train takes you from the restored New Hope State of 1891 across the trestle to which Pearl White was tied in the 1914 silent movie classic, *The Perils of Pauline,* and on through woodlands and countryside to Lahaska before returning. The 1920s passenger coaches are pulled by a 1925 Baldwin 2-8-0 locomo-

The New Hope & Ivyland Rail Road
(Photo by Michael Eagleson)

tive burning low-sulphur, low-smoke coal. There is a small museum of railroad history, as well as a gift shop, at the New Hope Station.

   Other attractions in New Hope include **Coryell's Ferry Boat Rides** on the Delaware River aboard a 40-foot pontoon boat. *Departures every 45 min. from noon until 7, daily April through Oct. Trips last 30 min. Tickets sold at Gerenser's Exotic Ice Cream, 22 S. Main St. (215-862-2050).* If you're in town after dusk you might want to take one of the eerie **Ghost Tours** arranged by a psychic investigator. *For information call 215-357-4558.* New Hope is famous for its quality **art galleries, antique shops,** and **boutiques** of all kinds; and has a broad choice of inns, restaurants, and cafés. Another enjoyable diversion is to stroll across the bridge to **Lambertville** in New Jersey, which has a lower-key atmosphere but many of the same type of attractions as New Hope.

LUMBERVILLE, a bit of Colonial charm set alongside the river and canal, makes a nice scenic side trip going about six miles north on narrow, winding State Route 32. Its country store has been around since 1770, and offers sandwiches for waterside picnics, bicycle rentals, and a variety of unusual goods. There are public outdoor tables by the locks, and you can walk along the towpath. A footbridge leads across the Delaware to New Jersey and the **Bull's Island Section** (609-397-2949) of the Delaware & Raritan Canal State Park, a haven for picnickers, birds, and birders alike. Canoeing, rafting, and innertubing on the Delaware can be enjoyed at **Point Pleasant,** 2 miles north of Lumberville on Route 32. *Point Pleasant Canoe & Tube, 215-297-TUBE, April through Oct.* Wine fanciers might continue another 5 miles north on Route 32 to Erwinna and the **Sand Castle Winery,** where you can taste the vinifera vintages on cellar and vineyard yours. *River Rd., behind the Golden Pheasant Inn, 215-294-9181. Open daily.* Erwinna also has a fine **covered bridge** dating from 1832, a half-mile west of the canal on Geigel Hill Road.

Heading **west** from New Hope on Route 202, the old Colonial road linking New York with Philadelphia, brings you to the **Bucks Country Vineyards.** Cellar tours, wine tasting, a wine museum, and an art gallery are featured at Pennsylvania's premier winery. *Open daily, phone 215-794-7449 or 800-523-2510.*

PEDDLER'S VILLAGE, 4 miles west of New Hope on route 202, is the star attraction of Lahaska, a village first settled around 1700 by Quakers from England. Originally a collection of barns and chicken coops, Peddler's Village has evolved into 30 acres of some 70 specialty shops, 6 restaurants, and a country inn arranged as a Colonial village around a common complete with a gazebo and a pond. All kinds of crafts, antiques, and unusual items can be found here; and there are frequent country festivals and special events to entertain you. *Peddler's Village, P.O. Box 218, Lahaska, PA 18931 (215-794-4000). Shops open daily 10–5:30, Fri. til 9, Sat. til 6, Sun. noon–5:30. Free parking. Narrow brick walks, steps into buildings, difficult for wheelchairs.*

Lahaska has many other shops as well, especially the 52 specialty stores at **Penn's Market** and the 14 antique dealers in the **Lahaska Antique Courte.** Just south of the village on Street Road is the **Quarry Valley Farm,** a real working farm with a barnyard full of animals that children can pet. They can also jump into the hayloft, ride ponies, climb around the old quarry, and play with farm implements of yesterday. This is a great treat for urbanized kids of all ages; and special events are scheduled throughout the year. *2302 Street Rd., Lahaska, PA 18931 (215-794-5882). Open daily all year round, 10–5. Adults $5, children under 12 $4.50.*

For another nearby attraction, continue 2 miles west on Route 202, then 2 miles south on Route 413 to the **Buckingham Valley Vineyards and Winery.** Free wine tastings and self-guided tours are offered at Bucks County's first winery. *Open Tues. through Fri., noon–6; Sat. 10–6; Sun. noon–4. (215-794-7188).*

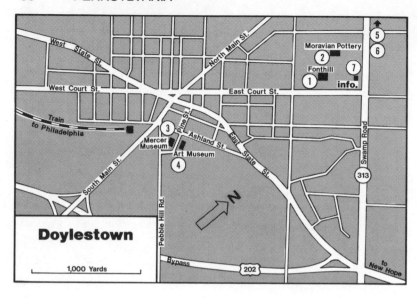

Trip A-14
Further Adventures in Bucks County

- DOYLESTOWN
- COVERED BRIDGE TOUR

DISTANCE: About 80 miles from Columbus Circle.

FOR THE DRIVER: Take the **New Jersey Turnpike** south to Exit 14, Newark Airport, then **I-78** west to Exit 30. Head south on **I-287** to Exit 13, then take **US-202** south toward Flemington. Continue south on 202 across the Delaware River and on to Doylestown. Turn right on **PA-313** (Swamp Rd.) and go north about a mile to East Court St., where you will find the **tourist office,** Fonthill, and the Moravian Pottery Works on the left.

A less touristed region of Bucks County that offers outstanding cultural attractions as well as rural beauty is featured on this continuation of the previous trip.

The Fonthill Museum

DOYLESTOWN, the seat of Bucks County, is a picturesque country town of beautifully preserved Colonial, Federal, and Victorian houses. A regional cultural center, it is best known for the works of its resident eccentric, Henry Chapman Mercer (1856–1930), a noted archaeologist, antiquarian, and leader of the Arts and Crafts Movement. Annual events include the Folk Fest in May, the Heart of Bucks Auto Show in summer, and the Bucks County Antiques Dealers' Show, also in summer. For further information, contact or visit the Bucks County Tourist Commission, 152 Swamp Road (Route 313), Doylestown, PA 18901 (215-345-4552). They are adjacent to the Moravian Pottery and Tile Works. The famed **Mercer Mile** tour begins with the:

Fonthill Museum (1), E. Court St., Doylestown, PA 18901 (215-348-9461). *Open Mon.–Sat, 10–5; Sun. noon–5; closed Thanksgiving, Christmas, New Year's. Adults $4, seniors $3.50, students $1.50. Guided tours only, last tour begins at 4; reservations advised. Not wheelchair-accessible.* Henry Chapman Mercer designed Fonthill, today a National Historic Landmark, as a home and showcase for his collection of tiles and prints from all over the world. The castle-like structure, begun in 1908, consists almost entirely of poured concrete and was conceived of as a "Castle for the New World." Each of the 40-odd rooms has a highly individual personality, with tiles sometimes depicting stories or historic events; and there are warrens, alcoves, and cubicles everywhere you turn on your fascinating tour of Fonthill.

Moravian Pottery and Tile Works (2), Swamp Rd. (Route 313), Doylestown, PA 18901 (215-345-6722). *Open daily 10–5, last tour at 4, closed selected holidays. Adults $2.50, seniors $2, youth $1. Guided tours every half-hour. Tile shop on site. Partially wheelchair-accessible.* A National Historic Landmark adjacent to the Fonthill Museum and the tourist office, this concrete Spanish-Mission-style tile works was built by Henry Mercer to revive the dying Pennsylvania-German art of tile making. Today it operates much as it did in Mercer's time, using the original formulas and methods. Over the years the tile works has furnished decorations for such notable installations as the Pennsylvania State Capitol, the Gardner Museum in Boston, and the John D. Rockefeller Estate in New York.

Mercer Museum and Spruance Library (3), Pine St., Doylestown, PA 18901 (215-345-0210). *Museum open Mon.–Sat. 10–5, Sun. noon–5, closed Thanksgiving, Christmas, New Year's. Library open Tues. 1–9, Wed.–Sat. 10–5. Admission to both: Adults $4, seniors $3.50, students $1.50. Museum has ramps and elevator; mostly wheelchair-accessible.* Another imposing concrete structure and National Historic Landmark, the Mercer Museum houses the tools and products of more than 60 trades and crafts. It was establishing by Henry Mercer to display his collection of over 40,000 Early American objects that tell the story of the nation's growth. Fortunately for succeeding generations, Dr. Mercer saw these artifacts as the stuff of history rather than yard sales. Henry Ford, a man of strong opinions, called this 6-story treasure trove the only museum in the country worth visiting. Don't miss the eerie 19th-century Vampire Killing Kit on the ground floor; or the prisoner's dock, gallows, and coffin on the 6th floor. Each year in May the museum hosts a Folk Fest featuring Early American craft demonstrations, picnics, music, dancing, sheep shearing, quilting, and the like.

The Spruance Library is a gold mine of information on the nation's past. It contains special collections on Bucks County history and genealogy, and on early American technology, culture, and folk art.

James A. Michener Art Museum (4), 138 S. Pine St., Doylestown, PA 18901 (215-340-9800). *Open Tues.–Fri. 10–4:30; Sat. and Sun. 10–5. Adults $3, seniors $2.50, students with ID $1.50. Wheelchair-accessible.* Just across the street from the Mercer Museum stands the old county jail, a handsome structure of 1884. Parts of this were placed on the National Register of Historic Buildings and Sites in 1985, the year the facility closed. In 1988 its preserved sections were converted into an art museum honoring and partly endowed by the famous author, James A. Michener, who grew up in Doylestown and later became a noted art collector. Although it has a growing permanent collection, the museum's focus is on changing exhibitions, some of which it creates itself or in cooperation with other museums.

National Shrine of Our Lady of Czestochowa (5), Ferry Rd., Beacon Hill, Doylestown, PA 18901 (215-345-0600). *Take Swamp Rd. north a mile or so, then Ferry Rd. west about 2 miles. Shrine and grounds open daily all year. Free. Largely wheelchair-accessible.* A Polish spiritual and pilgrimage center, established in 1955 by the Pauline Fathers and dedicated to Our Lady of Czestochowa (pronounced "Chen-sto-ho-va") in America. The present structure was completed in 1966 to commemorate the Millennium of Poland's baptism as a Christian nation. It houses a faithful reproduction of the Miraculous Painting of the Holy Mother, which is traditionally attributed to St. Luke and hangs in the Shrine of Czestochowa in Poland. The copy was blessed by Pope John XXIII in 1962.

A 6½-mile **side trip** northwest of Doylestown on Route 313 (Swamp Rd.) takes you to the village of Dublin, where you can turn left on Dublin Road to Green Hill Farms and the **Pearl S. Buck House** (6). This 1835 farmhouse, now a National Historic Landmark, was the home of the renowned author from 1935 until her death in 1973. The only woman to have ever won both the Nobel and Pulitzer prizes, Pearl S. Buck was raised in China and became famous for her classic novel *The Good Earth* in 1934. In 1964 she started a foundation to care for displaced children, which today operates the house and maintains its delightful blend of Asian and Western cultures. *520 Dublin Rd., Perkasie, PA 18944 (215-249-0100). Tours on Tues. through Sat., at 10:30, 1:30, and 2:30; on Sun. at 1:30 and 2:30. Closed Jan. and Feb., and on Mon. and major holidays. Adults $5, seniors and students $4.* Another nearby attraction on the way back to Doylestown is the **Peace Valley Winery,** where you can taste country wines made from premium grapes grown on the 36-acre vineyard. *300 Old Limekiln Rd.; 2 miles west of Route 313 on Stump Rd., then a bit south. (215-249-9058) Open Wed. through Sun., noon–6.*

BUCKS COUNTY COVERED BRIDGES TOUR, Bucks County Tourist Commission (7), 152 Swamp Rd. (Route 313), Doylestown, PA 18901 (215-345-4552). *Call or write for detailed brochure on self-guided auto mini-tours.* Covered bridges are a nostalgic part of America's heritage, evoking images of old-fashioned rural tranquility. A dozen of these romantic old spans still survive along the back roads of Bucks County and can be examined at leisure by following the directions in the *Bucks County Covered Bridges* brochure offered by the county tourist commission along with the official county road map. Seeing all 12 would take at least an entire day; fortunately, the most picturesque of these have been grouped into two self-guided mini-tours, of which the first is more scenic.

Don't just drive over the bridges—be sure to stop and walk across them, examining their clever "lattice truss" construction of timbers organized in a series of triangles that distribute stress to achieve great strength from simple materials. Although often called "kissing bridges," the spans were actually roofed for the practical purpose of protecting the supporting beams from the ravages of weather, thus insuring a long life.

Trip A-15
Across the Delaware
with General Washington

- WASHINGTON CROSSING STATE PARK, NJ
- WASHINGTON CROSSING HISTORIC PARK, PA

DISTANCE: About 70 miles from Columbus Circle.

FOR THE DRIVER: This trip takes you very close to Princeton (Trip A-11) and to other destinations in Bucks County (Trips A-13, A-14, A-16, A-17). If you are coming from or combining with any of those trips, consult a map for the best route to Pennsylvania or New Jersey sides of the Washington Crossing Area.

Coming from New York, take the **New Jersey Turnpike** to Exit 9, New Brunswick, then bear right after tollbooth onto **NJ-18,** and follow signs for **US-1** south to Trenton. Remain on US-1 to the junction with I-95/295 and take **I-95** west to last exit before Scudders Falls Bridge, **NJ-29.** Take 29 north about 4 miles to Washington Crossing State Park. Watch for stoplight at the junction with **Rte-546,** turn right here, and go about a mile east to the park headquarters.

Continue west across the Delaware on 546, which becomes **PA-532.** Just across the river, turn right (north) on **PA-32** and go a short distance to Washington Crossing Historic Park visitor center, on right, in McConkey's Ferry Section of park. There is a free parking lot across the street.

Continue about 4 miles north on 32, then turn left on Lurgan Rd. for about ¾ mile. A right turn leads up a steep, twisting lane to Bowman's Hill.

Return to 32 and continue north a few blocks to Thompson's Mill Section of the park.

When you leave here, you are just a few miles south of New Hope (see Trip A-13). If you don't want to return the way you came, continue north on **PA-32** to New Hope, pick up **US-202** north to Somerville, then **I-287** southeast to the **New Jersey Turnpike** and back on this to New York.

You are a little northwest of Trenton, capital of New Jersey and site of the famous Revolutionary battle where General Washington captured a Hessian garrison after crossing the icy Delaware River by night. There are numerous places of historic interest in Trenton, particularly the **Old Barracks Museum,** a 1758 structure built to house British troops during the French and Indian War. Costumed guides interpret life in Colonial and Revolutionary New Jersey. *Barrack St., Trenton, NJ 08608, (609-396-1776). Open Tues.–Sat. 11–5, Sun. 1–5, donation.* For further information contact the Mercer County Chamber of Commerce, 214 State St., Trenton, NJ 08608 (609-393-4143).

WASHINGTON CROSSING STATE PARK, Box 337, RD 1, Titusville, NJ 08560 (609-737-0623). *Grounds open daily all year, 8–8, Memorial Day to Labor Day, 8–dusk other times. Visitor Center (609-737-9304) open daily Memorial Day to Labor Day 9–5, 9–4 Wed.–Sun. other times. Ferry House open Memorial Day to Labor Day, Wed.–Sun. 9–4. Parking fee weekends and holidays from Memorial Day to Labor Day $4 per car; otherwise free. Picnic facilities and grills, fishing areas. Leashed pets only. Visitor Center and Ferry House wheelchair-accessible, some other facilities and parts of ground manageable for wheelchairs.*

This park of over 800 acres contains the site where General Washington and his troops landed after crossing the Delaware on Christmas night, 1776. You can stroll along Continental Lane following the route the soldiers took in their march on Trenton. At the tavern in the Ferry House State Historic Site, Washington strategized with his generals while waiting for his army to complete the crossing. Nearby, an overlook gives you a view of the Delaware and the landing site, which can be reached by footbridge. You can also visit the remnants of the Nelson House, believed to have been the site of the original ferry station, and see various historical exhibits at the flag museum, nature center, and visitor center. Native New Jersey trees and shrubs are on display at the George Washington Memorial Arboretum, and seedlings thrive at the State Forest Nursery. In summer, the 1,000-seat theater provides an attractive natural setting for dramas and musical productions.

WASHINGTON CROSSING HISTORIC PARK, PO Box 103, Washington Crossing, PA 18977 (215-493-4076). Located in Bucks County, PA, the park is divided into two riverfront sections about 4 miles apart, plus Bowman's Hill.

McConkey's Ferry Section, just across the river from New Jersey at the intersection of routes PA-32 and PA-532. *Grounds open all year daily 9–dusk. No admission fee for grounds. Buildings open all year Mon.–Sat. 9–5, Sun. noon–5, closed certain holidays except Christmas, Memorial Day, July 4, and Labor Day. Guided tours of buildings Mon.–Sat. at 9:30, 11, 12:30, 2, and 3:30; on Sun. at 12:30, 2, and 3:30. Adults $2.50, seniors $2, youths $1. Film show and visitor center free. Refreshments at the general store near the bridge. Picnic facilities. Visitor Center, Boat House, picnic area, some restrooms wheelchair-accessible.*

Here you can see, after only a few hours' drive, the tangible records of a great episode in American history, Washington's crossing of the Delaware on that stormy Christmas night in 1776. Here is the river, once filled with blocks of ice; here are the banks where the frostbitten Continentals embarked and landed; and here are the houses they used for shelter.

The tour begins at the **Memorial Building and Visitor Center,** near where the Continentals massed before their raid on the Hessian garrison in Trenton. Here, in Concentration Valley, the 2,400-odd patriots, beaten back in the disheartening campaigns of 1776, assembled to execute General Washington's bold strategy. At the Memorial Building, which houses the Visitor Center, park offices, a gallery with changing exhibits, and a theater with an exact copy of Emanuel Leutze's famous painting *Washington Crossing the Delaware* (the original hangs in the Metropolitan Museum in New York), you can watch a half-hour documentary film on the crossing.

Near the Memorial Building is the Point of Embarkation. Footpaths lead to a stone marker at the spot on the riverbank where the crossing began in 1776, and where the **Christmas Day Reenactment** begins each year. Volunteers in uniform climb into a Durham boat with "General Washington" and paddle across, hopefully under conditions less hazardous than those of 1776. The full-scale reproduction used in the reenactment is on display at the **Durham Boat House.** Durham boats were flat-bottomed barges about 60 feet long used for hauling iron ore on the river. They were propelled by oars or sails.

Not far from the boat house is **McConkey's Ferry Inn,** where General Washington may have eaten his Christmas meal before starting across the river. The inn served as a guardpost for the ferry landing during the Continental Army's encampment. In the vicinity of the inn are the **Taylorsville General Store** and several 19th-century houses,

The Thompson-Neely House

including Homewood (c. 1817), the completely restored residence of one of the founders of Taylorsville, a village now known as Washington Crossing.

Bowman's Hill Tower, *Open daily Apr. through Oct. and weekends in Nov., 10–5, and 10–6 on weekends during daylight saving time. Adults $2, seniors $1.50, children under 12 50¢. Not wheelchair-accessible.* Drive north on PA-32 for almost 4 miles, then turn left on Lurgan Rd. for about ¾ mile. Here an almost-hidden right turn leads up a steep, twisting lane to Bowman's Hill. This high ground was used by Washington's sentinels to observe enemy activity as it provides an unmatched panoramic sweep of the river valley. A commemorative fieldstone tower, 110 feet high, was built in 1930 and more recently equipped with an elevator. You can ride almost to the top, then climb up steep circular steps for a marvelous view. Return to route 32 and turn left.

Thompson's Mill Section, on PA-32 just north of Lurgan Rd. *Open all year, Mon.–Sat. 9–5, Sun. noon–5, closed certain holidays except Christmas, Memorial Day, July 4, and Labor Day. No admission fee for grounds. Tour of Thompson-Neely House: Adults $2.50, seniors $2, children $1. Free picnic facilities. Mostly wheelchair-accessible.* A fine example of early-18th-century Colonial architecture, the **Thompson-Neely House** was headquarters during the crucial months of December 1776 of General Stirling, who commanded the troops stationed along the Delaware to prevent a British crossing. Nearby is a restored, operating water-powered **grist mill** built in the 1830s, a restored 18th-century **barn** and, beyond the Delaware Canal, the **graves** of America's first unknown soldiers. Across the road is the **Bowman's Hill State Wildflower Preserve,** a 100-acre sanctuary devoted to the preservation of the native plants of Pennsylvania. It features miles of trails, exhibitions, and special events. The peak season for blooms is April through June.

Trip A-16
Fun with Bert and Ernie

- SESAME PLACE

DISTANCE: About 75 miles from Columbus Circle.

FOR THE DRIVER: Take the **New Jersey Turnpike** south to Exit 9, New Brunswick, bearing right after tollbooth onto **NJ-18 North.** Follow signs to **US-1 South,** taking that through Trenton, across the Delaware River into PA, and to the Oxford Valley Exit. Turn left onto Oxford Valley Road. Go to 3rd traffic light and turn right to **Sesame Place,** next to the Oxford Valley Mall.

You are still in Bucks County, right on the outskirts of Philadelphia. This trip is intended for those with youngters in tow; more adult themes in the same area are explored on Trips A-17 and A-18.

SESAME PLACE, P.O. Box L-579, Langhorne, PA 19047 (215-757-1100) *Open daily from early May through early Sept., then weekends until early Oct; 10–5 early and late season, 10–8 on weekends in late May and early June, 9–8 mid-June through Aug. Admission: Adults $15.95, children $17.95, seniors $10.95, children 2 and under free. Parking $3. Computer-use tokens 3 for $1. Water activities require proper bathing suit; changing rooms and lockers available, bring a towel. No pets allowed. Many facilities and restrooms wheelchair-accessible. Restaurant, cafeteria, snack carts, picnic tables on site. Average visit 5 hours.*
    Children from 3 to 13—and the adults who tag along—love Sesame Place, an action-oriented theme park that blends wholesome physical

Floating down Big Bird's Rambling River
(Photo © Sesame Place)

play and water activities with hands-on science exhibits, computer games, live entertainment, healthy foods, and environmental awareness. Who said that growing up isn't fun? What makes this place different from ordinary amusement parks is that it is largely kid-powered—there are no mechanical rides. Instead, your children and you can enjoy floating on an innertube down the water slides, over rapids, and along a rambling river. There is a cookie mountain to climb, suspended net tunnels to crawl through, and dozens of other energetic activities for all age groups. Sesame Island is a simulated tropical beach entered through a whimsical replica of a cruise ship. Indoors, guests can visit the Sesame Studio and participate in a pretend TV production, operate science exhibits, and play computer games programmed for various skill levels. And, of course, the whole gang's here—Big Bird, Ernie, Bert, Grover, Prairie Dawn, Cookie Monster, the Honkers, and all their pals.

Trip A-17
Memories of William Penn

- PENNSBURY MANOR
- HISTORIC FALLSINGTON

DISTANCE: About 75 miles from Columbus Circle.

FOR THE DRIVER: Take the **New Jersey Turnpike** south to Exit 6, bearing right toward the Pennsylvania Turnpike. Immediately across the Delaware River turn north on **US-13** for about 2 miles to Tully-town. Turn right through the town and follow Bordentown Rd. east across a lake for about 2 miles to Pennsbury Rd., where you turn right into **Pennsbury Manor.**

Leaving Pennsbury, turn right on Bordentown Rd. and then left on New Ford Rd. for about 2 miles. At the end, turn left onto Tybury Rd. for about 3 miles. The entrance into **Historic Fallsington** is about ½ mile beyond the intersection with PA-13, on the right just opposite New Falls Rd.

The shortest route home is to head north on Tyburn Rd. for a short distance, then take **US-1** east across the Delaware River and past Tren-ton. This continues north, connecting with the **New Jersey Turnpike** via **NJ-18** at New Brunswick.

Two historically important sights associated with William Penn, the founder of Pennsylvania, are explored on this trip to the southern end of Bucks County, just outside Philadelphia.

PENNSBURY MANOR, 400 Pennsbury Memorial Rd., Morrisville, PA 19067 (215-946-0400). *Open all year Tues.–Sat. 9–5, Sun. noon–5; closed Mon. and holidays except Memorial Day, July 4, and Labor Day. Call for current admission charges. Guided 1½-hour tours, last tour at 3:30. Restrooms and tour wheelchair-accessible except for 2nd floor of manor.*

"The Country Life is to be preferr'd; for there we see the Works of God; but in Cities little else but the Works of Men," wrote William Penn, Quaker, diplomat, and founder of Pennsylvania. No wonder he chose to live at Pennsbury, a (now reconstructed) manor house of 1683 on the Delaware River, surrounded by 43 acres of gardens, or-chards, and stately trees. The bake and brew house, the blacksmith's and joiner's shops, the replica of Penn's river barge, and the motley crew of farm animals give you a glimpse of the many activities that sustained the life of this country plantation. Inquire at Pennsbury about a package tour that includes Bristol and Andalusia, lunch at the King George II Inn in Bristol, and other attractions.

HISTORIC FALLSINGTON, 4 Yardley Ave., Fallsington, PA 19054 (215-295-6567). *Open daily mid-May to mid-Fall; Mon.–Wed. and Fri.–Sat. 10–4, Thurs. 10–7, Sun. noon–4. Closed Memorial Day, July 4, Labor Day. Guided tours hourly, reservations suggested, call for current rates. Buildings not wheelchair-accessible.*

Fallsington, settled in the late 17th century by followers of William Penn, is an unspoiled village that represents an enduring Quaker community and a uniquely American architectural heritage. Many of the houses are still occupied by descendants of the original settlers, and it's hard to believe that downtown Philadelphia is only minutes away. Three restored buildings are shown on the tours: the **Moon-Williamson House** (c. 1685), a pioneer log building, one of the oldest in Pennsylvania; the **Burges-Lippincott House,** an elegant, beautifully decorated home built in four stages from 1700 to 1829; and the **Stage-coach Tavern,** in continual operation from the 1790s until Prohibition. The **Gillingham Store,** rebuilt in 1910, is the headquarters of Historic Fallsington, Inc., and has a gift shop and information center.

Trip A-18
A Walking Tour of
America's Birthplace

- LIBERTY BELL
- INDEPENDENCE HALL
- HISTORIC PHILADELPHIA

DISTANCE: Central Philadelphia is about 90 miles from Columbus Circle.

FOR THE DRIVER: The easiest and least confusing route from the New York area is to take the **New Jersey Turnpike** south to Exit 4, then routes **NJ-73, NJ-38,** and **US-30** West across the Ben Franklin Bridge. Turn left on 6th St. to the underground parking facility at Independence Mall.

PUBLIC TRANSPORTATION: There are two ways to get to central Philadelphia by rail from New York City or other points along the Northeast Corridor. The fastest and most comfortable is via **AMTRAK** to 30th St. Station in Philadelphia, then SEPTA commuter train to Market East Station (or subway to 5th St., or taxi to Independence Mall). A much cheaper route, about 30 minutes longer, is to take a **New Jersey Transit** commuter train (buy a roundtrip off-peak ticket) from Pennsylvania Station in New York or other corridor points to Trenton. At Trenton buy a ticket from the platform machine for the connecting **SEPTA** commuter train to Philadelphia, getting off at the Market East Station, just four blocks from Independence Mall. There are also **Greyhound/Trailways** buses from New York to Philadelphia's bus terminal, located just behind the Market East commuter rail station.

A walk back in time through the beautifully-restored neighborhoods of Colonial Philadelphia is easily one of the most rewarding daytrips that can be made from the New York area, and an experience no American should miss. The sights along the way are varied enough to appeal to everyone from school-age children to the most sophisticated of adults.

Although it can be taken at any time of the year, consider making this daytrip during the off-season, after Labor Day and before May, when there are no waiting lines for the sights. Other than your transportation costs, this can be a very inexpensive excursion as only a few of the attractions charge any admission at all, and even these are quite modest. There are a number of budget places to eat in the neighborhood, along with some of Philadelphia's finest restaurants.

The suggested walking route is shown on the map by a heavy broken line, while the circled numbers refer to sights described in the text. Not including the side trip to Penn's Landing, the route is only about two miles long and level all the way. Most of the attractions are open daily, except that a few of the museums close on Mondays and/ or other days as noted. For further information contact the **Philadelphia Visitors Center,** 16th St. at John F. Kennedy Blvd., Philadelphia, PA 19102 (215-636-1666), or the Superintendent, **Independence National Historical Park,** 313 Walnut St., Philadelphia, PA 19106 (215-597-8974).

LIBERTY BELL PAVILION, (1), Market St. between 5th & 6th streets, on Independence Mall. *Open daily 9–5; early July to early Sept. 9–8. Free. Wheelchair-accessible.*

Housed in its own glass pavilion, the very symbol of American freedom is silhouetted against Independence Hall. There, on July 8, 1776, it was tolled to announce the first public reading of the Declaration of Independence, signed just four days earlier. The bell was originally cast in England in 1751 to commemorate the 50th anniversary of William Penn's Charter of Privileges guaranteeing certain freedoms for Pennsylvania residents. Recast in Philadelphia in 1753 after a defect was discovered, it carries the biblical quotation "Proclaim liberty throughout all the land, unto all the inhabitants thereof" (Leviticus 25:10). Its famous crack appeared well after the Revolution, and the bell has remained silent since 1846. Perhaps surprisingly for so important a treasure, you are actually encouraged to touch it.

INDEPENDENCE HALL, (2), Chestnut St. between 5th & 6th streets. *Open daily 9–5; early June to early Sept. 9–8. Visit by free guided tours only, departing from the southeast entrance about every 20 minutes and lasting about half an hour. Expect delays during the summer season. Bookstore on premises. Wheelchair-accessible.*

Built between 1732 and 1756 as the Pennsylvania State House, this elegant structure is where the Declaration of Independence was adopted in 1776, the Articles of Confederation were ratified in 1781, and the Constitution of the United States framed in 1787. Tours through its beautifully-restored interior take you first to the old **Pennsylvania**

Inside the Assembly Room

Supreme Court Chamber, arranged in the British manner with a bench for the judges, two jury boxes, and a prisoner's dock. The state coat of arms above the judges replaced that of King George III, which was dragged through the streets and burned following the public reading of the Declaration of Independence.

You will then visit the **Assembly Room,** where those momentous events of American history actually took place. Most of the original furnishings, both here and throughout the building, were destroyed by the occupying British in 1777; what you see today are authentic antiques similar to what would have been here. One of the few original pieces is the "Rising Sun" chair used by George Washington during the Constitutional Convention in 1787, which Benjamin Franklin said depicted a rising, not a setting, sun—surely a good omen for the new nation. The lovely silver inkstand in front of it was the one actually used to sign both the Declaration and the Constitution.

On the second floor is the **Long Gallery,** an enormous light-filled room that served in Colonial days as a banqueting hall, during the British occupation as a prison for captured American officers, and later as an art gallery.

Flanking Independence Hall are, to the west, the **Congress Hall** where the U.S. Congress met from 1790 to 1800 (House of Representatives on the first floor, Senate upstairs) and, to the east, the **Old City Hall** which housed both local government and the U.S. Supreme Court

Independence Hall from Independence Park

until the latter moved to Washington in 1800. (*Both buildings open daily 9–5. Free. Wheelchair-accessible*).

Independence Square, the park behind the hall, is where the Declaration of Independence was first read in public. Near its northeast corner is **Philosophical Hall**, headquarters of the American Philosophical Society, a scholarly organization founded in 1743 by Benjamin Franklin. (*Not open to the public*).

SECOND BANK OF THE UNITED STATES, (3), 420 Chestnut St. *Open daily 9–5. Free.*

Built between 1819 and 1824 to house the government's central bank, this handsome Greek Revival structure was modeled after the Parthenon in Athens. From 1845 until 1935 it served as a customs house, and in 1974 was restored as an art gallery. Step inside to see some 90 portraits of the founders of the United States, both the famous and the obscure, and be sure to examine the life-size wooden statue of George Washington by William Rush.

CARPENTERS' HALL, (4), 320 Chestnut St. (215-925-0167). *Open Tues.– Sun. 10–4, closed Mon., also closed Tues. in Dec. and Jan. Free.*

Still owned and operated by the Carpenters' Company, a trade guild founded in 1724 to promote construction skills, this Georgian structure was the setting for the First Continental Congress in 1774. It was

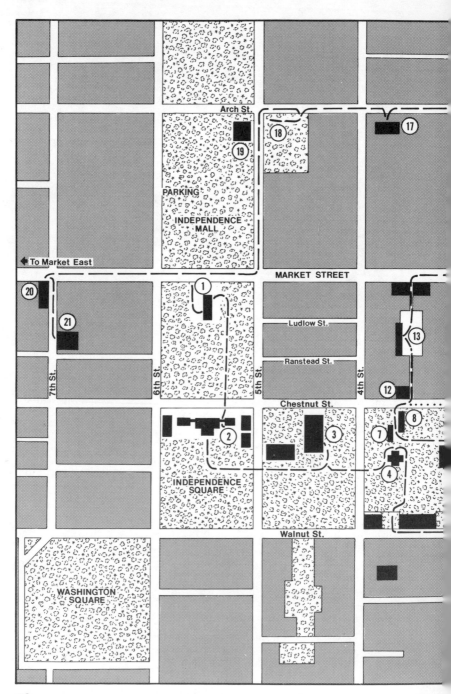

Arch St.

19

PARKING

INDEPENDENCE
MALL

18

17

To Market East

MARKET STREET

20

21

1

Ludlow St.

Ranstead St.

13

12

7th St.

6th St.

5th St.

4th St.

Chestnut St.

2

3

8

7

4

INDEPENDENCE
SQUARE

Walnut St.

WASHINGTON
SQUARE

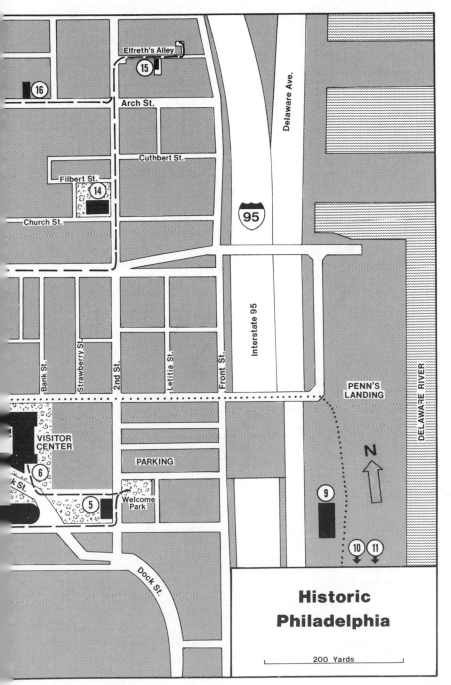

200 Yards

Historic Philadelphia

here that the colonists' grievances against the king were first aired and a declaration of rights sent to him, and it was here that the boycott against English goods began. Today, the hall houses changing exhibitions, models, period furniture, and a display of Colonial carpenters' tools.

Follow the map south through the 18th-century garden. Next to this, at the corner of 4th and Walnut streets, is the **Todd House.** This typical 18th-century middle-class home was the residence of Dolley Todd, who after her husband's death became the wife of James Madison, the fourth president of the United States. (*Ask at the Visitor Center, below, about a free tour that includes this house*). A few steps east on Walnut St. brings you to another row of modest 18th-century houses. The first is occupied by the **Pennsylvania Horticultural Society,** which has a splendid formal garden. (*325 Walnut St., 215-625-8250. Open Mon.–Fri., 9–5. Free*). To the right of it is the **Bishop White House** of 1787, an ornate upper-class residence where many of the nation's leaders were entertained. (*Ask at the Visitor Center, below, about a free tour that includes this house*).

The large Greek Revival structure at the corner of 3rd and Walnut streets is the former **Philadelphia Merchants' Exchange,** a center of commerce in the 19th century. It now houses offices of the National Park Service. (*Not open to the public*).

CITY TAVERN, (5), 2nd and Walnut streets (215-923-6059). *Open for patrons, daily 11:30–3:30 and 5–9, closing at 10 on Fri. and Sat.*

This was the favorite eating and drinking place for the nation's Founding Fathers during the 18th century. First built in 1773, it was demolished in 1854 and completely reconstructed in 1975. Once again operating as a restaurant, it is furnished with period reproductions and features mostly Colonial dishes served by staff in 18th-century dress. Reservations are suggested; prices moderate.

Catercorner from the tavern is **Welcome Park,** the site of William Penn's home and the spot where in 1701 he granted the famous Charter of Privileges to Pennsylvania residents. It is now arranged as an outdoor museum that describes the founding of Pennsylvania.

VISITOR CENTER, (6), 3rd and Chestnut streets (215-597-8974). *Open daily 9–5. Free. Wheelchair-accessible.*

A large, modern structure operated by the National Park Service, the center features a free 28-minute film, entitled *Independence,* on the founding of the nation. There is a self-operated interactive computer exhibit on the Constitution, information desks for both the park and the City of Philadelphia, free brochures and maps, and a bookstore. The Bicentennial Bell in the center's 130-foot tower was presented to the American people in July, 1976, by Britain's Queen Elizabeth II.

Follow the map past the **First Bank of the United States,** which from 1797 until 1811 was the central bank of the new nation. The pediment decorations above the Corinthian columns are carved in mahogany, and are among the very few such outdoor wooden sculptures to have survived from the 18th century. (*Not open to the public*).

MARINE CORPS MEMORIAL MUSEUM, (7), Carpenters' Court. *Open daily 9–5. Free.*

This reconstruction of a 1791 building once used by the War Department now houses a museum devoted to the history of the U.S. Marine Corps from 1775 to 1805.

ARMY-NAVY MUSEUM, (8), Chestnut St. at Carpenters' Court. *Open daily 9–5. Free.*

The development of the U.S. Army and Navy from 1775 until 1805 is explored with models, weapons, and other displays.

At this point you may want to make a **side trip** *to Penn's Landing on the Delaware River, which adds a little over a mile to the total walking tour distance. This extension features attractions numbered 9, 10, and 11, described below.*

PORT OF HISTORY MUSEUM, (9), Penn's Landing (215-925-3804). *Open Wed.–Sun., 10–4:30, closed holidays. Admission $2. Wheelchair-accessible.*

Changing exhibitions of both the arts and general-interest subjects are offered in this large, modern museum located at the spot where William Penn first came ashore in 1682 to found the colony of Pennsylvania.

GAZELA OF PHILADELPHIA, (10), Penn's Landing (215-923-9030). *Open when in port: Memorial Day to Labor Day, daily 10–6; remainder of year weekends only, noon–5.*

Over a century old, this Portuguese tall ship was still fishing for cod until 1969. Operated by volunteers as a training vessel, it regularly sails to other Atlantic Coast harbors to promote the Port of Philadelphia, one of the largest in the world. You're welcome aboard when it's in port.

U.S.S. *OLYMPIA* and U.S.S. *BECUNA*, (11), Penn's Landing (215-922-1898). *Open daily except Christmas and New Year's, 10–5, closing at 4 in the off-season. Joint admission: adults $3, seniors $2, children under 12 $1.50.*

The *Olympia* was Commodore Dewey's flagship in the Philippines during the Spanish-American War in 1898. Fully restored and open to your inspection, it is the only surviving capital ship from that era. Docked next to it is a World War II submarine, the U.S.S. *Becuna*, whose interior may be explored.

Return to Chestnut St. at Carpenters' Court to continue with the main tour.

PHILADELPHIA MARITIME MUSEUM, (12), 321 Chestnut St. (215-925-5439). *Open Tues.–Sat. 10–5, Sun. 1–5. Adults $2.50, seniors and children 12 and under $1.*

Three centuries of maritime life along the Delaware Bay and River are explored through a collection of ship models, paintings, instruments, sailors' gear, and artifacts in this nautical museum.

FRANKLIN COURT, (13), 316 Market St. *Open daily 9–5. Free. Museum is wheelchair-accessible.*

Little is known about the exact design of Benjamin Franklin's last Philadelphia home, which was torn down in 1812. Its foundation has, however, been unearthed and today a simple steel frame represents the house in its original setting. Adjacent to this a ramp leads down to the **Underground Museum,** where Franklin's amazingly varied achievements are celebrated through a collection of antiques, reproductions, and documents. A room full of high-tech gadgetry allows you to access opinions about the man, and a 20-minute film on his life is shown at frequent intervals.

The adjoining **row of houses** along Market Street were either built by or owned by Franklin. At number 322 is the restored office of *The Aurora*, a newspaper published by his grandson. Next door to this is an exhibit on Franklin's early career as a printer, followed by architectural and archaeological exhibitions. The **U.S. Post Office** at number 316 commemorates his role as postmaster by canceling stamps with the old postmark "B. Free Franklin." Authentically restored in the Colonial style, it is the only post office in the nation that does not display the U.S. flag, and the only one whose employees wear period costumes.

CHRIST CHURCH, (14), 2nd St. between Market and Arch streets. *Open for tourists Mon.–Sat. 9–5, Sun. 1–5. Free. Wheelchair accessible.*

Elfreth's Alley

Fifteen signers of the Declaration of Independence worshipped at this Georgian-style church, as did many prominent citizens. President George Washington had his own entrance door and box pew, and other pews were reserved for the Penn family, Benjamin Franklin, and other notables. Fully restored, the church serves an Episcopal congregation with Sunday services at 9 and 11.

ELFRETH'S ALLEY, (15), 2nd St. between Arch and Race streets (215-574-0560). *Alley always open, museum open Mar.–Dec. daily 10–4, weekends only in Jan. and Feb. Free.*

Dating from 1702, this is thought to be the oldest continuously-occupied residential street in America. Its 33 small houses were built between 1713 and 1811, and are today highly desirable city residences. The one at number 126, open to the public as a museum, is furnished in the Colonial style. Don't miss tiny Bladens Court, off to the left near the east end of the alley.

BETSY ROSS HOUSE, (16), 239 Arch St. (215-627-5343). *Open Tues.– Sun. 10–5. Free.*

According to tradition, Betsy Ross, a seamstress who lived in this house, is credited with sewing the first American flag. However accurate the story, the house is certainly filled with interesting memorabilia that makes it worth a visit.

FRIENDS' MEETING HOUSE, (17), Arch and 4th streets (215-627-2667). *Open Mon.–Sat. 10–4. Free tours.*

Built in 1804 to accommodate an annual meeting of the Society of Friends, this Quaker meeting house still serves its original purpose. There is a small exhibition and a slide show recalling the life of William Penn.

CHRIST CHURCH BURIAL GROUND, (18), Arch and 5th street. *Open mid-Apr. to mid-Oct., daily 9:30–4:30. Free.*

Benjamin Franklin and four other signers of the Declaration of Independence are buried in this oasis of quiet in the middle of town. Put a penny on his grave for good luck.

FREE QUAKER MEETING HOUSE, (19), Arch and 5th streets. *Open daily 9–5. Free.*

Rejecting their principle of pacifism, a group of "free," or "fighting," Quakers answered the call to arms during the Revolution. This caused them to be disowned, so they built their own meeting house in 1783. Later reconciled into the mainstream Quaker faith, their story is told here by exhibits and a slide show.

GRAFF HOUSE, (20), Market and 7th streets. *Open daily 9–5. Free. Wheelchair-accessible.*

In May, 1776, Thomas Jefferson rented two furnished rooms here in what was then the outskirts of Philadelphia. It was here that he drafted the Declaration of Independence, adopted with only a few changes on July 4th. The house you visit today is a total re-creation as the original was demolished in 1883. Jefferson's historic role is portrayed in a short film, and his rooms have been re-created with both period and reproduction furnishings.

ATWATER KENT MUSEUM, (21), 15 South 7th St. (215-922-3031). *Open Tues.–Sat., 9:30–4:45. Closed holidays. Free.*

Just a few steps from the Graff House, above, this is the museum of Philadelphia's history from the earliest days to the present. It is especially noted for its temporary exhibitions.

Area B

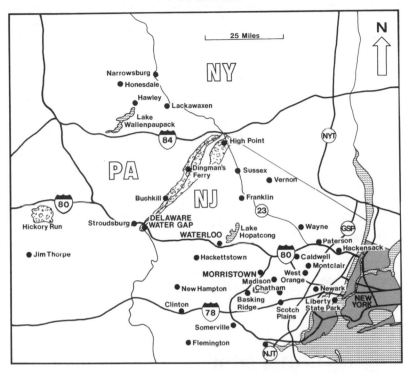

FROM THE STATUE OF
LIBERTY TO THE POCONOS

Here you can begin by exploring the part of New Jersey closest to New York City. Unlike the trips in Area A, which follow
one another in fairly straight lines, these come in clusters and
are spread out across some of New Jersey's more populated
regions. For the most part, the larger industrial cities are not
included because of their heavy traffic. You can gradually work
your way westward across the Delaware River into the Poconos, where the extraordinary scenic beauty, the unhurried
pace, and the great variety of recreational possibilities more
than justify the additional miles.

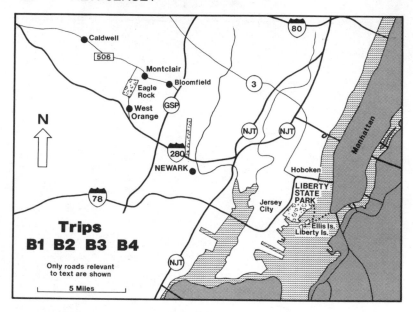

Trip B-1
On the Other Side
of the Golden Door

- LIBERTY STATE PARK
- STATUE OF LIBERTY
- ELLIS ISLAND

DISTANCE: About 10 miles from Columbus Circle.

FOR THE DRIVER: Liberty State Park is only a few minutes from the Holland Tunnel via **New Jersey Turnpike Extension** south to Exit 14B.

From the George Washington Bridge, take the New Jersey Turnpike south to Exit 14, then the Turnpike Extension to Bayonne and Jersey City, getting off at Exit 14B.

Leave your car at **Liberty State Park** and take the Circle Line boat to the **Statue of Liberty** and **Ellis Island**.

The Manhattan skyline from Liberty State Park

New Yorkers are notorious for never visiting the Statue of Liberty, probably because it's too close to home. Here's your chance to make more of a trip out of it by going via New Jersey's Liberty State Park and enjoying those attractions as well.

LIBERTY STATE PARK, Morris Pesin Drive, Jersey City, NJ 07305-4678 (201-915-3400). *Open daily all year, 8–10 Memorial Day to Labor Day, 8–8 other times. Parking fee. Visitor center, natural area, trails, observation points, picnic area, playground, refreshments, boating, fishing, bridle paths, cross-country skiing, swimming pool (Memorial Day–Labor Day, fee). Leashed pets only. Most facilities are wheelchair-accessible.*

Here's a glorious view you'll never forget. After your drive down State Flag Row (arranged in order of induction into the Union), you'll see the Statue of Liberty looming just 1,750 feet ahead. To the left lies Ellis Island, and beyond, the confluence of the Hudson and East rivers. Between them is all of lower Manhattan with its incomparable skyline. The Brooklyn Bridge is prominent, backed by the other bridges across the East River. To your right is the Verrazano Bridge linking Brooklyn with Staten Island. Finally, over the rooftops of Bayonne to the south, is the Bayonne Bridge, completing a giant arc linking three boroughs with New Jersey. The Staten Island Ferry and the popular sightseeing cruisers ply the waters of New York Harbor; tugs, cargo vessels, and, as an occasional bonus, one of the great ocean liners make a never-ending pageant on the waters.

Only 30 years ago this area of New Jersey was one of rotting docks, derelict boats, and marshlands. In the late 19th century it had been the site of a bustling commuter and freight rail terminal that handled tens of thousands of people each day, many of them immigrants who first set foot on the U.S. mainland here after being processed at Ellis Island. But as truck and highway transport gained ground, these facilities became obsolete and were gradually abandoned. In 1964 the State of New Jersey established Liberty State Park and began a major cleanup of the harbor area. The first phase of development was completed in time for the nation's bicentennial, and the park was improved for the Statue of Liberty centennial in 1986.

STATUE OF LIBERTY, Liberty Island, New York, NY 10004 (212-363-3200). *Open daily 9–5. Admission free. Snack bar, picnic area. Partially wheelchair-accessible. Circle Line boat from Liberty State Park operates year round, more frequently in summer. Fares, including Ellis Island and return: Adults $6, seniors $5, children 3–17 $3. For schedules call 212-269-5755 or 201-435-9499.*

New York Harbor's famous statue was given to America by the people of France in 1886. You can climb all 22 stories up into its crown for a stunning view, or ride the elevator to the top of its pedestal for a still-wonderful and infinitely less exhausting experience. In either case, expect long lines. There is also a fascinating exhibition on the construction and restoration of this symbol of American freedom.

ELLIS ISLAND NATIONAL MONUMENT, Ellis Island, New York, NY 10004 (212-363-6304). *Open daily except Christmas, 9–5. Admission free. Snack bar. Wheelchair-accessible. See Statue of Liberty entry for Circle Line boat information.*

The immigrant experience and the peopling of America is the theme of the newly-opened Ellis Island Immigration Museum, housed in the original buildings of the nation's most famous port of entry. Some 17 million people—the ancestors to nearly half of all living Americans—passed through this facility between 1892 and 1954 on their way to the American Dream. Their emotionally-charged story is told through artifacts, displays, a film, and in the very walls of the Great Hall itself.

Trip B-2
Art and Cherry Blossoms in Newark

- **NEWARK MUSEUM**
- **BRANCH BROOK PARK**

DISTANCE: About 15 miles from Columbus Circle.

FOR THE DRIVER: Take the **New Jersey Turnpike** to Exit 18 or 15W, then **I-280** west to Exit 15, Newark. Head south on Broad St. and turn right onto Washington St. The **Newark Museum** is at 49 Washington, facing Washington Park.

Head west on nearby Central Ave. and turn right at Belmont Ave., following it north past I-280, and then go left into **Branch Brook Park.**

To return, you can pick up I-280 at Exit 13, near the south end of the park.

PUBLIC TRANSPORTATION: Take a New Jersey Transit commuter train from Pennsylvania Station in New York, PATH train from other points in Manhattan, or commuter trains or buses in New Jersey to Newark's Penn Station. From there it's only a few blocks northwest to the Newark Museum. The park is also within a healthy walking distance, or you can take the Newark City Subway to the Branch Brook stop.

NEWARK MUSEUM, 49 Washington St., Newark, NJ 07101 (201-596-6550). *Open all year, Tues.–Sun., noon–5; closed major holidays. Free. Wheelchair-accessible.*

The Newark Museum has grown enormously in recent years, and is now the largest and probably the most important institution of its kind in the state. Among its many holdings is the foremost collection of Tibetan art and artifacts in the Western Hemisphere, a superb collection of American paintings and sculptures, plus Oriental and classical works. There's a planetarium with sky shows on weekends and holidays (nominal fee), a firefighters' museum, a one-room schoolhouse from 1784, a contemporary sculpture garden, a Native American gallery of costumes and crafts, a miniature zoo and aquarium, and—you name it, it's probably there.

The adjacent **Ballantine House,** reached internally, is an opulent Victorian mansion dating from 1885. It was built by beer baron John Ballantine, and reflects the kind of wealth that Newark knew in its heyday.

BRANCH BROOK PARK, Lake St., Newark, NJ 07104 (201-482-6400). *Open daily all year. Free entry, nominal fees for tennis and skating. Playgrounds and playing fields, cross-country trail, fitness course, jogging paths, fishing areas, skating rink, hard and clay tennis courts, bocce court, cricket crease, picnicking (no fires or grills allowed). Annual Cherry Blossom Festival, special events throughout the year. Leashed pets only. Largely wheelchair-accessible.*

Every spring in April the cherry blossoms appear throughout the New Jersey park system. The most lavish of these displays, surpassing even the glories of the Tidal Basin in Washington, D.C., can be seen at Branch Brook Park, where almost 3,000 cherry trees in 28 varieties create a canopy of hues from white to rose to deep pink. The Branch Brook cherry blossoms made their first notable appearance in the early 1940s, some 13 years after a substantial gift enabled the county parks commission to purchase 2,050 Japanese cherry trees. The trees came into their own as a tourist attraction after the anti-Japanese sentiment of World War II subsided, and they have been drawing people to Branch Brook in droves ever since.

The timing and duration of the blooming period depends upon the weather, but the flowers almost always appear by April 15, just in time for tax relief, and last for about 3 weeks. Some half million people have come to view the trees each spring in recent years, and the 360-acre park is especially crowded on weekends. Don't expect to stroll in solitude, but go anyway.

Apart from the cherry trees, Branch Brook is an attraction at any time of year. It was laid out by Frederick Law Olmsted, designer of New York's Central Park, Washington's Capitol grounds, and many other beautiful parks and estates.

Trip B-3
To the Laboratory of a Genius

- EDISON NATIONAL HISTORIC SITE
- EAGLE ROCK RESERVATION

DISTANCE: About 20 miles from Columbus Circle.

FOR THE DRIVER: Take the **Garden State Parkway** south to Exit 145 *or* the **New Jersey Turnpike** south to Exit 15W (Exit 18 if coming from Lincoln Tunnel), and pick up **I-280** west. Watch for Exit 10 for **Route 508,** West Orange. Get off 280 here. Immediately ahead is 508, North-field Ave. Turn right to Main St. at traffic light just ahead. Turn left on Main past municipal buildings and continue several blocks to the **Edison National Historic Site,** on the right.

From here, continue on Main St. briefly to Eagle Rock Ave., bear left on Eagle Rock, and follow it to the top of the hill and into **Eagle Rock Reservation.**

To return home, go south briefly on Prospect Ave. (the western boundary of the park) to the junction with I-280, then back as you came.

EDISON NATIONAL HISTORIC SITE, Main St. & Lakeside Ave., West Orange, NJ 07052 (taped message 201-736-5050, further information 201-736-0550). *Open daily all year 9–5, closed Thanksgiving, Christmas, New Year's. Adults 17–61 $2, others free. Guided 90-min. tours begin at 9:30, last tour at 3:30. Fully wheelchair-accessible.*

Every American who can should make this pilgrimage to the laboratory of the man whose imagination and ingenuity dramatically changed the world. Thomas Alva Edison came to West Orange in 1887, after he had invented the lightbulb in Menlo Park. This is where he perfected the motion picture camera and the phonograph, among other creations. You have an opportunity to get close to the man himself as you pass through his library and the old lab, where his coat hangs in its accustomed place and his tools lie ready at the workbench. In the theater you can watch Edwin S. Porter's *The Great Train Robbery* (1903), a landmark Edison production made here, and see informational material about Edison's life and times.

Ask at the Visitor Center by the lab about visits to nearby **Glenmont,** Edison's home, which has recently been restored. The number of visitors to this are restricted, so passes for the tours (*Wed.–Sun., 11–4*) are given on a first-come basis only. Edison bought this elegant Victorian house furnished, but added many characteristic personal touches of his own.

EAGLE ROCK RESERVATION, Eagle Rock Ave., West Orange, NJ 07052 (201-731-3000). *Open daily all year. Free. Wildlife preserve, picnic area (permit free), trails. Leashed pets only. Roads and lookout points are wheelchair-accessible.*

This 400-acre park has two popular lookout points that afford a good view of the local landscape and the distant New York skyscrapers.

Trip B-4
Art, History, and a President's Birthplace

- ISRAEL CRANE HOUSE
- MONTCLAIR ART MUSEUM
- GROVER CLEVELAND BIRTHPLACE

DISTANCE: About 20 miles from Columbus Circle.

FOR THE DRIVER: Take the **Garden State Parkway** south from the George Washington Bridge to Exit 148, Bloomfield Ave. *or* take **NJ-3** west from the Lincoln Tunnel, then the Garden State Parkway south as above. From Exit 148 head northwest on Bloomfield Ave. (Route 506) to Montclair. Shortly, at the traffic light, turn left on Orange Rd. and watch for the **Crane House,** on the right.

Continue down Orange Rd. to Elm St., turn left, and go back to Bloomfield Ave. Turn left and go down Bloomfield past Orange Rd., a block or so to the **Montclair Art Museum,** on the left.

Continue northwest on Bloomfield for about 3 miles to Caldwell. Shortly after you enter Caldwell, at Bloomfield and Arlington Ave., is the **Cleveland Birthplace.**

On this trip you are very close to the stops on Trip B-3, and may want to combine all or part of both trips. If you are coming from Eagle Rock Reservation, take Prospect Ave., at western edge of park, north about 2 miles to Bloomfield Ave. Turn right for art museum and Crane House, left for Cleveland Birthplace.

ISRAEL CRANE HOUSE, 110 Orange Rd., Montclair, NJ 07042 (201-744-1796). *Open Sept. through June, Sun. 2–5 and Wed. 1–4, other times by appointment; call ahead to be sure it's open. Closed July & Aug. except for special events. Adults $2, children 50¢. Not wheelchair-accessible.*

Headquarters of the Montclair Historical Society, this handsome Federal mansion was built in 1796 by Israel Crane, a successful businessman and a descendant of the founding family of Montclair (originally called Cranetown). A civic group saved the house from demolition in 1965 and moved it from Old Road to the present site. It is beautifully furnished in the varying styles of the period 1740–1840, and there are lovely herb and pleasure gardens on the grounds. Visitors can watch and participate in open-hearth cooking and see a variety of craft demonstrations including weaving, quilting, lacemaking, tinsmithing, blacksmithing, and basketry.

In the Victoriana House at 108 Orange Road are the Historical Society office and a research library with materials on Colonial and local history. Israel Crane's general store has been re-created in the **Country Store Museum and Gift Shop,** located in a house built in 1818 by Nathaniel Crane.

MONTCLAIR ART MUSEUM, South Mountain & Bloomfield Ave., Montclair, NJ 07042 (201-746-5555). *Open Tues.–Wed. and Fri.–Sat. 10–5, Thurs. 2–9, Sun. 2–5; closed Sat. during Aug. and Mon. all year. Adults $4, seniors and students $2, under 18 free; free to all on Thurs. Main floor is wheelchair-accessible.*

This is one of the finer small museums, with a permanent collection of over 6,000 works ranging from 19th-century portraiture and landscapes to abstract expressionism. The Hudson River School is well represented, as are some noted Montclair artists. Among the many American painters whose works hang here are Mary Cassatt, Edward Hopper, and Benjamin West. The museum also prides itself on its exhibits of Native American art, American costumes, English and Irish silver, and Chinese snuff bottles.

GROVER CLEVELAND BIRTHPLACE, 207 Bloomfield Ave., Caldwell, NJ 07006 (201-226-1810). *Open all year Wed.–Fri. 9–noon and 1–6, Sat. 9–noon and 1–5, Sun. 1–6; closed Thanksgiving, Christmas, New Year's.*

Closed when caretaker is away (call in advance). Free. Guided tour on request. Limited parking behind house. Steps into house, but will accommodate wheelchairs.

The Old Manse of the Caldwell First Presbyterian Church was just five years old when Grover Cleveland was born there in 1837. It's a homey place, furnished in late 19th-century style and maintained as a memorial to the only U.S. president born in New Jersey, though he lived in it for only four years. Personal mementos, pictures, and letters from the famous are displayed in wall cases.

Trip B-5
Into the Heart of the Great Swamp

- **GREAT SWAMP NATIONAL WILDLIFE REFUGE**

DISTANCE: About 40 miles from Columbus Circle.

FOR THE DRIVER: Take the **Garden State Parkway** south to Exit 142, *or* **New Jersey Turnpike** south to Exit 14, and pick up **I-78** west to Exit 48 (Chatham). Here take **NJ-24** northwest to Chatham, about 4 miles. In Chatham turn left on Fairmount Ave. at sign to Meyersville and go a little less than 2 miles to Southern Blvd. Turn right and go about ¾ mile to a sign for **Morris County Outdoor Education Center.** *Or,* from Chatham, remain on Fairmount Ave. and bear right onto Meyersville Rd. In Meyersville, turn right on New Vernon Rd. and go almost a mile to White Bridge Rd. Turn left on White Bridge, go just over a mile to Pleasant Plains Rd., and turn right. Shortly watch for signs to the south gate and refuge headquarters. For the **Somerset County Environmental Education Center,** continue on White Bridge Rd. across Pleasant Plains Rd. and watch for Lord Stirling Park and signs for center, just outside the refuge boundary on the right. To go directly from Meyersville to the self-service information booth at the **Wildlife Observation Center,** continue straight on New Vernon Rd. across White Bridge Rd. New Vernon becomes Long Hill Rd. and takes you to the observation center, just under a mile on the left.

Alternative route from the GWB via Interstate all the way: Take **I-80** west from the bridge to Exit 43, then **I-287** south to Exit 26, N. Maple Ave. Go south on N. Maple about ¾ mile to Madisonville Rd.,

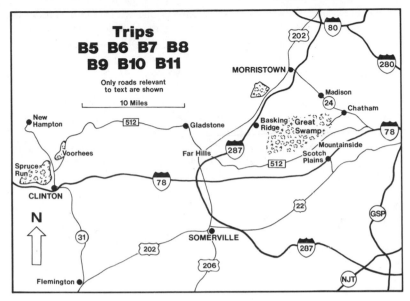

following signs for the Great Swamp. At Madisonville turn left and go about ½ mile to Pleasant Plains Rd. Turn right here and pass through the north gate to the refuge headquarters.

GREAT SWAMP NATIONAL WILDLIFE REFUGE, R.D. 1, Box 152, Basking Ridge, NJ 07920 (908-647-1222). *Open daily all year, dawn to dusk. Free. Visitors allowed in designated areas only. No bicycles or horses on trails. Picnicking, camping, and alcohol are not allowed. Smoking and pets allowed only in parking areas. Self-service information booth at the Wildlife Observation Center. Waterproof shoes recommended, insect repellent and protective clothing advisable May– Sept. Not wheelchair-accessible once off the paved roads.*

About 25,000 years ago, the Wisconsin Glacier reached its southernmost point of advance, looked around, and retreated, leaving the Great Swamp in its wake. In 1708 the Delaware Indians deeded a huge tract of land including the Great Swamp to the English in exchange for a barrel of rum, 15 kettles, 4 pistols, 4 cutlasses, assorted goods and sundries, and £30 sterling. Various attempts to log and farm the area proved unprofitable over the next two centuries. In 1959 a new airport for New York was proposed for the site, but the North American Wildlife Federation launched a successful campaign to block the project. The 3,000 acres purchased as a result of their efforts were donated to the Department of the Interior in 1960 and became the nucleus of today's 6,783-acre refuge.

Great Swamp is home to a great variety of flora and fauna, including swamp woodlands, hardwood stands, marshlands, over 200 species of birds, and numerous mammals, fish, reptiles and amphibians, among the latter the rare bog turtle and blue-spotted salamander. Since 1968 the eastern two-thirds of the refuge has been a designated wilderness area. Man-made structures and motorized equipment are prohibited, and the public is restricted to good old foot travel on more than 10 miles of trails. The western third is a wildlife management area regulated to maintain habitat and encourage breeding.

At the eastern end of the Great Swamp, just outside the refuge boundary, is the **Great Swamp Outdoor Education Center** (201-635-6629), operated by the Morris County Park Commission (201-326-7600). The center offers a varied program of weekend activities, guided tours and workshops, and maintains a mile-long trail and boardwalk into the swamp.

Outside the western boundary of the swamp is the **Somerset County Environmental Education Center** (908-766-2489), a solar research station and park offering walking trails, field trips, and special programs.

Trip B-6
On the Outskirts of
the Great Swamp

- MUSEUM OF EARLY TRADES AND CRAFTS
- BASKING RIDGE
- U.S. GOLF ASSOCIATION GOLF HOUSE
- U.S. EQUESTRIAN TEAM HEADQUARTERS

DISTANCE: The farthest point is about 50 miles from Columbus Circle.

FOR THE DRIVER: Take the **Garden State Parkway** south to Exit 142 *or* the **New Jersey Turnpike** south to Exit 14, and pick up **I-78** west to Exit 48. Here take **NJ-24** northwest to Madison, about 6 miles. Go through downtown Madison on 24 (which becomes Main St.) to the junction with Green Village Rd. On the left is the **Museum of Early Trades and Crafts.**

Continue on 24 to Morristown (Trips B-7 and B-8). Go around Morristown Green and follow **US-202** south for about 6 miles through an area of small towns and antique shops. Watch for the Old Mill Inn on the left, opposite Van Dorn Mill, on the right. At the stoplight, turn left onto North Finley Ave. and go about a mile to North Maple Ave. Here is the church and the cemetery where the **Basking Ridge** Oak stands. Drive or walk up the hill in front of the church for a good view of the center of town.

Return to US-202 and continue south about 6 miles to Far Hills. Turn left on **Route 512** and go about 2 miles to the **Golf House.**

Go back on 512, continuing through Far Hills towards Pottersville. Near Peapack 512 veers left (watch for sign) to Gladstone. In Gladstone turn left on Pottersville Rd. (still Rte. 512), go through first light, then go about ½ mile to the third driveway on the left, entrance to the **U.S. Equestrian Team Headquarters.**

MUSEUM OF EARLY TRADES AND CRAFTS, Main St. & Green Village Rd., Madison, NJ 07940 (201-377-2982). *Open all year, Tues.–Sat. 10–4, Sun. 2–5; closed Mon. & major holidays. Adults $2, children $1. Guided tours by appointment. Will accommodate wheelchairs.*

This eye-catching limestone building, almost a small castle, houses displays depicting New Jersey life from the 1600s to the 1800s. The exhibits include a schoolroom, a cobbler's shop, a kitchen, a general store, and an interesting array of period tools and the products they fashioned for the early New Jersey villagers. The building itself is a turn-of-the-century gem.

BASKING RIDGE is a small, historic town proud of its past and heedful of the present, making certain its appearance remains unchanged and attractive. On the way into town you will pass the **Van Dorn Mill** of 1843, an architectural landmark and symbol of New Jersey farming. Markers along the main street tell of the earliest settlement here in 1720, point out the site of the Widow White's tavern, where the treasonous General Charles Lee was ignominiously captured by the British in 1776, and inform us that today's Presbyterian church supplanted a log church that had been erected under an old oak tree. In the adjoining cemetery this ancient tree, known as the **Basking Ridge Oak,** still stands. It is said to be second in size only to the Salem Oak. For further information, contact the Basking Ridge Association, Basking Ridge, NJ 07920 (908-647-6470).

U.S. GOLF ASSOCIATION GOLF HOUSE, Liberty Corner Rd., Far Hills, NJ 07931 (908-234-2300). *Open all year, Mon.–Fri. 9–5, Sat.–Sun. 10–4; closed major holidays. Free. A few steps into the building, but the* *displays and gift shop are all on the main floor.*

In 1972 the United States Golf Association moved from New York into the red brick Georgian Colonial estate once owned by the W. J. Sloane family of Far Hills. Part of the building is now a museum that charts the history of golf from its origins to the present day. Fascinating displays depict the evolution of golfing equipment, the rules of the game, and clothing worn on the links. You will also see trophies, photographs, pictures of golf courses, and clubs and balls used by today's champions. There is a valuable golfing reference library, and a gift shop that sells golf-related memorabilia and artwork.

U.S. EQUESTRIAN TEAM HEADQUARTERS, Gladstone, NJ 07934 (908-234-1251). *Open all year Mon.–Sat. 8:30–4:30; closed major holidays. Free. Call in advance to make sure the team is not on tour. Stables and some activities are wheelchair-accessible.*

This is an extraordinary treat for horse lovers. Here you can watch the U.S. riding teams train for the Pan American and Olympic games. The horses work out in the morning, and rehearsals for the contests include dressage, show jumping, three-day eventing, and driving. The organization has a long record of major awards.

Trip B-7
The Continental Trail After Trenton, Before Yorktown

- **MORRISTOWN NATIONAL HISTORICAL PARK**

DISTANCE: About 45 miles from Columbus Circle.

FOR THE DRIVER: Take **I-80** west from the George Washington Bridge to Exit 43, then **I-287** south to Exit 32, Morristown. From the exit ramp turn left on Ridgedale to Morris Ave., then left again on Morris Ave., crossing I-287 and passing the Ford Mansion to Washington Place. Here turn left to the parking lot behind the mansion. The route is well marked with brown signs directing you to **Washington's Headquarters.** At the **Historical Museum** pick up a brochure for a self-guided tour through the rest of the park. Note that you are now within a short drive of the sites on trips B-6 and B-8.

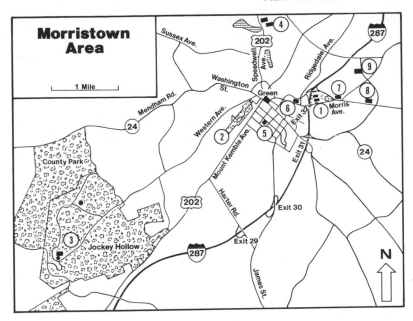

Continue west across I-287 through the center of Morristown. From the main square take Washington St., then make a left on Western Ave., followed by another left at Ann St. that leads steeply uphill to **Fort Nonsense.**

Return to Western Ave. and follow south to **Jockey Hollow.**

MORRISTOWN NATIONAL HISTORICAL PARK, Washington Place, Morristown, NJ 07960 (201-539-2085). *Grounds open all year daily 9–sunset; Historical Museum and Ford Mansion daily 9–5; Jockey Hollow Visitor Center and Wick House May–Oct daily 9–5, limited times rest of year; all buildings closed Thanksgiving, Christmas, New Year's. No park entry fee; combination admission to Historical Museum and Ford Mansion $1, under 16 and over 62 free. Free parking. Brochures for self-guided auto tour of the park are available at the Historical Museum and Visitor Center. Leashed pets only. Museum, first floor of Ford Mansion, and Visitor Center are wheelchair-accessible.*

Created by an Act of Congress in 1933, Morristown National Historical Park occupies some 1,600 acres that played a crucial role in the Revolutionary War. Twice, in 1777 and again in 1779–80, the Continental Army wintered here under conditions of extreme hardship. Washington chose Morristown because it is protected on the east by swamplands and by the Watchung ridges, which afforded an excellent vantage point for keeping watch on the large British force in New York City. But these strategic advantages were almost outweighed by the bitter cold weather, chronic shortages of food and clothing, and by outbreaks of disease—perhaps harsher enemies than the British. Though no decisive battles occurred at Morristown, the two winter encampments were in many ways the greatest test of Washington's leadership and the courage of his men.

Begin your tour in the **Historical Museum** at **Washington's Headquarters** (1), which displays Washington memorabilia, period weapons, and a 104-pound link of the chain that was stretched across the Hudson from West Point to Constitution Island to block British warships (see Trip C-12). A 15-minute film recalls the harsh winter of 1779–80 and shows the dramatic contrast between the lives of the officers and those of the ordinary soldiers. Dioramas depict Washington's meeting with Lafayette and other events, and there is a Gilbert Stuart painting of Washington, but not the one immortalized on the dollar bill.

Just beyond the museum stands the **Ford Mansion,** which served as General Washington's headquarters. Fully restored to its 1780 condition, it may be seen on guided tours that begin at the museum. This gracious Colonial house was built by Jacob Ford, Jr. between 1772 and

The Ford Mansion

Inside the Ford Mansion—George Washington slept here

1774, and was one of the grandest homes in Morristown at the time. When the Revolution began, Ford opened a gunpowder mill to supply the patriot army, in which he became a colonel. He took sick and died during the ill-fated New Jersey "Mud Rounds" campaign in the winter of 1776. Two years later his widow squeezed herself, her three children, and any belongings she valued (some of the patriots were prone to pilfering) into two rooms and offered the rest of the house to General Washington for use as his headquarters. Here he spent one of the worst winters of the 18th century, when no less than 28 blizzards blasted Morristown and compounded the miseries of his men; here he met with foreign dignitaries, including the young Marquis de Lafayette bringing welcome news of French support; and here he fired off an endless stream of letters pleading provisions for the army from Congress and the states.

The next stop on the tour is **Fort Nonsense** (2), a hill about a mile and a half away that offers a commanding view of the surrounding countryside. Legend has it that Washington ordered the hill fortified to keep his troops occupied and take take their minds off their troubles (which included a smallpox epidemic) during the first encampment of 1777. In fact, the fort had great strategic value and was the site of a beacon that was part of an alarm system stretching all the way to the Hudson Highlands (see Madam Brett Homestead, Trip D-9). Today, little trace remains of the earthworks and redoubt, but the view is still grand.

A few miles south of Fort Nonsense is **Jockey Hollow** (3), site of the 1779–80 encampment. Here Washington's troops felled some 900 acres of timber to build huts and keep themselves in firewood. Washington issued strict specifications for the construction of the huts, which were to be well drained and ventilated to avoid the outbreak of disease that had decimated his troops at Valley Forge two years earlier. By January 1780, nearly 1,200 huts housed some 10,000 men, making Jockey Hollow the sixth-largest city in the United States. There are replicas of the soldiers' huts at Sugar Loaf Hill and markers throughout the hollow noting the locations of the various brigades. Sugar Loaf Hill, in particular, recalls the hardships of the Continental Army: in 1780 the troops of the Pennsylvania Line, stationed here, put down a mutiny by the First Connecticut Brigade; the following year they themselves mutinied, demanding back pay and redress of their many grievances. Near Sugar Loaf Hill is the Grand Parade, a large field where the troops drilled when not confined to their huts by snowdrifts.

Also in Jockey Hollow is the **Wick House,** which served as headquarters for Major General Arthur St. Clair in 1779–80. This house was owned by Henry Wick, a prosperous farmer, and is very different from the Ford Mansion in its homey, comfortable air. Wick lived here with his daughter Temperance, who distinguished herself, so the story goes, by hiding her horse in a closet when Colonial troops came to requisition it.

Trip B-8
More to See in Morristown

- HISTORIC SPEEDWELL
- MACCULLOCH HALL
- SCHUYLER-HAMILTON HOUSE
- ACORN HALL
- MORRIS MUSEUM
- FRELINGHUYSEN ARBORETUM

DISTANCE: About 45 miles from Columbus Circle.

FOR THE DRIVER: Take **I-80** west from the George Washington Bridge to Exit 43, then **I-287** south to Exit 35, NJ-10 and Whippany. Go west on 10 (away from Whippany) about 1½ miles to the junction with **US-**

202. Turn left and go south on 202 towards Morristown. Cross Hanover Ave. and watch for **Historic Speedwell,** shortly on the left (202 becomes Speedwell Ave.).

Continue south on Speedwell to the Morristown Green and bear right onto Bank St. for 2 blocks. Turn left on Macculloch Ave. for 2 blocks to **Macculloch Hall.**

Continue east for 2 blocks and turn left onto Madison St., which becomes Elm St. At Morris St. turn right, under the railroad trestle, then go a short block past it to Olyphant Place. Turn left here to **Schuyler-Hamilton House.**

Return to Morris Ave., turn left, and continue across I-287 past Washington's Headquarters (Trip B-7). Shortly come to a 3-way split. Staying in righthand lane, you can go left around the jughandle following sign for U-Turn, then passing the Governor Morris Inn to **Acorn Hall,** on the right.

Continue back on Morris Ave. At the 3-way split, bear right through a stoplight onto Columbia Road. Go uphill and turn left at first light onto Normandy Heights Rd., then make an immediate left to the **Morris Museum.**

From the museum turn left on Normandy Heights Rd. and continue to Whippany Rd. Turn left on Whippany and proceed briefly to Hanover Ave. Turn left on Hanover and go a short distance to the **Frelinghuysen Arboretum** on the left.

Not only George Washington stayed in Morristown—so did several other famous people. Here's a chance to explore one of New Jersey's most interesting communities. Note that four of its attractions have rather limited opening times, so you probably won't be able to see them all in one day. The site numbers in the text correspond to numbers on the map for Trip B-7. For further information contact the Historic Morris Area Convention & Visitors Bureau, 10 Park Ave. at Columbia Turnpike, Morristown, NJ 07960 (201-539-9105).

HISTORIC SPEEDWELL (4), 333 Speedwell Ave., Morristown, NJ 07960 (201-540-0211). *Open May through Oct., Thurs.–Fri. noon–4, Sat.–Sun. 1–5, last admission one hour before closing. Adults $3, seniors $2, children $1. Free parking at entrance. No pets, no smoking or photographing inside buildings. Vail House is partially wheelchair-accessible.*

Historic Speedwell preserves the site of two major technological innovations that helped fuel America's Industrial Revolution in the early 19th century. Judge Stephen Vail, self-made man and family patriarch, built the Speedwell Iron Works next to his Homestead Farm here along the Whippany River. In 1818–19 this foundry cast most of

The Cotton Factory at Speedwell

the machinery for the *S.S. Savannah,* the first transatlantic steamship. Later, in 1837, his son Alfred began a collaboration with the artist and inventor Samuel F. B. Morse, and in January 1838 the first successful demonstration of Morse's electromagnetic telegraph took place in the cotton factory, where some of the original wiring may still be seen nailed to the wall. The message that day was "A patient waiter is no loser," courtesy of Judge Vail. "What hath God wrought" came six years later.

A National Historic Site organized in 1966, Speedwell consists of nine buildings, including the Vail House, the cotton factory, a water-powered wheelhouse, a granary, a carriage house, and three historic houses relocated from various parts of Morristown to avoid demolition. There are comprehensive displays on the development of both the steamship engine and the telegraph, a guided tour of the fully-restored Vail House with its original paintings by Morse, a gift shop, and a self-guided tour of the entire complex.

MACCULLOCH HALL (5), 45 Macculloch Ave., Morristown, NJ 07960 (201-538-2404). *Open April to mid-Dec., Sun. & Thurs. 2–4:30, closed holidays. Adults $3, seniors $2, students $1.*

George Macculloch, the originator of the Morris Canal (see Trip B-16), built this handsome Federal mansion between 1806 and 1815, and it remained the home of his descendants until the middle of the 20th century. Filled with an eclectic assortment of the American and Europeans decorative arts from the 18th and 19th centuries, it is most noted for its collection of famous cartoons by Thomas Nast, who lived across the street. This 19-century illustrator created the universal image of Santa Claus that everyone knows so well, gave the Democratic Party its donkey, and helped toppled the corrupt political regime of Boss Tweed in New York City. Another treasure in the house is the original portrait of George Washington by Rembrandt Peale.

SCHUYLER-HAMILTON HOUSE (6), 5 Olyphant Place, Morristown, NJ 07960 (201-267-4039). *Open all year Tues. & Sun. 2–5, and by appointment. Adults $1, children under 12 free. Many steps, difficult for wheelchairs.*

This Colonial house and its garden was the setting for the courtship of Betsy Schuyler by Alexander Hamilton, then a colonel in the Continental Army, stationed in the nearby Ford Mansion (see Trip B-7) as part of General Washington's staff. The house has period furnishings and is maintained by the local chapter of the D.A.R.

ACORN HALL (7), 68 Morris Ave., Morristown, NJ 07960 (201-267-3465). *Open Mar.–Dec. Thus. 11–3, Sun. 1:30–4; gardens open daily dawn–dusk; house and gardens closed Jan.–Feb. and major holidays. Adults $2, children 50¢. Steps into house, interior difficult for wheelchairs.*

This beautifully preserved Victorian house (1853) is the headquarters of the Morris County Historical Society. The scrollwork embellishments on the exterior are a good indication of what to expect inside. There are many priceless furnishings, including a Rococo Revival parlor set, a printed velvet rug identical to one displayed at London's Crystal Palace Exhibition in 1851–52, and some porcelains given to Commodore Perry, a relative of the second owner, when he opened Japan to Western trade in 1854.

Acorn Hall takes its name from the majestic, centuries-old red oak that stands near the driveway. The Home Garden Club of Morristown has restored the grounds to re-create a period garden of extraordinary variety and beauty, well worth the trip in itself.

MORRIS MUSEUM (8), 6 Normandy Heights Rd., Morristown, NJ 07960 (201-538-0454). *Open all year, Mon.–Sat. 10–5, Sun. 1–5. Adults $2, seniors and children $1. Ramp into building, elevator for wheelchairs.*

This wonderful museum, in an imposing red-brick mansion, holds just about everything from fossils to live animals, art to archaeology, old-time toys to computers. The museum sponsors a lively program of concerts, lectures, workshops, and special events; and there are lots of activities geared towards kids, including a special room for preschoolers.

FRELINGHUYSEN ARBORETUM (9), 53 East Hanover Ave., Morristown, NJ 07960 (201-326-7600). *Open daily 9–4:30. Free. Hiking trails, nature programs, concerts, special events. No pets. Braille Trail is wheelchair-accessible.*

The Morris County Park Commission has its headquarters here in an 1891 country estate, a lovely specimen of Victorian architecture that also houses a fine horticultural library. Elaborate gardens, flowering shrubs, and brilliant displays of roses make the grounds worth visiting at almost any time of the year. There are 127 acres of forest and gardens crisscrossed by well-marked trails.

Trip B-9
From a Stage Coach Stop
to the High Hills

- STAGE HOUSE INN AND VILLAGE
- TERRY LOU ZOO
- WATCHUNG RESERVATION
- TRAILSIDE NATURE AND SCIENCE CENTER

DISTANCE: About 30 miles from Columbus Circle.

FOR THE DRIVER: Take the **Garden State Parkway** south to Exit 140 *or* the **New Jersey Turnpike** south to Exit 14. From either, take **US-22** west toward Somerville. After passing New Providence Rd., watch for sign on US-22 to take Mountain Ave. to Scotch Plains. Turn left on this into town, and again left on Park Ave. to Front St. and the **Stage House Inn and Village.**

Continue on Front St. for several blocks to Terrill Rd., where you turn left to the end at Raritan Rd. On the right is the **Terry Lou Zoo.**

Return on Terrill to US-22, turn right (east) and go back past Scotch Plains to Mountainside/New Providence Rd. exit. Take the main road up the mountain to the **Watchung Reservation.** Turn right onto Tracy Drive, then take the third exit out of the traffic circle. When the road turns sharply left, turn right to the **Trailside** parking lot.

STAGE HOUSE INN AND VILLAGE, Front St. & Park Ave., Scotch Plains, NJ 07076 (908-322-4224). *Shops open all year Mon.–Sat. during business hours. Inn open daily 11:30–9:30, Fri.–Sat. until 10:30. Mostly wheelchair-accessible.*

This collection of restored 18th-century buildings holds a number of small shops surrounding a courtyard and offering early crafts, leatherwork, antiques, silverware, and the like. The Stage House Inn, built in 1737, once served weary travelers taking the two-day trip between New York and Philadelphia on the Swift Sure Stage Line along the Old York Road. Today, it is a well-known restaurant. Across the street is the **Osborn Cannonball House** (open Sept.–June, 2–4 Sun. only, 908-889-1928), hit by cannon fire during the Battle of Short Hills in 1777.

TERRY LOU ZOO, 1451 Raritan Rd., Scotch Plains, NJ 07076 (908-322-7180). *Open daily except in winter, weekdays, 10–4, weekends and holidays 10–6. Adults $6, children 1–12 $3, under 1 free. Largely wheelchair-accessible.*

This privately-owned zoo has an outstanding collection of tropical birds and game, including lions, tigers, hippos, elephants, giraffes, and orangutans. Its design allows a closer look at the animals than is the case in more conventional zoos. If you happen to have small kids in tow, they'll certainly enjoy the petting area and pony rides.

WATCHUNG RESERVATION, Mountainside, NJ 07092. *Open daily all year. Free. Hiking trails, cross-country ski trails, picnic facilities and fireplaces, fishing and boating by permit at Lake Surprise, stables (fee) and bridle paths. Leashed pets only. Difficult for wheelchairs. For further information, contact the Union County Dept. of Parks & Recreation, Union County Admin. Bldg., Elizabeth, NJ 07207 (908-527-4900).*

There is much to do in this scenic 2,000-acre preserve that stretches along the Watchung Ridges overlooking Blue Brook Valley. In season there's a wonderful rhododendron display, usually in peak season a little past mid-May. An observation tower 575 feet above sea level provides an excellent view and a good lookout for bird migrations. The 10-mile Sierra Loop and other marked hiking trails, the mile-long Lake Surprise, and the 30 miles of bridle paths are also popular attractions. Much of the reservation has been left in its natural state, and many Indian trails have been preserved. The name Watchung, meaning "high hills," was also left by the Indians, and sometimes in these quiet woods you get the feeling they're not so far away from their old camping grounds.

TRAILSIDE NATURE AND SCIENCE CENTER, Coles Ave. & New Providence Rd., Mountainside, NJ 07092 (908-789-3670). *Visitor center and museum open 1–5 daily April through mid-Nov., weekends only the rest of the year, closed holidays. Free except for planetarium shows. Mostly wheelchair-accessible.*

   Trailside, located in the Watchung Reservation, was New Jersey's first nature center. Designed by the noted architect Michael Graves, it first opened in 1941 and has been offering fascinating exhibits on animals, and birds, plants, minerals, and other natural wonders ever since.

Trip B-10
George and Martha and Gardens of the World

- WALLACE HOUSE STATE HISTORIC SITE
- OLD DUTCH PARSONAGE STATE HISTORIC SITE
- DUKE GARDENS

DISTANCE: About 45 miles from Columbus Circle.

FOR THE DRIVER: Take the **Garden State Parkway** south to Exit 142 *or* the **New Jersey Turnpike** south to Exit 14. From either, take **I-78** west to Exit 30, then **I-287** south to Exit 13. Continue on **US-202/206** south towards Princeton, staying on 206 when it branches off from 202. Shortly on 206, just beyond the railroad overpass, is Somerset St. Turn left for a block, then right at Middagh to the end. Turn left on Washington Place for the **Wallace House** and **Old Dutch Parsonage.**

   Go back to US-206 and continue south about a mile to the **Duke Gardens.**

Here's a great trip to take in the dreary off-season, when the exotic indoor gardens are open. Don't forget to make advance reservations for them, however.

WALLACE HOUSE STATE HISTORIC SITE, 38 Washington Place, Somerville, NJ 08876 (908-725-1015). *Open all year Wed.–Fri. 9–5, Sat. 10–5, Sun. 1–5; closed Thanksgiving, Christmas, New Year's. Free. Not wheelchair-accessible.*

General Washington made this Colonial house his headquarters in 1778, just after it was built. He and Mrs. Washington stayed here into the spring of 1779 while the Continental Army was camped at Middle Brook (now Somerville), experiencing remarkably moderate weather in contrast to the two brutal winters at Morristown (see Trip B-7). A tour acquaints you with both the military and social life of the house during the Revolution. Although not the ones used by Washington, the period furnishings are authentic, and the typical 18th-century kitchen has a special interest.

OLD DUTCH PARSONAGE STATE HISTORIC SITE, 65 Washington Place, Somerville, NJ 08876 (908-725-1015). *Located across the street from the Wallace House, same information as above; check at the Wallace House for the caretaker.*

In this brick structure, built in 1751 and moved from its original site, the Reverend John Frelinghuysen established the first Dutch Reformed theological seminary in the New World. The seminary became Queens College and later Rutgers University. One of the occupants of the parsonage, the Reverend Jacob Hardenburgh, was a friend of Washington's. An interesting novelty is the smokehouse, usually built outdoors but here installed on the third floor, perhaps because of the constant wartime foraging.

DUKE GARDENS, Route 206 South, Somerville, NJ 08876 (908-722-3700). *Open for guided tours Oct. through May, daily 12–4; closed June through Sept., Thanksgiving, Christmas, New Year's; advance reservations required. Adults $5, seniors and children $2.50, under 6 free. No high heels, no cameras, no pets. Cobbled paths, narrow walks, some stairs; very difficult for wheelchairs.*

An acre of exquisite gardens in 11 different styles flourishes here under glass in carefully controlled temperatures. This magnificent collection of international flora includes a lush tropical jungle, a starkly beautiful patch of Arizona desert, a formal French parterre garden, a Chinese grotto, an English summer garden, a Japanese garden, and an Indo-Persian display. Duke Gardens is one of the few attractions closed in summer and open in winter; it's a perfect escape from the city during those long gray months that never seem to end. Note again that advance reservations are required at all times.

Trip B-11
Shops and Houses
out of America's Past

- CLINTON HISTORICAL MUSEUM VILLAGE
- HUNTERDON ART CENTER
- TOWNSHIP OF LEBANON MUSEUM

DISTANCE: The farthest point, New Hampton, is about 70 miles from Columbus Circle.

FOR THE DRIVER: Take the **New Jersey Turnpike** south to Exit 14, or the **Garden State Parkway** south to Exit 142A. From either, pick up **I-78** west to Exit 15, the second exit for Clinton. Turn right from the ramp onto West Main Street, go about ¼ mile, and turn left at the Clinton House Inn to the **Clinton Historical Museum Village,** just before the bridge.

Cross the Raritan River to the **Hunterdon Art Center,** just opposite the museum village, on Center Street.

Return to Main Street and turn left through the shopping area for about a block. Turn left on Leigh Street and follow it out of town to **NJ-31.** From here you can head south back to I-78, or head north to the two state parks and New Hampton.

Continue north on NJ-31 to **Spruce Run State Park** or turn right onto **Route 513,** which leads through High Bridge to the **Voorhees State Park.**

For the **Township of Lebanon Museum,** continue north on NJ-31 past the Hampton turnoff, then turn right on Musconetcong River Road to New Hampton.

With its mixture of Colonial and Victorian buildings nestled by the placid banks of the Raritan River, Clinton easily ranks among New Jersey's more attractive small towns. What makes it especially interesting for daytrippers, however, is the restored museum village with its red mill of 1812, an art center, the appealing shops along Main Street, and a number of colorful restaurants including an old stagecoach inn from 1743. Clinton is not nearly as overexposed or commercialized as some of the other preserved old towns in the region, and certainly makes a pleasant respite from urban life.

The Old Red Mill and the Hunterdon Art Center

CLINTON HISTORICAL MUSEUM VILLAGE, 56 Main St., Clinton, NJ 08809 (908-735-4101). *Open April through Oct., Tues.–Sun. 10–4. Adults $3, seniors $1.50, children $1, under 6 free. Concerts and special events throughout the season. Some wheelchair-accessible facilities and activities.*

You don't have to be an antiquarian to enjoy the Old Red Mill and reconstructed village set in a 10-acre park complete with waterfall and 150-foot limestone cliffs. Life in bygone times is re-created in the mill, where the waterwheel still turns as it did in the days when grain, flaxseed, limestone, graphite, and talc were processed here. You can also visit a blacksmith's shop, a turn-of-the-century general store and post office, an 1860 little red schoolhouse, a log cabin, old lime kilns, a herb garden, and the gift shop.

HUNTERDON ART CENTER, 7 Center St., Clinton, NJ 08809 (908-735-8415). *Open all year, Tues. through Fri., noon–4:30; weekends 1–5; closed major holidays. Donation. Wheelchair-accessible.*

This large, cool, barnlike gallery on the South Branch of the Raritan River was once a gristmill (1837). Now it houses exhibits, a small theater, and displays of arts and crafts by prominent contemporary artists (some works are for sale). The center sponsors a variety of workshops and concerts throughout the year.

SPRUCE RUN STATE PARK, Box 289A Van Syckels Rd., Clinton, NJ 08809 (908-638-8572).

This State recreation area just north of Clinton surrounds a reservoir and offers picnic areas with grills and shelters, boating, swimming, fishing, and a range of winter sports. Special consideration was given to wheelchair accessibility in the design of Spruce Run.

VOORHEES STATE PARK, R.D. 2, Box 80, Rt. 513, Glen Gardner, NJ 08826 (908-638-6969).

A smaller and less "civilized" park, Voorhees has picnic areas, hiking trails, a scenic overlook, and a playground for children. It is partially wheelchair-accessible.

TOWNSHIP OF LEBANON MUSEUM, Musconetcong River Rd., New Hampton, NJ 08827 (908-537-6464). *Open all year, Tues. and Thurs. 9:30–5, Sat. 1–5. Free. Workshops, craft classes, lectures, special events. Main floor is wheelchair-accessible.*

Put on your pinafores, hitch up your suspenders, pack your McGuffey's Readers, and grab your slates—you don't want to be late for the Museum at New Hampton, a 19th-century schoolhouse with a vintage, no-nonsense, Three-R's classroom featuring original books, old-style desks, and a potbellied stove. The building, constructed in 1823 as a one-room school, was enlarged in the 1870s, and the second floor is now used for changing exhibits of such esoterica as poison bottles, Hunterdon County milk bottles and clothespin dolls.

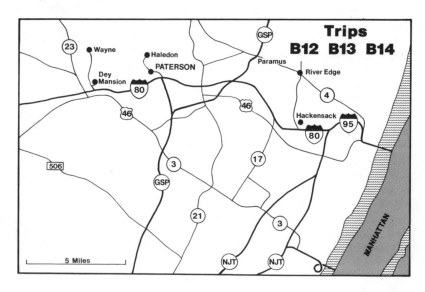

Trip B-12
A Fascinating Sub Trip

- U.S.S. *LING* SUBMARINE
- VON STEUBEN HOUSE STATE HISTORIC SITE
- VAN SAUN COUNTY PARK AND ZOO

DISTANCE: About 15 miles from Columbus Circle.

FOR THE DRIVER: Take **I-80** west from the George Washington Bridge to Exit 66, Hudson St., just across the Hackensack River. Coming off ramp, turn left on Vreeland at the stop sign, and go a block to Hudson St. Turn left and go to fifth light on Hudson, turning right here onto East Kansas, then turn left at light onto River St. The **Ling** is docked at Borg Park, about ¼ mile on the right.

From the *Ling*, turn right on River St. **(Route 503)** and follow it north. About ¼ mile past the junction with NJ-4, turn right on Main St. in River Edge. Continue to a dead end and the **Steuben House.**

Go back to **NJ-4** and go west to the Forest Ave. exit. At the traffic light remain on Forest and continue north briefly to **Van Saun County Park** on the right.

To return to New York, go east on NJ-4 back to the George Washington Bridge.

U.S.S. *Ling*, New Jersey Naval Museum, Court & River St., Hackensack, NJ 07601 (201-342-3268). *Open daily 10–5 except major holidays. Sometimes closed on Mon. & Tues. in winter. Adults $3, children $2. Guided 45-minute tours. Not wheelchair-accessible.*

The *Ling* is a real submarine, used in World War II. Later on it became part of the reserve fleet, then a training vessel. Since 1973 she has been berthed on the Hackensack River, donated as a memorial to those who lost their lives in submarine service. The 312-foot-long vessel is kept in perfect working condition, and you can tour the crew quarters, the engine rooms, the torpedo rooms, and more. Visitors learn about some of the problems of submarine warfare, and some of the improvements that have been made since the *Ling* was built. Ashore, there's a small museum with related displays. The ship is heated, but in winter it's wise to dress warmly. As for agility, it helps to have some, but many senior citizens have made the tour and enjoyed every minute.

108   NEW JERSEY

VON STEUBEN HOUSE STATE HISTORIC SITE, 1209 Main St., River Edge, NJ 07661 (201-487-1739). *Open all year Wed.–Sun. 10–noon and 1–5, Sun. 2–5; closed Thanksgiving, Christmas, New Year's. No ramps, but will accommodate wheelchairs.*

Built in 1695, this attractive dwelling was enlarged by the Zabriskie family in 1752 and is sometimes known as the Zabriskie House. Because the Zabriskies were Tories, the house was confiscated during the Revolution and given to Baron von Steuben in gratitude for his help in training the Continental Army. The Baron eventually chose not to live in the house and sold it back to the Zabriskies. Today it is the headquarters of the Bergen County Historical Society. VIsitors will find a good sampling of period furniture, glassware, antiques, toys, and Indian artifacts.

VAN SAUN COUNTY PARK AND ZOO, 216 Forest Ave., Paramus, NJ 07652 (201-262-3771). *Grounds open daily all year, dawn to dusk. Picnic facilities, fishing, playgrounds, bike trail, ice skating, tennis (fee). Zoo is wheelchair-accessible, park largely barrier-free.*

This popular park is likely to be crowded at the height of the summer season, but the kids will enjoy the recently-expanded zoo, the 1860s farmyard display, the miniature train ride, and even the large walk-through aviary. Van Saun is also worth a visit in the spring, when the early gardens bloom. Particularly attractive is the garden at Washington Spring, from whose waters the general is said to have drunk.

Inside the Paterson Museum

Trip B-13
Discovering the
"Cradle of American Industry"

- THE GREAT FALLS
- S.U.M. HISTORIC DISTRICT
- THE PATERSON MUSEUM
- AMERICAN LABOR MUSEUM

DISTANCE: About 20 miles from Columbus Circle.

FOR THE DRIVER: Take **I-80** west from the George Washington Bridge to Exit 57B and follow Main St. north into Paterson. Turn left on Market St., then right on Spruce St. to the Visitor Center at the **Great Falls.**

From the falls, cross the Passaic River on Wayne Ave. and turn left on Front St. briefly to Preakness Ave. Turn right, proceed a few blocks to Union Ave., and turn right again. Shortly, at West Broadway, turn left. At the third light make a sharp right onto Barbour St., then the second left onto Mason Ave. The **American Labor Museum** is on the left at Norwood St.

PUBLIC TRANSPORTATION: Buses depart New York City's Port Authority Bus Terminal and points in New Jersey frequently for Paterson, where they stop at the Paterson Bus Terminal on Broadway, near the Great Falls. **Trains** operated by New Jersey Transit leave Hoboken (connection to midtown Manhattan via PATH trains) frequently for Paterson, whose train station is within walking distance of the Great Falls by following Market St. west and Spruce St. north.

History may not be quaint in gritty Paterson, but it's for real and it's intensely interesting. This is where America's Industrial Revolution began in the late 18th century when the enormous waterpower potential of the Great Falls was first harnessed. Much of its 19th-century industrialization has survived intact and may be explored on self-guided walking tours, along with the impressive Great Falls themselves.

GREAT FALLS HISTORIC DISTRICT, 65 McBride Ave. Extension, Paterson, NJ 07501 (201-279-9587). *Visitor Center (1) open weekdays 9–4; offers free brochure and map for do-it-yourself walking tours. Guided tours for groups by appointment only, may be customized to suit special interests.*

Two hundred feet wide and 77 feet high, the **Great Falls** (2) of the Passaic River can be counted on for a spectacular display in any season. They were visited in 1778 by George Washington, the Marquis de Lafayette, and Alexander Hamilton. Attracted by the tremendous power of the falls, Hamilton later became one of the founders of the **Society for Useful Manufactures (S.U.M.),** which established Paterson in 1791 as the first planned industrial city in the newly-independent United States. Pierre L'Enfant, planner of Washington, D.C., designed raceways (now renovated) for the various mills, and Paterson grew rapidly. In 1835 Samuel Colt began manufacturing his revolvers here; then the silk boom made Paterson into America's "Silk City." The iron industry was turning out Rogers locomotives at a great rate by the 19th century, and the aeronautics industry came to town after World War I.

Changing technologies gradually made the mills and factories of the Great Falls district obsolete; today it is designated a National Historic Landmark preserving an important chapter in American industrial history. You can walk along the old cobbled streets, see the houses of workmen and mill owners, and visit the **Paterson Museum.** A footbridge over the falls affords a magnificent view. The **Hydroelectric Plant** (3) of 1914, one of the oldest in America, has been recently renovated and is once again "on line," generating electricity for the people of Paterson *(open Wed. 10–2).* And, should you get hungry, there's the **Farmer's Market** (4) just a few blocks away, along with a good selection of ethnic restaurants.

PATERSON MUSEUM (5), Thomas Rogers Building, 2 Market St., Paterson, NJ 07501, (201-881-3874). *Open all year, Tues.–Fri. 10–4, Sat.–Sun. 12:30–4:30, closed Mon. and holidays. Suggested donation: $1 adults, children free. Fully wheelchair-accessible.*

Organized in 1925, the Paterson Museum began rather humbly as a collection of rocks and artifacts dug up by local residents and donated to the public library. Growing steadily in size and scope, it was relocated in 1982 into the restored Thomas Rogers Locomotive Erecting Shop (1873) in the Great Falls Historic District. In addition to an exceptional collection of rocks, minerals, and gems, there are archaeological and natural history displays along with exhibits that show Paterson's evolution as a textile and manufacturing center. You can also see the shell of the 14-foot prototype submarine built in 1878 by John P. Holland, an underwater pioneer, and a slightly later model, Hol-

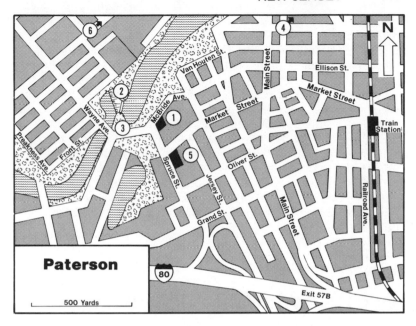

Paterson

500 Yards

land's *Fenian Ram,* intended by its designer to sink the British navy, thereby winning freedom for Ireland. There is also a magnificent collection of Colt revolvers and, outside, some locally-built steam locomotives.

AMERICAN LABOR MUSEUM (6), Botto House National landmark, 83 Norwood St., Haledon, NJ 07580 (201-595-7953). *Open all year Wed.– Sun. 1–4, closed Mon., Tues., and major holidays except Labor Day. Adults $1.50, children under 12 free.*

America is a nation of immigrants, built by the sweat and toil of men, women, and children from all over the world. Interestingly, the American Labor Museum in Haledon is one of the very few institutions in the United States dedicated to the history of working people—their lives on and off the job, their culture, their organizing struggles, their aspirations. The museum building itself is a peculiarly apt symbol: in 1908, after emigrating from Italy and laboring 12 hours a day, 6 days a week, for 15 years in New Jersey's textile mills, Pietro and Maria Botto built this house, 12 rooms of their own with garden, the American Dream come true. They installed a grape arbor and bocce court in the garden and ran the house as a kind of social center for fellow Italian immigrants. In 1913, when more than 24,000 workers struck the Paterson silk mills, the Bottos offered their house as a gathering place, and for six historic months it was the scene of meetings, rallies, strategy sessions, and stirring oratory from some of the champions of the cause, including Elizabeth Gurley Flynn, John Reed, Big Bill Haywood, and Upton Sinclair. The Paterson strike was a turning point in the battle for the 8-hour day and other labor reforms.

Through its varied collections, exhibits, ethnic celebrations, lectures, seminars, and workshops, the American Labor Museum re-creates these events and the texture of working people's lives around the turn of the century. For those interested in delving further, there are extensive pictorial and archival materials in the library, open by appointment.

For a rare slice of ordinary life during the decades of this country's industrial transformation, or for a rare visit to a historic site in New Jersey where George Washington *did not* sleep, go to the American Labor Museum.

Trip B-14
Two Restored Colonial Houses
Near the City

- DEY MANSION
- VAN RIPER-HOPPER HOUSE

DISTANCE: About 25 miles from Columbus Circle.

FOR THE DRIVER: Take **I-80** west from the George Washington Bridge through Paterson to second exit for **Route 62,** marked "62 South, Little Falls." Almost at once follow small sign and fork right on **US-46** towards Dover. Shortly exit, right, to Riverview Drive and stay on it about a mile, following signs to Wayne. At the intersection just before a golf course is Totowa Rd. Turn right here to **Dey Mansion,** on the left.

Go back to Riverview Drive, turn right, and proceed briefly to Valley Rd. Turn right and continue on Valley Rd. several miles to its end. Here turn right onto Berdan Ave. and watch for the **Wayne Museum,** on the left.

On this trip you are very close to the Paterson sites described on Trip B-13.

DEY MANSION, 199 Totowa Rd., Wayne, NJ 07470 (201-696-1776). *Open all year, Wed.–Fri. 1–4:30, Sat. 10–noon & 1:4:30, Sun. 1–4:30; closed Mon., Tues., New Year's, Thanksgiving, Christmas. Adults $1, under 10 free; additional fees for special events. Guided tours lasting about 40 minutes, picnic area. Not wheelchair-accessible.*

Located in Preakness Valley Park, this attractive Georgian mansion was built in 1740 by Dirck Dey (pronounced "Die"), a prosperous Dutch gentleman. A knowledgeable builder, Dey used the finest fieldstone, Flemish brick, and hand-hewn timbers in the construction of the house. His son, Colonel Theunis Dey, became a friend of George Washington's during the Revolution, and when the Continental Army was camped in the Preakness Valley, he offered the general the use of the house as his headquarters. Washington was here in July 1780, when he received news of the French allies' landing on Rhode Island with badly needed supplies and reinforcements, and he returned that fall after the failure of Benedict Arnold's treason at West Point. The mansion, maintained by the Passaic County Park Commission, holds great appeal for anyone interested in furnishings; all the articles are period originals in perfect condition. The outbuildings, including a plantation house, barn, wagon shed, smokehouse, forge, and springhouse, have also been restored.

VAN RIPER-HOPPER HOUSE / WAYNE MUSEUM, 533 Berdan Ave., Wayne, NJ 07470 (201-694-7192). *Open all year, Fri.–Tues. 1–5; closed New Year's, Thanksgiving, Christmas. Free. Difficult for wheelchairs.*

The Dutch colonial farmhouse, whose original portion was built in 1786, stands on land once belonging to the Lenni Lenape Indians. An excellent example of careful planning, the house faces south in order to take advantage of the sun's light and heat. There are furnishings dating from the 1780s to the 1880s, an exhibit room with changing displays, a herb garden, and special programs throughout the year.

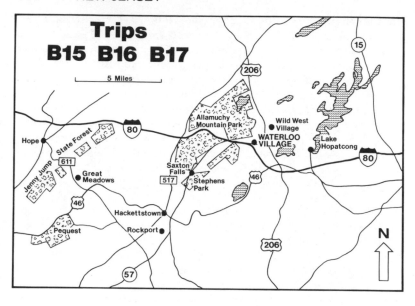

Holding up the stagecoach
(Photo courtesy of Wild West Village)

Trip B-15
Westward Ho!

- LAKE HOPATCONG
- HOPATCONG STATE PARK
- WILD WEST CITY

DISTANCE: About 55 miles from Columbus Circle.

FOR THE DRIVER: TAKE **I-80** west from the George Washington Bridge to Exit 28, proceed to the stoplight, turn left, and go about ½ mile to **Hopatcong State Park** and lake. From here you can take a scenic drive around the lake.

Go back to I-80 and head west to the junction with **US-206 N.** Take 206 north towards Newton, passing the turnoff to Waterloo Village (Trip B-16). A little beyond, on the right, is the road to **Wild West Village.**

LAKE HOPATCONG is New Jersey's largest lake and one of its most popular resort areas. It is 900 feet above sea level and nine miles long, with 40 miles of shoreline. Recreational opportunities abound: swimming (there are 10 public beaches), fishing, boating, water skiing, horseback riding, tennis, golf, ice fishing, ice boating, etc. For further information contact the Skylands Regional Tourism Council, 49 High St., P.O. Box 916, Newton, NJ 07860 (201-579-3933).

HOPATCONG STATE PARK, Landing, NJ 07850 (201-398-7010). *Grounds open daily all year, 8–8 Memorial Day to Labor Day, 8–4:30 at other times; beach open 10–6 daily Memorial Day to Labor Day. Parking fee Memorial Day to Labor Day $5 per car weekends and holidays, $3 weekdays, no fee at other times. Swimming, fishing, boat launching ramp (rentals available at nearby marinas outside park), picnic facilities and grills, playgrounds. No alcohol, no hunting. Leashed pets only, no pets at beach. Partially barrier-free, well-graded lawn to swimming area, wheelchair-accessible picnic facilities and restrooms.*

This scenic 113-acre park is a good place to get your feet wet in Lake Hopatcong. It contains a section of the old Morris Canal (see Trip B-16), which was the chief means of moving coal and ore across the state from the 1830s to the 1880s.

WILD WEST CITY, Route 206, Netcong, NJ 07857 (201-347-8900). *Open daily mid-June to Labor Day, 10:30–6; weekends May to mid-June and Labor Day through Oct. (weekends school groups only). Adults $6.40, children under 12 $5.90; train, stagecoach, or pony rides $1 each. Birthday parties and hayrides on request. Most facilities are wheelchair-accessible.*

Here's a place that looks just like the set of your favorite TV westerns. Try the horseback, pony or hay rides, take a foray into Indian territory on an old Iron Horse, watch the famous gunfight at the OK Corral, and beware of gunslingers on the stagecoach. Top off the day by swinging into the Golden Nugget Saloon for a meal and a show.

Trip B-16
New Jersey, Too,
Has its Waterloo

- WATERLOO VILLAGE RESTORATION
- ALLAMUCHY MOUNTAIN STATE PARK

DISTANCE: About 60 miles from Columbus Circle.

FOR THE DRIVER: Take **I-80** west of the George Washington Bridge to Exit 25, **US-206.** Take 206 north to second traffic light and turn left at the sign for Waterloo Village, in Allamuchy Mountain State Park.

From the village, turn left on the park road and go south to Saxton Falls and the Stephens Section of the park.

Of all the restored historic villages within daytrip range of New York, Waterloo is arguably the most enjoyable. From an authentically reconstructed Indian settlement of 1625 to the cheerful ambiance of the Towpath Tavern next to the locks on the Morris Canal, Waterloo offers a broad scope of experiences covering nearly three centuries of America's heritage. It is also home to a world-famous music festival held each summer, with offerings from top rock stars to the Metropolitan Opera.

The blacksmith's shop at Waterloo

WATERLOO VILLAGE RESTORATION, Stanhope, NJ 07874 (201-347-0900). *Open Tues.–Sun. 10–6, mid-April through Sept.; Tues.–Sun. 10–5, Oct.–Dec.; closed Mondays, Easter, Thanksgiving, Christmas, and Jan. to mid-April. The Village is open on holiday Mondays and closed the following Tuesday. Admission: Tues.–Fri. Adults $6, seniors $4.50, children 6–12 $3; Weekends, adults $7.50, seniors $5, children 6–12 $3. Luncheons, beer and wine are available at the Towpath Tavern; light lunches and drinks at the Outdoor Grill from mid-April through Oct. Picnicking on the grounds is permitted. Maps provided for self-guided tours. Many special events. Dogs are not allowed. Dirt roads, much walking involved, many steps, difficult for wheelchairs.*

Originally inhabited by the Lenape Indians, the land around what is now Waterloo was attractive to early settlers because of its fertile soil, water power, timber, and iron ore. By 1760, an iron-making community called Andover Forge developed on the site of the present village. In 1778 the ironworks was confiscated from its pro-British owner and used to produce armaments for the Revolutionary Army. The name was later changed to Waterloo in honor of Wellington's defeat of Napoleon at Waterloo, Belgium, in 1815.

Prosperity came in 1831 with the opening of the Morris Canal, which carried boats more than a hundred miles across northern New Jersey from Phillipsburg on the Delaware to New York Bay. Lying at a junc-

In the Lenape Indian Village

tion of the canal where boats were lifted across the mountain on an inclined plane, Waterloo became a busy inland port, and later an important railway depot. All of this came to an end in 1901 when a new rail route was developed; the now-obsolete canal ceasing operations in 1927. An attempt to develop Waterloo into an exclusive lakeside community was foiled by the stock market crash of 1929. After World War II, the site was taken over by a foundation and restorations begun, opening to the public in 1964.

There are over 20 original buildings that may be visited on the self-guided walking tour. Dating from the Colonial, Federal, and Victorian periods, these include several furnished houses, a general store, a stagecoach inn, a working blacksmith's shop, an operating saw mill and grist mill, a farmstead and barn, a wood-working shop, an apothecary, the Canal Museum, and the Indian Museum. The old trades are demonstrated by skilled artisans in period costumes, who will gladly answer your questions.

Waterloo's latest attraction is an authentically re-created **Lenape Indian Village** on an island in the lake. Guides in Indian dress explain how Native Americans lived here in the early 17th century, and of course are a big hit with young children. A simulated archaeological site with half-buried Indian artifacts lies near the village, on the mainland.

You might want to finish your tour with a visit to the **Towpath Tavern,** where you can enjoy snacks or drinks next to the locks of the canal.

ALLAMUCHY MOUNTAIN STATE PARK, Hackettstown, NJ 07840 (908-852-3790). *Open daily all year, daylight hours. Free. Picnic areas, fishing, hiking, camping (fee), playground, cross-country skiing, sledding. Leashed pets only, no pets in campgrounds. Stephens Section is partially barrier-free and wheelchair-accessible.*

This attractive 6,000-acre park is mainly a wilderness area. The large northern section, where Waterloo Village is located, has hiking trails and good fishing at Saxton Falls, a waterfall on the Musconetcong River. Most of the park's facilities are located in the Stephens Section, about a mile below.

Trip B-17
Fish, Fowl, and the Legend of Jenny

- ROCKPORT GAME FARM
- PEQUEST TROUT HATCHERY
- LAND OF MAKE BELIEVE
- JENNY JUMP STATE FOREST

DISTANCE: About 65 miles from Columbus Circle.

FOR THE DRIVER: Take **I-80** west from the George Washington Bridge to Exit 26, Hackettstown/**US-46.** Follow 46 southwest to Hackettstown. Turn left at light onto Grand Ave. and go abut 3 miles south to **Rockport Game Farm,** well marked by signs.

Return to Hackettstown and US-46. Continue west on 46 about 10 miles to **Pequest Hatchery,** again well marked by signs.

I lead back east on 46 a few miles to Great Meadows. Here turn left on **Route 611** (St. Peter and Paul Church on corner) and go north about 2 miles to the **Land of Make Believe,** entrance on right.

Continue north on 611 about 2 miles to State Park Rd. and **Jenny Jump.** From here, for return trip, continue north to Hope and I-80, and back to GWB.

ROCKPORT GAME FARM, Box 27A, Rockport Rd., Hackettstown, NJ 07840 (908-852-3461). *Open daily all year. Free.*

Acres of pheasants await you here after a beautiful drive through the Jersey hills. This sea of feathers makes an imposing sight, and the farm also keeps some exotic birds, deer, and other game. There's not much to see when the birds are young and kept indoors, but the drive alone is well worth the trip.

PEQUEST TROUT HATCHERY and NATURAL RESOURCE EDUCA-TION CENTER, Pequest Rd., Oxford, NJ 07863 (908-637-4125). *Open all year Fri.–Sun. 10–4. Free. Tours, slide shows. Wheelchair-accessible.*

This could just be the hit of today's trip. It's a must for the fishermen in the family, but even the amateur will be impressed. Anglers (and cooks) will stand drooling at the sight of thousands of trout that will soon stock the New Jersey waters. Indoors, the first steps in the hatching process (September–October) may be observed through glass partitions, and there are special programs and videos at the Natural Resource Education Center. Your visit to Pequest may inspire you to head up the road to Allamuchy Mountain State Park (Trip B-16) and try your luck in the Musconetcong.

LAND OF MAKE BELIEVE, Great Meadows Rd., Hope, NJ 07844 (908-459-5100). *Open 10–5 Memorial Day weekend and weekends in June, daily 10–5 (6 on weekends) late June to Labor Day, Sun. only 10–5 Labor Day through Sept.; closed other times. Adults $8.50, children $10.50 (fee covers all rides and activities). Picnic area, refreshment stand, gift shop. Many facilities are wheelchair-accessible.*

Nestled at the foot of Jenny Jump Mountain, this family amusement park is just the place for kids who want to visit Santa at the North Pole, pilot the Red Baron or a restored World War II DC-3, take a Civil War train ride or the Alfalfa Express hayride, converse with a talking scarecrow and a talking horse, or frighten themselves silly in the Haunted House. There's also a restored house where Jenny may have lived at the time of her legendary jump (see below).

JENNY JUMP STATE FOREST, P.O. Box, Hope NJ 07844 (908-459-4366). *Open daily all year, daylight hours. Free. Picnics, camping (fee), hiking and nature trails, playground, cross-country skiing, sledding. Leashed pets only, no pets in campgrounds. Park office and restrooms are wheelchair-accessible.*

The settler looked up in horror to where his daughter was picking berries above the clearing, saw the raised tomahawks of the Indians coming up behind her, and cried out "Jump, Jenny, jump!" Legend

has it that Jenny did. A small but exceedingly scenic park commemorates this tale, and you're invited to explore either by car or on foot.
Here lived the Minsi (Wolf) tribe of the Lenape Indians. Campsites
now rest on ground where Indian artifacts have been found. The main
attraction is the superb view from the well-marked drives and trails.

Trip B-18
Rumpelstiltskin, Rocks and Recreation

- FAIRY TALE FOREST
- FRANKLIN MINERAL MUSEUM
- ACTION PARK / VERNON VALLEY GREAT GORGE

DISTANCE: About 55 miles from Columbus Circle.

FOR THE DRIVER: From the George Washington Bridge take **I-80** west
to Exit 53 and pick up **NJ-23** north through Butler for about 18 miles
to Oak Ridge Rd. From here follow signs to the **Fairy Tale Forest,** on
the left.

Continue on 23 north towards Franklin and Sussex. Coming into
Franklin, just past the junction with Route 517 is a small shopping
center. Continue briefly on 23 to Buckwheat Rd. and turn left, following signs for the **Franklin Mineral Museum.**

Return to NJ-23 and continue northwest to the junction with **NJ-
94.** Turn right here and head north about 4 miles to **Action Park** and
Great Gorge, well marked by signs.

There are fun-filled activities for people of all ages on this enjoyable
excursion into New Jersey's Skylands Region.

FAIRY TALE FOREST, Oak Ridge Rd., Oak Ridge, NJ 07438 (201-697-
5656). *Open Easter through October: daily mid-June to Labor Day, Mon.–
Sat. 10–5, Sun. & holidays 10–6; weekends 10–5 Easter to mid-June
and Labor Day through Oct.; gate closes an hour before closing time.
Adults $6.50, children $5.25. Snack bar, picnic area, souvenir shop.
Paved walks are manageable for wheelchairs.*

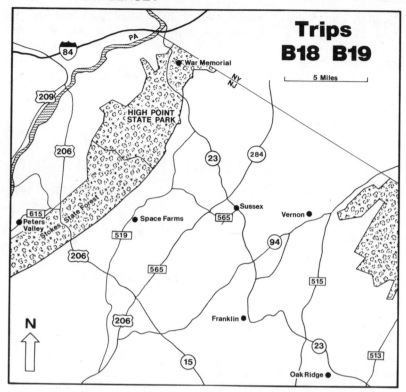

Children can hardly wait to enter this enchanted woodland filled with scenes and characters from their favorite stories. Hand-crafted life-size characters inhabit the castles, cottages, and gingerbread houses that dot this 20-acre storybook land. The kids can visit Rapunzel's tower, the Old Woman's shoe, Goldilocks' cabin, Jack's beanstalk, and a three-ring circus, renewing their acquaintance with Red Riding Hood, Snow White, Humpty Dumpty, Little Miss Muffet, contrary Mary, and other fairy-tale notables along the way. There's also a merry-go-round, a fire engine, and the Candy Rock Train. Grab your glass slippers and follow the breadcrumbs to Oak Ridge!

FRANKLIN MINERAL MUSEUM, Evans St., Franklin, NJ 07416 (201-827-3481). *Open mid-Apr. to mid-Nov.: mid-Apr. through June and Sept. to mid-Nov. Fri.–Sat. 10–4, Sun. 12:30–4:30; July–Aug. Wed.–Sat. 10–4, Sun. 12:30–4:30; closed Easter. Museum admission $2 adults, $1 children; same fees charged again for admission to Buckwheat Dump. Guided tours, gift shop. Museum is wheelchair-accessible, but not dump.*

There are some 300 different minerals on display here, almost all of them from the Franklin-Ogdensburg area, the beneficiary of a unique sequence of geological events that began about a billion years ago. In the course of these unimaginable eons, several major periods of mountain building produced the world's richest zinc ore body, along with 26 minerals not found anywhere else on Earth. Recently (in the last million years or so, that is), glaciation, erosion, and weathering have continued the process of mineral formation, and new specimens are still being discovered.

The **Franklin Mineral Museum** contains permanent and traveling collections, as well as what may be the most spectacular display of fluorescent minerals to be found anywhere. The **replica mine** simulates the operations of the New Jersey Zinc Company, which donated all of the equipment and materials used in the reconstruction. The museum also administers the **Buckwheat Dump,** where you can prospect on your own and take home up to 20 pounds of minerals (10 pounds for kids). You're welcome to bring your own gear, or rent or purchase ultraviolet lamps and other equipment at the gift shop.

ACTION PARK / VERNON VALLEY GREAT GORGE, Rt. 94, Vernon, NJ 07462 (general information 201-827-2000, ski conditions and year-round activities 201-827-3900).

Action Park. *Open July 1 to Labor Day daily; late May through June and fall weekends; call for current schedules. Admission: adults $19, children $15, $16 on weekends. Some activities extra. No pets, no food or beverages allowed in park; picnic area and refreshments available nearby. Partially wheelchair-accessible.* The *New York Times* called Action Park "the most distinctive expression of the amusement park in our age"—and they're not talking Ferris wheels and Kewpie dolls. With more than 75 different activities and the world's largest water park at your disposal, you can easily spend an entire day in this beautiful mountain setting. For a break from Grand Prix race driving, bungee jumping, the Tidal Wave Pool, speedboats, the Alpine Slide, and other self-operated macho thrills, try the scenic sky ride, various live entertainments, or quench your thirst at the brewery. As you might have guessed, this park is aimed primarily at young adults looking for an exciting time.

Vernon Valley Great Gorge. *Generally open daily Thanksgiving to April; call for current schedules and rates. Ski lessons, equipment rentals, patrolled slopes, lodges, spa, nursery, cafeteria, bar, evening entertainment.* Here, spread over 3 mountains, are some 25 miles of interconnected skiing terrain, with 17 lifts and 52 trails graded for difficulty. The vertical drop exceeds 1,000 feet, while the world's largest snowmaking system can lay 8 miles of 3-foot-deep fresh snow overnight.

Trip B-19
A Private Zoo in Natural Surroundings and the Highest Point in New Jersey

- SPACE FARMS ZOO
- HIGH POINT STATE PARK
- STOKES STATE FOREST

DISTANCE: About 75 miles from Columbus Circle.

FOR THE DRIVER: Take **I-80** west from the George Washington Bridge to Exit 53 and pick up **NJ-23** north to Sussex. At the junction with **Route 565,** turn left, following signs to **Space Farms.** Shortly make a right-angle turn and continue straight ahead to **Route 519,** turning left and proceeding to farms as indicated by signs.

Go north on 519 about 5 miles to NJ-23, then north on 23 another few miles to **High Point State Park,** *or* go south on 519 about 6 miles to **US-206,** then north on 206 about 3 miles into **Stokes State Forest.** High Point borders Stokes on the south, and you can drive from one to the other on interconnected park roads, taking a scenic route along the crest of the mountain. Ask for maps at park offices.

Peters Valley Crafts Center, described on Trip B-20, is very close to Stokes State Forest. If you prefer to include it on this trip instead, head north on 206 to the junction with **Route 521.** Turn left here and go about a mile to the junction of **Route 615,** then left again about 2 miles on 615 to Peters Valley, near Layton.

SPACE FARMS ZOO & MUSEUM, R.D. 6, Box 135, Beemerville Rd., Sussex, NJ 07461 (201-875-8000). *Open 9–5 daily May through Oct. Adults $7.50, children 3–12 $3.50. Picnic area, playground, restaurant, gift shop. Grounds somewhat hilly but manageable for wheelchairs, buildings wheelchair-accessible.*

The denizens of Space Farms are not extraterrestrials, but over 500 native North American mammals, birds, and reptiles, along with a few exotic species from foreign parts, all collected by the Space family. The Spaces have been operating the 400-acre farm since 1927 and pride themselves on their tradition of "tender, loving care in tune with nature." In addition to viewing the animals in their natural habitat, you can visit the museum buildings and see Grandpa Ralph Space's remarkable collection of Americana—antique cars, toys, dolls, clocks, muskets, inventions, gadgets, Indian artifacts, and everything but the kitchen sink (that's in Grandma Space's restaurant, serving short-order specialities with an old-fashioned touch).

HIGH POINT STATE PARK, R.R. 4, Box 287, Sussex, NJ 07461 (201-875-4800). *Open daily all year, daylight hours. Admission Memorial Day to Labor Day and weekends in May and Oct., $3 per car weekdays, $4 weekends and holidays; other times $1 per person, under 12 and over 62 free. Picnicking, refreshments, swimming and bathhouse, hiking and nature trails, boating, fishing, camping (fee), cross-country skiing, ice skating, ice fishing, snowmobiling, sledding, dog sledding. Leashed pets only. Wheelchair-accessible beach and restrooms.*

The highest point in New Jersey (1,803 feet) lies in this beautiful 14,000-acre park. From the top of the 200-foot **War Memorial** that marks the spot, you can see the Delaware River, the Poconos, the Catskills, and the juncture of three states—New York, New Jersey and Pennsylvania. The 80-mile view is especially magnificent in laurel time and in the fall. Part of the **Appalachian Trail** winds through High Point, and spring-fed **Lake Marcia** provides a refreshing dip.

STOKES STATE FOREST, R.R. 2, Box 260, Branchville, NJ 07826 (201-948-3820). *Open daily all year. Free admission to park; Memorial Day to Labor Day admission to Stony Lake day use area $2 per car weekdays, $4 weekends and holidays. Picnicking, playground, refreshments, swimming and bathhouse, boating, camping (fee), fishing, hiking and nature trails, bridle paths, cross-country skiing, ice skating, ice fishing, sledding. Stony Lake, picnic areas, and newer buildings are wheelchair-accessible.*

This park of over 15,000 acres on the Kittatinny Ridge offers some of the finest scenery in New Jersey. Don't miss the **Tillman Ravine,** a natural gorge in the southern corner of the park, or the 1,600-foot-high **Sunrise Mountain,** with superb views of the surrounding landscape.

Trip B-20
A Majestic Gateway
to the Poconos

- DELAWARE WATER GAP NATIONAL RECREATION AREA
- BUSHKILL FALLS
- DINGMANS FALLS
- PETERS VALLEY CRAFTS CENTER
- MILLBROOK VILLAGE

DISTANCE: Delaware Water Gap is about 80 miles from Columbus Circle, while the leisurely drive through the National Recreation Area adds another 50 miles or so in all.

FOR THE DRIVER: Take **I-80** west from the George Washington Bridge all the way to Exit 1, the last exit in New Jersey, just before the Delaware River. Get off here and follow the road under the highway to the **Kittatinny Point Visitor Center** (1), where you can get a free map and current information about the National Recreation Area as well as have a good view of the Delaware Water Gap.

Return to I-80 and head west across the toll bridge into Pennsylvania. Take the first exit and turn right past the Pennsylvania Visitor Information Center to the old resort of **Shawnee-on-Delaware.** Continue on a narrow, winding road into the Pennsylvania side of the National Recreation Area. After about 9 miles you'll come to **US-209,** a busy highway lined with commercial establishments.

Turn right onto US-209 and follow it north for about 1½ miles until you reach a well-marked left turn for **Bushkill Falls** (2).

Return to US-209 and take it north about 12 miles to Dingmans Ferry, where you can turn left to **Dingmans Falls** (3).

Return to Dingmans Ferry and turn right on PA-739-S, crossing the toll bridge over the Delaware into the New Jersey side of the National Recreation Area. Continue on to the **Peters Valley Crafts Center** (4) near Layton.

A road through the National Recreation Area leads south about 12 miles to **Millbrook Village** (5).

Continue south through the park for another 11 miles to **I-80** for the drive home.

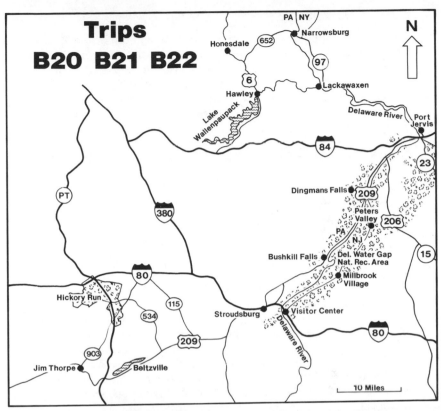

Trips
B20 B21 B22

Honesdale

PA NY

Narrowsburg

652

97

6

Hawley

Lackawaxen

Lake Wallenpaupack

Delaware River

Port Jervis

84

23

PT

380

Dingmans Falls

209

Peters Valley

206

PA

NJ

15

Bushkill Falls

Del. Water Gap Nat. Rec. Area

80

Millbrook Village

Hickory Run

534

115

Stroudsburg

Visitor Center

209

Delaware River

80

903

Jim Thorpe

Beltzville

N

10 Miles

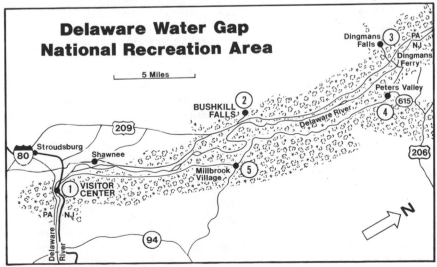

Delaware Water Gap
National Recreation Area

Dingmans Falls

3

PA

NJ

Dingmans Ferry

5 Miles

Peters Valley

615

BUSHKILL FALLS

2

Delaware River

4

209

Stroudsburg

Shawnee

206

80

Millbrook Village

5

1 VISITOR CENTER

PA NJ

Delaware River

94

N

128   NEW JERSEY/PENNSYLVANIA

This glorious one-day excursion meanders in and out of the 35-mile-long Delaware River Gap National Recreation Area, taking you through some of the best scenery in the Northwest. Along the way you can visit some spectacular waterfalls, a crafts community, and a restored 19th-century village. For the most part, busy and commercialized roads are avoided. It is an especially nice trip to take during the fall foliage season.

DELAWARE WATER GAP NATIONAL RECREATION AREA, Bushkill, PA 18324 (717-588-2435). *Grounds open daily all year; Kittatinny Point Visitor Center (1) open April–Oct daily 9–5, Nov.–Mar. weekends only 9–4:30; Dingmans Falls Visitor Center (3) open April–Oct. daily 9–5, Nov.–Dec. weekends only 9–4:30. No fees. Picnicking, swimming, camping (state forest only), fishing, boating, canoeing (rentals available outside park), hiking trails, nature trails, bicycling, rock climbing, ice skating, cross-country skiing, snowmobiling; all in designated areas only. Detailed park maps, trail and river guides available at the Kittatinny Point Visitor Center (1). Leashed pets only. Some facilities manageable for wheelchairs.*

Stretching for 35 miles along the banks of the Delaware River, these 70,000 largely unspoiled acres hold a wealth of scenic and recreational opportunities. The most spectacular sight is the **Delaware Water Gap** (1) itself, where over countless millennia, the Delaware River carved a path between the Kittatinny Ridge in New Jersey and the Pocono Mountain Plateau in Pennsylvania. The gap, about 900 feet across at river level, widens to span a mile at the crest, making a dramatic cleft in these ancient mountains, which were once as high as the Rockies. There are three marked gap overlooks; one on the site of the old Kittatinny House, a popular resort hotel destroyed by fire in 1931, one at Point of Gap, and one at Arrow Island.

Wildlife bounds here; and you can hike along marked trails graded for difficulty, including a 25-mile section of the Appalachian Trail. The **Dingmans Fall Trail** (3), an easy hike through a picturesque gorge leads to the Pocono's highest waterfalls, Dingmans and the aptly named Silver Thread Falls (see below). There's a visitor center here with exhibits and audio-visual programs. Two educational centers in the middle of the park, operated by local schools in cooperation with the National Park Service, offer year-round environmental programs: **Pocono Environmental Education Center,** Rd 2, Box 1010, Dingmans Ferry, PA 18328 (717-828-2319), and **Walpack Valley Environmental Education Center,** Box 134, Walpack Center, NJ 07881 (201-948-5749). There's no camping in the National Recreation Area itself, but the **Worthington State Forest** (201-841-9575), located within its boundaries at the southern end, allows camping, as do High Point State Park and Stokes

Along the trail at Bushkill Falls

State Forest, outside the boundaries to the north.

In addition to the natural attractions, there are two developed park sites of historic interest. Slateford Farm is a partially restored 19th-century house with outbuildings near the site of an old slate quarry. **Millbrook Village** (5) (see below), a small rural town left behind by the march of progress, has been restored to life as a 19th-century village, with homes, general store, church, school, blacksmith's shop, grist-mill, and other buildings. Two other major attractions, **Bushkill Falls** (2) and the **Peters Valley Crafts Center** (4), are just on the boundary of the park and are described below.

BUSHKILL FALLS (2), Bushkill Falls Rd., Bushkill, PA 18324 (717-588-6682). *Open April–Nov. daily 9–dusk. Adults $4.50, seniors 62 and older $3.75, children 6–12 $1, under 6 free. Picnic area and grills, nature trails, wildlife exhibit, fishing, 2-seater paddleboat rentals, miniature golf, shops, snack bar. Good walking shoes essential. Shops and restrooms are wheelchair-accessible, but not falls.*

Bushkill Falls, the "Niagara of Pennsylvania," has been a classic tourist attraction since 1904, when the Peters family first opened their natural haven to the public. They still own it and have made few changes (other than trail improvements) in the decades since. This is a won-

130   NEW JERSEY/PENNSYLVANIA

derful escape into an earlier time when a stunning waterfall in a near-primeval setting was all it took to keep folks happy.

From the entrance, there are four trails to and around the falls. The easiest of these goes to a scenic overlook at the top of the 100-foot-high main falls, can easily be done in 15 minutes, and involves no climbing. The **"Popular Route"** takes you to the bottom of the main falls and up the other side to some upper falls before returning about 45 minutes later. This can be extended by including the new **Pennell Falls Trail.** Serious hikers will enjoy the gorgeous **Bridal Veil Falls Trail,** which winds through the bounder-strewn gorge past all eight waterfalls and takes about two hours, including roughly 200 feet of vertical ascent. All of the trails end at the snack bar and old-fashioned pavilion, where you can enjoy lunch, soft drinks, or beer. There are several other simple amusements near the parking lot, like miniature golf and paddle boats on a pond.

DINGMANS FALLS (3), a bit more than a mile west of Dingmans Ferry, is within the National Recreation Area and may be visited at any time during daylight hours. There is no admission charge. Its Visitor Center is open daily from April through October, and on weekends in November and December. From the parking lot, a half-mile-long nature trail leads through a picturesque gorge dotted with stands of the hemlock and rhododendron to the Pocono's highest waterfalls, **Dingmans** and the aptly-named **Silver Thread Falls.**

PETERS VALLEY CRAFTS CENTER (4), Route 615, Layton, NJ 07851 (201-948-5200). *Store and gallery open daily all year 10–5. Store is wheelchair-accessible.*

Located on the edge of the National Recreation Area, Peters Valley is a year-round residential community where skilled artisans are invited to live and work in exchange for teaching workshops in their various specialities. Workshops have covered such topics as hand-forged tools, the "lost wax" process of ceramic shell casting, contemporary teapots, kiln building, goldsmithing, enameling, electoforming and electroplating, landscape and portrait photography, quilting, collage art, handbound books, knotting and coiling, embroidery, silk painting, rustic furniture, and joinery. The gallery and store feature work by resident craftspeople and other nationally-known artists. This visit may also be taken as part of Trip B-19.

MILLBROOK VILLAGE (5), Old Mine Rd., 11 miles northeast of I-80. *Grounds open daily, village open late June–Labor Day daily 9–5, Sept.–Oct. Wed.–Sun. 9–5. No admission charge. Phone the Kittatinny Point Visitor Center (908-496-4459) for current activities.*

A small hamlet that developed around a mill built in 1832, Mill-brook flourished during the mid-19th century. By the early 1900s, however, it fell into an irreversible decline. What you see today is a skillful re-creation of a late-19th-century rural community, peopled by guides in period costume who demonstrate the crafts of yesteryear. It is located within the National Recreation Area and is operated by the National Park Service.

Trip B-21
From Stroudsburg West

- QUIET VALLEY LIVING HISTORICAL FARM
- OLD MAUCH CHUNK
- HICKORY RUN STATE PARK

DISTANCE: From Columbus Circle to Stroudsburg is about 85 miles, from there to Old Mauch Chunk another 35 miles.

FOR THE DRIVER: Take **I-80** west from the George Washington Bridge through New Jersey and across the Delaware into Pennsylvania. At Stroudsburg take Exit 46S onto **US-209 South.** Take Shafer School House Rd. exit off 209 briefly to Business Route 209. Turn left here, following well-marked route to **Quiet Valley.**

Go back to 209 South and continue through Brodheadsville and across the Pennsylvania Turnpike N.E. Extension. Just before this is the **Beltzville State Park** (215-377-0045), with fishing, hiking, swimming, winter sports, and other activities. About 2 miles after the turnpike, 209 turns sharply right and goes north into **Jim Thorpe,** the site of **Old Mauch Chunk.**

Take **PA-903** north out of Jim Thorpe and go about 15 miles, crossing the turnpike, to **PA-534.** Turn left and go through Albrightsville back across the turnpike to **Hickory Run State Park.**

For the return trip, go back on 534 to the junction with 903. Turn left on 903 and go north to the junction with **PA-115.** Turn left on 115 and go a mile or so to the junction with I-80 east to New York.

On this trip you can take an hour's drive from Stroudsburg, gateway to the Poconos, west to the town of Jim Thorpe in Carbon County. For further information, contact the Pocono Mountains Vacation Bureau, 1004, Main St., Stroudsburg, PA 18360 (717-424-6050 *or* 800-PO-CONOS), and their Carbon County office, P.O. Box 27, Jim Thorpe, PA 18229 (717-325-3673).

QUIET VALLEY LIVING HISTORICAL FARM, 1000 Turkey Hill Rd., Stroudsburg, PA 18360 (717-992-6161). *Open daily June 20 through Labor Day, Mon.–Sat. 9:30–5:30, Sun. 1–5:30; Adults $5, children 3–12, $3, under 3 free. Annual Harvest Festival on weekend before Columbus Day, other special events and workshops throughout the year. Continuous guided tours; last tour leaves at 4. Picnic area. No pets. Will accommodate wheelchairs and other handicaps; call in advance.*

Quiet Valley is a journey back in time to a self-sufficient Colonial farm run much as it was in 1765 when a hardworking Pennsylvania Dutch family first settled here. The costumed staff members are more than tour guides; they are actors playing the roles of family members going about their daily chores of spinning, weaving, meat smoking, gardening, and tending the animals. As they take you through the farm's 14 buildings, some original, they describe their lives as colonists and demonstrate such skills as forging (not money), wool dyeing, candle dipping, and broom making. In the age of mass production, these activities may come as a revelation to the kids, who will also enjoy petting the animals and trying the hay jump in the barn.

JIM THORPE, as the historic town of **Mauch Chunk** is now known, lies a little beyond the normal daytrip range, but it's a unique place that's well worth the extra mileage. It takes its name from the great Native American athlete who astonished the world with an unprecedented record-breaking performance at the 1912 Olympics. Jim Thorpe was not born here, nor did he ever pass through here while he was alive. The story of how the town came to be named for him is a story of hard times: hard times for the man, who was unfairly stripped of his Olympic medals (since restored) on a technicality, and hard times for Mauch Chunk (the Indian name for "Bear Mountain"), Upper Mauch Chunk, and East Mauch Chunk, booming coal and railroad towns in the 19th century, declining and economically strapped in the 20th. In 1953 Jim Thorpe died in poverty after a long, painful illness, and his wife sought to have him buried with a public memorial in his home state, Oklahoma. Oklahoma said no. Hearing of the plight of the Mauch Chunks, Mrs. Thorpe proposed to lend the towns her husband's name in return for their assistance in memorializing him. Though the towns had been squabbling for years, their citizens were inspired by this

Basket weaving at Quiet Village
(Photo courtesy of Quiet Village Living Historical Farm)

idea, transcended their differences, and merged to become Jim Thorpe, Pennsylvania.

Jim Thorpe lies at the bottom of a gorge on the Lehigh River, flanked by sheer mountainsides, in a region sometimes known as the "Switzerland of America." The town's appearance is as fascinating as the story of its name. In its heyday it spawned a slew of self-made millionaires who built the palatial residences and impressive public buildings you see today. Perhaps the most striking of these is the **Asa Packer Mansion** *(open daily June–Oct., weekends mid-Apr.–May, 1–5. Adults $4, students $2. Phone 717-325-3229),* an Italianate extravagance built by the founder of Lehigh University, who came to Mauch Chunk penniless in 1828 and became a wealthy railroad tycoon. **St. Mark's Episcopal Church** *(Open daily June–Oct., weekends mid-Apr.–May. Donation $2.50. Tours at 1:15, 2, 2:45, 3:30.),* commissioned in 1869 as a memorial by Asa Packer's widow, is a striking Gothic Revival structure built into a hillside, and is noted for its early Tiffany windows. The fine townhouses on **Millionaires Row** contrast with the humbler residences on **Stone Row,** where Asa Packer's foremen and engineers lived. There's railroad history in the bricks of the **Jersey Central Rail-**

road Station of 1888, which now houses the **Tourist Welcoming Center.** The folks there will gladly give you a map and brochure about the town. **Steam train rides** are offered on weekends from mid-May through September, with special excursions in spring, October, and December *(Rail Tours Inc., 717-325-3673)*. Railfans and hikers might also explore the bed of the historic **Switchback Gravity Railroad,** completed in 1827 as the first of its kind in America.

The **Lehigh River** offers some terrific whitewater rafting. If you want to shoot the rapids, try **Jim Thorpe River Adventures** *(717-325-2570 or 800-424-RAFT)* or **Pocono Whitewater Rafting Center** *(717-325-3656)*. There's also recreation at man-made **Mauch Chunk Lake** three miles west of town, and a great view from **Flagstaff Mountain Park,** some 1,400 feet above it.

HICKORY RUN STATE PARK, R.D. 1, Box 81, White Haven, PA 18661 (717-443-9991). *Open daily all year. No entry fee. Picnicking, playgrounds and fields, nature center, hiking trails, swimming beach (Memorial Day to Labor Day), fishing, camping (fee), snack bar, ice fishing, ice skating, sledding, snowmobiling, cross-country skiing. Leashed pets in day-use area, not pets on beach or campsites. Picnic area, restrooms, and beach are wheelchair-accessible.*

Here are 15,500 acres of wooded hills threaded with clear streams and waterfalls. The park's special feature is a lake 2,000 feet long and 500 feet wide, with scenically contoured shores and trees stretching down to where the water should be—but there's no water. Instead, boulders: pinkish, rounded, and piled up like heaps of jellybeans. This is the glacial **Boulder Field,** a National Natural Landmark. One of the more startling views is of energetic "swimmers" clambering across the lake to the opposite shore.

Trip B-22
A Scenic Drive to the Pocono's "Big Lake"

- ## LAKE WALLENPAUPACK AND ENVIRONS

DISTANCE: From Columbus Circle to the lake is about 110 miles.

FOR THE DRIVER: Since this trip is planned mainly for the enjoyment of the drive itself, the directions are incorporated with the brief descriptions of the principal attractions along the route, given below. The site numbers correspond to the numbers on the trip map.

Lake Wallenpaupack is the centerpiece of this trip to the northeast Poconos. From here you can make a loop back into New York State to see some of the sights just across the Delaware in the southernmost Catskills region (see Trips C-15 to C-20 for the Catskills). For further information about the lake area, contact the Lake Wallenpaupack Association, P.O. Box 398, Hawley, PA 18428 (717-226-2141), or the Pocono Mountains Vacation Bureau, 1004 Main St., Stroudsburg, PA 18360 (717-424-6050 or 800-POCONOS); for the New York area, contact the Sullivan County Office of Public Information, County Government Center, Monticello, NY 12701 (914-794-3000 X160 or 800-882-CATS in NYS, 800-343-INFO outside NYS).

LAKE WALLENPAUPACK (1) is 5,600 acres of tempting blue water with 52 miles of shoreline and the Pocono Mountains as a backdrop. The lake region was home to the Minisink, Lenape, and Paupack Indians; "Wallenpaupack" is a Lenape word meaning "stream of swift and slow waters." And it *was* a stream, until the Pennsylvania Power and Light Company dammed it in 1926. Today the lake is a major year-round recreation area, and the hydroelectric plant is used mainly during periods of peak demand.

To reach Lake Wallenpaupack, take **I-80** west from the George Washington Bridge to Exit 53 west of Paterson. Here you pick up **NJ-23** northwest to Port Jervis and the junction with **I-84.** Take 84 west to Exit 6 and follow **PA-507** northeast along the southern shore of the lake. Shortly after the exit there are signs and a turnoff, left, for the **Claws 'N' Paws Wild Animal Park** (2), about 6 miles northwest and

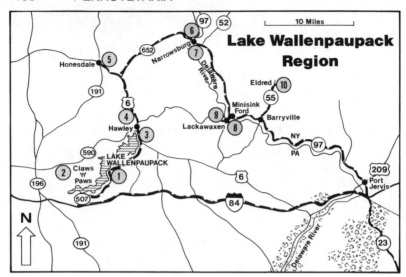

always a hit with the kids. In addition to a tiger, wolf, bear, puma, performing chimps, et al, there's the usual collection of tame deer and llamas to pet, along with a chance to caress a python or alligator. *Open May through Oct., daily 10–6. Admission fees. (717-698-6154).*

There are a number of resorts and recreation areas around the lake. Going northeast on 507, you will come to several places that offer cruises on the lake, waterskiing, boat rentals, jet skis, and the like. Two of these are Wallenpaupack Scenic Boat Rides at Paupack (717-226-6211), and Pocono Action Sports near Hawley (717-857-1976).

Continue on 507 to the northeast end of the lake, where the dam is located. At the junction with **US-6,** turn left on 6 and go about ½ mile to the **Pennsylvania Power and Light Company Visitor Center** (3). Here you can see exhibits on the hydroelectric dam and recreation area. *Open daily, free. (717-226-3702).*

Continuing on US-6 north to Hawley, you'll pass a junction with PA-590 on the left. This goes around the lake on the north side and is an alternative route to Claws 'N' Paws, about 12 miles southwest on 590. Just northwest of Hawley on US-6 is a red railroad car, the **Gravity Coach** (4), which ran between Pittston and Hawley from 1850 to 1880. It was part of the Pennsylvania Gravity Railroad, operating on 22 inclined planes from Hawley to Scranton. The cars, loaded with coal and passengers, were hauled uphill by stationary engines and went downhill on their own with Galilean gusto.

From Hawley, continue west on US-6 for about 12 miles to Honesdale, founded in 1826 by the Delaware & Hudson Canal Company and named for the company's president, Philip Hone. In town, at 810 Main St., is the **Wayne County Historical Society Museum** (5), housed in the old canal company office. *Open Apr.–Dec., Mon.–Sat.; Jan.–Mar., Tues., Thurs., Sat.; closed some major holidays. (717-253-3240).* A little farther on US-6, across a bridge, is a replica of the **Stourbridge Lion** of 1829, the first operating steam locomotive in the United States, shortly supplanted by mules when the railbed proved too weak to hold it. If you're tired of driving, **Stourbridge Rail Excursions** can take you on a scenic ride to Lackawaxen, but call ahead for schedules and prices *(717-253-1960)*.

Now go back southeast on US-6 for about 4 miles to the junction with **PA-652.** Turn left here and go about 10 miles northeast across the Delaware to Narrowsburg, New York. Bear left after the bridge and turn left at the second stoplight onto **NY-97.** Here you'll find the **Fort Delaware Museum of Colonial History** (6), a replica of a 1755 stockade, maintained by Sullivan County in honor of the Connecticut Yankees who settled the Delaware Valley. Costumed staff members demonstrate how the original occupants of this frontier fortification actually lived, and there are special events throughout the summer. *Open daily late June to Labor Day, weekends only Memorial Day to late June. Nominal admission fee. (914-252-6660).*

There's fine canoeing and kayaking around Narrowsburg; with a choice of white water or gentle currents, and of numerous rental and tour facilities in the area, including **Lander's Delaware River Trips** (7) *(914-252-3925,* a few miles south of the fort.

Continuing south about 10 miles on 97, you'll come to Minisink Ford. Here, opposite Minisink Battleground Park, is the **Roebling Bridge** (8) of 1848, the first suspension bridge designed by John Roebling—a smaller version of his most famous creation, the Brooklyn Bridge. Actually, this bridge was originally constructed as a aqueduct for the Delaware and Hudson Canal. Walk or drive across it to Lackawaxen, Pennsylvania, and turn right to the **Zane Grey Museum** (9) in the former home of the New York dentist who penned *Riders of the Purple Sage* and 102 other books at the rate of 100,000 words a month. It was here in Lackawaxen, said America's most prolific author of westerns, that he first experienced *really* wild country. *Open daily Memorial Day to Labor Day, weekends only Apr.–May and Sept.–Oct., by appointment other times. Free. (717-685-4871).*

Back across the bridge, continue south on 97 a few miles to the junction with **NY-55** in Barryville. Turn left here and go north 7 miles to the **Eldred Preserve** (10), where the main attraction is year-round trout fishing at three stocked ponds in 2,000 acres of rustic woodlands. Eldred also offers lodging and dining, tennis, swimming, hiking, and other recreational facilities *(914-557-8316)*.

To return to New York City from Eldred, go back to 97, take it south to Port Jervis, and head back on NJ-23 to I-80 east.

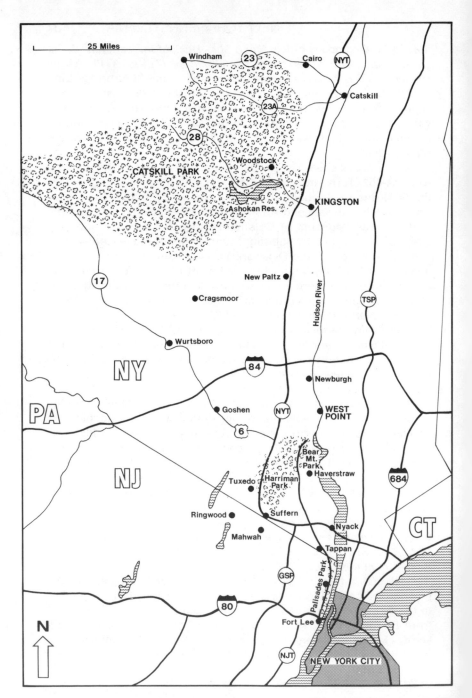

25 Miles

Windham · ——23—— Cairo · NYT

Catskill ·

23A

28

Woodstock ·

CATSKILL PARK

Ashokan Res. · KINGSTON ·

New Paltz ·

Hudson River

17

· Cragsmoor

TSP

· Wurtsboro

NY

84

· Newburgh

PA

Goshen · NYT WEST POINT ·

6

684

NJ

Bear Mt. Park

· Haverstraw

Tuxedo · Harriman Park

CT

Ringwood · · Suffern

· Nyack

Mahwah · Tappan ·

Palisades Park

GSP

80

N ↑ Fort Lee ·

NJT NEW YORK CITY

Area C

The view from State Line Lookout

UP THE HUDSON
ON THE WEST BANK

To many New Yorkers the Hudson is the Enchanted Valley, a wizard's mixture of history and legend; evoking memories of Dutch mariners, British grenadiers, Continental veterans; conjuring vistas of Bear Mountain, the wooded Highlands, the Catskills rising in the west. Houses of stone that have lasted 300 years, miles of apple orchards and vineyards, parks and waters for outdoor fun, embellished by the imagination of Washington Irving and Fenimore Cooper—from Manhattan to Rip Van Winkle's hideout, every mile is an exhilarating experience.

Trip C-1
On a Clear Day,
a Remarkable Panorama

- PALISADES INTERSTATE PARK
- ROCKEFELLER LOOKOUT
- ALPINE LOOKOUT
- STATE LINE LOOKOUT

DISTANCE: About 15 miles from Columbus Circle to the farthest point.

FOR THE DRIVER: From either level of the George Washington Bridge, follow signs for the **Palisades Interstate Parkway,** which runs the length of the park. Rockefeller Lookout is about 3 miles north, just off the parkway on the right. Alpine Lookout is another 3 miles north on the right; park headquarters is just above, off Exit 2 on right; and State Line Lookout is off Exit 3 on the right, about 3 miles north of Alpine.

PALISADES INTERSTATE PARK, NEW JERSEY SECTION, P.O. Box 155, Alpine, NJ 07620 (201-768-1360). *Grounds open daily all year, weather permitting, daylight hours. Park headquarters open all year Mon.–Fri. 8:30–4:30. Free except for areas in Trips C-2 and C-3. No climbing, no alcohol, no picnicking except in designated areas (see Trip C-2); no ground fires, no pets in picnic areas or developed areas, leashed pets only on trails. Some facilities are wheelchair-accessible.*

Discovered in 1524 by Giovanni da Verrazano, the Palisades ("fence of stakes") are volcanically-formed basalt cliffs overlooking the Hudson River. In 1900 Congress established the Palisades Interstate Park Commission to protect the cliffs from destruction by quarrying. The park consists of over 80,000 acres of land in New York (Trips C-4, C-5, C-7, and C-8) and New Jersey; the 2,500-acre New Jersey Section, extending about 11 miles from Fort Lee (Trip C-3) to the New York State Line, is a National Historic Landmark and a National Natural Landmark. Here, minutes from Manhattan, you can stand on cliffs 300 to over 500 feet high as you survey a panorama that includes the mighty Hudson, the New York skyscrapers, Long Island, Westchester, and far beyond. Looking straight down, you'll have awesome views of the tops of trees that literally grow up the sides of the precipice. Below,

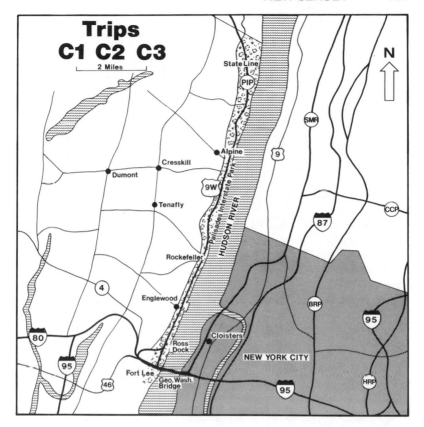

along the shore, are picnic grounds and boat basins (Trip C-2).

The New Jersey Section contains two designated National Recreation Trails, the Long Path and the Shore Trail, both beginning at the George Washington Bridge. The famous **Long Path,** marked by blue squares, winds along the clifftops past Rockefeller, Alpine, and State Line lookouts, crosses into New York, and continues through Harriman State Park into the Catskills; when complete, it will link New York City with the Adirondacks and Lake Placid, some 400 miles away. The **Shore Trail** follows the low route to the New York State Line and is marked by white squares. Six sets of stairs marked by overlapping blue and white squares connect the two trails. Average hiking time is 30 minutes per mile; camping, cooking, and cliff climbing are prohibited, and hikers must be off the trail by dark. For further hiking information and detailed maps, contact the New York-New Jersey Trail Conference, G.P.O. Box 2250, New York, NY 10116 (212-685-9699).

Many cultural, educational, and recreational programs take place in the park throughout the year. Call or write park headquarters for a calendar of events.

Rockefeller Lookout. *20-minute parking limit, no fee. One curb, but fair wheelchair access to vista points.* You're across the Hudson from the Riverdale section of the Bronx, just above Manhattan Island. To the right is the George Washington Bridge, and behind it, the New York skyscrapers. Beyond them is the Long Island Sound and Long Island. The hills north of the bridge rise to become Washington Heights, highest point on Manhattan. During the Revolution this was the site of Fort Washington, one of the city's ill-fated defenses. Fort Tryon Park stretches along the clifftops, and at the upper end stands the Cloisters, a medieval museum maintained by the Metropolitan Museum of Art.

Underneath the New York end of the bridge at Jeffreys Hook you can just make out the Little Red Lighthouse, slated for demolition when the bridge went up, but spared through protests and publicity. Look straight down the side of the cliffs for staggeringly effective views of treetops mingling with gigantic columns of rock.

Alpine Lookout. *20-minute parking limit, no fee. Steps and gravelly walk to promontory.* On your way here from the Rockefeller Lookout, you'll pass the Greenbrook Sanctuary of the Palisades Nature Association (call or stop by park headquarters for hours and further information). At the lookout, part of the Long Path takes you to the very edge of the cliffs, among the craggy pillars that poured out of the earth and solidified so many eons ago. That's Yonkers across the river (Trip D-1).

State Line Lookout. *1-hour parking limit, no fee. Hiking, cross-country skiing, refreshments, special events. Restrooms wheelchair-accessible.* You're now across from Hastings-on-Hudson, and 532 feet tall. The best view is to the north where the Tappan Zee Bridge carries the New York Thruway across three miles of river between Tarrytown and Nyack. The Long Path still clings to the top of the cliffs—why not join it for a hike?

Trip C-2
Exploring the Palisades from Below

- PALISADES INTERSTATE PARK
- ROSS DOCK
- ENGLEWOOD AREA
- UNDERCLIFF
- ALPINE AREA

DISTANCE: About 10 miles from Columbus Circle to the farthest point.

FOR THE DRIVER: From the George Washington Bridge follow signs for the **Palisades Interstate Parkway.** Go north to Exit 1 and follow signs for Henry Hudson Drive and Englewood Area, at the bottom of the cliff. Ross Dock is about 1½ mile south, Undercliff is just above Englewood, and Alpine about 5 miles north of Undercliff, all via Henry Hudson Drive.

Note that the Henry Hudson Drive is closed completely from early Nov. to mid-Apr. Otherwise, it is open during daylight hours to cars only, except on weekend and holiday mornings when the Englewood-Alpine section is reserved for joggers, bicycles, and pedestrians. During this time you can drive to Alpine via the parkway to Exit 2.

PALISADES INTERSTATE PARK, NEW JERSEY SECTION (See Trip C-1 for general information). *Shore areas open during daylight hours, weather permitting; times and facilities vary as noted and by staff availability. Alcohol, picnicking and barbecuing (no ground fires, bring your own grill and charcoal) permitted in these 4 areas only. Fishing and crabbing from sea walls, docks, and shoreline permitted in season. No swimming, no climbing, no pets.*

Ross Dock. *Open (when collector is on duty) weekends and holidays mid-Apr. to early May and in Oct., daily early May through Sept. Parking fee: cars $3, motorcycles $2. Picnicking, hiking, fishing, playgrounds, basketball court. Picnic area wheelchair-accessible.* This is the first picnic area you reach after coming over the George Washington Bridge. The view is especially interesting because you're almost beneath the bridge.

Englewood Area. *Open daily all year. Parking fee: weekends and holidays most of Apr. and most of Oct., daily late Apr. to early Oct.,* cars $3, motorcycles $2; other times free. Picnicking, hiking, fishing, playground, boat basin, refreshment stand in season. Picnic area and restrooms wheelchair-accessible. Here is the park's largest picnic area, with fine views and a trail to the clifftops. The Dyckman Street Ferry used to dock at Englewood.

Undercliff. Open (when collector is on duty) weekends and holidays Memorial Day to Labor Day. Parking fee: cars $3, motorcycles $2. Picnicking, hiking, fishing. Picnic area wheelchair-accessible. This small area on the cliff side of Henry Hudson Drive has fine views and trails leading down to the river.

Alpine Area. Open daily all year. Parking fee: weekends and holidays early Apr. to early May and early Sept. to late Oct., daily early May to early Sept., cars $3, motorcycles $2. Picnicking, hiking, fishing, playground, boat basin, special events, outdoor concerts. Picnic area and restrooms wheelchair-accessible. Above you hang the great cliffs, with trees growing at all angles from the rock crevices. Man-made embellishments include picturesque pavilions and the historic Blackledge-Kearny House (c. 1750), once Cornwallis's headquarters. Trails lead along the river bank and right up the side of the Palisades. If these seem pretty steep, you might note that during the Revolution the British soldiers climbed them, carrying all their equipment, on their way to capture Fort Lee.

A soldier's hut at Fort Lee Historic Park

Trip C-3
Vistas of Past and Present
Just Across the Bridge

- **FORT LEE HISTORIC PARK**

DISTANCE: Less than 10 miles from Columbus Circle.

FOR THE DRIVER: Take the **upper level** of the George Washington Bridge to the first Fort Lee exit, after the exit for the Palisades Interstate Parkway. Bear right and go down the ramp to Hudson Terrace, at the traffic light. Turn right and go about 50 feet past the next light to the park entrance, on left.

FORT LEE HISTORIC PARK, Hudson Terrace, Fort Lee, NJ 07024 (201-461-1776). *Grounds open daily all year, daylight hours. Visitor Center open Mar.–Dec., Wed.–Sun. 10–5. Closed Jan.–Feb. Parking fee $2. Picnicking (no grills or fires). No climbing, no bicycles, no pets. Visitor Center main floor and restrooms wheelchair-accessible, wide paved paths with ramps through grounds.*
Fort Lee played a disheartening role in the early phases of the American Revolution, when the British were fighting for control of the Hudson. In July 1776, to block them, George Washington ordered the fortification of a number of sites on both sides of the river, including this fort named for General Charles Lee, a mercurial man who envied Washington and whose treason almost handed the British a victory at the Battle of Monmouth later that year. In August a large British force landed on Long Island and drove the American defenders across Brooklyn into Manhattan. Throughout the fall skirmishes raged where skyscrapers now stand, and Washington fell back to Harlem Heights and White Plains (Trip D-3). In November the Americans suffered a major defeat at Fort Washington, in what is today upper Manhattan. With its sister fort in British hands, Fort Lee lost its strategic importance and was already being evacuated when a surprise attack forced a hasty fight, resulting in further losses of men and badly needed supplies. That December, as Washington retreated deeper into New Jersey, Tom Paine penned the famous line "These are the times that try men's souls."

Fort Lee Historic Park, administered by the Palisades Interstate Park Commission, commemorates those trying times. The **Visitor Center,** just east of the original fort, features historic exhibits, audiovisual displays, and a short film (shown only on weekends). Outside, two overlooks give spectacular views of the George Washington Bridge, the New York skyline, and the Hudson River (minus the attacking British armada). Winding trails take you through the southern part of the 33-acre park to reconstructed gun batteries and an 18th-century soldier's hut where demonstrations of Colonial life are staged. Of course, momentous battles still rage in this area daily during the rush hour, but it's hard to imagine it as a wilderness outpost of America's war for independence.

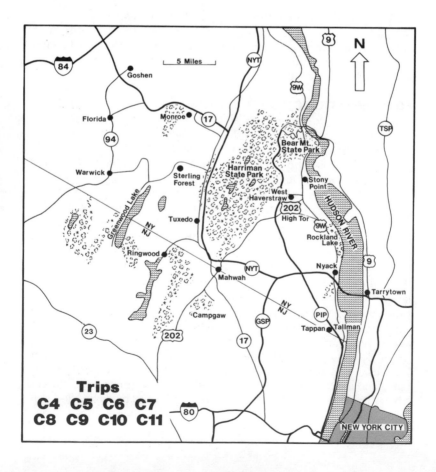

Trip C-4
The End of the Road
for Major André

- GEORGE WASHINGTON MASONIC SHRINE
- ANDRÉ HILL
- TALLMAN MOUNTAIN STATE PARK

DISTANCE: About 20 miles from Columbus Circle.

FOR THE DRIVER: From the George Washington Bridge take the **Palisades Interstate Parkway** north to Exit 4, **US-9W,** then 9W north towards Nyack. Shortly, at traffic light, turn left on Oak Tree Rd. and follow it a block past the junction with NY-303 to the **De Wint House** entrance on the left.

Return to Oak Tree Rd., turn left, and continue until it merges with Main St. in Tappan. For **André Hill,** turn left on Main and continue uphill bearing right. There's a marker at the execution site.

Go back on Oak Tree Rd. past De Wint House and return to the junction with US-9W. Continue north briefly to the **Tallman Mountain State Park,** on the right.

GEORGE WASHINGTON MASONIC SHRINE / DE WINT HOUSE, 20 Livingston Ave., Tappan, NY 10983 (914-359-1359). *Open all year daily 10–4, closed Christmas. Donations. Pets discouraged. Will accommodate wheelchairs.*

General Washington made the De Wint House (c. 1700) his headquarters five times, and he was here the last week of September 1780, when Major John André, accused as a spy in the Benedict Arnold conspiracy to betray West Point, was captured and brought to Tappan. A military court appointed by Washington held an inquiry on September 29 and determined that André should be hung as a spy. Washington is said to have signed the order for his execution at a table now in this house. The house was subsequently bought by the Masons and is preserved as a memorial to Washington, a member. On the grounds is a carriage house (1800) containing historic artifacts.

ANDRÉ HILL, Tappan, NY. British headquarters in New York tried but failed to secure André's release through a prisoner exchange. André wrote to General Washington asking for a soldier's death by shooting, but his request was denied on the grounds that he had been condemned as a spy and must suffer a spy's punishment. On October 2, 1780, resplendent in the full dress uniform of a British officer, he was taken from his place of detention in a local tavern, escorted up the hill to the drumbeat of "The Dead March," and hanged. A charming and cultivated man, he was mourned by many on both sides and became something of a romantic figure after his execution. André was buried where he died; in 1821 his remains were moved to Westminster Abbey in London.

TALLMAN MOUNTAIN STATE PARK, Sparkill, NY (914-359-0544). *Part of the Palisades Interstate Parks; see Trip C-5 for general information and fees. Park vehicle-use fee in effect mid-June to early Sept. Picnicking, hiking trails, playground, handball, tennis, swimming pool, refreshments in season.*

This scenic park, administered by the Palisades Interstate Park Commission, is a stone's throw from the northern tip of the New Jersey section of the Palisades (Trips C-1 and C-2), and right across the river from Sunnyside, home of Washington Irving (Trip D-2).

Trip C-5
Up the Hudson to High Tor

- PALISADES INTERSTATE PARKS
- NYACK BEACH STATE PARK
- ROCKLAND LAKE STATE PARK
- HIGH TOR STATE PARK

DISTANCE: The farthest point is about 35 miles from Columbus Circle.

FOR THE DRIVER: From the George Washington Bridge, take the **Palisades Interstate Parkway** north to Exit 4 and pick up **US-9W** north to Nyack. In town turn right on High St., just after the junction with NY59, and proceed to Broadway. Turn left and follow Broadway into **Nyack Beach State Park.**

Go back down Broadway about a mile and turn right on Old Mountain Rd., continuing uphill to the top. Follow signs to US-9W and head north on 9W about a mile to **Rockland Lake State Park.**

Continue north on 9W to the junction with **NY-304** to New City. Turn left on 304 to Ridge Rd. (1st small road), then turn right on Ridge and go to the end at South Mountain Rd. Turn left on South Mountain for a mile or so to **High Tor State Park,** on the right.

From here you can go back to South Mountain Rd. and turn left back to US-9W the way you came, *or* turn right on South Mountain to Central Highway, then right over Little Tor Mountain to the junction with US-202. A right turn here leads back to US-9W south, *or* you can turn left on 202 to the Palisades Interstate Parkway for the return trip.

This area can also be accessed via the New York State Thruway and the Tappan Zee Bridge.

PALISADES INTERSTATE PARKS, Bear Mountain State Park, Bear Mountain, NY 10911 (914-786-2701). *Open daily all year, daylight hours. Vehicle use fees in season. No ground fires; cooking permitted in park grills and fireplaces. No camping except in Harriman State Park (Trip C-8). Leashed pets only. All parks within the system have wheelchair-accessible restrooms and ramps at parking lots, beach areas, pools, and picnic areas. Some of the pools and beaches may be closed at times due to a shortage of lifeguards; check in advance.*

The three parks on this trip, as well as Tallman Mountain State Park on the last trip and many of the parks and historic sites on the next several trips, are administered by the Palisades Interstate Park Commission. Unlike the New Jersey Section of the Palisades (Trips C-1 and C-2), the New York parks are scattered throughout several counties. Exact opening and closing dates and operating hours tend to vary slightly from year to year; park activities are free except for vehicle fees in season, pools, etc. For further information call the specific park that interests you or contact the Palisades Interstate Park Commission at the Bear Mountain headquarters.

Nyack Beach State Park, Upper Nyack, NY (914-358-1316). *Park vehicle-use fee in effect weekends Memorial day to mid-June and Labor Day to early Oct., daily mid-June to Labor Day. Picnicking, hiking trails, ballfields, fishing, boat launching ramp, cross-country skiing.* This small 61-acre park is hard to beat for scenery. The main attraction is the river itself (no swimming allowed); kids love to play on its banks, adults think first of the fishing. Trails start here for a hike to Rockland Lake, just north, or a trek to High Tor.

Rockland Lake State Park, Congers, NY (914-268-3020). *Park vehicle-use fee in effect weekends Memorial Day to mid-June, daily mid-June to Labor Day. Picnicking, hiking and exercise trails, swimming* *pools, playing fields, basketball courts, boat launching ramp, fishing, ice skating, sledding, cross-country skiing, nature center, rowboat rentals, tennis courts (fee), golf courses (fee, equipment rentals, lessons), refreshment stands in season. Golf, tennis, fishing, and boating season Apr.–Nov. No pets.* Built around an attractive small lake, this park provides a wide range of activities. A network of trails spreads out in several directions for hiking, and the nature center has a boardwalk into a swamp area where plants of the region are marked for identification. Wildfowl gather here and during the winter are a constant attraction.

High Tor State Park, Haverstraw, NY (914-634-8074). *Park vehicle-use fee in effect daily mid-June to Labor Day. Picnicking, hiking, swimming pool, refreshment stand in season.* Located up the side of the famous High Tor Mountain, this rugged park is popular mainly for hiking and swimming. Hiking here is for the more experienced. You can climb High Tor or Low Tor, or take any of the connecting trails south to Hook Mountain, Rockland Lake, or Nyack Beach State Parks. The Long Path goes through High Tor on its way west to Harriman State Park (Trip C-8).

Trip C-6
Religious Tranquility,
Revolutionary Turmoil

- MARIAN SHRINE
- STONY POINT BATTLEFIELD

DISTANCE: About 40 miles from Columbus Circle.

FOR THE DRIVER: From the George Washington Bridge take the **Palisades Interstate Parkway** north to Exit 13, Willow Grove Rd. Turn right (east) on Willow Grove and go about a mile to Filors Lane. Turn right and proceed to the **Marian Shrine,** shortly on the right.

From the shrine turn right on Filors Lane and continue east to **US-9W.** Go north on 9W to the turnoff for **Stony Point Battlefield,** on the right shortly after the junction with NY-210.

You can return on 9W south *or* take it back to the junction with NY-210, turn right, and go west about 2½ miles to Palisades Interstate Parkway South.

This area is also accessible via the New York State Thruway and the Tappan Zee Bridge.

MARIAN SHRINE, Filors Lane, West Haverstraw, NY 10993 (914-947-2200). *Open May–Oct. daily 9–6; closed other times. Weekday services at noon (mass) and 3:30; weekend masses (11, noon); blessing of pilgrims in morning; tours, procession, benediction in afternoon. Picnicking allowed, pets discouraged. Well-paved walks, ramp to main building, annual handicapped day.*

Here a beautiful woodland path winds past 15 white Carrara marble statues that comprise the Rosary. While not as spectacular as Graymoor, the Franciscan monastery across the river to the north (Trip D-8), the Marian Shrine has an intimacy all its own; the guardians are the Salesians of St. John Bosco. Visitors may attend mass at an outdoor altar under a marble dome. There's a good deal of walking, as the statues are spaced some distance apart. The expressions on the finely-sculpted faces make a good subject for photographers, and there are lovely views of the Hudson and the distant mountains.

STONY POINT BATTLEFIELD STATE HISTORIC SITE, P.O. Box 182, Stony Point, NY 10980 (914-786-2521). *Grounds open May–Oct. daily 8:30–5, museum Wed.–Sun. 9–4:30. Free. Picnicking (no cooking), self-guided tours, special events. Leashed pets only. Parking, building entrances, and most public areas and restrooms are wheelchair-accessible.*

This site, administered by the Palisades Interstate Park Commission, commemorates the night of July 15–16, 1779, when General "Mad" Anthony Wayne and his Light Infantry stormed the British garrison at Stony Point and recaptured the fort. It was a classic surprise attack, mounted by way of a sandbar traversible only at very low tides, with the soldiers using bayonets for silence. The victory gave a tremendous boost to American morale. Today, markers enable you to walk out the battle: you learn where the Americans made their assault on the seemingly impregnable fort, where the outer and inner lines of the British abatis were located, where the final hand-to-hand combat took place. At the tip of the point is a picturesque lighthouse from 1826.

In the museum you'll find documents on the history of Stony Point, maps of the battleground, audiovisual displays, and costumed interpreters. There's also material on the Arnold-André treachery (trips C-4, C-12) (look for a self-portrait by André) and artifacts from the war. Outside, you have fine vistas of Haverstraw Bay and the lower Hudson Valley.

Trip C-7
A Trip to Bear Mountain

- BEAR MOUNTAIN STATE PARK
- BEAR MOUNTAIN INN

DISTANCE: About 45 miles from Columbus Circle.

FOR THE DRIVER: From the George Washington Bridge take the **Palisades Interstate Parkway** north to its end at the Bear Mountain traffic circle. Turn right to the inn and parking lot. At the south end of the parking lot turn right onto Seven Lakes Parkway and proceed to **Perkins Memorial Drive,** shortly on the right.

Note that at the Bear Mountain circle you can drive over the Bear Mountain Bridge to the east bank of the Hudson and some of the sites in Area D. Just south of the bridge is Iona Island, once a navy base where bombs and ammunition were assembled during both World Wars. In the mid-1960s the navy gave Iona to the Palisades Interstate Park Commission for development as a recreation area, but nothing came of these plans. It is now a winter sanctuary for the endangered bald eagle. The island itself is closed to the public but can be viewed from the causeway.

Bear Mountain is also accessible via the New York State Thruway and the Tappan Zee Bridge.

BEAR MOUNTAIN STATE PARK, Bear Mountain, NY 10911 (914-786-2701). *Part of Palisades Interstate Parks; see Trip C-5 for general information. Park vehicle-use fee in effect all year, daily early May to Labor Day, weekends and holidays only at other times. Perkins Memorial Drive open daily late Mar. to early Oct. Trailside Museum and Zoo open all year daily 9–5. Picnicking (cooking permitted, but bring your own grill; no cooking facilities in park), hiking trails, playing fields, fishing, swimming pool (Memorial Day to Labor Day), roller and ice skating, sledding, cross-country skiing, boat rentals (Apr.–Oct.), miniature golf (fee), year-round refreshment stand. Annual Christmas festival and winter ski jumping tournaments.*

Bear Mountain State Park, New York City's year-round playground, covers more than 5,000 acres of the Highlands that gave the Hudson its reputation as the Rhine of America. The popular **Trailside Museum and Zoo** has exhibits on the history and natural history of the area.

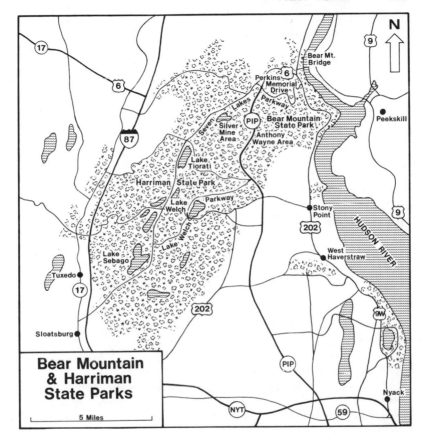

N

Bear Mountain & Harriman State Parks

5 Miles

The beautiful scenery and wide variety of activities attracts great throngs, so try to plan your trip for a weekday.

One of the best mountain drives available near the city is the ride to the top of Bear Mountain on **Perkins Memorial Drive.** Along the way there are continual vistas from scenic overlooks, and historic markers telling of battles that took place directly below. From the **observation tower** atop the mountain you can see the High Point tower in New Jersey (Trip B-19), the New York skyscrapers, and, much closer, Anthony's Nose just across the river and Sugar Loaf Hill to the north. There are picnic areas below the tower, and a road to the scenic drive leading to the well-photographed overlook above Bear Mountain Inn.

BEAR MOUNTAIN INN, Bear Mountain, NY 10911 (914-786-2731). *Open all year for lodging and dining. Dining hours 8–11 a.m., noon–3 p.m., 5–8 p.m. (10 on weekends). Inquire about overnight rates, weekend*

*packages, seasonal specials. Wheelchair-accessible parking and rest-
rooms, sidewalk ramps, elevator to dining room, level grounds.*

Operated as a concession within Bear Mountain State Park, the inn
has a long tradition of hospitality and fine dining. Overlooking Hessian Lake, surrounded by majestic mountains, it's a perfect place for
a meal or drink. A major attraction is the entertainment on Friday and
Saturday evenings.

Trip C-8
More of the Great Outdoors

- ## HARRIMAN STATE PARK

DISTANCE: About 40 miles from Columbus Circle to the Anthony
Wayne Area, another 2–10 miles to the other sites.

FOR THE DRIVER: From the George Washington Bridge, take the **Palisades Interstate Parkway** north to Exit 15 and the **Anthony Wayne
Area.** From there follow signs to the **Seven Lakes Parkway** and turn
left. The **Silver Mine Area** is about 2 miles south, and **Lake Tiorati**
another 1½ miles south.

Continue south on Seven Lakes past lakes Askoti and Skannatati
(fishing only), Lake Kanawauke (picnicking and hiking; vehicle use fee
in effect mid-June to Labor Day), and the junction with NY-210. Just
beyond this is **Lake Sebago.** From here, go back up the Seven Lakes
Parkway to **Lake Welch Parkway** and turn right to **Lake Welch,** about
2½ miles.

If you are not going to the Anthony Wayne or Silver Mine areas,
there are more direct routes to the lakes. From the Palisades Interstate
Parkway Exit 13, go west on Gate Hill Rd. and NY-210 to Lake Welch.
Turn left off 210 onto Johnstown Rd. to Lake Sebago. For Lake Tiorati,
take Palisades Parkway Exit 14A and go west on Tiorati Rd. to the lake.
Just after the exit you can also turn left on Lake Welch Parkway to Lake
Welch.

Harriman State Park is also accessible via the New York Thruway
and the Tappan Zee Bridge.

HARRIMAN STATE PARK, Harriman, NY (914-786-2701). *Part of the Palisades Interstate Parks; see Trip C-5 for general information.*

Adjacent to Bear Mountain State Park on the southwest, Harriman is a much larger area (over 46,000 acres) and includes more rugged terrain and many undeveloped areas. Like Bear Mountain, it offers a wide range of activities and facilities for year-round use.

Anthony Wayne Area (914-942-2650). *Park vehicle-use fee in effect daily mid-June to Labor Day. Picnicking, hiking trails, playground, swimming pool (may be closed), cross-country skiing, refreshment stand in summer. No pets.* With attractive picnic and play areas fanning out around a large pool, this is a good spot for those who don't like things too rustic.

Silver Mine Area (914-429-2608). *Park vehicle-use fee in effect daily mid-June to Labor Day. Picnicking, hiking, fishing.* This is a lovely woodland park by a picturesque mountain lake. Paths and picnic areas all around the lake make it a fine place to spend an afternoon. Fall foliage is outstanding here.

Lake Tiorati (914-351-2568). *Beach vehicle-use fee in effect weekends and holidays Memorial Day to mid-June, daily mid-June to Labor Day. Picnicking, hiking trials, swimming beach, boat launching ramp, fishing, ice skating on lake, tent camping sites (fee), refreshment stand in summer.* A large, clear lake, Tiorati offers a refreshing swim, and little tufts of islands provide intriguing destinations for fishermen.

Lake Sebago (914-351-2583). *Beach vehicle-use fee in effect daily mid-June to Labor Day. Picnicking, hiking trails, playing fields, swimming beach, fishing, boat rentals, boat launching ramp, ice skating on lake, cross-country skiing, refreshment stand in season, cabin rentals in season (call Sebago Cabins, 914-351-2360). No pets.* One of the larger beaches in the area, this is another superb setting, with fine walks and good views all around.

Lake Welch (914-947-2444). *Beach vehicle-use fee in effect weekends and holidays Memorial Day to mid-June, daily mid-June to Labor Day. Picnicking, hiking trails, playing fields, swimming beach, fishing, boat launching ramp, boat rentals, snowmobile trail, refreshment stand in summer, tent and trailer camping at Beaver Pond (fee, reserve in advance).* This is another large beach area, able to handle the biggest summer crowds. The swimming and boating are excellent, and there's a lovely hedged lawn for sunbathing.

Trip C-9
Good Manors in Northern Jersey

- RINGWOOD STATE PARK
- RINGWOOD MANOR
- SHEPHERD LAKE
- SKYLANDS MANOR

DISTANCE: About 40 miles from Columbus Circle.

FOR THE DRIVER: Take the **New York Thruway** north towards Albany to Exit 15 at Suffern. Here pick up **NY-17** north to the Ringwood-West Milford exit (Sloatsburg Rd.) and turn left for nearly 3 miles into **Ringwood State Park.** Entrance to **Shepherd Lake** is off this road on the left, entrance to **Ringwood Manor** is a little farther, on the right, and entrance to **Skylands Manor** is beyond Ringwood at Morris Rd.

RINGWOOD STATE PARK, Box 1304, Ringwood, NJ 07456 (201-962-7031). *Grounds open all year daily dawn–dusk. Fees charged separately for each section from Memorial Day to Labor Day. Leashed pets only. Special events throughout the year. Partially barrier-free.*
    Ringwood Manor Section. *Manor open May–Oct., Tues.–Sun. 10–4; closed Mon. Entry fee $4 per car weekends and holidays, $3 weekday (Tues. free). Picnic area, hiking and nature trails, fishing in Ringwood River, ice fishing, sledding, cross-country skiing, refreshment stand. Manor entrance is wheelchair-accessible.* A picturesque park with a millpond and formal gardens surrounds a 78-room **manor house** built in the 18th century and Victorianized in the 19th. Some of the rooms are furnished with valuable pieces collected by two well-known families over the years: Peter Cooper, founder of Cooper Union and one-time presidential candidate, lived at Ringwood as did his son-in-law, Abraham Hewitt, a mayor of New York City. General Washington made it his headquarters occasionally. Outside, a waterwheel stands on the site of an old iron forge.
    Shepherd Lake Section. *Entry fee Memorial Day to Labor Day $4 per car weekends and holidays, $3 weekdays (Tues. free). Picnic facilities (fireplaces), hiking, playground, swimming, fishing, boating (ramp and rentals), ice skating, ice fishing, sledding, cross-country skiing, year-round trap and skeet shooting (fee, 201-962-6377), refreshment stand. Swimming area and restrooms wheelchair-accessible.* Here, some

541 acres of the Ramapo Mountains are yours to enjoy. The lake is spring-fed, and the fishing is excellent if you like trout, pickerel, and northern pike. Hiking trails into the mountains afford good views at elevations of 500 to 1,040 feet above sea level.

Skylands Manor Section. *Manor house open by appointment only. Entry fee $4 per car weekends and holidays, $3 weekdays (Tues. free). Hiking trails, ice fishing, cross-country skiing, snowmobile trails, sledding. House is manageable for wheelchairs.* Skylands Manor House is a beautiful rustic estate built in 1924 and patterned after an English baronial mansion. The 44 rooms are unfurnished, but the walls, ceilings, fireplaces, stained-glass windows, and paneling, imported from European castles, are noteworthy. The elegantly-landscaped **gardens** are especially popular in the springtime. Here are more good hiking trails with splendid views of the surrounding country.

Trip C-10
Certain Reservations
in the Ramapos

- CAMPGAW MOUNTAIN RESERVATION
- DARLINGTON COUNTY PARK
- RAMAPO VALLEY RESERVATION
- BERGEN COUNTY WILDLIFE CENTER

DISTANCE: About 40 miles from Columbus Circle.

FOR THE DRIVER: Take the **New York Thruway** north towards Albany to Exit 15 at Suffern. Here pick up **NY-17** south to New Jersey, then **US-202** southwest about 2 miles to Darlington Ave. Turn left and go a short distance to a fork in the road. Bear right uphill on Campgaw Rd. for the **Campgaw Mountain Reservation;** bear left, continuing on Darlington, for **Darlington County Park.**

Go back to US-202 (Ramapo Valley Rd.), turn left, and continue briefly to the entrance of the **Ramapo Valley Reservation,** on the right.

Continue south on 202 to Oakland and the junction with **NJ-208.** A right turn here will take you to the scenic Skyline Drive through the Ramapo Mountain State Forest (201-337-0960), a beautiful and largely undeveloped wilderness area. For the **Bergen County Wildlife Center,** turn left on 208, towards New York City, and go about 2 miles to Summit Ave. exit, on the right. Get off 208 here and bear left, crossing back over 208 to Franklin Ave. Turn right on Franklin and follow it through the center of Wyckoff, across a small railroad track, and across Godwin Ave. about 4 blocks to Crescent Ave. Turn right here and watch for a sign to the center, almost immediately on the left.

CAMPGAW MOUNTAIN COUNTY RESERVATION, Campgaw Rd., Mahwah, NJ 07443 (201-327-7804). *Open daily all year, daylight hours. No entry fee. Picnicking, hiking trails, playgrounds, bridle paths, camping (fee), snowmobiling, downhill skiing mid-Dec. to mid-Mar. (call 201-327-7800 or -7801 for snow conditions and fees). Leashed pets only. Wheelchair-accessible restrooms, easy paved roads.*

Here's a good place for a not-too-strenuous hike along old Indian trails that wind through hemlock groves or skirt the swamplands. The park contains a wildlife refuge and plenty of play areas for the kids. **Campgaw Mountain Ski Area,** with a 1,650-foot main slope and snow-making facilities, is a popular and reasonably-priced attraction in winter.

DARLINGTON COUNTY PARK, Darlington Ave., Mahwah, NJ 07443 (201-327-3500). *Open Apr. to late Nov. daily 10 to sunset, weather permitting. Admission charged during swimming season. Picnicking (bring your own grill), swimming, fishing, playing fields, handball courts, basketball courts, tennis courts, golf course (fee), snack bar. No pets. Wheelchair-accessible restrooms, ramps to beach area.*

There are three lakes here, two for swimming and one for fishing. Adjacent to Campgaw Mountain, the park provides a beautiful setting for family outings.

RAMAPO VALLEY RESERVATION, Ramapo Valley Rd., Mahwah, NJ (201-825-1388). *Open all year daily 8–4:30. Free. No cars beyond the entrance, no swimming; picnic areas, hiking trails, fishing, canoeing, camping. Leashed pets only. Difficult for wheelchairs.*

Here are some trails for the more adventuresome, under really tall timber. There's more climbing than walking, and the boulders are piled high. Among several hikes is one up the mountainside to a clear lake a mile or so away, not from the Skylands section of Ringwood State Park (Trip C-9).

BERGEN COUNTY WILDLIFE CENTER, Crescent Ave., Wyckoff, NJ 07481 (201-891-5571). *Grounds open all year daily, 8–8 in summer, 8– sunset at other times. Buildings open all year daily 8–4:45. Free. No pets. Building fully wheelchair-accessible and barrier-free.*

This is a fine place to take the kids for an all-around introduction to Mother Nature. The 81-acre grounds feature a nature trail, a wildlife pond, and seasonal displays of rhododendron, azaleas, and wildflowers. There's some captive wildlife on view, and the museum has an observatory, informative natural-history exhibits, and two large aquariums, one for saltwater species and the other for their freshwater cousins.

Trip C-11
To Standardbred Country via
Merrie Olde England

- NEW YORK RENAISSANCE FESTIVAL
- HALL OF FAME OF THE TROTTER
- GOSHEN HISTORIC TRACK
- MUSEUM VILLAGE IN ORANGE COUNTY

DISTANCE: About 70 miles from Columbus Circle to the Museum Village via Sterling Forest and Goshen.

FOR THE DRIVER: Take the **NEW YORK THRUWAY** north towards Albany to Exit 15 at Suffern and pick up **NY-17** north for about 10 miles to the junction with **NY-17A/210.** Turn left and go about 3 miles west to Sterling Forest and the **New York Renaissance Festival.** In winter there's downhill skiing here at Sterling Forest Ski Center (914-351-2163).

Continue on 17A/210 to the junction with Route 5 at Greenwood Lake, where the cannon Molly Pitcher used during the Battle of Monmouth was cast. Here 210 branches off to the left, and you may want to follow it south for a scenic drive into New Jersey, where it becomes NJ-511 and takes you to a nice family recreation area at the southern end of Greenwood Lake. From here, you can follow 511 to Awosting Rd., turn left, and return to NY-17A/210 via Awosting, East Shore, and Sterling Forest roads; or you can remain on 511 to the turnoff for Ringwood (Trip C-9); or you can remain on 511 to Wanaque Reservoir, impressive not only for its 28-billion-gallon capacity but also for its beauty in fall and its apparent attractiveness to aliens (numerous flying saucers have been sighted in the area). As you proceed around the reservoir on 511, you will meet Skyline Drive, which goes through Ramapo Mountain State Forest (Trip C-10).

From the junction of 17A/210 and Route 5, continue on 17A about 6 miles to Warwick, passing Mount Peter Ski Area (914-986-4992), another nice spot to hit the slopes in winter. In **Warwick** there are a number of interesting buildings maintained by the Warwick Historical Society (914-986-2720): Shingle House on Forester Ave., the oldest house in the village, said to have been roofed and sided with shingles all made from a single tree; the 1810 House on Main St., with some fine Duncan Phyfe pieces and displays of Americana; and the Old School Baptist Meeting House on Church St.

In Warwick 17A meets NY-94, and the two become Main St. Go north on this about 6 miles to Florida, where 94 branches off to the right. Go straight and continue on 17A about 4½ miles to **Goshen.** In Goshen at the junction with NY-17/US-6, 17A becomes NY-207. Continue through the stoplight to the entrance of the **Goshen Historic Track;** just beyond this is the **Hall of Fame of the Trotter.**

Go back to the junction with NY-17/US-6 (Quickway) and take it east about 10 miles, passing Goosepond Mountain State Park, an unspoiled wilderness tract with hiking trails and bridle paths. Get off the Quickway at Exit 129, Museum Village Rd., and follow signs to the **Museum Village of Orange County.**

For the return trip, continue east on the Quickway to the Thruway.

NEW YORK RENAISSANCE FESTIVAL, Route 17A, Sterling Forest, Tuxedo, NY 11978 (914-351-5171, in NYC 212-645-1630). *Festival runs for 7 or 8 weekends beginning in early Aug., 11–6, schedule varies, check in advance. Jousts are held about 5 p.m. Admission (includes entertainment): Adults $12.50, seniors $10, children 6–12 $5, under 6 free. Special Short Line Festival Bus from Port Authority Bus Terminal in Manhattan (212-736-4700). Food and drink available, or you can bring your own. Grounds and restrooms are wheelchair-accessible.*

If you think that all the romance has gone out of the world, try shedding your cares and a few centuries at the New York Renaissance Festival, where you can thrill to the spectacle of knights in shining armor jousting on horseback as in days of yore, lend an ear to the strolling minstrels, laugh along with the jesters and mimes, sate yourself on hearty fare and noble drink, fritter away your farthings at the gaming tables, and watch the Equity players strut and fret their hour upon the stage at the Globe Theater. Struth, all this and more, as you like it, in the lovely setting of Sterling Forest. The festival is now in its 15th year, and going strong.

HALL OF FAME OF THE TROTTER, 240 Main St., Goshen, NY 10924 (914-294-6330). *Open all year Mon.–Sat. 10–5, Sun. noon–5; closed Thanksgiving, Christmas, New Year's. Adults $2, children $1; tours by appointment. No steps into building, wide aisles on 1st floor; no wheelchair access to 2nd floor.*

The former Good Time Stable has been converted into a museum dedicated to the Standardbred trotters who made this area famous. More than 100 exhibits in the large box stalls and hay chutes capture the flavor of harness racing and tell the story of this quintessential American sport, the great national pastime of the 19th century, still entertaining millions of enthusiastic fans today. There's an original painting of Hambletonian, the Standardbred "daddy of 'em all," as well as Currier and Ives lithographs, wood carvings, bronzes, and statuary. Dioramas and films depict the immortal horses and drivers, and there are lifelike statuettes of the sport's great personalities in the United States Harness Writers Association Living Hall of Fame. You can browse in the Peter D. Haughton Memorial Library or in the Weathervane Shop, which sells horseshoes, jewelry, and all manner of items related to harness horses.

GOSHEN HISTORIC TRACK, Park Place, Goshen, NY 10924 (914-294-5333). *Open for walking tours all year daily 9–5. Racing in spring and summer; schedule and fees vary (check in advance). Picnicking, refreshment stand, special events all season. Grounds easy for wheelchairs; grandstand not wheelchair-accessible, but races can be watched from other locations.*

This National Historic Landmark, harness racing's oldest track (1838), still offers an exciting program of Grand Circuit races, Sire Stakes events, trotting bred exhibition races, and matinee races where amateur drivers vie for the coveted trophy—a horse blanket. Even if there are no races scheduled on the famous half-mile during your visit, you can see the horses in their stables and watch them go through their paces during the daily workout.

MUSEUM VILLAGE IN ORANGE COUNTY, Museum Village Rd., Monroe, NY 10950 (914-782-8247). *Open May to early Dec.: May–June and Sept.–Dec. Wed.–Fri. 10–2, Sat. & Sun. noon–5; July–Aug. Wed.–Fri. 10–5, Sat. & Sun. noon–5; open Mon. holiday weekends, otherwise closed Mon.–Tues. Adults $7, seniors $5, children 6–15 $4, under 6 free. Picnic area, snack bar, shops, special events all year. No pets. Will accommodate wheelchairs, call in advance.*

Here's an outdoor museum that gives you a vivid taste of life in preindustrial America. At 33 buildings clustered around the Village Green, you can see demonstrations of such indispensable 19th-century skills as weaving, blacksmithing, cobbling, wood carving, sheep shearing, sausage stuffing, and the making of candles, brooms, soap, cider, and other basics. A collection of steam and gas engines heralds the arrival of 20th-century technology, while a natural history exhibit takes you back to prehistoric times and for once invites you to "please touch" the bones of a well-preserved mastodon.

The Museum Village specializes in such contrasts, with exhibits that remind you how laborious life was before the invention of modern appliances like the vacuum and the Cuisinart, but may also make you long for the simpler days of Dr. Daniel's Housecleaning Fluid and Gargle. Throughout the year there are special events, including antique shows, Christmas shopping and caroling, festive dinners, Halloween tricks and treats, and an annual kite-flying day where you can buy or build your own aerodynamic contribution to the Hudson Valley skies.

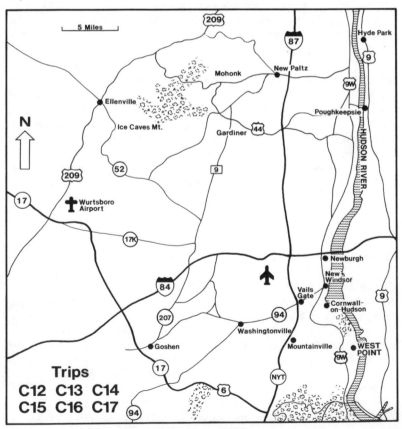

Trip C-12
Duty, Honor, Country

- UNITED STATES MILITARY ACADEMY
- WEST POINT MUSEUM
- WEST POINT CHAPELS
- FORT PUTNAM

DISTANCE: About 50 miles from Columbus Circle.

FOR THE DRIVER: From the George Washington Bridge, take the **Palisades Interstate Parkway** north to the Bear Mountain traffic circle. Follow signs for **US-9W** north to West Point. Go a few miles on 9W to the junction with **NY-218** and turn right to Highland Falls and **West Point.** When the road forks, follow the sign on the right to the main gate (Thayer Gate South). The **Visitor Center** and **Museum** are just outside the gate.

After entering the grounds, turn left on Mills Rd., just before Cavalry Flats. Follow signs for through traffic, bearing right. Just before Lusk Reservoir and Michie Stadium (where Army home games are played), on left, are signs for **Fort Putnam.** Beyond the stadium, on the right, is a sign for **Cadet Chapel.** Continue downhill for the Jewish Chapel and the Catholic Chapel, both on the left.

At the bottom of the hill a right turn on Washington Rd. takes you past Trophy Point and parade grounds to Thayer Hall on Cullum Rd. A left goes to the Old Cadet Chapel and through the grounds to Washington Gate, where you can pick up US-9W south for the return trip. To add a beautiful drive, turn right at Washington Gate and go over Storm King Mountain on NY-216 past a sign for the Museum of the Hudson Highlands (Trip C-13) to the junction with US-9W.

UNITED STATES MILITARY ACADEMY, West Point, NY 10996 (914-938-2638). *Grounds open all year daily dawn–dusk. Visitor Center open all year daily 9–4:45; closed Thanksgiving, Christmas, New Year's. All facilities and parking free. Self-guided tour, picnic areas, gift shops, restaurant and café at Hotel Thayer on grounds (open daily all year). Leashed pets only. Many areas wheelchair-accessible. Commercial guided tours available through West Point Tours Inc. (914-561-2671), not affiliated with academy, leave from Visitor Center daily in summer and weekends in off-season.*

West Point, site of the military academy established by an Act of Congress in 1802, figured prominently in the Revolutionary War, though it was never a battleground. It was one of four strategically situated fortifications along the mid-Hudson, and it was here, in 1778, that the great 150-ton chain was laid across the river to Constitution Island to block British ships. It was as commander of West Point in 1780 that General Benedict Arnold made his name a synonym for "traitor" by plotting to betray the Point into British hands.

The Hudson bends sharply here before continuing towards Pough-keepsie, providing fine scenic views at Trophy Point, where you can see some of the 300-pound links of the river chain and a battle monument to the Civil War dead. There are many other monuments and memorials scattered throughout the grounds, including a 9-foot bronze American Soldier by Felix Deweldon, designer of the Iwo Jima Flag Raising Memorial. If your timing is right, you can watch the current crop of cadets drilling on the Plain, the same parade ground where Baron von Steuben drilled the ragtag soldiers of the Continental Army. The **Visitor Information Center** just outside Thayer Gate is the best place to start your visit. Here you can see displays and a film on cadet training, pick up maps and brochures for a self-guided tour, or join a guided bus tour.

West Point Museum. *Open all year daily 10:30–4:15; closed Christmas, New Year's. Wheelchair-accessible.* "Weapons change," said General George S. Patton, "but man who uses them changes not at all." This quotation is called to mind as you view an imposing array of military arms, flags, uniforms, and memorabilia. There are dioramas of past wars, military miniatures, and weapons from the war with Spain, the Boxer Rebellion, the Civil War, Vietnam. Other displays include a 6-ton World War I tank, George Washington's personal "gentleman's pistols," and Napoleon's sword and pistols. The collection of military battle art is the largest such collection in the United States.

West Point Chapels. *Open all year daily 8:30–4:15. No photographing during services.* Cadet Chapel, built in 1910, is an impressive cross-shaped structure in "military Gothic," with an exceptionally large pipe organ and magnificent stained-glass windows. It holds services on Sundays at 10:30 a.m. (also summer services at Trophy Point). Catholic Chapel, another fine building, holds Sunday services at 8, 9, 10:30, noon, and 5. Jewish Chapel has a gallery museum that chronicles Jewish participation in America's military history. Services are at 7:30 Friday evenings. Old Cadet Chapel, dating from 1836, holds a Lutheran service Sunday mornings at 10:30. In the chapel is a file with the names of those buried in the adjoining cemetery, including Revolutionary War heroine Margaret Corbin, General Custer, General Winfield Scott, and astronaut Edward White, killed in a space test in 1967.

Fort Putnam. *Open mid-Apr. to mid-Nov. daily 10:30–4.* This restored Revolutionary War fort offers period exhibits and a commanding view of West Point and the Hudson River. The fort was built in 1778–79 to provide protection for Fort Clinton, downriver near what is now the Trailside Museum in Bear Mountain State Park (Trip C-7).

Trip C-13
The Army's Winter of Discontent

- WASHINGTON'S HEADQUARTERS STATE HISTORIC SITE
- KNOX'S HEADQUARTERS STATE HISTORIC SITE
- NEW WINDSOR CANTONMENT
- MUSEUM OF THE HUDSON HIGHLANDS

DISTANCE: About 60 miles from Columbus Circle to the farthest point.

FOR THE DRIVER: From the George Washington Bridge, take the **Palisades Interstate Parkway** north to the Bear Mountain traffic circle and pick up **US-9W** north for 16 miles to Newburgh. At Broadway (NY-17K) turn right to Liberty St., then right on Liberty for 2 blocks to **Washington's Headquarters.**

Go back to US-9W and take it south to **NY-94.** Turn right on 94 and go 2–3 miles to Forge Hill and **Knox Headquarters.**

Continue briefly on 94 to the junction with NY-32 and **NY-300** (Temple Hill Rd.). Turn right on 300 and go about a mile to the **New Windsor Cantonment,** on the right.

Go back down NY-300 to the junction with NY-94 and **NY-32.** Take 32 south past the turnoff for Storm King Art Center (Trip C-14) to the T-junction just beyond (NY-107, not marked). Turn left here and proceed into Cornwall-on-Hudson. The road merges shortly with **NY-218;** proceed on this, bearing right, to Payson Rd., and turn right here, following signs for **Museum of the Hudson Highlands.**

For your return trip, continue on 218 over Storm King Mountain to the junction with US-9W south.

Other routes to this area are via the New York Thruway-Tappan Zee Bridge, or the Taconic State Parkway and west on I-84.

WASHINGTON'S HEADQUARTERS STATE HISTORIC SITE, 84 Liberty St., Newburgh, NY 12550 (914-562-1195). *Open mid-Apr. to late Oct. Wed.–Sat. 10–5, Sun. 1–5; groups by appointment at other times; closed Thanksgiving, Christmas, New Year's. Free. Parking, house, and museum 1st floor are wheelchair-accessible.*

In the fall of 1782, after 7 years of war, more than 8,000 soldiers and officers of the Continental Army camped in the Newburgh area to await news of the peace negotiations in Paris. The three historic sites on this trip, all administered by the Palisades Interstate Park Commission, tell the story of this last long encampment of Washington's army.

The Jonathan Hasbrouck House in Newburgh served as Washington's headquarters from April 1782 to August 1783. Here he issued orders, declined a suggestion that he become America's first king, and in general spent the days none too happily, if you can judge from a letter he wrote on January 10, 1783: "Time will pass heavily on in this dreary mansion in which we are fast locked by frost and snow." The house, begun in 1725 and completed by 1770, is furnished as it might have been when Washington was here. It stands on seven acres overlooking the Hudson. On the grounds is the 53-foot Tower of Victory, erected to commemorate the 100th anniversary of the disbanding of the Continental Army. Nearby is a museum with exhibits and audiovisual displays.

KNOX'S HEADQUARTERS, Vails Gate, NY 12584 (914-561-5498). *Open Apr.–Oct. Wed.–Sat. 10–5, Sun. 1–5; closed otherwise except by appointment. Free. Picnicking, craft demonstrations, concerts, special events. Partially wheelchair-accessible, interior difficult.*

This attractive Georgian house of stone and frame construction was the home of John Ellison, an 18th-century merchant. General Horatio Gates used it as his headquarters in the winter of 1782–83, while he was in command of the New Windsor Cantonment. Earlier in the war it sheltered Generals Henry Knox and Nathanael Greene. A short walk from the house is the **Jane Colden Native Plant Sanctuary,** a beautiful sight in spring when the wildflowers bloom, and just beyond are the ruins of the Ellison gristmill and an old stone bridge to the main road.

NEW WINDSOR CANTONMENT, Vails Gate, NY 12584 (914-561-1765). *Open mid-Apr. to late Oct. Wed.–Sat. 10–5, Sun. 1–5. Free. Picnicking, military demonstrations, special events. Leashed pets only. Wheelchair-accessible.*

Some 8,000 soldiers of the Continental Army spent the last months of the Revolutionary War on this site, living in 800 log huts and waiting for news of peace. The winter was a hard one; the men were in rags, and their meager pay was long overdue. Some of the officers began circulating mutinous documents known as the Newburgh Addresses, calling on the army to take matters into its own hands. Washington showed a fine political instinct in his handling of the situation, sympathizing with their grievances while appealing to their patriotism. In the end the officers unanimously reaffirmed their support for their general and the cause for which they had fought so long. On April 19, 1783, exactly 8 years after "the shot heard round the world" was fired at Concord, the Cessation of Hostilities was announced to the army, and the soldiers dispersed to their homes in the newly independent United States of America.

Today at New Windsor Cantonment the daily routine of the Continental Army's last encampment is re-created in a "living history area." Every afternoon uniformed interpreters hold a military drill and demonstrate the firing of Revolutionary War muskets and cannon. At the Visitor Center there are audiovisual displays and two floors of exhibits, including the original medal created by Washington for enlisted men, the Badge of Military Merit, predecessor of the Purple Heart.

MUSEUM OF THE HUDSON HIGHLANDS, The Boulevard, Cornwall-on-Hudson, NY 12520 (914-534-7781). *Open all year daily 10–4; closed July 4, Thanksgiving, Christmas, New Year's. Free. No pets. Wheelchair-accessible.*

In a granite gorge on the side of a mountain, surrounded by self-guiding nature trails, stands a prize-winning piece of architecture housing a unique museum with natural history displays, cultural exhibits, and an assortment of live animals native to the region. The walls are adorned with attractive murals, and an exhibit area depicts habitats of the Hudson Valley.

Trip C-14
Vintage Art and Wine

- STORM KING ART CENTER
- BROTHERHOOD WINERY

DISTANCE: About 55 miles from Columbus Circle.

FOR THE DRIVER: Take the **New York State Thruway** north towards Albany to Exit 16. Immediately after the toll turn right off Quickway (US-6/NY-17) and go north 10 miles on **NY-32,** watching for blue-and-white signs to **Storm King Art Center.** Just past the T-junction (NY-107, not marked), cross a green steel bridge over a small creek and turn left on Orrs Mills Rd. Go a mile to the 1st left, Old Pleasant Hill Rd., turn here, and go a half-mile to the art center, on left.

Go back to NY-32 and continue north to the junction with **NY-94** in Vails Gate (Trip C-13). Make a left on 94 and continue west to Washingtonville. Just before the center of town is North St. Turn right and drive up the block to **Brotherhood Winery,** entrance on right.

For the return trip, continue into Washingtonville on 94 to the junction with **NY-208** and take this south about 6 miles to the Quickway. Heading east on this soon brings you to the N.Y.S. Thruway.

STORM KING ART CENTER, Old Pleasant Hill Rd., Mountainville, NY 10953 (914-534-3115). *Grounds open early Apr. to late Nov., daily noon–5:30; building open mid-May to late Oct., daily noon–5:30. Adults $5; seniors, students, children $3; under 5 free. Picnic area. No pets on grounds. Wheelchair-accessible.*

More than 100 large-scale contemporary sculptures are on display here in 350 acres of landscaped gardens overlooking Schunemunk Mountain. The museum, an elegant cut-stone mansion in the Normandy style, houses a superb collection of sculptures by well-known American and European artists. The center's impressive permanent holdings are supplemented by loans from other museums and changing sculpture exhibits throughout the year. From the gardens you can look out through five enormous granite Ionic columns to magnificent vistas of rolling foothills. If your thirst for scenic beauty still isn't quenched, you can take a hike through the Mountainville Nature Conservancy of the Storm King Art Center, about 4 miles west of here (the museum staff will be happy to supply directions).

BROTHERHOOD WINERY, 35 North St., Washingtonville, NY 10992 (914-496-9101). *Open May to Oct. daily 11–6; Nov.– Apr. weekends noon–5; closed major holidays. Free parking. Frequent tours $3 per person. No pets. Wheelchair-accessible parking, tour difficult for wheelchairs.*

This is the oldest winery in America, but if you're expecting hilly vineyards with rows of brown-robed monks picturesquely plucking grapes, forget it. Only the name Brotherhood remains in this modern commercial enterprise to remind you that the original cellars were built by French monks in the early 1700s. The tour takes you on a long subterranean ramble through dank caverns among the great white-oak aging casks. You'll visit the processing/bottling plant and see a slide presentation on wine and champagne making over the years, with tips on the proper way to serve and enjoy the fruits of the vine. Eventually you're invited to sample the merchandise. The winery is busiest during the fall harvest, when the grapes are brought in by truck, but any season is good for the tour, and there are special events throughout the year (theater/lunch programs, Maine clambakes, grape stomps, feasts in the Bacchus Room, etc.). No matter when you go, bring a jacket or sweater; even in summer the cellars are cool.

Trip C-15
Two Breathtaking Introductions
to the Catskills

- WURTSBORO AIRPORT
- ICE CAVES MOUNTAIN

DISTANCE: About 95 miles from Columbus Circle.

FOR THE DRIVER: Take the **New York State Thruway** north towards Albany to Exit 16, then the **Quickway** (US-6/NY-17) west to Exit 113. Here take **US-209** north 2½ miles to the **Wurtsboro Airport.**

Continue north on 209 to Ellenville. In town turn right on **NY-52** and go about 5 miles to the turnoff for Cragsmoor and **Ice Caves Mountain,** on left, then another few miles to the entrance and scenic drive.

You're approaching the Catskill Mountains, a region that's almost (but not quite) beyond practical daytrip range of New York City. There's a wealth of beautiful scenery, cultural attractions, and historic sites here; you'll explore some of the highlights and take some lovely drives. Bear in mind that as you go up, the temperature goes down; the mountains are generally 10 to 15 degrees cooler than the valley.

In this and the next few trips, you're nearing the southern Catskills, home of those famed resort hotels that have nurtured so many comedians. Each resort is a self-contained world of its own, and there are many such worlds to choose from if you've got the time for more than a daytrip. For further information about accommodations and about the southern Catskills generally, contact the Chamber of Commerce of Ulster County, 7 Albany Ave., Kingston, NY 12401 (914-338-5100), the Ulster County Public Information Office, County Office Building, Box 1800, Kingston, NY 12401 (914-331-9300), and the Sullivan County Office of Public Information, County Government Center, Monticello, NY 12701 (914-794-3000, X5010). There are also two toll-free Catskill information numbers: in New York State 800-882-CATS, outside New York State 800-343-INFO.

WURTSBORO AIRPORT, Route 209, Wurtsboro, NY 12790 (914-888-2791). *Open daily all year, weather permitting, 9–6 (or dusk, whichever comes first); closed Thanksgiving, Christmas, New Year's. Sailplane demonstration rides (15–20 minutes) $30, introductory lesson (15–20 minutes) $35, varying fees for more advanced instruction. Will accommodate handicapped persons if able to sit in plane.*

Whether you want to experience the thrilling sensation of soaring like a bird, or simply watch this fascinating sport from the sidelines, you'll find your visit here intriguing. Graceful, slim-lined Schweizer sailplanes are towed into the air by high-performance Cessnas, then released to glide, silhouetted against magnificent mountain scenery. Wurtsboro has been a soaring site since 1927 and offers instructional programs for experienced pilots as well as beginners.

ICE CAVES MOUNTAIN, Box 11, Cragsmoor, NY 12420 (914-647-7989). *Open Apr.–Oct. daily 9–dusk. Adults $7, children 6–12 $3.50, under 6 free. Self-guided tour, picnic area. Leashed pets only. Scenic drive to Sam's Point and top of mountain, but no wheelchair access to caves.*

This National Natural Landmark in the Shawangunk (pronounced "Shongum") Mountains offers marvels formed by millions of years of geological activity. A beautiful drive up the mountain takes you to **Sam's Point,** a massive stone plateau jutting a half-mile (2,255 feet) into the sky and affording a spectacular panoramic view of five states. According to legend, a trapper named Sam jumped from here to escape an Indian war party and lived to tell about it, but you won't want to try this unless you've brought along a sailplane from Wurtsboro.

Beyond Sam's Point a trail leads past attractions like Crystal Chasm, the Balanced Rock, and Rainbow Tunnel to the glacial **caves** where the ice never melts. You can listen through a crack to the voice of the Lost River, discover caverns, underground lakes, and cool grottos; and find stone shapes for every fantasy among the rugged rock formations. You can walk the well-maintained trail in a half-hour or so, but why hurry? Near the top of the mountain is Lake Maratanza, a haven for migratory birds and the water supply for Ellenville.

Trip C-16
A Huguenot Haven on the Hudson

- HUGUENOT STREET
- LOCUST LAWN
- WIDMARK HONEY FARMS

DISTANCE: About 80 miles from Columbus Circle.

FOR THE DRIVER: Take the **New York State Thruway** north towards Albany to Exit 18 at New Paltz. Go west into town on **NY-299** (Main St.) to the junction with **NY-32.** Turn right and go north on 32 to **Huguenot Street,** shortly on the left.

Go back to 32 and continue 4 miles south to **Locust Lawn.**

Turn west on the **Minnewaska Trail** (US-44/NY-55) for a few miles to the **Widmark Farm.**

The historic sites on this trip are owned and operated by the Huguenot Historical Society, P.O. Box 339, New Paltz, NY 12561 (914-255-1660), one of those dedicated local organizations that do so much to preserve the nation's history. The Huguenots, French followers of John Calvin, suffered heavy persecution at the hands of France's King Louis XIV during the 17th century. Many thousands of them fled, including the 12 families who settled along the Hudson in 1677 and named their community after *die Pfalz,* an area of Germany bordering on the Rhine, where they had found temporary refuge before sailing to the New World.

HUGUENOT STREET, New Paltz, NY. *Open Memorial Day through Sept., Wed.–Sun. 10–4; closed Mon.–Tues. Complete 2¼-hour tours at 10:30 and 1:30, Adults $5, seniors $4, children 7–12 $2, under 7 free; short 1¼-hour tours $2.50 per person; individual houses $2 per person. Tours depart from Deyo Hall on Broadhead Ave., just off Huguenot St. No pets. Deyo Hall, gift shop, and restroom wheelchair-accessible; 4 houses are accessible to handicapped.*

Here is the oldest street in America where the original houses still stand intact. The land was purchased by the Duzine (the heads of the 12 founding Huguenot families) from the Esopus Indians in 1677, for once on generous terms. At first the families lived in log huts, gradually replaced by the sturdy stone structures you see here today, among them the **Jean Hasbrouck House** (1692–1712),in the medieval Flemish style; the **Bevier-Elting House** (1698) with its large windows and roomy porch; **DuBois Fort** (1705), built to satisfy the English governor's demand for "a place of Retreat and Safe-guard;" and the **French Church** (1717), reconstructed in 1972 after 10 years of painstaking research. Most of the houses were continually occupied by the descendants of the builders for 250 years, and the furnishings include heirlooms considered too precious to be left behind during the long flight from France.

LOCUST LAWN, Gardiner, NY 12561 (914-255-6070). *Open Memorial Day through Sept., Wed.–Sun. 10–4; closed Mon.–Tues. Guided tours Adults $2, children under 14 $1. Wildlife sanctuary, nature trails. No ramps into buildings; difficult for wheelchairs.*

This handsome Federal mansion was built in 1814 by Colonel Josiah Hasbrouck, a descendant of one of the original Huguenot families that settled around New Paltz. Hasbrouck fought in the Revolutionary War, served in Congress, and was one of the wealthiest men of his day; as is apparent from the beautiful furnishings, fine china, and paintings (including portraits by Ammi Phillips and works of the Hudson River School) that adorn his home. The marbelized plaster walls in the central hall were the trademark of the well-known architect Cromwell of Newburgh. The outbuildings include a slaughterhouse, smokehouse, and carriage house.

Also on the grounds, near Plattekill Brook, is a much older building, the **Terwilliger Homestead,** reflecting Hudson River Valley, French Huguenot, and Dutch architectural styles. Evert Terwilliger, who began the house in 1738, is buried here with his wife and slaves. Just west of Locust Lawn is the **Little Wings Wildlife Sanctuary,** where woodland trails offer pleasant strolls and a chance to observe some of the 28 species of resident birds.

WIDMARK HONEY FARMS, Routes 44/55, Gardiner, NY (914-255-6400). *Open daily all year, 10–8. Demonstrations mid-May through mid-Oct., weekends and holidays only, at 3 p.m. Wheelchair-accessible.*

A working honey bee farm operated by the family for four generations, this attraction is complete with black bears to steal the honey. There are bee demonstrations, bear performances, honey for sale, and animals to pet.

Trip C-17
Sparkling Blue Waters,
Clear Mountain Air

* MOHONK MOUNTAIN HOUSE

DISTANCE: About 90 miles from Columbus Circle.

FOR THE DRIVER: Take the **New York State Thruway** north towards Albany to Exit 18 at New Paltz. Turn left on **NY-299** (Main St.) and follow it west through New Paltz. Cross a bridge over the Wallkill River, take the first right after the bridge, and go about $\frac{1}{4}$ mile to a fork in the road. Bear left at the fork and proceed up Mountain Rest Rd. to the **Mohonk Gatehouse.** Day visitors must park here; you can begin your walk at this point or take the shuttle bus *(service daily in summer, weekends off-season, $2 round trip)* to the Picnic Lodge.

MOHONK MOUNTAIN HOUSE, Lake Mohonk, New Paltz, NY 12561 (914-255-1000 or 800-722-6646). *Open daily all year for lodging, dining, activities. Day visits: $20 per person for lunch and access to grounds; $7 per person weekends and holidays, $5 weekdays, for hiking pass and use of picnic lodge. No swimming for day visitors; overnight guests have priority in use of other facilities. Picnicking, hiking trails, game room, boat rentals ($7 per hour), carriage rides ($12 per person per hour), 9-hold golf course (Apr.–Oct.; $7.50 per round weekdays, $8.50 weekends, carts $8 per round), clay tennis courts (May–Nov.; $10 per court per hour), platform tennis (no charge), horseback riding (Apr.–Oct.; $20 per hour), cross-country skiing (equipment rentals $18–$29 per day), ice skating (skate rentals $3 per hour), fitness center with masseuse (fees). Special events and programs all year. Inquire about*

Mohonk has hardly changed since the 1890s

daily and weekly rates, special packages. No pets. Building and some paths are wheelchair-accessible.

One of the last great late-19th-century mountain resorts, Mohonk is an enormous, rambling Victorian castle overlooking a small, clear, deep freshwater lake. This improbable and quite fantastic structure was built as a retreat by Alfred Smiley and his twin brother, Albert, Quakers dedicated to the cause of world peace, and is still run by the Smiley family. In 1986 it was officially awarded National Historic Landmark status. More than 85 miles of trails and carriage roads wind through some 5,000 acres of stunning Shawangunk mountain scenery in the Mohonk Preserve, a haven for hikers, naturalists, bird watchers, and rock climbers eager to test their mettle on the sheer Trapps cliffs. The marvelous view from **Sky Top Tower** encompasses several states and is especially gorgeous in spring when the laurel blooms and in fall when the foliage turns.

Among the places to visit is the **Picnic Lodge** *(10–5 daily in summer, weekends and holidays in spring and fall)*, a day visitor center with a selection of food, picnic tables, and restrooms. The **Barn Museum** *(closed Fridays)*, near the stables, has a collection of Mohonk memorabilia and features both blacksmithing and pottery demonstrations. Plants are sold at the **Greenhouse,** next to the prizewinning **Gardens.**

Mohonk runs a plethora of programs offering something for everyone virtually year-round: nature outings, Hudson Valley heritage tours, Tower of Babble intensive foreign language study, chamber music, cooking classes, stargazing, sports tournaments, children's activities, an Odyssey program with Dave Berry, and the annual Mystery Weekend, where guests divide into teams to solve a dastardly crime concocted by mystery writer Donald E. Westlake. Day visitors can participate in some of these programs, but many last several days and most require advance reservations.

Mohonk is proud of its traditions and dedicated to the preservation of its beautiful surroundings. In 1992 world peace may look further away than it was in 1869 when Alfred Smiley first looked out over the Shawangunks from Sky Top, but a day's peace is no further away than the mountain house he built.

Trip C-18
Historic Kingston,
New York's First Capital

- **HISTORIC STOCKADE WALKING TOUR**
- **SENATE HOUSE STATE HISTORIC SITE**
- **VOLUNTEER FIREMEN'S HALL AND MUSEUM**
- **OLD DUTCH CHURCH**

DISTANCE: About 95 miles from Columbus Circle.

FOR THE DRIVER: Take the **New York State Thruway** north towards Albany to Exit 19. Follow signs for Kingston; halfway around the traffic circle, exit at Washington Ave. Go two blocks to North Front St., turn left, and go four blocks to Fair St. Park as close to here as possible.

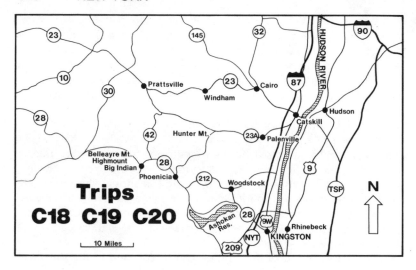

Continue on foot a block to Clinton Ave. and turn right to the **Visitor Center.** The **Senate House** is nearby on Fair St., near the corner of North Front. Just down the block, across John St., is the **Firemen's Hall.** From here go to the next corner and turn right to the **Old Dutch Church** at Main and Wall streets.

Note that you are only minutes from Rondout Landing and the sites on Trip C-19, which can easily be combined with this trip.

KINGSTON URBAN CULTURAL PARK VISITOR CENTER, 308 Clinton Ave., Kingston, NY 12401 (914-331-9506). *Open May–Dec., Wed.–Sat. & Mon. 11–5, Sun. 1–5; Jan.–Apr., Thurs.–Sun. 11–5. Free. Wheelchair-accessible.*

Here you can get a brochure for a self-guided **Historic Stockade Walking Tour,** learn about Kingston's colorful past as a transportation hub during the early growth of the nation, and see exhibits on local history.

SENATE HOUSE STATE HISTORIC SITE, 312 Fair St., Kingston, NY 12401 (914-338-2786). *Open mid-April to late Oct., Wed.–Sat. 10–5, Sun. 1–5. Free. Can accommodate wheelchairs; call in advance.*

The Senate House, administered by the Palisades Interstate Park Commission, holds an important place in the history of New York State. Built by Wessell Ten Broeck in 1676 of rock-cut limestone, with one wall of Holland brick, it was already a century old when the first state legislature convened here on September 9, 1777. On October 7 the legislature adjourned upon learning that British troops were moving up the Hudson towards Kingston, and on October 16 the British landed and set the town afire. The house was damaged in the fire and repaired by its owner, Abraham Van Gaasbeek. Only the porch is "new"—it dates from 1888. There's a lovely rose garden behind the house, and the museum has historical exhibits and a collection of paintings by John Vanderlyn, a Kingston native and a student of Gilbert Stuart's.

VOLUNTEER FIREMEN'S HALL AND MUSEUM, 265 Fair St., Kingston, NY 12401 (914-331-0866). *Open Apr.–Oct., Sat.–SUn., 1–4. Free. First floor manageable for wheelchairs.*

In 1981 Kingston's seven volunteer fire companies and the Exempt Firemen's Association leased this 1857 fire station of the Wiltwyck Hose Company from the city as a meeting hall. As a labor of love, the members turned the first floor into a museum and opened it to the public. In the parlor you'll find hand-carved black walnut furniture and the inevitable firehouse player piano (it works). Also on display is an extensive collection of antique fire-fighting equipment, memorabilia, and prints. Books and documents testify to the valor of the early firemen and trace the history of fire fighting in Kingston, which began when the city ordered a fire engine from England in 1754. Three years and many fires later, this primitive but functional apparatus arrived and served admirably for two decades, until it went up in smoke when the British burned Kingston in 1777.

OLD DUTCH CHURCH, Main & Wall Sts., Kingston, NY 12401 (914-338-6759). *Open year round, Mon.–Fri. 9–2. Free. Partially wheelchair-accessible.*

This attractive 19th-century church is home to one of the oldest congregations in America, established in 1659. The church museum holds artifacts and documents of historical interest, including a letter from George Washington. George Clinton, first governor of New York (1777–1795), vice-president under Jefferson and Madison, and one of the earliest New York politicians to manipulate election results (in the 1792 gubernatorial race against John Jay), is buried in the cemetery.

Trip C-19
Solitude and Scenery
Along the Historic Hudson

- SLABSIDES
- HUDSON RIVER MARITIME CENTER
- TROLLEY MUSEUM OF NEW YORK
- HUDSON RIVER CRUISES

DISTANCE: About 95 miles from Columbus Circle.

FOR THE DRIVER: Take the **New York State Thruway** north towards Albany to Exit 18 at New Paltz. Here go east on **NY-299** to the junction with **US-9W.** Turn left and go north about 4 miles to West Park. Beyond the main part of town, at Park Lane, turn left and continue, bearing left, as Park Lane becomes Floyd Ackert Rd. At the sign for the **Burroughs** sanctuary, park on the road and walk a half-mile on Burroughs Drive to the cabin.

Return to 9W and continue north about 8 miles. After passing through Port Ewen, cross the bridge over Rondout Creek, proceed to the light at the bottom of the hill, and turn left on Garraghan Drive. Go about two blocks to the end of the street and turn left at the light, onto Broadway. Follow Broadway to the waterfront, turn left, and park. The **Maritime Center** is right here, and the **Trolley Museum** is just beyond.

If you're coming from the Senate House or other sites on Trip C-18, follow Clinton Ave. south, make a left on St. James St., then a right on Broadway. This leads southeast through most of Kingston to the Rondout waterfront district, as above.

SLABSIDES, West Park, NY 12493 (914-384-6556). *Grounds and trails open daily all year, tours by appointment only; open houses twice a year, on 3rd Sat. in May and 1st Sat. in Oct. Free. No picnicking, no smoking, no fires, no pets. Not wheelchair-accessible.*

John Burroughs (1837–1921) was a great American naturalist who lived on a farm near Esopus and wrote expressively in a Thoreauvian vein. He decided to convert a marshy woodland area near his home into a garden, and the results were so attractive that he knew he must build a retreat here. With the help of a local carpenter, he fashioned a rustic cabin and even made some of his own furniture. Burroughs came to this sanctuary often, sometimes bringing his friends—among them Teddy Roosevelt, Thomas Edison, Henry Ford, fellow naturalist John Muir, and Walt Whitman, whose poetic gift Burroughs was the first to recognize.

Today the "Sage of Slabsides" is no more, but the feeling of quiet and solitude remains. By far the best means of appreciating Slabsides is on the tour held but twice a year. The John Burroughs Natural History Society and the John Burroughs Association, composed of friends who made possible the preservation of the cabin, meet at Slabsides twice a year, and the public is welcome to attend.

RONDOUT WATERFRONT DISTRICT, Kingston, NY. Kingston's historic port on Rondout Creek has been revitalized as an urban cultural park, and today it once again bustles with activity, as it did in the days when the Rondout linked the city with the Delaware & Hudson Canal. There are many fine shops, restaurants, and galleries in the beautiful section of town.

Hudson River Maritime Center, 1 Rondout Landing, Kingston, NY 12401 (914-338-0071). *Open May–Oct., Wed.–Fri. & Mon. 11–5, Sat.–Sun. 10–5. Donation. Ramp into building, parts of the interior are manageable for wheelchairs.* Here is a living museum of Hudson River maritime history, started out of a storefront in 1980, now the hub of the waterfront renaissance. In the museum you can see a variety of marine artifacts and exhibits, with special attention to the steamboat era and the days of the elegant paddlewheeler *Mary Powell,* queen of the Hudson from the Civil War until after World War I. Outside you can watch shipwrights at work building and rigging all sorts of craft, from shad boats to vessels of the kind that sailed the Hudson a century ago. There are also outdoor floating displays, and more exhibits in the restored **Kingston Lighthouse,** accessible via a short, pleasant ride on the museum boat, the *Rondout Belle.*

Many yachts, sailboats, tugs, launches, cruisers, and coastal liners make Rondout Landing a port of call. A number of Hudson River cruise ships leave from here, including the *Rip Van Winkle* (see below). Every year the center sponsors two delightful events: the Shad Festival, during the running of the shad in spring, with the day's catch donated by the local fishermen, pan-fried before your eyes, and served up to the accompaniment of sea chanteys; and the Pumpkin Festival, when the sloop *Clearwater* sails up the Hudson and unloads its cargo of soon-to-be jack-o'-lanterns in a great gold-orange heap for the inspection of the valley's children.

Trolley Museum of New York, 89 East Strand, Kingston, NY 12401 (914-331-3399). *Open Memorial Day to Columbus Day, noon to 5 on* *weekends and holidays; noon–5 on Thurs.–Mon. during July–Aug. Adults $1, children 50c. Visitor center and gift car are wheelchair-accessible.* Landlubbers will appreciate this museum on wheels, an old-time trolley offering a 1½-mile scenic ride along the Hudson. There's a selection of antique cars on display, as well as more trolley lore in the visitor center.

Hudson River Cruises, Rondout Landing, Kingston, NY 12401 (914-255-6515). *Operates May through Oct.: weekends in May–June and Sept.–Oct., 6 days a week in July–Aug. Inquire about current schedules and fares. No pets. Not wheelchair-accessible.* Here's a relaxing, delightful way to take in the sights and sounds of the Hudson River Valley. You'll have to get up with the sun to make it to Kingston by departure time, but this day-long cruise to West Point aboard the 350-passenger *Rip Van Winkle* is well worth the effort. A guide regales you with a capsule history as you glide past wild stretches of shoreline, dramatic mountains (including the aptly named Storm King), vineyards and orchards, lavish estates, quaint lighthouses, island castles, and soaring bridges. You can loll on deck while the boat docks at West Point (Trip C-12), or purchase tickets for a tour of the U.S. Military Academy before heading back up the legendary river.

Trip C-20
Deeper into the Catskills

- **ONTEORA TRAIL**
- **RIP VAN WINKLE TRAIL**
- **MOHICAN TRAIL**

DISTANCE: About 95 miles from Columbus Circle to Kingston, about 120 miles to Catskill.

FOR THE DRIVER: Since this trip is planned mainly for the enjoyment of the drive itself, the directions are incorporated with the brief descriptions of the principal attractions along the route, given below.

On this trip you'll be moving into the heart of the Catskill Mountains, taking in some truly magnificent scenery and passing many points of interest along the way. Remember that this area is in a different weather pattern from New York City. Spring comes late here; by the same token, two or three weeks before the leaves turn in the city they'll be at their peak in the mountains. For further information about the northern and western Catskills, contact the Greene County Promotion Department, Box 527, Catskill, NY 12414 (518-943-3223), and the Delaware County Chamber of Commerce, 97 Main St., Delhi, NY 13753 (607-746-2281). The toll-free information number for the southern Catskills can also give you information on the entire Catskills area: in NYS 800-882-CATS, outside NYS 800-343-INFO.

ONTEORA TRAIL, NY-28 from Kingston. Kingston, explored on the last two trips, is one of the gateways to the Catskills. From the **New York State Thruway** Exit 19 at Kingston, you'll drive west on **NY-28,** but first go three miles south on Old Route 209 to Hurley, capital of New York for one month in 1777 after Kingston was burned by the British, birthplace of Sojourner Truth, and a station on the Underground Railroad. Here you can visit the **Hurley Patentee Manor** (914-331-5414), a Dutch cottage built in 1696 and enlarged in 1745 as an English country mansion. Once a year, on the second Saturday in July, the town dresses up in 17th-century garb for Stone House Day (914-331-4121), when the public is invited to tour 10 privately-owned Dutch stone houses (be sure to look for the witch-catcher in the chimney of the Polly Crispell House). Brochures for a self-guided walking or driving tour are available in town or from the Hurley Heritage Society, Box 661, Hurley, NY 12443.

Returning on Old 209 to NY-28, turn left and go west. Almost immediately you'll enter the **Catskill Forest Preserve** (518-457-2500), an enormous tract of almost 700,000 acres where you can hike through some of the wildest, most unspoiled country in the East. Part of the State Forest Preserves, the park stretches across Ulster and Greene counties into Sullivan and Delaware counties; most of the sites on this drive and the next lie within its boundaries.

Proceeding west on NY-28 for several miles, you'll come to the tip of the 12-mile-long **Ashokan Reservoir** (914-657-2304), whence comes a large proportion of New York City's daily water supply. The underground hydroelectric plant is not open to the public, and there's no picnicking here, but fishing and boating are allowed by permit. Or you can just look: mountains unfold in all directions, cloud formations and reflections in the clear waters are superb. Often when the fall foliage has petered out along the Thruway and across the river, this area is still ablaze with color. You can continue along the north side of the reservoir on NY-28 or take the southern route around it on 28A, which brings you back to 28 on the other side of Boiceville.

Continuing west on NY-28 from the eastern end of the reservoir, you come to the attractive small town of West Hurley. Just beyond is the junction with **NY-375**. Take this north about 3 miles for a side trip to Woodstock.

Woodstock has been a mecca for artists since 1902, when Ralph Radcliffe Whitehead, a student of John Ruskin's, established the Byrd-cliffe Crafts Colony here. The **Woodstock Artists Association** at 28 Tinker St. (914-679-2940), founded in 1920, still thrives, offering a sum-mer lecture series and changing exhibits. You can also visit the Wood-stock Guild of Craftsmen (914-679-2079), which stages multimedia events in its Kleinert Gallery (914-679-2079) and operates a co-op shop selling locally-made crafts. Boutiques, galleries, restaurants, and cafés can be found along Mill Hill Road and its continuation, Tinker St. For further information contact the Woodstock Chamber of Commerce, Box 36, Woodstock, NY 12498 (914-679-6234). By the way, that infamous hippie happening of 1969 actually happened on a farm about 60 miles west of here, so don't blame the locals.

Back on NY-28, continue west to Boiceville, at the western end of the reservoir. Here you can stop at the **Totem Indian Trading Post and Museum** (914-657-2531) to see a display of totem poles, an Indian statue garden, and a collection of Indian artifacts, crafts, clothing, and jewelry.

Another 8 or 9 miles on 28 brings you to Phoenicia, where you can hike, swim, camp, and find a variety of winter activities at **Romer Mountain Park** (914-688-7440), or board the **Catskill Mountain Rail-road** (914-688-7400) for a scenic 2.8-mile ride along Esopus Creek. This is trout country, but fly fishermen aren't the only ones who flock to the creek; the untamed waters makes it a favorite haunt of innertu-bers. If you haven't brought your own tube, you can rent one in the park or at several shops in the area. Note that NY-214 goes north from Phoenicia to Hunter Mountain and NY-23A (see next drive).

About 13 miles west of Phoenicia, still on NY-28, you'll come to Highmount, where you can hit the slopes at two fine ski facilities: **Belleayre Mountain Ski Center** (914-254-5601; ski phone 800-942-6904 in NYS, 800-431-6012 outside NYS) and **Highmount Ski Center** (914-254-5265). Belleayre has cross-country skiing too, and in summer you can picnic here and take a scenic chairlift ride to the summit.

You're now at the edge of Catskill Park. This drive ends here, but NY-28 goes on through Delaware County to Oneonta.

RIP VAN WINKLE TRAIL, NY-23A from Catskill. From the **New York State Thruway** Exit 21 you can drive west along this stunning wilder-ness route through Greene County, legendary home of Rip Van Win-kle. Leaving the Thruway puts you in the town of **Catskill,** where art enthusiasts will want to visit the **Thomas Cole House** at 218 Spring St.

(518-943-6533). Cole, the founder of the Hudson River School, lived here from 1836 to 1848 and did some of his most important work in the studio. Catskill also hosts an annual summer Old Catskill Days Festival (518-943-4591).

Heading west from Catskill to Palenville, **NY-23A** crosses **NY-32**, which goes north to Cairo and NY-23 (see next drive). Along the way are many lovely waterfalls and some interesting attractions. Left off 32 is a turnoff for the **Catskill Game Farm** (518-678-9595), which more than 35 years ago began a conservation project to preserve species endangered in the wild and today has large breeding herds of rare and vanishing animals. There are more than 2,000 furred and feathered creatures here, including rhinos, giraffes, zebras, cheetahs, and tame deer for the children to pet. (*Open mid-Apr. through Oct., daily 9–6*). Just up the road a piece on 32 is **Carson City** (518-678-5518), an old Wild West town with gunslingers, can-can girls, museum, and Indian show (*June to Sept., daily 10–5*); and just beyond that is the **Catskill Reptile Institute** (518-678-5590), with a complete line of ophidians, from snakes in the grass to the deadly king cobra.

Back on 23A, a little west of the junction with 32, you'll come to **Palenville,** whose annual Circus Arts Festival (518-678-9021) is a real treat for big-top aficionados. Also here is the Palenville Interarts Colony (518-678-9021), with music, dance, drama, mime, and experimental theater performances by the Bond Street Theater Coalition (518-678-3332).

Leaving Palenville, 23A takes you into **Catskill Park** (see previous drive) and on to **Haines Falls.** The falls, high and beautiful, are off the route a little in Twilight Park. Tucked away in the forest, accessible by trail from the North Lake State Park off 23A in Haines Falls, is New York's highest waterfall, **Kaaterskill,** which James Fenimore Cooper described so vividly in *Leatherstocking Tales.*

From Haines Falls continue west on 23A to Hunter, where a tempting array of activities awaits you at the Catskills' second-highest mountain (4,025 feet). **Hunter Mountain Ski Bowl** (518-263-4223, ski phone 800-FOR-SNOW), a vast three-mountain complex with 46 slopes and trails plus snowmaking facilities that insure over 140 ski days per season, can easily accommodate thousands of skiers an hour. In summer and fall you can take the **Hunter Mountain Sky Ride** for wonderful views of the Catskills. The well-known Hunter Mountain Festivals (518-263-3800) run virtually nonstop from late June through Labor Day and include an Italian Festival, German Alps Festival, Country Music Festival, National Polka Festival, International Celtic Festival, and Indian Festival.

NY-23A continues another 13 miles or so through Lexington to Prattsville, where it merges with the next route, NY-23.

MOHICAN TRAIL, NY-23 from Catskill. From the **New York State Thruway** Exit 21 you again head west from Catskill, through more gorgeous mountain scenery, but now you're north of where you were on the last drive. Soon you will pass Leeds, with the oldest stone bridge in New York (1780), and South Cairo, with its slightly incongruous Mahayan Buddhist Temple, an ornate specimen of Chinese architecture.

Approaching **Cairo,** you'll pass the junction with NY-32, where you can go south to the Catskill Game Farm, Carson City, and the Catskill Reptile Institute (see previous drive).

From Cairo you can make side trips south a few miles on NY-24 to Purling and the old gristmill at **Shinglekill Falls,** or north about 7 miles on NY-145 to **East Durham,** "The Emerald Isle of the Catskills," which hosts a major Irish Festival and Irish Feis (518-634-7100). Also here, on Wright St., is the **Butterfly Museum and Farm** (518-634-7759), where they'll give you a home where the viceroys roam while the monarchs and swallowtails play. No, really, it *is* a butterfly farm, a tribute to the life's work of butterfly collector and cultivator Max Richter, and a boardinghouse into the bargain.

Continuing west on 23, wind you way up to Windham, where you'll find a fine downhill skiing facility, **Ski Windham** (518-734-4300; ski phone 800-729-SKIW). There's a classy atmosphere at this once private ski club, which has a 3,050-foot mountain and excellent snowmaking facilities.

NY-23 continues west to Prattsville, where it meets NY-23A, on the previous drive. You can turn left here and make a circle around the heart of Greene County by going east on 23A back to Catskill, or continue west to Prattsville, Oneonta, and beyond.

Area D

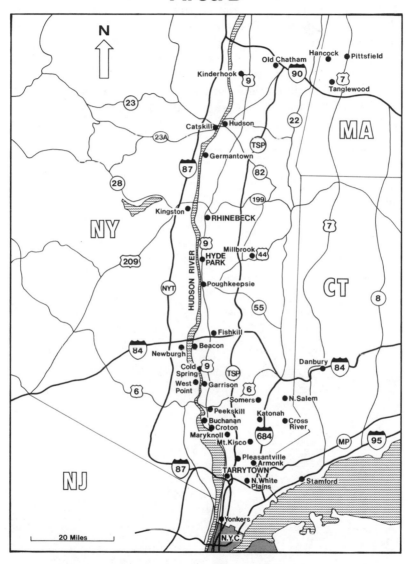

ALONG THE EAST BANK
OF THE HUDSON

Here are lands of great natural beauty, hills and valleys endowed with folklore, Colonial settlements, Revolutionary memorials, parks and reservations. You can follow the Hudson River northward through historic Westchester County into Putnam and Dutchess counties. Proceeding inland across the southeastern strip of New York State above Long Island, you'll soon reach attractions near the border of Connecticut.

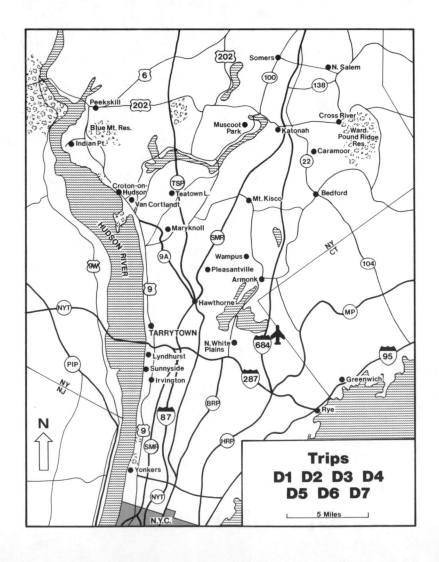

Trips
D1 D2 D3 D4
D5 D6 D7

5 Miles

Trip D-1
A Trip to De Jonkheer's Town

- PHILIPSE MANOR HALL
- HUDSON RIVER MUSEUM
- UNTERMYER PARK AND GARDENS
- SHERWOOD HOUSE

DISTANCE: About 15 miles from Columbus Circle.

FOR THE DRIVER: Take the **Saw Mill River Parkway** north to the Yonkers Ave. exit, immediately after the junction with the Cross County Parkway, *or* take the **New York State Thruway** north to Exit 4 and the Cross County briefly to the Saw Mill River Pkwy. north to the Yonkers Ave. exit, passing the exit off the Thruway for **Yonkers Raceway** (914-968-4200), famed home of night harness racing.

Coming off the ramp, turn right on Yonkers Ave., then right at the stoplight onto Ashburton Ave., following it as it goes right at the top of the hill, then left downhill. Continue on Ashburton about a mile to Warburton Ave. Turn left on Warburton and go three blocks south to Dock St. and **Philipse Manor,** at Larkin Plaza.

Go back on Warburton past Ashburton, then north about 6 blocks to Trevor Park and the **Hudson River Museum,** shortly after Warburton crosses Glenwood Ave.

Continue north on Warburton just over a mile to Odell Ave. Turn right and follow Odell uphill to North Broadway (US-9). Turn right on N. Broadway and go about a half-mile south to **Untermyer Park and Gardens,** just past the hospital.

Go back to Odell and turn right, crossing the Saw Mill River Parkway to Saw Mill River Road (NY-9A). Turn right, go about a half-mile south to Tuckahoe Rd., and turn left, following signs for the Thruway. Beyond the Thruway entrance watch for a sign to Sprain Brook Parkway south. Just before the ramp is a small road, on the right, to **Sherwood House.**

The next several trips take you to Westchester County, land of the Manhattan and Mohican Indians before the Dutch West India Company bought and battled them out, site of George Washington's desperate struggle to keep the British at bay in the early years of the

Revolution, home of America's first internationally acknowledged writer, Washington Irving. For further information contact the Westchester Tourism Council, 148 Martine Ave., White Plains, NY 10601 (914-948-0047), and the Hudson River Valley Association, 42 Catharine St., Poughkeepsie, NY 12601 (914-452-4910).

PHILIPSE MANOR HALL STATE HISTORIC SITE, Warburton Ave. & Dock St., Yonkers, NY 10701 (914-965-4027). *Grounds open all year daily; manor open late May to late Oct., Wed.–Sun. noon–5. Free. Guided tours by appointment. Wheelchair-accessible.*

This handsome Georgian manor house was begun in 1682 by Frederick Philipse, a Dutch immigrant who became Peter Stuyvesant's carpenter-contractor and, under the British, first lord of the manor of Philipsburg. By trading and shipping he made himself an owner of houses, mills, and 90,000 acres on both sides of the Hudson up to Croton. During the Revolution the Philipse family remained loyal to the Crown, and the manor was confiscated. George Washington is said to have been interested in Mary Philipse, sister of the lord of the manor. At one time the house served as the Town Hall of Yonkers, and the northern wing was stripped to create a courtroom and a council chamber. In addition to its intristic architectural interest, the house contains exhibits on the painstaking restoration process, historical exhibits, and the Cochran portrait collection, including works by Copley, Gilbert Stuart, Charles Willson Peale, Rembrandt Peale, and Benjamin West.

HUDSON RIVER MUSEUM, Trevor Park-on-Hudson, 511 Warburton Ave., Yonkers, NY 10701 (914-963-4550). *Open all year, Wed.–Sat. 10–5, Sun. noon–5, closed major holidays. Adults $4, children under 12 $1, planetarium shows additional. Concerts, lectures, café, gift shop, summer jazz and chamber music concerts, special events throughout the year. Wheelchair-accessible.*

With its triple focus on art, local history, and science, the Hudson River Museum is a fascinating place to spend a day. Here you can go from Indian relics to contemporary art, from the *Half Moon* to the Space Age. In the modern buildings you'll find galleries with changing exhibits in a wide variety of media, from ceramics to video, and the **Andrus Space Transit Planetarium,** with excellent programs on astronomy and the latest developments in space science. Its new star projector makes it one of the most sophisticated planetariums in the Northeast. You can also tour the adjoining **John Bond Trevor Mansion** (1876), a beautifully preserved Hudson River Eastlake château. You'll also get a marvelous view of the Palisades (Trips C-1 and C-2) across the river.

UNTERMYER PARK AND GARDENS, N. Broadway and Greystone Pl., Yonkers, NY 10701. *Open all year daily. Flat but gravelly; difficult for wheelchairs, but manageable with help.*

This elaborate formal garden is perched on one of the highest natural elevations in the Hudson River Valley, on the grounds of the former Greystone estate, owned by New York governor Samuel Tilden and then by Samuel Untermyer, a self-made millionaire. It was Untermyer who developed the Grecian Gardens and willed the property to the city of Yonkers as a public park. A massive restoration project in the 1970s has repaired the fountain network, Greek Temple and statues, Assyrian Portal, ornate marble mosaics, and other striking features of the Grand Beaux Arts landscape design, one of the few in America.

SHERWOOD HOUSE, 340 Tuckahoe Rd., Yonkers, NY 10707 (914-965-7300). *Open May–Oct., Sat.–Sun. 2–5. Adults $1, children 50¢; additional fees for some special programs. Craft demonstrations, annual festivals. Not wheelchair-accessible.*

One of the few pre-Revolutionary structures in the area, this Colonial farmhouse has been restored by the Yonkers Historical Society. Escorted by costumed guides, visitors will see the large fireplace and beehive bake oven, historical exhibits, and many fine antiques. The main part of the house was built in 1740 by Thomas Sherwood, a tenant farmer on the Philipse Manor, and was purchased by his son Stephen when the Philipse lands were sold at auction after the Revolution. In the early 1800s Dr. John Ingersoll bought the house and built an addition for use as an office, charging his patients 50 cents a visit ($1 for house calls). Sherwood House is on the National Register of Historic Places.

Trip D-2
A Day in Sleepy Hollow

- SUNNYSIDE
- LYNDHURST
- HISTORICAL SOCIETY OF THE TARRYTOWNS
- UNION CHURCH OF POCANTICO HILLS
- PHILIPSBURG MANOR
- OLD DUTCH CHURCH

DISTANCE: About 25 miles from Columbus Circle.

FOR THE DRIVER: Take the **New York State Thruway** north to Exit 9 at Tarrytown and pick up **US-9** (Broadway) south a mile to **Sunnyside,** on the right.

Go back to US-9, turn left, and go north ¾ mile to **Lyndhurst,** on the left.

Continue north on 9 about a mile past the junction with the Thruway to Neperan Rd. Turn right uphill and go two blocks to Grove St. and the **Historical Society.**

Go back to US-9, turn right, and go north briefly to the junction with **NY-448.** Turn right here and go 1½ miles east to the **Union Church.** Return to 9.

Near the junction with 448 is **Patriot's Park,** on the left just off US-9, with a statue marking the capture of Major André. A little farther north is **Philipsburg Manor,** at the foot of the hill. Just beyond, across the Headless Horseman Bridge, is the entrance to the **Old Dutch Church** and sleepy Hollow Cemetery.

PUBLIC TRANSPORTATION: This area is served by frequent commuter trains operated by the Metro-North Railroad from Grand Central Terminal in Manhattan. For schedules call 800-638-7646 or 212-532-4900. Unless you don't mind walking a few miles, you'll need a taxi between the sites. For Sunnyside, get off at Irvington; use the Tarrytown or Philipse Manor stations for the other locations.

Overlooking the widest section of the Hudson River at the point where it is spanned by the majestic Tappan Zee Bridge, the old village of Tarrytown is steeped in history and preserves several of the most in-

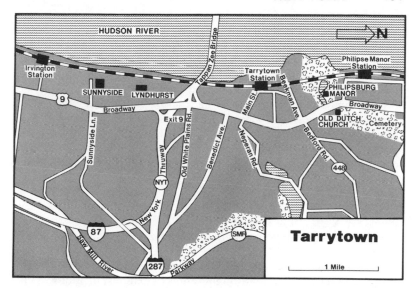

triguing sites from America's past. Its name may derive from the Dutch word *tarwe*, meaning "wheat," or, as Washington Irving conjectured, from the tendency of the early menfolk to tarry too long in the local tavern. In any case, you'll want to tarry too, so allow plenty of time for these treats.

SUNNYSIDE, West Sunnyside Lane, Tarrytown, NY 10591 (914-631-8200). *Open Mar.–Dec., daily except Tues., 10–5; last tour at 4; closed Thanksgiving and Christmas. Guided tours. Adults $6, seniors $5, children 6–17 $3. No pets. Difficult for wheelchairs, call in advance.*

Washington Irving, the first American to achieve a literary reputation abroad, made his home here in what he described as "a little old-fashioned stone mansion, all made up of gable ends, and as full of angles and corners as an old cocked hat." An apt description of this most picturesque of houses, and an apt dwelling for the author of "The Legend of Sleepy Hollow" and "Rip Van Winkle." Sunnyside is just as it was in Irving's day, and you can look out over the same views he loved so much, of the Tappan Zee and the beautiful clear pond he called his "little Mediterranean."

LYNDHURST, 635 S. Broadway, Tarrytown, NY 10591 (914-631-0046). *Open May–Oct. and Dec., daily except Mon., 10–5; Nov., Jan.–Apr. Sat.–Sun. 10–5. Guided tours. Adults $6, seniors $5, children $3. Gift shop, evening concerts in July, special events. No pets. Partially wheelchair-accessible.*

This masterpiece of Gothic Revival architecture, maintained by the National Trust for Historic Preservation, was designed by Alexander Jackson Davis for New York City mayor William Paulding and was later owned by merchant George Merritt and railroad speculator Jay Gould. The interior is not so much a restoration as a reconciliation among the styles of the three families who lived here. Apparently nothing was ever thrown away, so the place is a treasure house of Victorian elegance. There are Tiffany glass windows, rugs of silk and silver thread, paintings by well-known artists, examples of *trompe l'oeil* decor (wood painted to look like marble, ceilings painted to look like wood), and many other striking details. Its setting on 65 landscaped acres overlooking the Hudson is spectacular.

HISTORICAL SOCIETY OF THE TARRYTOWNS, 1 Grove St., Tarrytown, NY 10591 (914-631-8374). *Open all year Tues.–Sat. 2–4; closed major holidays. Donations accepted. Gift shop. Not wheelchair-accessible.*

This museum in the elegant 1848 home of the first president of the Village of Tarrytown contains eight rooms of exhibits, including a Victorian parlor, the Room of the Old Tarrytowns, a weapon room, two American Indian rooms, a children's room filled with dolls and toys, and the Captor's Room, where paintings, lithographs, and documents record the capture of Major John André by three local militiamen in September 1780 (see Trip C-4). The building itself is in the Italianate Victorian style with a dormered mansard roof reflecting the influence of the French Second Empire. Down the street at 19 Grove the Historical Society maintains a research center with an extensive library, map collections, and the Requa Archaeological Laboratory and Library, housing 35,000 artifacts recovered during a 7-year dig at the Requa tenant farmstead on the Philipsburg Manor grounds.

The Historical Society buildings are only two of the many interesting architectural specimens that abound in Tarrytown. The society will happily supply you with a brochure outlining walking or driving tours of the town's landmarks and historic districts.

UNION CHURCH OF POCANTICO HILLS, North Tarrytown, NY. *Open Apr.–Dec., Wed.–Fri. 1–4; Sun. 2–5; closed holidays. Tours $3. Will accommodate wheelchairs. Tours and further information available through Historic Hudson Valley, 150 White Plains Rd., Tarrytown, NY 10591 (914-631-8200).*

In the sanctuary of this lovely stone church you can go back for a moment far beyond Colonial days to the time of the Old Testament prophets depicted on seven extraordinary stained-glass windows created by Marc Chagall. The stained glass gives a special translucence

Philipsburg Manor across the millpond
(Photo courtesy of Historic Hudson Valley)

to the unmistakable forms and palette of this modern master. There are also two other windows by Chagall on biblical themes, and a hauntingly beautiful rose window by Matisse, commissioned as a memorial to Abby Aldrich Rockefeller.

PHILIPSBURG MANOR, Upper Mills, North Tarrytown, NY (914-631-8200). *Open Mar.–Dec., daily except Tues., 10–5; last tour at 4, closed Thanksgiving and Christmas. Guided tours. Adults $6, seniors $5, students $3. Visitor center with 15-minute film, exhibitions, picnic facilities. No pets. Partially wheelchair-accessible.*

This Dutch Colonial farm and trade center was one of the headquarters of the Philipse family's 90,000-acre empire on the Hudson (see Trip D-1). The stone manor house has been restored to its appearance in 1720, and the farm still operates much as it did then: costumed farmers till the soil, milkmaids tend the cows and the great millstones of the water-driven gristmill turn wheat into flour. Philipsburg is rich in history and lore. It was here that Major André was captured after conspiring with Benedict Arnold to betray West Point (see Trip C-4); it was here, with the Headless Horseman hot on his heels, that Ichabod Crane tried but failed to get over the millpond bridge. Today you see much the same landscape that Ichabod saw in his headlong flight, and you can walk over the Headless Horseman Bridge to the Old Dutch Church and cemetery (see below).

OLD DUTCH CHURCH, Broadway & Pierson, North Tarrytown, NY 10591. *Maintained under auspices of the First Reformed Church of North Tarrytown (914-631-1123). Tours by appointment, May–Oct., daily except Mon. Grounds open daily all year.*

This ancient landmark in Sleepy Hollow stands on a hill that was partly cut away to accommodate US-9, which crosses the Headless Horseman Bridge over the Pocantico River just below. The church was built by Frederick Philipse around 1685 for his family and the tenants of the manor. The belfry atop the gambrel roof contains the original bell cast in Holland with the legend, in Latin, "If God be for us, who can be against us?" Philipse and his wife, Catherine Van Cortland, are buried under the chancel. Just north of the church is **Sleepy Hollow Cemetery,** the "sequestered glen" that Washington Irving called "one of the quietest places in the whole world." Today the author rests here, and so do William Rockefeller, Andrew Carnegie, Samuel Gompers, and many others, famous and little-known.

Trip D-3
In Washington's Footsteps
at White Plains

- WASHINGTON'S HEADQUARTERS MUSEUM
- MILLER HILL RESTORATION

DISTANCE: About 25 miles from Columbus Circle.

FOR THE DRIVER: Take the **Bronx River Parkway** north to Exit 26, Virginia Rd. Turn right on Virginia Rd., proceed across railroad tracks, and watch for **Washington's Headquarters Museum,** shortly on the left.

Continue a short distance on Virginia Rd., watching for signs on the left to **Miller Hill.**

PUBLIC TRANSPORTATION: North White Plains is served by commuter trains operated by the Metro-North Railroad from Grand Central Terminal in Manhattan.

WASHINGTON'S HEADQUARTERS MUSEUM, 140 Virginia Rd., North White Plains, NY (914-949-1236). *Open all year Wed.–Sun. 10–4. Free. Self-guided tour, curator on duty. Special events, tours by appointment. Partially wheelchair-accessible.*

George Washington slept here in this white clapboard house, the center of a busy 100-acre Colonial farm owned by Elijah and Ann Miller. The original portion was built in 1738, with the west wing added in 1770. During the Battle of White Plains in October-November 1776, the Miller home served as headquarters for Washington, whose rag-tag army had just been driven out of New York City by British forces under General Howe. The American troops retreated up the Bronx River Valley and established a line of defense on Chatterton Hill in what is now northern White Plains. It took the British only 15 minutes to dislodge them from this position, but then a timely rainstorm forced a lull in the battle. Washington used the opportunity to regroup his men on Miller Hill, which was much steeper and easier to defend. From here they were able to repulse the combined British and Hessian forces, and Howe finally retreated at daybreak on November 5.

The Miller homestead was right in the thick of the action, and today you can see it much as it looked when Washington stayed here. Everything on view is authentic or an exact duplicate: Washington used the table and chair in the parlor; the clothes press in the bedroom belonged to Ann Miller's father and bears a musket pellet authenticating its patriot pedigree; Mrs. Miller baked in the brick beehive oven in the kitchen, still in occasional use for samplings of baked beans, cookies, and breads; and the Miller family laundry was done in the large wooden box in the kitchen, with a bell tied to the stick "agitator" to make sure the child-powered "washing machine" completed its cycle. In the 1970s the house was renovated by the Historic Workshop of the National Trust for Historic Preservation in Tarrytown, and it now shows the original look of the floorboards, walls, doors, and trim. The White Plains chapter of the D.A.R. donated the furniture and keeps it in perfect condition. Be sure to pay your respects to the huge sycamore whose boughs shade the western corner of the house, and whose roots have lifted the bedroom floor 4 inches. It's said to be some 300 years old, and it's been inducted into the Hall of Fame for Trees in Washington, D.C.

MILLER HILL RESTORATION, North White Plains, NY. *Open daily all year for viewing. Free.*

Here the final shots of the Battle of White Plains were fired. Restored earthworks show where Washington's troops dug in and held off the Redcoats, while a battle diagram enables you to follow the course of the combat.

Trip D-4
Across Westchester
by Pond, Marsh, and Lake

- WAMPUS POND
- MARSH SANCTUARY
- TEATOWN LAKE RESERVATION

DISTANCE: About 30 miles from Columbus Circle to Wampus Pond, another 15 to Teatown via Marsh.

FOR THE DRIVER: Take the **New York State Thruway** north to Exit 8. Here take **I-287** east to White Plains and pick up **I-684** north towards Brewster. Go about 6 miles to the exit for Armonk and **NY-22.** Take 22 west briefly into Armonk and turn right at the junction with **NY-128,** Armonk Rd. About 1½ miles up 128 is **Wampus Pond.** Note that Armonk is very close to the Connecticut border and some of the sites on the early trips in Area E.

Continue north on 128 a few miles to **NY-117,** Bedford Rd., and turn right here briefly to **NY-172,** still Bedford Rd. Turn right on 172 and watch for Brookside section of the **Marsh Sanctuary** at McLain St., shortly on the left. To reach the woodlands and marsh area, continue on 172 to Sarles St., turn right, and go about two miles to the entrance, marked by orange posts.

Go back on 172 to the junction with 117, turn right, and continue north briefly into Mt. Kisco. Turn left on **NY-133** and proceed west past the Saw Mill River Parkway about a mile to Seven Bridges Rd. Turn right and go to the end at the Croton Reservoir, then turn left on **NY-100** briefly to **NY-134.** Turn right on 134 and proceed across the Taconic State Parkway, passing the **Kitchawan Field Station** (914-941-8886), a lovely wooded area operated by the Brooklyn Botanic Garden. Shortly after 134 crosses the Taconic, watch for Spring Valley Rd., one of several small roads on the right. Turn here for the **Teatown Lake Reservation.**

WAMPUS POND, Route 128, Armonk, NY 10504 (914-273-3230). *Open all year daily dawn–dusk. Parking fee May–Sept. Picnicking, fishing, boat rentals and ramp, ice skating. Leashed pets only. Not wheelchair-accessible.*

Here's a small, scenic park a little off the beaten track. It's a nice place to picnic or plunk your line in the pond and wait for the one that got away.

MARSH SANCTUARY, Route 172, Mt. Kisco, NY 10549 (914-241-2808). *Grounds open all year daily dawn–dusk; museum open all year Mon.– Fri. 9–4. Free. No pets. Not wheelchair-accessible.*

On a rustic hillside surrounded by blossoming shrubs and wild-flowers stands, of all things, a small Greek amphitheater. Built in 1913, it is the setting for a variety of activities, both cultural and botanical. The sanctuary has two parts. Brookside, the more developed one, has 15 acres of gardens and trails. The other consists of some 75 acres of woods and marshland accessible by trail and boardwalk, providing opportunities for serious study of plant and bird life.

TEATOWN LAKE RESERVATION, Spring Valley Rd., Ossining, NY 10562 (914-762-2912). *Grounds open all year daily dawn–dusk; museum open all year Tues.–Sat. 9–5. Free. No pets. Partially wheelchair-accessible.*

This Nature Education and Environmental Field Station is devoted to environmental preservation and sponsors an ambitious range of school and community programs, in addition to seminars and slide programs for the general public. It's an ideal setting for such an endeavor: the 400 acres of serene woodlands crisscrossed by 12 miles of trails are calculated to induce an appreciation for nature in even the most hardened urbanite. Teatown is a perfect place for nature walks and relaxed contemplation. There's also a fine museum with changing natural history exhibits and a small animal rehabilitation program for injured wildlife.

By the way, there's a wonderful story behind the name Teatown. Some time before the American Revolution, a Bronx merchant moved to the area, bringing with him a stash of tea. The local women, catching wind of the sudden appearance of this rare commodity, stormed the merchant's farm and were held at bay by the women of the household. The stalemate was finally broken when the merchant capitulated to the irate ladies and agreed to ship in a steady supply of black-market tea.

Trip D-5
To the Manor House

- VAN CORTLANDT MANOR
- CROTON POINT PARK
- CROTON GORGE
- INDIAN POINT ENERGY EDUCATION CENTER
- BLUE MOUNTAIN RESERVATION

DISTANCE: About 40 miles from Columbus Circle to the farthest point.

FOR THE DRIVER: Take the **Saw Mill River Parkway** to the Hawthorne Interchange and pick up **NY-9A** north for about 7 miles until it merges with **US-9.** Continue north briefly to Croton Point Ave. A right turn here, followed by another right at the first light, takes you to the **Van Cortlandt Manor.**

Return on Croton Point Ave., cross US-9, and proceed across the railroad tracks to **Croton Point Park.**

Go back to US-9, turn left, and go north briefly to the next exit, **NY-129.** Turn right and go northeast on 129 about 2 miles to the **Croton Gorge** entrance, just below the dam. A little past the park entrance, on the right, is Croton Dam Rd., which takes you across the top of the dam for good views.

Return to 9, turn right, and go north about 3 miles to the exit for Montrose and Buchanan. Turn left here onto 9A and go past the veteran's hospital to Dutch St. Turn left on Dutch to **George's Island.**

Go back to 9A, turn left, and continue a short way to a group of traffic lights; at the third light, on Bleakley Ave., turn left and follow signs for about a mile to the Con Ed plant at Indian Point.

Return to 9A, turn left, and drive to Welcher Ave. Turn right and proceed uphill, crossing Washington St. Signs here direct you to the **Blue Mountain Reservation.**

This scenic excursion takes you to one of the best Colonial restorations in the Hudson Valley, offers a choice of four natural beauty spots, and, to finish things off with a bang, throws in a visit to a nuclear power station.

VAN CORTLANDT MANOR, S. Riverside Ave., Croton-on-Hudson, NY (914-631-8200). *Open Mar.–Dec., daily except Tues., 10–5; last tour at 4; closed Thanksgiving and Christmas. Guided tours. Adults $6, seniors $5, students 6–17 $3. No pets. Picnic area. Special events. Special arrangements for disabled, call in advance.*

Situated on a rise at the confluence of the Croton and Hudson rivers, this handsome manor was the home of Philip Van Cortlandt, scion of a powerful New York family, hero of the Revolutionary War, and member of Congress. The house has been carefully restored and beautifully furnished, and there's a flavor here that puts the visitor right back among the industrious Dutch occupants. You can watch demonstrations of crafts and cooking, and examine priceless antique furnishings, many from the original estate.

Stroll down the **Long Walk** through gardens and orchards to the atmospheric **Ferry House,** a popular stop for weary travelers on the old Albany Post Road, with a Tap Room for the noisier, bawdier crowd, and a Common Room reserved for meals and games for the quieter patrons.

CROTON POINT PARK, P.O. Box 64, Croton-on-Hudson, NY 10520 (914-271-3293). *Grounds open all year daily dawn–dusk; parking fee May–Sept. Beach open late June to Labor Day, fee. Picnicking, playing fields, hiking, canoe launching ramp (fee), camping (fee), fishing, refreshment stand. No pets. Wheelchair-accessible parking and restrooms.*

This popular recreation area of more than 500 acres offers fine views up and down the Hudson, and in winter you can often see ice boating. It was off this point, in September 1780, that the British man-of-war *Vulture* lay at anchor waiting to pick up Major John André after his secret interview with Benedict Arnold near Haverstraw. But when Americans at King's Ferry opened fire with a small howitzer, the ship had to drop downriver; André was compelled to take the land route and was captured at Tarrytown (Trip D-2).

CROTON GORGE, P.O. Box 64, Croton-on-Hudson, NY 10520 (914-271-3293). *Grounds open all year daily dawn–dusk. Parking fee May–Sept. Picnicking, play areas, hiking, fishing, cross-country skiing, sledding. Leashed pets only. Wheelchair-accessible parking.*

Hugging the side of Croton Dam, this little park is a small patch of wilderness in the very heart of suburbia. When the reservoir is high, water cascades over the dam in a sparkling display of freedom on its way to the Old Croton Aqueduct and thence to the taps of New York City. The view from the top of the dam is worth the climb, but you can drive there too.

GEORGE'S ISLAND PARK, Dutch St., Montrose, NY 10548 (914-737-7530). *Grounds open all year daily dawn–dusk. Parking fee May–Sept. Picnicking, playing fields, hiking, fishing, launching ramp (fee). Leashed pets only. Wheelchair-accessible parking and restrooms.*

Here is a particularly scenic park on Montrose Point, across from Stony Point (Trip C-6). Trails extend along the crest of rocky shores dotted with intriguing little coves and patches of beach. Many species of small wildlife and birds make their homes here.

INDIAN POINT ENERGY EDUCATION CENTER, Bleakley Ave., Buchanan, NY 10511 (914-737-8174). *Open all year Mon.–Fri. 8:30–4:30, closed holidays. Free. Partial wheelchair access; ramps into building, all 3 levels can be reached.*

Con Ed's nuclear power plant at Indian Point offers a variety of exhibits, films, and discussions on atomic energy. You can also see the control room simulator used to train plant operators, a working solar energy system, a wind-operated generator, and displays on energy conservation, the environment, and on the history and ecology of the Hudson River Valley. Whatever your position on nuclear power, Indian Point provides an opportunity to learn more about how the awesome power of the atom is harnessed.

BLUE MOUNTAIN RESERVATION, Welcher Ave., Peekskill, NY 10566 (914-737-2194). *Grounds open all year daily dawn–dusk. Parking fee May–Sept. Beach open mid-June to Labor Day, Tues.–Sun. (fee). Picnicking, hiking, playgrounds, bridle paths, fishing, ice skating, cross-country skiing, sledding, refreshment stand. No pets. Parking, restrooms, and beach are wheelchair-accessible.*

Two of Westchester's highest peaks are within this forest preserve. You can hike to Blue Mountain (680 feet) and Mount Spitzenberg (560 feet), or ride up on the bridle paths instead. Swimming is in Loundsbury Pond. The Sportsman Center (914-737-7450) has safe and diversified target ranges for trap and skeet shooting, rifles, pistols, and archery (fees vary with activity).

Trip D-6
History, Art, and Music
in Upper Westchester

- JOHN JAY HOMESTEAD
- WARD POUND RIDGE RESERVATION
- CARAMOOR CENTER
- BEDFORD COURTHOUSE MUSEUM
- KATONAH GALLERY
- MUSCOOT FARM PARK

DISTANCE: About 45 miles from Columbus Circle to Katonah.

FOR THE DRIVER: Take the **Hutchinson River Parkway** north to **I-684** north, *or* the **Saw Mill River Parkway** north past the Hawthorne Interchange to **I-684** north. Follow 684 to Exit 6 for Katonah-Cross River. Here go east on **NY-35** to the junction with **NY-22** (Jay St.). For the **John Jay Homestead,** turn right on 22 and go about 1½ miles south to the entrance, on the left. For **Ward Pound Ridge Reservation,** continue east on 35 abut 3 miles to Cross River and the park entrance.

From the John Jay Homestead, continue south on 22 about a mile to the junction with Girdle Ridge Rd., turn left, and go a half-mile to **Caramoor** gates, on the right.

Return to 22 and go south about 3 miles to **Bedford Courthouse,** in the center of Bedford Village.

Go north on 22 back to the junction with 35. Turn left and go west across I-684 briefly to Bedford Rd. (NY-117). Turn left and proceed to **Katonah Gallery,** shortly on the left.

Go back to 35, turn left, and continue west about ¾ mile to the junction with **NY-100.** Turn left on 100 and follow it into **Muscoot Farm Park.**

JOHN JAY HOMESTEAD STATE HISTORIC SITE, Katonah, NY 10536 (914-232-5651). *Grounds open all year daily 8–dusk. Building open May to mid-Dec., Wed.–Sat. 10–4 and Sun. noon–4, closed on holidays except in summer. Tours by appointment. Free. Concerts, nature walks, holiday programs, special events all year. Steps into house, but wheelchairs can get around first floor once inside.*

John Jay, America's first Chief Justice, was a towering figure in the early history of the nation. He was a principal negotiator of the peace treaty that ended the Revolution, coauthor with Madison and Hamilton of the *Federalist Papers* arguing for ratification of the Constitution, and author of the 1794 treaty with England that bears his name. He also served the State of New York in many different capacities. After 27 years of public life he retired to this homestead, built on land purchased by his maternal grandfather, Jacobus Van Cortlandt, from the Indian sachem Katonah in 1703. Jay's descendants lived here continuously until 1953, and the house is furnished primarily with their belongings. The rear of the original farmhouse has been extensively restored, and the Iselin room has been turned into a family portrait gallery that includes paintings by John Trumbull and Gilbert Stuart.

WARD POUND RIDGE RESERVATION, Routes 35 & 121, Cross River, NY 10518 (914-763-3493). *Grounds open all year daily dawn–dusk; parking fee May–Sept. Trailside Museum (914-763-3993) open all year Wed.–Sun. 10–4; free. Picknicking, hiking, bridle paths, fishing, camping (fee), snowmobiling, sledding, cross-country skiing, refreshment stand. Leashed pets only. Wheelchair-accessible parking.*

Over 4,000 acres of park spread over a scenic mountain provide a great place to spend the day. There are miles of trails with lovely vistas, two rivers for fishing, and the small-but-interesting **Trailside Nature Museum,** with natural history exhibits and various interpretive programs.

CARAMOOR CENTER FOR MUSIC AND THE ARTS, P.O. Box R, Katonah, NY 10536 (914-232-5035). *Museum open June–Aug., Thurs. & Sat. 11–4, Sun. 1–4, Wed. & Fri. by appointment. Nov.–Apr. by appointment only on Mon.–Fri. Open holidays in season. Adults $4, children under 12 $2; guided tours, picnicking. Annual music festival June through Aug. Museum and festival are wheelchair-accessible; call in advance.*

The former home of New York lawyer Walter T. Rosen, a lavish Mediterranean-style estate built between 1930 and 1939, today operates as a museum housing his extensive collection of paintings, sculpture, Italian Renaissance furniture, medieval tapestries, and Chinese art. Here you can wander through entire rooms from European villas and palaces, stroll through the impressive formal gardens, and picnic in the apple orchard. In summer the highly respected **Caramoor Music Festival** brings some of the world's best classical artists to this lovely setting in the rolling hills of northern Westchester.

BEDFORD COURTHOUSE MUSEUM, Bedford Village, NY 10506 (914-234-9781). *Open Apr. to Dec., Wed.–Sun. 2–5; closed major holidays. Adults 75¢, seniors and children under 12 25¢. Partially wheelchair-accessible.*

Begin your tour of this 1787 courthouse, the oldest in the nation, in the courtroom where, over 150 years ago, John Jay's son William was one of the presiding judges. Typical accoutrements of a court of the stagecoach period surround the bench. Upstairs there are two original jail cells and a museum with memorabilia covering 300 years of town history. The museum, maintained by the Bedford Historical Society, was formerly located in the little stone school (1829) across the green, now restored as a typical **one-room schoolhouse** of the 19th century (open same hours as museum, no additional charge).

KATONAH GALLERY, 28 Bedford Rd., Katonah, NY 10536 (914-232-9555). *Open all year Tues.–Fri. 1–5, Sat. 10–5, Sun. 1–5; closed Mon. and during installation of new exhibits (check in advance). Free. Festivals and special events during exhibits. Wheelchair-accessible.*

Established in 1953, the Katonah Gallery has mounted five or more major exhibits annually for over three decades. There is no permanent collection here; instead the staff researches and creates exhibits assembled from the holdings of museums and private collectors around the country.

MUSCOOT FARM PARK, Route 100, Somers, NY 10589 (914-232-7118). *Open all year Wed.–Sun. 10–4. Free. Picnicking, fishing. Leashed pets only. Partially wheelchair-accessible.*

This 777-acre spread re-creates farm life at the turn of the century. You can see the 28-room main house and original outbuildings, farm animals, antique cultivating equipment, and, on weekends, demonstrations of beekeeping, sheep shearing, blacksmithing, and other vanishing skills of America's rural past.

Trip D-7
American Enterprise, Oriental Gardens

- READER'S DIGEST
- HISTORIC ELEPHANT HOTEL AND CIRCUS MUSEUM
- HAMMOND MUSEUM AND ORIENTAL STROLL GAR-DENS

DISTANCE: About 55 miles from Columbus Circle to the farthest point.

FOR THE DRIVER: Take the **Saw Mill River Parkway** north to the Hawthorne Interchange and continue north on the parkway for another 4 miles. At Roaring Book Rd. and Reader's Digest Rd. turn right to the **Reader's Digest Headquarters.**

Go back to the parkway, turn right, and continue north towards Brewster and the junction with **I-684.** Go about 5 miles north on I-684 to the junction with **NY-116.** Turn left and go west on 116 into Somers and the junction with **NY-100/US-202.** Turn left on these briefly to where they branch; here is the **Historic Elephant Hotel and Circus Museum.**

Go back to NY-116, turn right, and proceed past I-684 and Titicus Reservoir to **NY-124,** at the top of the hill. Turn left, go $\frac{1}{4}$ mile to Deveau Rd., and turn right on Deveau to the **Hammond Museum.**

READER'S DIGEST, Pleasantville, NY 10570 (914-238-1000). *Open all year Mon.–Fri. during business hours; tours by appointment only. Call at least a week in advance. Free. Not wheelchair-accessible.*

Motorists driving along the Saw Mill River Parkway in Westchester have long been familiar with the outlines of some red-brick buildings grouped around a main building with a handsome white cupola. This is the headquarters of one of the world's most widely read magazines, the *Reader's Digest.* On this guided tour you can visit the offices, scan the corridors for the Most Unforgettable Character, and soak up Life in These United States. Besides the luxurious furnishings, many of them antiques, you'll find a notable collection of French Impressionist and modernist paintings. You won't get to see how they condense those books, though—the printing is not done on the premises.

HISTORIC ELEPHANT HOTEL AND CIRCUS MUSEUM, Somers, NY
10589 (914-277-4977). *Open all year Fri. 2–4 and by appointment. Free.
Not wheelchair-accessible.*

Show-biz history was made in this small town. Once the center of
a thriving cattle industry, it won national attention around 1810 when
a farmer named Hachaliah Bailey (no relation to James Bailey of Barnum
& Bailey fame) came into possession of an elephant, Old Bet, the second ever seen in the United States. His brother, a sea captain, had
bought her in London and shipped her up the Hudson to Ossining.
The elephant caused such a sensation that Bailey took her on tour and
exhibited her for a fee. In Maine poor Bet was foraging for a snack in
a tasty-looking potato field, and the farmer shot her. Despite Bet's
unhappy end, Bailey's neighbors were inspired by his example, rounded
up the most exotic four-footed critters they could find, and started
road shows, making Somers a hotbed of circus entrepreneurship. From
his profits Bailey built the Elephant Hotel, today the Somers Town
Hall, housing offices and a museum with old posters, circus para-
phernalia, and a display of miniatures collected by circus people on
their travels. In 1829 Bailey raised a monument to Old Bet in front of
the building, a large effigy made of wooden blocks standing high on
a granite plinth.

HAMMOND MUSEUM AND ORIENTAL STROLL GARDENS, Deveau
Rd., North Salem, NY 10560 (914-669-5135). *Museum open May through
Dec. Wed.–Sun. 11–5; gardens open May through Oct. Wed.–Sun.
11–5; both closed Mon.–Tues. except on legal holidays. Separate ad-
missions: Museum, adults $3, children under 12 $1; gardens, adults $2,
children $1. No pets. Not suitable for children under 7. Museum is
wheelchair accessible, gardens have one major wheelchair-accessible
path.*

Here, apart from the rush of life, you can stroll through 3½ acres of
artfully landscaped Oriental gardens that transport you to another
world, another culture, another time. You'll come upon rippling waterfalls, a river of blue lava stones gliding past banks of miniature plants,
an island garden of rock ruled by Jizo, patron saint of children. Adjacent to the gardens is a museum of the humanities founded in 1957
by Natalie Hays Hammond in memory of her parents. A showcase for
art treasures from around the world, it mounts a major exhibit every
year on themes ranging from heraldry to ecology, from needlepoint
to world religions. The museum also sponors a program of dramatic
readings, concerts, lectures, ballets, period plays, and masques. At
Hammond, all these disparate forms of expression receive their due
as different ways of telling the human story.

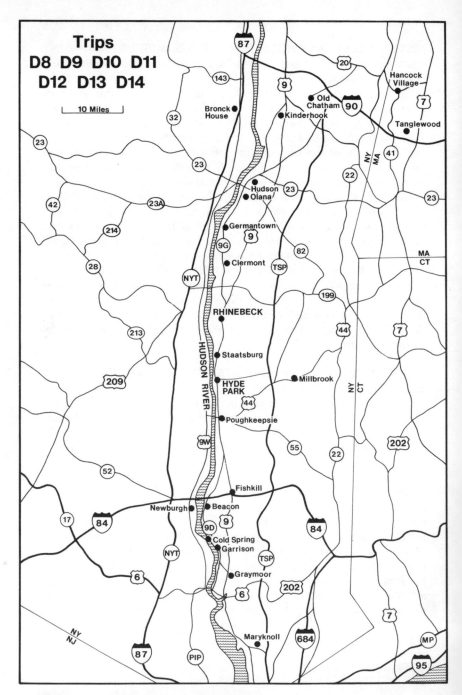

Trips
D8 D9 D10 D11
D12 D13 D14

10 Miles

87

20

143

9

Hancock
Village

7

32

Bronck
House

Old
Chatham

90

23

Kinderhook

Tanglewood

23

41

NY
MA

22

23

42

23A

Hudson
Olana

23

214

Germantown

9

28

9G

82

MA
CT

Clermont

TSP

NYT

199

213

RHINEBECK

44

7

HUDSON RIVER

Staatsburg

209

HYDE
PARK

Millbrook

NY
CT

44

Poughkeepsie

9W

55

202

52

22

Fishkill

84

Newburgh

Beacon

17

84

9

9D

Cold Spring

NYT

Garrison

6

TSP

Graymoor

202

6

7

NY
NJ

Maryknoll

684

MP

87

PIP

95

Trip D-8
From Mary's Lovely Knoll
to Beautiful Boscobel

- MARYKNOLL SEMINARY
- GRAYMOOR
- BOSCOBEL
- FOUNDRY SCHOOL MUSEUM

DISTANCE: About 55 miles from Columbus Circle to the farthest point.

FOR THE DRIVER: Take the **Saw Mill River Parkway** north to the Hawthorne Interchange and pick up **NY-9A** north about 4½ miles to **NY-133.** Turn right, towards Millwood, drive a few blocks to Brookside Lane, and turn left to **Maryknoll,** across Ryder Ave.

From Maryknoll turn right on Ryder back to 9A and follow it north, merging with **US-9** and continuing through Peekskill across a small bridge to a traffic circle. Continue north on US-9 about 4 miles to **Graymoor,** on the right.

Just beyond Graymoor, **NY-403** branches left off 9 to Garrison. Take 403 to the junction with **NY-9D** and turn right, going north on 9D past Garrison to **Boscobel,** on the left.

When you leave Boscobel, continue north on 9D, which bears left, then right, into Cold Spring. Make a sharp left onto Chestnut St. to the **Foundry School Museum.**

A little north of the museum on 9D, at a traffic light, is the junction with NY-301. A right turn here will take you east to the **Clarence Fahnestock Memorial State Park** (914-225-7207), a popular 4,000-acre recreation area with picnicking, hiking, bridle paths, swimming beach, boat rentals and ramp, and camping. *Or* you can turn left at the light onto Main St. for a brief side trip to an unusual **scenic vista.** Go as far as you can, then turn left on Lunn Terrace, crossing the railroad tracks to Market St. Turn right on Market back to Main St., then left to the waterfront. Here, on the banks of the Hudson, you'll find a 1920s bandstand and a lovely view across the river to Crow's Nest and Breakneck mountains, Storm King Mountain to your right, and West Point (Trip C-12) below. A left on Market St. will take you to the restored Chapel of Our Lady, the oldest Catholic church in New York outside Manhattan.

From the junction of 9D and 301, you can easily continue north on 9D to the Madam Brett and Van Wyck homesteads, first stops on the next trip.

MARYKNOLL SEMINARY, Maryknoll, NY 10545 (914-941-7590). *Open all year daily 9–5; gift shop open Mon.–Sat. 2–5, Sun. 1–4:30. No admission fee. Pets discouraged. Partially wheelchair-accessible; call in advance.*

Maryknoll is the headquarters of the Catholic Foreign Mission Society of America. At the seminary on the west property and across the road at the Maryknoll Sisters Center, priests and nuns are trained for service in foreign missions. From here they go out to all corners of the world to work among the poor and oppressed in churches, schools, health clinics, farms, and community projects. Here you can see photo exhibits on the Maryknoll missions around the globe, stop at the various chapels and shrines, and climb to the upper cloister for splendid views of the countryside. The international gift shop at the Sisters Center has an unusual and intriguing selection of items.

GRAYMOOR CHRISTIAN UNITY CENTER, Garrison, NY 10524 (914-424-3671). *Grounds open all year; inquire about services, tours, pilgrimages, weekend retreats, weekly meetings, special programs. Picnic facilities. Pets discouraged. Grounds and some buildings are manageable for wheelchairs.*

Here, situated on top of a high hill, commanding a magnificent view, is the monastery of the Franciscan Friars of the Atonement. Pilgrims from around the world come here to attend services, visit the shrines and chapels, and make the Stations of the Cross at the Crucifixion Group. The Unity Center is an interfaith conference and retreat facility where people of all beliefs can heed the injunction of Isaiah 2:3, "Come, let us go up the mountain of the Lord."

BOSCOBEL, Route 9D, Garrison, NY 10524 (914-265-3638). *Open Apr.–Oct., Wed.–Mon. 10–4:30; Nov., Dec., Mar., Wed.–Mon. 10–3:30; closed Tues., Jan., Feb., holidays. Guided tours only. Adults $6, seniors $5, children 6–14 $3, under 6 free. Gift shop. Concerts, special events throughout the year. No pets, no spike heels. Grounds are wheelchair-accessible; mansion difficult for wheelchairs.*

A flawless example of New York Federal architecture, Boscobel (1804) overlooks a rocky gorge in the Hudson Highlands where the river cuts through the Appalachian Mountain range. This is indeed a *bosco bello,* "beautiful wood." Boscobel's builder, States Morris Dyckman, wanted the finest of everything for his dream house, and despite his wife's pleas for economy, he spared no expense. This, he told her, would be their "last sacrifice to Folly." Today, you can be glad he had his way.

Both the building and its interior were patterned after the style of Robert Adam—delicate, flowery, pleasing to the eye. The mantels and moldings are exquisitely designed; the furnishings include Duncan Phyfe pieces and much of Dyckman's original china, silver, and library. Outside across the portico are carvings resembling graceful draperies of wood. You can also tour the stunning formal rose gardens, the orangerie and herb garden, and several original outbuildings, including the "necessary house.'

After visiting Boscobel, you will wince to learn that it nearly fell victim to the wrecker's ball in the 1950s. It now stands 15 miles north of its original site, whence it was transported piece by piece and restored with generous support from Lila Acheson Wallace, founder of the *Reader's Digest* (Trip D-7).

FOUNDRY SCHOOL MUSEUM, 63 Chestnut St., Cold Spring, NY 10516 (914-265-4010). *Open Mar.–Dec., Wed. & Thurs. 1–4 & 7–9, Sun. 2–5; groups by appointment; closed Christmas. Free, donations accepted. No ramps into building, but can accommodate wheelchairs.*

This small museum, operated by the Putnam County Historical Society, is a treasure house filled with Americana and fascinating exhibits on local history and industry. It's located in a refurbished 150-year-old schoolhouse originally used by the children of the factory workers at the neighboring West Point Foundry. Permanent exhibits include paintings, scale models of a Hudson River sloop and the grand old paddlewheeler *Mary Powell,* and artifacts connected with foundry operations, both military and household. There's good material for research in the libaray and archives.

Trip D-9
Bound for Poughkeepsie

- MADAM BRETT HOMESTEAD
- VAN WYCK HOMESTEAD MUSEUM
- LOCUST GROVE / YOUNG-MORSE HISTORIC SITE
- GLEBE HOUSE
- VASSAR COLLEGE

DISTANCE: About 75 miles from Columbus Circle.

FOR THE DRIVER: Take the **Saw Mill River Parkway** to the Hawthorne Interchange and pick up the **Taconic State Parkway** north to
the junction with **NY-301.** Drive west on 301 through Fahnestock Park
across US-9 to the junction with **NY-9D** in Cold Spring. Here you are
very close to the last stops on Trip D-8. Turn right and go into Beacon
on 9D (Wolcott Ave.). A few blocks ahead, across a small bridge, is
Teller Ave. Turn right here and proceed to the **Madam Brett Homestead,** at Van Nydeck Ave.

Continue to the stoplight and go straight on what is now Business
Route 52 until it merges with **NY-52** into Fishkill. At the junction with
US-9, turn right on 9 and go about a mile south, just past the junction
with I-84, to the **Van Wyck Homestead** entrance on Snook Rd.

Go back to US-9 and go north about 9 miles to **Locust Grove,** at
the Beachwood Ave. stoplight.

Continue north on 9 into downtown Poughkeepsie. Take the exit
for US-44/NY-55 and go east to White St. Turn left and go a block to
Main St. and the **Clinton House.** Turn right on Main and go 2 blocks
to the **Glebe House,** on the left.

Continue down Main St. to Raymond Ave., turn right, and go about
a mile to **Vassar,** main entrance on the left.

Now you're in Dutchess County, an area rich in history, scenic beauty,
culture, and old money. For further information contact the Dutchess
County Tourism Promotion Agency, P.O. Box 2025, 532 Albany Post
Rd., Hyde Park, NY 12538 (914-229-0033).

MADAM BRETT HOMESTEAD, 50 Van Nydeck Ave., Beacon, NY 12508
(914-831-6533). *Open May through Oct., Sat. & Sun. 1–4, or by appointment. Adults $2, students 13–18 $1, under 13 50¢. Two steps into*

building; wheelchairs can navigate 1st floor once up steps.

Here is the oldest standing building in Dutchess County. Catheryna and Roger Brett moved into this house on Christmas Day, 1709, and it was occupied by their direct descendants for seven generations thereafter, until 1954. During the Revolutionary War, Beacon was a link in a long chain of alarm pyres stretching from the Hudson Highlands south to Morristown, New Jersey (trips B-7 and B-8), erected at General Washington's command to warn of the approach of British troops. The Brett Homestead served as a supply depot for the Continental Army, and the lady of the house, Catheryna's granddaughter, entertained Washington, Lafayette, and von Steuben here. Today the house and formal gardens are maintained by the local chapter of the D.A.R.

VAN WYCK HOMESTEAD MUSEUM, Fishkill Historical Society, Box 133, Fishkill, NY 12524 (914-896-9560). *Open Memorial Day to Labor Day, Sat–Sun. 1–5 and by appointment. Steps into building; difficult for wheelchairs.*

This Dutch Colonial house stands on grounds purchased from the Wappinger Indians in the 1680s by Francis Rombout, who struck a deal for "all the lands he could see" and then climbed to the top of Mount Beacon to enlarge his prospects. Rombout's daughter, Catheryna Brett, inherited his property and in 1732 sold 959 acres of it to Cornelius Van Wyck, who built a three-room house that is still the east wing of the present structure. During the Revolution, Fishkill served as Washington's Northern Army headquarters, and the Van Wyck house was requisitioned for military use. After the war it reverted to the Van Wyck family, who lived here for the next 150 years, until the Fishkill Historical Society acquired the house and turned it into a Revolutionary War museum.

LOCUST GROVE / YOUNG-MORSE HISTORIC SITE, 370 South Rd., Poughkeepsie, NY 12602 (914-454-4500). *Open Memorial Day through Sept., Wed–Sun. and holidays 10–4. Adults $4, seniors $3.50, children 7–16 $1, under 7 free. Guided tours, last tour starts at 3. Picnic facilities, hiking trails. No ramps, but 1st floor manageable for wheelchairs once up porch steps.*

Since the Locust Grove property was granted to Colonel Peter Schuyler in 1688, it has passed through many hands, including those of Samuel F. B. Morse (see Trip B-8), inventor of the telegraph, who bought it in 1847 and remodeled the house as a Tuscan villa. The dining room addition and the large collection of fine furnishings were the work of the Young family, who owned Locust Grove from 1901 to 1975 and set aside a trust to maintain it as a historic site and wildlife sanctuary. Today, you can see early telegraph equipment, Morse memorabilia, period furnishings, and changing exhibits from the Young collection of dolls, fans, costumes, books, and assorted Americana.

CLINTON HOUSE STATE HISTORIC SITE, 549 Main St., Poughkeep-sie, NY 12601 (914-471-1630). *Open all year Mon.–Fri. 9:30–4, closed major holidays. Ramp into building; will accommodate wheelchairs (call in advance). Address inquiries to Dutchess County Historical Society, P.O. Box 88, Poughkeepsie, NY 12602.*

This museum is named for New York's first governor, George Clinton, who used it as his office when Poughkeepsie was the temporary state capital in 1777. It is operated by the Dutchess County Historical Society primarily as a research facility and has an excellent collection of manuscripts, books, maps, and other documents on local history.

GLEBE HOUSE, 635 Main St., Poughkeepsie, NY 12601 (914-454-0605). *Open July–Aug. Sun. 1–4 and by appointment; call Clinton House (above) for arrangements. Partially wheelchair-accessible.*

Glebe House has a colorful history dating from pre-Revolutionary times, when it was built as the rectory of the Episcopal Church. In its first decade it was home to the Reverend John Beardsley, exiled in 1777 for his vigorous support of the Crown. Thereafter, though "glebe" means "parsonage," the house was put to more profane uses, serving as a rectory again for only four years. During the Revolution it was occupied by quartermasters of the Continental Army; in 1796 it was purchased by Peter DeReimer, whose daughter Elsie eloped from an upstairs window three years later; in the late 19th century the property went into decline and had a checkered career as a beer garden and picnic grove, among other things. Today it has been restored to reflect the life of a middle-class family in the early 1800s.

VASSAR COLLEGE, Press and Information Office, Poughkeepsie, NY 12601 (914-452-7000). *Buildings open during the academic year Mon.–Fri. 8:30–5, and by appointment in summer. Free. Fully wheelchair-accessible.*

Founded by Poughkeepsie brewer Matthew Vassar in 1861, Vassar College was a pioneering experiment in higher education for women. Today it is a coeducational college known for its academic quality and the beauty of its 1,000-acre campus. More than 200 species of trees, some exotic, offer their shade to 100 distinctive buildings designed by such noted architects as James Renwick, Jr. (the 1865 Main Building, after the Tuileries, reportedly planned so that it could be converted to a brewery if females proved uneducable), Marcel Breuer (Ferry House), and Eero Saarinen (Noyes House). The Norman-style chapel

musicworks
in the Berkshires
P.O. Box 199
Richmond, MA 01254

Non-Profit Org.
U.S. Postage
PAID
Richmond, MA
Permit No. 6

ADDRESS SERVICE REQUESTED

*************AUTO**3-DIGIT 012   T4   P1
ELIOT AND HELEN KRANCER
29 BLUNT RD
GREAT BARRINGTON MA 01230-9023

has five Tiffany windows, and the great stained-glass window in Thompson Library depicts Elena Lucrezia Cornaro Piscopia receiving the first doctorate awarded to a woman (by the University of Padua in 1678). The $7.2 million Seeley G. Mudd Chemistry Building, opened in 1984, boasts the latest in energy-saving technology and laboratory equipment. Of particular interest is the **Vassar College Art Gallery,** with a fine permanent collection of 8,500 works, including 19th-century English drawings, 20th-century art, Hudson River landscapes, Rembrandt etchings, and Dürer engravings.

Trip D-10
"I Will Arise and Go Now, and Go to Innisfree . . ."

- ## INNISFREE GARDEN

DISTANCE: About 80 miles from Columbus Circle.

FOR THE DRIVER: Take the **Saw Mill River Parkway** north to the Hawthorne Interchange and pick up the **Taconic State Parkway** north to Poughkeepsie and the exit for **US-44.** Take 44 east to Millbrook and watch for Tyrrel Rd. on the right, just beyond the junction with NY-82. Turn here and follow signs to **Innisfree.**

Innisfree is about 15 miles northeast of Poughkeepsie and about 12 miles east of Hyde Park. It can easily be combined with one or more of the stops on trips D-9 and D-11.

INNISFREE GARDEN, Millbrook, NY 12545 (914-677-8000). *Open May–Oct.; Wed.–Fri. 10–4, Sat.–Sun. 11–5. Adults over 16 $2 on Sat. & Sun.; otherwise free. No pets. Not wheelchair-accessible.*

The late Walter Beck was a landscape artist in the most literal sense. He spent the better part of a lifetime studying Oriental techniques of painting, calligraphy, and gardening; and in 1930 he began applying them to the creation of what is sometimes known in the East as a cup garden. With nature as his canvas, he used rocks, terraces, and retaining walls to create areas of tension and motion around streams, waterfalls, and the lake that forms the first "floor" of his garden. The result of his 22 years of work at Innisfree was an exquisitely wrought garden "painting" that still delights the eye and mind.

Trip D-11
F.D.R. and the C.I.A.

- FRANKLIN D. ROOSEVELT NATIONAL HISTORIC SITE
- VANDERBILT MANSION
- CULINARY INSTITUTE OF AMERICA

DISTANCE: About 80 miles from Columbus Circle.

FOR THE DRIVER: Take the **Saw Mill River Parkway** north to the Hawthorne Interchange and pick up the **Taconic State Parkway** north to the **Salt Point Turnpike** exit above Poughkeepsie. Go west on this to **US-9,** turn left, and go south about 2 miles to the **F.D.R. Home** at Hyde Park. The **Library** is here also; ask for directions to nearby **Val-Kill.**

From the F.D.R. Home turn left on 9 and go north about 2 miles to the **Vanderbilt Mansion,** entrance on the left.

From the mansion, turn right on 9 and go about 4 miles south of the F.D.R. Home to the **Culinary Institute of America.**

The Franklin D. and Eleanor Roosevelt National Historic Sites, together with the Roosevelt Library and Museum, constitute a moving memorial to the First Family that saw the nation through the Depression and the Second World War. The nearby Vanderbilt Mansion is, among other things, an apt expression of the class interests President Roosevelt was often accused of betraying by his social and economic policies. If you plan your trip far enough ahead and make reservations, you can really make a day of it by having lunch or dinner at the world-renowned Culinary Institute of America.

HOME OF FRANKLIN D. ROOSEVELT NATIONAL HISTORIC SITE, Route 9, Hyde Park, NY 12538 (914-229-9115). *Open Apr.–Oct. daily 9–5; Nov.–Mar. Thurs.–Mon. 9–5; closed Tues. & Wed. in winter, Thanksgiving, Christmas, New Year's. Adults $4, under 16 and over 62 free. Wheelchair-accessible.*

Franklin Delano Roosevelt was born in this house on January 30, 1882, and kept it as his family home all his life. With the inimitable recorded voice of Eleanor Roosevelt as a guide, revealing anecdotes

214

about this room or that, you may have the uncanny feeling that you're really visiting the living family, not just the house. You'll see some magnificent furnishings: the beautifully wrought Dresden chandelier and mantel set bought by Roosevelt's father in 1866, fine pieces from Italy and the Netherlands, a Gilbert Stuart painting of one of F.D.R.'s illustrious ancestors.

Echoes of more recent history are heard in Roosevelt's office, his "Summer White House," where in June 1942 he and Winston Churchill signed the agreement that led to the development of the atomic bomb. Upstairs, you'll find the boyhood room used by Roosevelt and his sons after him. Perhaps the most moving is F.D.R.'s own bedroom, with his favorite photos, Fala's leash and blanket on the chair where the little Scottie always slept, and the books and magazines the president left scattered about on his last visit here in March 1945, shortly before his death.

The name Roosevelt, from the Dutch, means "field of roses." How fitting, then, that in a beautiful garden of roses, surrounded by century-old hemlocks and perennial flower beds, both Franklin and Eleanor now rest. The tombstone is of Imperial Danby, the same white marble used in the Thomas Jefferson Memorial in Washington. A sundial stands just beyond the graves; at its base is a small plaque flush with the ground and hard to see from the walk. Here, still close to his master, lies Fala.

Franklin D. Roosevelt Library and Museum, near the house. *Open year round daily 9–5; closed Thanksgiving, Christmas, New Year's.* Those who experienced the Roosevelt years will be reminded of many things here as they peruse newsworthy gifts from foreign rulers, oddities (remember him as the Sphinx?), family heirlooms, photos, naval paintings, ship models, and more. Be sure to go downstairs to see the Ford specially fitted for Roosevelt to drive after he contracted polio. The F.D.R. Library was the first presidential library and houses Roosevelt's papers.

Eleanor Roosevelt National Historic Site, 2 miles east of the F.D.R. home, ask for driving directions. *Open May.–Oct. daily 9–5; Nov., Dec., Mar. weekends only 9-5; closed major holidays.* Eleanor Roosevelt was a tireless worker for social justice and political reform. During F.D.R.'s 12 years as presdient, she performed with dignity and grace the difficult role of First Lady to "that man in the White House." It was here at her country retreat, **Val-Kill,** that she relaxed from the cares of public life and entertained friends, relatives, and a fair contingent of foreign dignitaries. Val-Kill was dedicated as a memorial to Eleanor Roosevelt and opened to the public on October 11, 1984, the centennial of her birth. It reflects both her personal tastes and her work for the wide range of causes she adopted.

VANDERBILT MANSION NATIONAL HISTORIC SITE, Route 9, Hyde Park, NY 12538 (914-229-9115). *Open Apr.–Oct. daily 9–5; Nov.–Mar. Thurs.–Mon. 9–5; closed Tues. & Wed. in winter, Thanksgiving, Christmas, New Year's. Adults $2, under 16 and over 62 free. Partially wheelchair-accessible.*

A turn-of-the-century palatial mansion, this relic of the Gilded Age is considered to be one of the best examples of the Beaux-Arts style in the country. Designed by the architectural firm of McKim, Mead and White, with interiors by the leading decorators of the time, it was the country home of a grandson of the railroad baron Cornelius Vanderbilt, and it expresses the influence of European art on American wealth in those days. It is filled with fine marble, mahogany woodwork, throne chairs, tapestries, beaded crystal chandeliers, heavily napped rugs (one weighs 2,300 pounds), and hand-embroidered silk. The glittering opulence impresses, in different ways, everyone who visits the mansion—which, with 59 rooms, 22 fireplaces, and quarters for 60 servants, is considered the most *modest* of the various Vanderbilt estates.

CULINARY INSTITUTE OF AMERICA, Hyde Park, NY 12538 (914-471-6608). *Escoffier Restaurant (moderately expensive) open Tues.–Sat.; American Bounty Restaurant (moderate) open Tues.–Sat.; St. Andrew's Café (casual, inexpensive); all closed 3 weeks in July, 2 weeks at Christmas, major holidays. Advance reservations are essential. Smoking prohibited. Jacket required at Esoffier and American Bounty restaurants. All are wheelchair-accessible.*

Do you worry about the state of the world? Suffer from indigestion every time you watch the news? Relax. Since 1946, thousands of C.I.A. graduates have filled key positions in the world's finest restaurants, hotels, private clubs, resorts, and corporate dining rooms. Strategically placed on the proverbial way to a man's heart, these products of C.I.A. training labor ceaselessly to make the world safe for gastronomy.

The Culinary Institute of America was founded after World War II as a storefront school for 16 returning veterans. Today it has almost as many students as Vassar, all learning the myriad arts of fine cooking and dining, and all eager to practice on you. It's a fair enough exchange: without hocking the family jewels, you can dine sumptuously at the Escoffier, a 3-star restaurant offering *haute cuisine;* savor an array of regional specialities at the American Bounty Restaurant; or partake guiltlessly of gourmet health food at St. Andrew's Café. The meals—about 4,000 of them a day—are prepared by the students under the watchful eyes of 90 chefs and instructors from many different countries. Tours of the facilities are reserved for prospective students or groups by advance arrangement, but visitors are welcome to browse in the well-stocked bookstore, which also sells a line of kitchen accessories not readily available elsewhere.

The C.I.A.'s weekly shopping list includes 1,500 pounds of sugar, 1,500 pounds of flour, 2,200 dozen eggs, 400 pounds of bananas, 100 pounds of garlic, 2,000 pounds of butter, and no guns.

Trip D-12
Rhinebeck from Below—and Above

- MILLS-NORRIE STATE PARK
- MILLS MANSION STATE HISTORIC SITE
- OLD RHINEBECK AERODROME

DISTANCE: About 95 miles from Columbus Circle to Rhinebeck.

FOR THE DRIVER: Take the **Saw Mill River Parkway** north to the Hawthorne Interchange and pick up the **Taconic State Parkway** north to the **Salt Point Turnpike** exit above Poughkeepsie. Go west on this to **US-9,** turn right, and go north past the Vanderbilt Mansion (Trip D-11) about 4 miles to the **Mills-Norrie State Park,** entrance on the left. This puts you in the Norrie section of the park; **Mills Mansion** is about a mile north off US-9.

Continue north on 9 a few miles to Rhinebeck. At the junction of 9 and NY-308 is the **Beekman Arms Inn** (914-876-7077), built in 1700 and said to be the oldest continuously operating hotel in the country. Its Tap Room is an attractive and popular spot for drinks and dining. Rhinebeck is a picturesque old town, and you may want to spend some time here shopping, sightseeing, or attending one of the events at the Dutchess County Fairgrounds, which hosts an antiques show and a well-known juried crafts show in addition to the annual fair. For further information, contact the Rhinebeck Chamber of Commerce, P.O. Box 42, Rhinebeck, NY 12572 (914-876-4778).

From the Beekman Arms, continue north on US-9 past the junction with US-9G a short way to Stone Church Rd., opposite a church. Turn right here and follow signs to the **Old Rhinebeck Aerodrome.**

For a different route home, continue north briefly on US-9 to the junction with **NY-199** in Red Hook, another quaint town full of antique shops, surrounded by farms where you can pick your own fresh produce in season. As perhaps you've noticed, in the Hudson River Valley there are many mansions, and another of these, **Montgomery Place** (914-758-5461; *open Apr.–Oct., Wed.–Mon.; Mar. & Nov.–Dec. weekends*), is a few miles west of Red Hook via 199. To return to New York City, turn right on 199 and go east about 5 or 6 miles to the Taconic State Parkway.

MILLS-NORRIE STATE PARK, Staatsburg, NY 12580 (914-889-4646). *Open all year daily, daylight hours. No entry fee. Picnicking and grills, playground, hiking trails, fishing, marina, camping and cabins (fees), snowmobiling, sledding, cross-country skiing, refreshment stand. Leashed pets only, no pets in picnic areas or campsites. Picnic areas and restrooms are wheelchair-accessible.*

This attractive park on the Hudson offers fine facilities for a day's outing. There are really two parks here, one the Mills Historic Site (see below), and the other the Norrie recreation area. On the grounds of the Norrie section is the Norrie Point Inn, formerly a popular spot for waterfront dining and dancing, now an environmental education center run by the Dutchess County Community College.

MILLS MANSION STATE HISTORIC SITE, Old Albany Post Rd., Staatsburg, NY 12580 (914-889-4100). *Grounds open all year daily, daylight hours. Mansion open May–Labor Day, Wed.–Sat. 10–5, Sun. noon–5; Labor Day–Oct., Wed.–Sun., noon–5. Free. Picnicking, golf (fee). No pets. Will accommodate wheelchairs; call in advance.*

The Mills Mansion was originally a Greek Revival structure built in 1832 by Morgan Lewis, Revolutionary War officer and governor of New York from 1804 to 1807. It was later the home of Ogden and Ruth Livingston Mills, who hired the noted architectural firm McKim, Mead and White to enlarge and remodel it in the Neoclassical style. Mills was a prominent financier, his wife was a member of an established New York political family, and their son served as Secretary of the Treasury under Herbert Hoover. The mansion reflects the lifestyle of America's wealthy and powerful over several generations. The gorgeous marble fireplaces, rich wood paneling, and gilded plasterwork make an appropriate setting for Flemish tapestries, fine artwork, and ornate furnishings in the Louis XV and Louis XVI styles. The grounds are beautifully landscaped and afford a sweeping panorama of the Hudson.

OLD RHINEBECK AERODROME, Stone Church Rd., Rhinebeck, NY 12572 (914-758-8610). *Open mid-May through Oct. daily 10–5. Air shows mid-June to mid-Oct., Sat.–Sun. 2:30; pre-show activities begin at 2.*

A 1917 Fokker Triplane in mock combat over Rhinebeck (Photo courtesy of Old Rhinebeck Aerodome)

Tours July–Aug. Mon.–Fri. 1 p.m. Daily admission: Adults $4, children 6–10 $2, Air shows: adults $9, children $4. Open-cockpit rides before and after air shows $25 per person. Free parking, picnic facilities. Show and displays are wheelchair-accessible.

This one-of-a-kind "museum in the sky" is a showcase for Cole Palen's collection of vintage aircraft dating from 1900 to 1937. Palen sank everything he had into acquiring and maintaining these rare specimens, which take to the air every weekend in season for a thrilling 1½-hour show. The daring young men in their flying machines, sporting aviator garb out of World War I, are aided in takeoffs and landings by a ground crew that apparently knows exactly how to handle planes without brakes or automatic starters, on runways of dirt that slope just enough to give the necessary boost. Before and after the show, you can take a barnstorming ride in a 1929 open-cockpit biplane piloted by a dead ringer for Eddie Rickenbacker. The planes, some of which have starred in movie and TV productions, are on display for your inspection every day during the season.

Trip D-13
Up the Hudson to Hudson

- CLERMONT STATE HISTORIC SITE
- OLANA STATE HISTORIC SITE
- AMERICAN MUSEUM OF FIRE FIGHTING

DISTANCE: About 120 miles from Columbus Circle.

FOR THE DRIVER: Take the **Saw Mill River Parkway** north to the Hawthorne Interchange and pick up the **Taconic State Parkway** north towards Albany. At the junction with **NY-199** turn left and proceed west past the junction with US-9 in Red Hook to the junction with **NY-9G.** Turn right and go north on 9G. Just over the Columbia County line (see Trip D-14), turn left on Route 6 and follow signs to **Clermont,** entrance on the right.

Continue north on 9G about 15 miles. As the Rip Van Winkle Bridge comes into view, watch for the road to **Olana,** on the right about a mile before the bridge.

Return to 9G, turn right, and go north briefly to the junction with NY-23. Bear left and continue north to Hudson on what is now 9G/23B (Columbia St.). Soon you will pick up signs to the Firemen's Home. Follow these, continuing a block beyond the point where 9G/23B turns right. The next corner is State St. Turn right past the library, then bear left on Carroll to the next corner, Short St. Turn left (this is now Harry Howard Ave.) and proceed to the top of the hill and the Firemen's Home, on the left. Drive to the parking lot at the right of the buildings. The **American Museum of Fire Fighting** is in the last building on the left.

For the return trip, go back on 9G/23B and follow 23B east towards Claverack. This joins NY-23, which continues east to the Taconic State Parkway.

CLERMONT STATE HISTORIC SITE, Box 215, Germantown, NY 12526 (518-537-4240). *Grounds open all year daily 8:30 to sunset. Mansion open May–Oct., Wed.–Sat. 10–5, Sun. 1–5, including holidays. Guided tours. Picnicking, hiking, cross-country skiing. Special events throughout year. Leashed pets only, no pets in picnic area. Wheelchair-accessible.*

Here is the ancestral estate of Robert R. Livingston, a member of the Continental Congress, one of the five framers of the Declaration

220

of Independence, and a man with a finger in many another historic pie. As first chancellor of New York State, he administered the presidential oath of office to George Washington, and as minister to France under Thomas Jefferson, he negotiated the Louisiana Purchase. In 1802 he agreed to finance Robert Fulton in the experiments that led to the first commercially practical steamboat. Fulton named the boat *Clermont* in Livingston's honor, and it stopped at the estate on its maiden voyage up the Hudson in 1807.

Originally built in 1730, the house was burned by the British in 1777 in reprisal for Livingston's staunch advocacy of American independence, and rebuilt largely through the determined efforts of Livingston's wife, Margaret Beekman Livingston. Clermont remained in the hands of the Livingston family until 1962, when the State of New York acquired it, restored it to its appearance in 1930, and opened it as a public park and memorial to one of its first families. Today you can tour the house, stroll through the lovely restored gardens, and picnic on the grounds, enjoying a glorious view of the Hudson to the Catskills rising in the west.

OLANA STATE HISTORIC SITE, Route 9G, Hudson, NY 12534 (518-828-0135). *Grounds open all year daily 8:30–sunset, free. House open Memorial Day through Oct.: Memorial Day to Labor Day Wed.–Sat. 10–4, Sun. noon–4; Labor Day–Oct. Wed.–Sun. noon–4. Admission to house by guided tour only, adults $2, children $1; tours begin every 20 minutes, maximum 12 persons per tour; advance reservations strongly recommended. Picnicking, carriage trails, ice skating, cross-country skiing. Concerts and special events throughout the season. Leashed pets only on grounds, no photographing in house. Grounds difficult for wheelchairs, but house is accessible.*

"As the good woman said of her mock-turtle soup, 'I made out of my own head.' " Thus, with what can only be called magnificent understatement, did Frederick Edwin Church describe his 31 years of work on Olana, the striking castle he designed and built on an Italian layout with strong Persian decorative elements. Church was a noted painter of the Hudson River School and studied with its founder, Thomas Cole, who first introduced him to the site where Olana now stands. Like the other members of the school, Church painted native American landscapes and Hudson River scenes, but he had a preference for foreign and exotic subjects—a preference aptly reflected in Olana, in contrast to the homey, plain, and very American-looking residence of Thomas Cole across the river in Catskill (Trip C-20).

The main portion of Olana was built between 1870 and 1876, with some additions in the 1880s. As Church constantly reworked his paintings, so he constantly fashioned and refashioned Olana, proclaiming it "finished" only in 1891, when he turned it over to his son. The interior, meticulously restored just as Church planned it, is a marvel of intricately patterned tiles, gilded arches, vibrant colors, exquisite furnishings from Persia, Kashmir, and other Near Eastern lands. Church's work—some of which adorns Olana's walls, along with two paintings by Thomas Cole—is noted for its delicate rendering of light, and this same sensitivity is displayed in the design and placement of the windows, each framing a scenic view, each capturing a different quality of light.

Church lavished equal attention on his 250 acres of property, which was farmland when he purchased it in the 1860s. Today it is a beautiful woodland, each of the thousands of trees selected by Church and planted with a painterly eye for composition. He even created the beautifully contoured lake at the foot of the hill to "balance" the view of the Hudson against the Catskills. Indeed, driving through Olana's grounds is like driving through one of Church's paintings—a romantic landscape conceived in the artist's mind's eye and executed with utmost care on the canvas of the Hudson River Valley.

AMERICAN MUSEUM OF FIRE FIGHTING, 117 Harry Howard Ave., Hudson, NY 12534 (518-828-7695). *Open Apr. through Oct. Tues.–Sun. 9–4:30. Free. Wheelchair-accessible.*

This museum, operated by the Firemen's Association of the State of New York, contains one of the oldest and largest collections of firefighting equipment and memorabilia in the country. There are thousands of items here, from firehats, badges, banners, and speaking trumpets to paintings, prints, and lithographs. And, of course, the engines, scores of them, stalwart antiques spanning two centuries of fire fighting, from the horse-drawn days through the steam era to the early motorized trucks of the 1920s. The oldest specimen is the Newsham engine, built in England in 1725, imported to New York in 1731, and in continuous service for the next 154 years. Fittingly, the museum is located in the Firemen's Home, close to some of the men who used the equipment to battle the flames of yesteryear.

Trip D-14
Bound for the Berkshires

- ## UPPER COLUMBIA COUNTY

DISTANCE: about 145 miles from Columbus Circle to the farthest point.

FOR THE DRIVER: Since this trip is planned mainly for the enjoyment of the drive itself, the directions are incorporated with the brief descriptions of the principal attractions along the route, given below.

The last trip crossed from Dutchess County into Columbia County, a lovely area between the Catskills and the Berkshires. It's a bit far for a daytrip from New York City, but you'll have time to take a spin through the countryside north of Hudson and then east to the Massachusetts line. For further information, contact Columbia County Tourism, 401 State St., Hudson, NY 12534 (518-828-3375 or 800-777-9247); for more on the many scenic, cultural, and recreational attractions of the popular Berkshires region, which is mainly in Massachusetts but includes parts of eastern Columbia County, contact the Berkshire Visitors Bureau, Berkshire Common, Pittsfield, MA 01201 (413-443-9186).

Begin your trip at Kinderhook, birthplace of Martin Van Buren, the eight president of the United States, and the first president to be born an American citizen. You can easily reach Kinderhook by continuing north on **US-9** from Hudson, last stop on Trip D-13 (note also that the Rip Van Winkle Bridge runs from Hudson across the river to Catskill and some of the sites on Trip C-20). If you're coming directly from the city, take the **Saw Mill River Parkway** north to the Hawthorne Interchange and pick up the **Taconic State Parkway** north to **NY-23,** about 6 miles past the exit for **Lake Taghkanic State Park** (518-851-3631), with year-round fishing and facilities for a wide range of winter and summer sports. Turn left on 23 and go west to Hudson, where you'll pick up **US-9** north for about 11 miles to Kinderhook. On the left as you come into town is the **James Vanderpoel House** (518-758-9265), an 1819 building in the Federal style, maintained by the Columbia County Historical Society as a museum. In addition to a fine collection of Duncan Phyfe and Chippendale furniture, the museum has materials on local history and documents relating to Martin Van Buren. It's a good place to get directions for a walking tour of **Kinderhook,** a town frequented by Washington Irving, his fictional creation Ichabod Crane, and the pre-treasonous Benedict Arnold, among others. The society also operates the **Luykas Van Alen House** (518-758-9265), a little south of town on NY-9H. Built in 1737, it has been restored as a museum of 18th-century Dutch culture and Hudson Valley art. *(Both sites are usually open Memorial Day to Labor Day, Wed.–Sat. and Mon. 11–5, Sun. 1–5.)*

By the way, anyone with a particular interest in the Dutch influence on the development of the Hudson Valley will also enjoy the **Bronck House Museum** (518-731-8862), almost directly across the river from Kinderhook, about 10 miles north of Catskill (Trip C-20) off US-9W, accessible via the Rip Van Winkle Bridge. This complex of stone houses and farm buildings was begun in 1663 by Pieter Bronck, whose father, a Dane in the employ of the Dutch West India Company, settled in and gave the family name to the Bronx. The buildings, all carefully researched and restored by the Green County Historical Society, include two vintage Hudson Valley Dutch stone houses; several Dutch barns, among them the unique 13-sided Freedom Barn, with one wall for each of the 13 original states; and a "stepmother's house," built in the 1820s in deference to the sensibilities of the Bronck daughters, who refused to live under the same roof with their father's second wife. There are many interesting artifacts and period tools on display here, as well as a fine collection of paintings by such noted American artists as Thomas Cole, Ammi Phillips, Ezra Ames, and John Frederick Rensett. *(Usually open May–Sept., Tues.–Sat. 10–5, Sun. 2–6.)*

Back on the east side of the Hudson, a little south of the Van Alen House on **NY-9H,** is the **Martin Van Buren National Historic Site** (518-758—9689). Van Buren bought this 1797 estate, known as Lindenwald, in 1839 during his term as president. The house can be seen on tours, and the gardens are lovely. *(Open mid-Apr. through Oct., daily 9–4:30; Nov. Wed.–Sun.)*

From Lindenwald, head back on 9H past the junction with 9 to **Route 28B.** Turn right here and go east through Valatie and Chatham Center, continuing on what is now Route 13. A mile or so past Chatham Center, on the left just below the Berkshire spur of the New York Thruway, is the **Shaker Museum** (518-794-9100) at Old Chatham. Here, spread through eight buildings, is an extensive collection of artifacts, crafts, tools, documents, and books relating to the American settlements of the United Society of Believers in Christ's Second Appearing, popularly known as Shakers because of the trembling ecstatic displays that accompanied their religious worship. An offshoot of the English Quakers, the Shakers believed that the Deity was both male and female, and that their leader, Mother Ann Lee (1736–1784), was the incarnation of the female divine principle, as Jesus had been the incarnation of the male. Persecuted in England, Mother Ann and eight followers emigrated to America in 1774 and settled at Watervleit, New York, near Albany. By 1850, when the movement reached its height, there were some 6,000 Shakers living in 18 communities, mostly in the Northeast. They practiced equality of the sexes, open confession of sins, communal ownership of property, pacifism, and celibacy, perpetuating themselves by conversion and the adoption of orphans. They were also an ingenious people, noted for their many practical inventions and the beautiful simplicity of their furniture designs. Today, though the Shaker movement has all but died out, the culture, craftsmanship, and ideals of these gentle people continue to fascinate. *(Open May–Oct. daily 10–5).*

The Shaker Museum provides an excellent introduction to Shaker history. Now deepen your acquaintance by driving northeast from Old Chatham on **Route 13** past the New York Thruway a few miles to the junction with US-20 at Brainard. Here turn right and go east through New Lebanon, site of the first permanent Shaker community (1787), continuing across the Massachusetts line to the **Hancock Shaker Village** (413-443-0188), at the junction of US-20 and MA-41. This settlement, established in 1790, remained an active Shaker community until 1960 and was known to its inhabitants as the City of Peace. Today you can tour 20 original buildings and watch craftspeople preserving the Shaker traditions of fine workmanship. The village also sponsors a busy program of special events, and some of the crafts and furniture are for sale in the restored 1910 horse barn. *(Open Memorial Day to Oct., daily 9:30–5; Apr., May, Nov. daily 10–3. Adults $7, children 6–12 $3).*

The drive to the Hancock Shaker Village takes you along the southern edge of **Pittsfield State Forest** (413-442-8992), a 10,000-acre tract that has camping and recreational facilities and is especially beautiful during azalea time, usually late May to mid-June. At the village, you are only five miles west of **Pittsfield,** with its many museums, ski areas, and historic buildings, including **Arrowhead** (413-442-1793), the house where Herman Melville lived while writing *Moby Dick.* About seven miles south of Pittsfield is **Tanglewood** (413-637-1940), former home of Nathaniel Hawthorne, present home of the famed Berkshire Music Festival, held annually in summer.

These are only a few of the attractions of the Berkshire region of Massachusetts. You can't begin to explore them all in the space of a day, but now you'll have your bearings when you come back with more time at your disposal.

From Pittsfield, the quickest route home is to go south on **US-7** and then **US-20** to Lee and pick up **I-90,** Massachusetts Turnpike west towards Albany. This becomes the **New York Thruway,** which takes you to the **Taconic State Parkway** south and back to New York City.

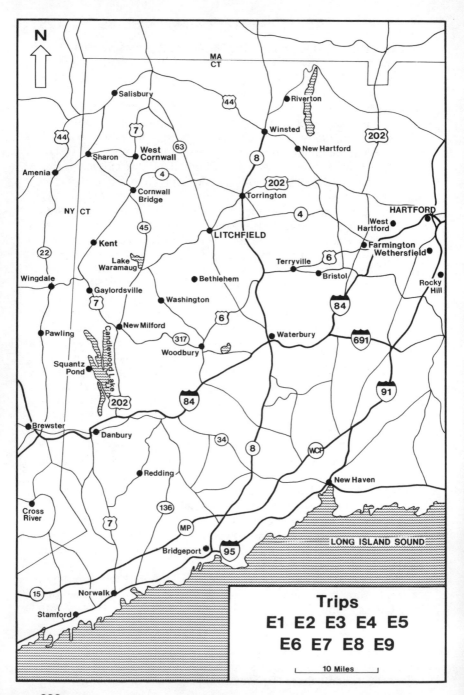

N

MA
CT

Salisbury

44

7

63

Amenia

44

Sharon

West
Cornwall

4

NY CT

Cornwall
Bridge

45

Kent

22

Lake
Waramaug

Wingdale

Gaylordsville

7

Washington

New Milford

317

Pawling

Squantz
Pond

Woodbury

202

Brewster

Danbury

34

Cross
River

Redding

7

136

15

Norwalk

Stamford

MP

Bridgeport

95

Riverton

Winsted

202

New Hartford

8

Torrington

202

4

LITCHFIELD

HARTFORD

West
Hartford

Farmington
Wethersfield

Terryville

6

Bristol

84

Rocky
Hill

Bethlehem

6

Waterbury

691

91

8

WCH

New Haven

LONG ISLAND SOUND

Trips
E1 E2 E3 E4 E5
E6 E7 E8 E9

10 Miles

Area E

Bull's Bridge near Kent, Connecticut
(Photo courtesy of Litchfield Hills Travel Council)

INTO MIDDLE AND UPPER CONNECTICUT

The next trips take you across the New York line into Connecticut, mainly the middle and upper regions of the western part of the state. Most of these trips are full-day extensions covering territory beyond an average short drive from New York City. However, fast roads allow you to reach a wide variety of attractions easily.

The excursions begin on the New York side of the line and move into Connecticut. For hundreds of unspoiled Colonial towns filled with pre-Revolutionary homes, for entire areas that have been designated historic districts, for the quietly beautiful New England countryside, these drives are unexcelled.

Trip E-1
Local Heroes

- SOUTHEAST MUSEUM
- SQUANTZ POND STATE PARK

DISTANCE: About 75 miles from Columbus Circle to the farthest point.

FOR THE DRIVER: Take **I-684** north to Brewster. Just after the exit for I-84 to Danbury, take the Brewster exit for **US-6** west and US-202/NY-22 south. After they branch, remain on 6 (Main St.) briefly into tiny downtown Brewster, where it's hard to miss the **Southeast Museum.**

Go back as you came to the junction of 6, 202, and 22. Bear left and go north on 22 briefly to **Route 54,** Milltown Rd. Turn right and follow this across the New York State line to the junction with **CT-39,** Bull Pond Rd. Turn left and proceed north and east on 39 about 8 miles to **Squantz Pond State Park.**

SOUTHEAST MUSEUM, Main St., Brewster, NY 10509 (914-279-7500). *Open Mar. to Dec., Tues.–Thurs., noon–4; Sat.–Sun. 2–4. Free. Special events throughout the season. Not wheelchair-accessible.*

This fine regional history museum was founded in 1963 when the tiny town of Southeast was observing its tricentennial. Preparing for the celebration, the townsfolk began rifling through their attics and basements in quest of historic artifacts and were so impressed with the results that they decided to open a museum in the Old Town Hall of Southeast (1896).

There are four permanent exhibits on display here: the David McLane railroad exhibit on the history of the Harlem Line (now Metro-North Railroad), which runs between New York City and Brewster; an exhibit on condensed milk, invented in 1863 by Gail Borden, who opened a factory that operated here for 50 years; a collection of circus memorabilia from the days when the Brewster area was home base for various local traveling menageries (see Historic Elephant Hotel and Circus Museum, Trip D-7); and the Trainer collection of rare minerals from the Tilly Foster iron mine, active through most of the 19th century, until it collapsed in 1897. In addition, the museum mounts several exhibits a year on changing themes, drawing on its extensive collection of antique farm implements, old quilts, period clothing, and assorted Americana reflecting 19th-century material culture.

SQUANTZ POND STATE PARK, Route 39, R.F.D. 3, New Fairfield, CT 06810 (203-797-4165). *Open all year daily 8–sunset. Use fee Memorial Day to Labor Day $2 per car weekdays, $4 weekends and holidays; otherwise free. Picnicking, hiking trails, swimming, scuba diving, fishing, canoe rentals, ice skating, food concession. No pets. Wheelchair-accessible facilities.*

Here's a scenic 172-acre park in a picturesque region of rural Connecticut. It's a fine place for picnicking or nature photography after an afternoon of absorbing the multifarious facts of local history. The drive to Squantz Pond, partially along the shores of **Candlewood Lake** (203-797-4632), is especially pretty. Connecticut's largest lake, Candlewood is 14 miles long with more than 60 miles of shoreline, and offers further opportunities for swimming, fishing, boating, and picnicking.

Trip E-2
To the Connecticut Berkshires

- MUSEUM OF NATURAL HISTORY
- WEBATUCK CRAFT VILLAGE
- MACEDONIA BROOK STATE PARK
- SLOANE-STANLEY MUSEUM
- KENT FALLS STATE PARK
- NORTHEAST AUDUBON SOCIETY CENTER
- HOUSATONIC MEADOWS STATE PARK
- LAKE WARAMAUG STATE PARK

DISTANCE: About 100 miles from Columbus Circle to the farthest point.

FOR THE DRIVER: Take **I-684** north to Brewster. Here pick up **NY-22** and continue north about 11 miles towards Pawling. At the junction with NY-55, continue north on 22/55 merged, shortly coming to Quaker Hill Rd. Turn right here at the stoplight and sign for the **Museum of Natural History,** Akin Free Library.

Return to 22/55, turn right, and continue north 5 or 6 miles. At Wingdale, just beyond the State Hospital, 55 goes on ahead and 22 forks left. *Here you have several choices.* If it's blueberry season (usually mid-July into August), you can follow 22 to the blinking light, turn left at the sign to Wingdale, and drive about 4 miles up a winding road to **Blueberry Park** (914-782-8664), where you can pluck to your heart's content. You pay by the amount you pick—at lot less than at city markets, and freshness is guaranteed. Best to bring your own containers and wear comfortable shoes. If you continue north on 22 through the blinking light for about 15 miles, you can have a different kind of experience with the fruits of the vine at **Cascade Mountain Vineyards** (914-373-9021) on Flint Hill Rd. in Amenia, New York. The drive up to this 110-acre winery is lovely, and when you get there you can take a free tour, taste some of the prize-winning wines, and savor other local delicacies. *(Open year round, daily 10–6).* Note that Amenia is only a few miles from Sharon, Connecticut; if you go to the vineyards, you can drive over 'to Sharon and continue this trip from there (see directions below).

From the junction of 22 and 55 at Wingdale, proceed east on 55 towards Connecticut, following signs to the **Webatuck Craft Village.**

Continue east on 55 across the Connecticut line to the junction with **US-7** in the quaint village of Gaylordsville. For the next stops in this trip, you turn left here and go north on 7, *but* you may also want to drive south about 7 miles to New Milford, passing **Voltaire's** (203-354- 4200), with an exceptional selection of craft items for sale and changing fine arts exhibits in the gallery; at the junction with **US-202,** turn left and go east briefly to New Milford Green, surrounded by antique shops, restaurants, boutiques, and historic buildings, including the **New Milford Historical Society Museum** (203-354-3069), with fine collections of portraits, miniatures, furniture, china, antique clothing, dolls, and toys.

From the junction of 55 and 7 in Gaylordsville, go north on 7 towards Kent, passing Bull's Bridge Rd., where a left turn will take you across the Housatonic on **Bull's Bridge,** one of two covered bridges in Connecticut still open to automobile traffic (you'll come to the other one soon). Over 200 years old, it's a favorite subject for photographers.

Continue north on 7 about 4 miles to the junction with **CT-341** in Kent. Here turn left and proceed briefly to **Macedonia Brook State Park,** entrance on the right. Return to 7 and Kent Center, where there are a number of fine shops and galleries, including the **Paris-New York-Kent Gallery** (203-927-3357), praised by the *New York Times* as a "top-quality private art gallery," and the **House of Books** (203-927-4104), specializing in books by local authors and limited-edition prints by Eric Sloane and David Armstrong. The **Sloane-Stanley Museum** is about 2 miles north of Kent Center on US-7, and another 3 or 4 miles north of that, on the right, is **Kent Falls State Park.**

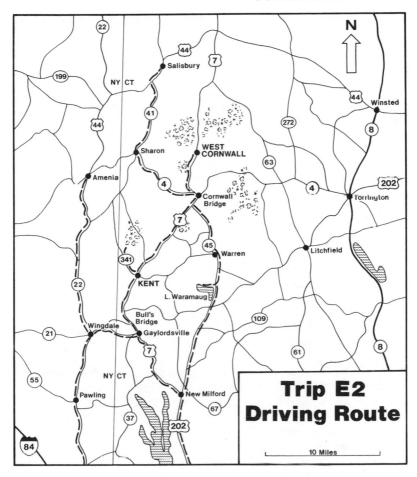

Trip E2
Driving Route

10 Miles

From Kent Falls, continue north on 7 for several miles to Cornwall Bridge and the junction with **CT-4,** passing **Cornwall Bridge Pottery** (203-672-6545), where you can watch pots fired in a 35-foot-long wood-burning kiln and inspect the many beautiful items in the showroom. *At the junction with 4, you again have several choices.* A left turn onto 4 takes you to the **Northeast Audubon Center** in Sharon, another quintessential New England village with many lovely 19th-century homes and the inevitable green and Congregational church. A little farther on 4, past the distinctive Hotchkiss Clock Tower, is the junction with **CT-343,** where you can turn left and go west briefly to the **Sharon Playhouse** (203-364-5909), a professional summer theater and art gallery. Note that in Sharon you are about 10 miles south of Salisbury via CT-41/US-44. Here is yet another lovely old town, in a particularly scenic area, and if you're taking this drive in the fall, you may catch the famed Salisbury Antiques Fair, one of the oldest such fairs in Connecticut.

If you've gone to Sharon, return on CT-4 to Cornwall Bridge and the junction with US-7. Turn left and go north on 7 into **Housatonic Meadows State Park.** A little beyond the north end of the park is the postcard-pretty village of West Cornwall, where you'll find the second covered bridge over the Housatonic. This one, designed by covered-bridge maven Ithiel Town, has been in continuous use since 1837. Also here, in the enter of West Cornwall, is the **Cornwall Bridge Pottery Store** (203-672-6545), an outlet for the work done at Cornwall Bridge Pottery (see above) as well as for fine ceramics, glassware, fabrics, and paintings by other craftspeople and artists.

From West Cornwall, go back down 7 through Cornwall Bridge and continue south briefly to the junction with **CT-45.** Turn left and go south on 45 through Warren to Lake Waramaug Rd., just before New Preston. Turn right here to **Lake Waramaug State Park.**

For the quickest route back to New York City, continue south briefly on 45 to the junction with US-202, then south on US-202 through New Milford, where 202 merges with US-7, to Danbury. Here take **I-84** west into New York and pick up **I-684** south.

On this trip you can take a long ride all the way to the northwest corner of Connecticut, singling out some of the highlights along the route. If you're just out for a scenic drive, you can cover the distance in a day, but if you're interested in spending more time at the various stops, you might want to divide this into two or more trips, and perhaps include some of the attractions and side trips mentioned in "For the Driver," above. For further information about western Connecticut, contact the Litchfield Hills Travel Council, P.O. Box 1776, Marbledale, CT 06777 (203-868-2214). They'll be happy to send you a variety of thorough, informative, lively brochures and a calendar of events for the very eventful region.

MUSEUM OF NATURAL HISTORY, Akin Free Library, Quaker Hill, Pawling, NY 12564 (914-855-5099). *Museum open mid-May to mid-Oct. Thurs.–Sun. 2–4, closed holidays. Library open all year, mid-May to mid-Oct. Thurs.–Sun. 2–4, other times Sat.–Sun. 2–4. Museum exhibits are wheelchair-accessible.*

Mrs. Olive Gunnison, longtime resident of Quaker Hill, spent the better part of a lifetime acquiring specimens of rocks, minerals, insects, and birds from all over the world. This museum houses her personal collection, informatively displayed in four large rooms. There is also a room devoted to the history of Quaker Hill, which takes its name from the band of Quakers who settled here in the early 1700s. Today their meetinghouse still stands, surrounded by picturesque countryside and beautiful estates that have attracted many famous residents over the years, including Lowell Thomas, Edward R. Murrow, and Thomas E. Dewey. The Akin Free Library has extensive materials on local history and genealogy.

WEBATUCK CRAFT VILLAGE, Webatuck Rd., Wingdale, NY 12594 (914-832-6464). *Open daily 10–4. Free admission. Picnicking, fishing, special exhibits. Many steps, uneven paths; difficult for wheelchairs.*

Here's a good place for an afternoon of shopping in a relaxed, scenic setting. Spread over the grounds of Hunt Country Furniture, the Webatuck Craft Village has a silversmith, a potter, a stained-glass artisan, and several other shops featuring crafts and gift items. The furniture showroom, a converted 1747 inn with the original flooring and chestnut beams, displays a variety of hand-crafted pine, oak, and cherry furniture in original designs.

MACEDONIA BROOK STATE PARK, Kent, CT 06757 (203-927-3238). *Open all year daily 8–sunset. Free. Picnicking, hiking trails, playing field, fishing, camping (fee), cross-country skiing. Leashed pets only, in picnic areas only. Wheelchair-accessible facilities.*

A gift to the state from the White Memorial Foundation in Litchfield (Trip E-5), these 2,300 acres contain excellent trout streams, bubbling natural springs, and two peaks affording superb views of the Catskills and the Taconic Mountains from an elevation of about 1,400 feet.

SLOANE-STANLEY MUSEUM, Kent, CT 06757 (203-927-3849 or 566-3005). *Open mid-May through Oct. Wed.–Sun. 10–4. Adults $3, seniors $1.50, children 6–17 $1.50. Partially manageable for wheelchairs.*

This extensive collection of early American farm implements, tools, and paintings, housed in a New England barn, was brought together by the late Eric Sloane, author and artist, on land donated by the Stanley tool manufacturing company of New Britain. Captions accompany the tools, which are displayed in such a way as to demonstrate how they were used. In the early 18th century, Kent was a center of the iron ore industry, and the ruins of the old Kent blast furnace (1826–1892) are here on the museum grounds, along with an early New England log cabin replica built by Eric Sloane.

KENT FALLS STATE PARK, Kent, CT 06757 (203-927-3238). *Open all year daily 8–sunset. Free. Picnicking, hiking trails, playing field, fishing. Leashed pets only, in picnic areas only. Partially wheelchair-accessible.*

Here Connecticut's loveliest waterfall cascades down several levels to a brook. A wide, winding path leads to the head of the falls, which are particularly beautiful in spring when the water is high and in fall when the leaves turn. All around are pine forests with inviting trails for hiking.

NORTHEAST AUDUBON CENTER, Route 4, Sharon, CT 06069 (203-364-0520). *Trails open all year daily dawn–dusk. Building open all year daily, Mon.–Sat. 9–5, Sun. 1–5; closed major holidays. Museum admission $2 adults, $1 children, free to Audubon Society members. Self-guided tour, picnic tables, gift shop, bookstore. No pets. Building not wheelchair-accessible; easy trail for young and elderly may be manageable for some wheelchairs.*

This 684-acre sanctuary of the National Audubon Society is a good place for birdwatching, observation of the spring and fall migrations, or quiet walks through meadows and forests dotted with lakes, ponds, and brooks. The museum and interpretive center has both live and static natural history exhibits, a Children's Discovery Room, and the Hal Borland Seasonal Room.

HOUSATONIC MEADOWS STATE PARK, Sharon, CT 06069 (203-927-3238). *Open all year daily 8–sunset. Picnicking, hiking trails, fishing, boating, camping (fees), cross-country skiing. Free. Leashed pets only, in picnic areas only. Partially wheelchair-accessible.*

This 452-acre park along the rushing Housatonic River is noted for a 2-mile stretch of water reserved for fly fishing. Non-anglers will enjoy the beautiful woods and fine hiking trails.

LAKE WARAMAUG STATE PARK, Kent, CT, 06757 (203-868-0223). *Open all year daily 8–sunset. Use fee Memorial Day to Labor Day $1 per car weekdays, $2 weekends and holidays; otherwise free. Picnicking, hiking trails, playing field, swimming, scuba diving, fishing, camping (fees), ice skating, cross-country skiing, food concession. Leashed pets only, in picnic areas only. Partially wheelchair-accessible.*

Waramaug, an Indian word meaning "good fishing place," is an apt name for Connecticut's third-largest natural lake, and one of its most beautiful. This 95-acre park located on its northwest shore hosts the annual Women's National Rowing Regatta in May.

Inside the Sloane-Stanley Museum
(Photo courtesy of Litchfield Hills Travel Council)

Trip E-3
On General Putnam's Trail

- ● DANBURY SCOTT-FANTON MUSEUM
- ● PUTNAM MEMORIAL STATE PARK

DISTANCE: About 65 miles from Columbus Circle.

FOR THE DRIVER: Take **I-684** north to Brewster. Here pick up **I-84** east to Danbury. Get off at Exit 5, turn right at the stoplight onto Main St., and proceed down Main about two miles to the **Scott-Fanton Museum,** on the left just past St. Peter's Church. Note that Danbury is at the southern tip of Candlewood Lake, about 8 miles south of Squantz Pond State Park (Trip E-1), and about the same distance north of Ridgefield (Trip F-5).

Continue on Main St. to the end, passing Rogers Park, where the Ives House is located. Turn left here at the stoplight onto South St. Proceed a few miles on South St. (which becomes CT-53) to the junction with **CT-302.** Bear left and go through Bethel to the junction with **CT-58.** Turn right and go south about two miles to **Putnam Memorial State Park.**

There are a number of other historical and cultural sties in the Danbury-Bethel area, as well as an array of municipal parks, lakes, and golf courses. For further information, contact the Housatonic Valley Tourism Commission, Box 406, Danbury, CT 06810 (203-743-0546).

DANBURY SCOTT-FANTON MUSEUM, 43 Main St., Danbury CT 06810 (203-743-5200). *Open all year Wed.–Sun. 2–5; closed major holidays. Donations accepted. Historic buildings not wheelchair-accessible; Huntington Hall has a few steps, but exhibits are on one level.*

An important supply depot for the Continental Army during the American Revolution, Danbury was looted and burned by British and Hessian forces in 1777. In the early 1970s, history sleuths were surprised to find evidence that the Scott-Fanton House, presumed to have been spared the torch because of Tory ownership, was actually built around 1785 by John Rider, a carpenter and ardent patriot. Restored to its appearance around the time of Rider's death in 1833, the house contains authentic furnishings, a large collection of carpenter's and joiner's tools, and a costume display.

The Danbury Historical Society also owns the house in Rogers Park where Charles Ives was born in 1874. Ives, considered the father of modern American music, won a Pulitzer Prize for his Third Symphony in 1947. His parlor was moved to the Scott-Fanton House, where you can see the composer's piano along with other memorabilia.

Behind the Scott-Fanton House is the Dodd Shop, with exhibits showing the development of the hat industry in Danbury from the humble three-a-day output of Zadoc Benedict's 1790 factory to the booming mechanized production that made it the "Hat Capital of the World" from the early 20th century into the 1950s. Also behind the house is Huntington Hall, a modern building with changing exhibits and a research library.

PUTNAM MEMORIAL STATE PARK, Redding, CT 06875 (203-938-2285). *Grounds open all year daily 8–sunset; museum open mid-Apr. to mid-Sept. daily 8–4, mid-Sept. to mid-Oct. Sat.–Sun. 8–4. Free. Picnicking, playing field, hiking and nature trails, fishing, ice skating. Leashed pets only, in picnic areas only. Museum and picnic area wheeelchair-accessible.*

In the winter of 1778–79, several thousand Continental troops under the command of General Israel Putnam wintered near Danbury on this site, which is now preserved as a Revolutionary War memorial. Some of the foundations and chimneys of the original soldier cabins are still visible, and the museum houses other relics of the encampment. An oak tree that sprouted from an acorn of the famous Charter Oak of Hartford (Trip E-9) flourishes in the park, and there's a scenic picnic and play area around a small lake.

Trip E-4
From Glebe to Crèche to Wigwam

- GLEBE HOUSE
- FLANDERS NATURE CENTER
- ABBEY OF REGINA LAUDIS
- GUNN HISTORICAL MUSEUM
- AMERICAN INDIAN ARCHAEOLOGICAL INSTITUTE

DISTANCE: About 90 miles from Columbus Circle to the farthest point.

FOR THE DRIVER: Take **I-684** north to Brewster. Here pick up **I-84** east to Danbury. Continue past Danbury to Exit 15 at Southbury and take **US-6** east (actually going north at this point) about 4 miles to Woodbury. Watch for a sign for the Woodbury Historic District and Pilgrim's Mall, on the left. Just after the mall parking lot, take an immediate left on Hollow Rd. to **Glebe House.** This section of US-6 (Main St. in Woodbury), often referred to as Antique Avenue, is lined with what is possibly the densest concentration of antique shops in Connecticut.

 Your route to Glebe House, US-6 between Southbury and Woodbury, is a lovely stretch of road passing many fine old houses. During the Revolutionary War it was a major thoroughfare for the Continental Army, and General Rochambeau marched his troops along it in 1781 to join General Washington for the Yorktown campaign, the closing battle of the war. But there's more here than historic reverberations. Shortly after leaving I-84, just beyond Southbury Plaza, a left turn off US-6 takes you to the **Heritage Village Shoppes,** a pleasant shopping area with specialty stores, restaurants, and art galleries. Farther along

6, at the junction with CT-64, a right turn takes you to **Lake Quassa-paug** ("clear water") in Middlebury, open to the public for swimming and boating. On its shores is **Quassy Amusement Park** (203-758-2913 or 800-FOR-PARK), an old-fashioned family attraction with over 30 rides, games, arcade, swimming, and special events.

From Glebe House, continue east on US-6 about a mile to Flanders Rd., just outside Woodbury Center. Turn left here and go about 3 miles to Church Hill Rd., a dirt road leading to the office of **Flanders Nature Center.**

Continue on Flanders Rd. a mile or so to the **Abbey of Regina Laudis.**

From the abbey, continue on Flanders Rd. about 1½ miles to **CT-61,** turn left on 61, and continue north through Bethlehem to the junction with **CT-109** in Morris. Turn left on 109 towards Washington Depot. At the junction with **CT-47,** turn left and continue south on 47 after 109 branches right, proceeding to Washington Green and the **Gunn Historical Museum.**

Continue south on 47 briefly to the junction with **CT-199.** Turn right and go 1¼ miles to a sign for the **American Indian Archaeological Institute.**

For the return trip, go back on 199 to the junction with 47 and take 47 north a few miles to the junction with **US-202** A right turn here takes you to **Mount Tom State Park** (203-868-0223), with swimming, boating, picnicking, and other recreational facilities. A left turn takes you south via US-202 and US-7 to I-84 west to I-684 south and back to New York, City.

GLEBE HOUSE, Hollow Rd., Woodbury, CT 06798 (203-263-2855). *Open Apr.–Nov., Wed.–Sun., 1–4; rest of year by appointment. Suggested donation $2 adults, 50¢ children. Will accommodate wheelchairs.*

This picturesque building, some of it dating from 1690, was part of the glebe (minister's farm) of Woodbury's first Episcopal priest, John Rutgers Marshall, who took up residence here in 1771. Marshall, like many other Anglicans, was a Tory sympathizer who vigorously opposed American independence and wrote pamphlets attacking the ideas of Thomas Paine. It is sometimes said that Marshall built a secret tunnel in Glebe House to escape in case of trouble, but researchers now believe that this "tunnel," really little more than a basement crawl space, predates Marshall's occupancy. In 1783, when the cause of American independence was won, a group of American clergymen met at Glebe House and elected Samuel Seabury first American bishop of the Protestant Episcopal Church.

Like many of the homes in Woodbury's historical district, Glebe House was built by a local housemaker called Herd (who lived in the nearby red house on Hollow Road, now maintained by the Old Wood-bury Historical Society). The gambrel roof and other additions to the central room dates from the 1730s or 1740s. Today, the house has period furnishings, documents relating to the development of the Episcopal Church in America, and charming Colonial gardens. Costumed guides occasionally give tours and re-create the life of the household during Colonial times.

FLANDERS NATURE CENTER, Flanders Rd., Woodbury, CT 06798 (203-263-3711). *Trails open all year daily dawn–dusk; trailside center Sat. 9–5.; office Mon.–Fri. 9–5. Free. No horses on trails, no pets on Church Hill Rd. trail. Difficult for wheelchairs.*

This 1,000-acre wildlife sanctuary and outdoor education laboratory offers a choice of two hiking trails through varied terrain and habitats. The wildflower trail is delightful in spring, and the marsh walk is particularly popular with birdwatchers. There are some good exhibits at the trailside environmental center, along with a small natural history museum.

ABBEY OF REGINA LAUDIS, Bethlehem, CT 06751 (203-266-7727). *Grounds open all year daily; art shop (203-266-7637) open all year Tues.–Sun. 11–noon and 1:30–4; crèche on display late Apr. to mid-Jan. daily 11–4. Donations accepted. Annual Abbey Fair in early Aug. Difficult for wheelchairs.*

The main attraction of this Benedictine abbey in Bethlehem is, appropriately enough, a nativity scene crafted by artists of 18th-century Naples. The Neapolitan crèche is displayed in an antique barn perhaps not so unlike that faraway stable where the Christ child was born. Also here is the Little Art Shop of the Abbey of Regina Laudis, selling religious articles, wool from the abbey sheep, and many items handcrafted by the Benedictine nuns. Visitors are welcome to attend mass or vespers at the chapel.

GUNN HISTORICAL MUSEUM, Wykeham Rd., Washington, CT 06793 (203-868-7756). *Open Apr.–Dec.; Thurs., Fri., Sat.; noon–4. Donation. Difficult for wheelchairs.*

Here's an interesting place, a 1781 house crammed with artifacts reflecting life in Washington in the 18th and 19th centuries—furniture, paintings, toys, dolls and dollhouses, gowns, thimbles, needlework, spinning wheels, tools, kitchenware, china, and more. In addition, there are exhibits on the history of Washington since Colonial times.

AMERICAN INDIAN ARCHAEOLOGICAL INSTITUTE, Curtis Rd., Washington CT 06793 (203-868-0518). *Open all year daily, Mon.–Sat.*

10–5, Sun. noon–5, closed New Year's, Easter, Thanksgiving, Christmas. Adults $3, children 6–16 $2, under 6 free. Tours by appointment, gift shop, craft workshops, weekend film series. Wheelchair access into building, all exhibits on one level.

The American Indian Archaeological Institute is a serious research and educational facility devoted to the history of America's original inhabitants and the study of early cultures. The exhibits include a mastodon skeleton 12,000 years old, 10,000-year-old Paleo-Indian artifacts from the oldest known Indian campsite in Connecticut, a simulated dig site, and a reconstructed Indian village with wigwams and a longhouse, the distinctive bark-covered structure that symbolized the mutual responsibilities of the Five Nations of the Iroquois Confederacy. There are nature trails on the grounds, and the institute borders the **Steep Rock Reservation,** a 600-acre preserve with hiking trails and picnic facilities.

Trip E-5
A Day in Litchfield

- **LOURDES IN LITCHFIELD SHRINE**
- **LITCHFIELD HISTORICAL SOCIETY MUSEUM**
- **TAPPING REEVE HOUSE AND LAW SCHOOL**
- **WHITE MEMORIAL FOUNDATION**

DISTANCE: About 100 miles from Columbus Circle.

FOR THE DRIVER: Take **I-684** north to Brewster. Here pick up **I-84** east to Waterbury and take Exit 19 to **CT-8** north. Before continuing north towards Litchfield, you may want to take a side trip off CT-8 at Exit 33 to Waterbury's **Mattatuck Museum** (203-753-0381) at 144 West Main. Here, in addition to notable collections of decorative and fine arts and a junior museum with Indian and Colonial displays, is the fascinating Waterbury Industrial History Exhibit, which portrays the development of Connecticut's fourth-largest city as a center for the production of brass and brass objects, from buttons to shell housings. For further information on Waterbury, contact the Waterbury Convention and Visitors Commission, 83 Bank St., Waterbury, CT 06702 (203-597-9527).

The Congregational Church in Litchfield
(Photo courtesy of Litchfield Hills Travel Council)

Continue north on CT-8 about 16 miles to Exit 42. Here take **CT-118** west towards Litchfield. About a mile before Litchfield Center, just past the junction with Ct-254, is Chestnut Hill Rd., where a left turn takes you to the **Haight Vineyard and Winery** (203-567-4045) for free tours and tastings. A little beyond the turnoff for Haight is the **Lourdes in Litchfield Shrine,** just off 118 on the right.

From Lourdes, continue west briefly on 118 to the junction with US-202. Here, on the village green, is Litchfield's stately **Congregational Church** (1829), one of the most photographed churches in New England. Continue on 202 to the other side of the green and the junction with CT-63 (North St. above 202, South St. below). Here, on the corner, is the **Litchfield Historical Society Museum.** If you park near the green, you can walk to various historic sites in Litchfield. Many of these are still privately owned homes, but once a year, usually on the first or second Saturday in July, they are open to the public for tours; inquire at the Historical Society Museum.

From the museum, go down South St. past the Samuel Seymour House (now the rectory of the Episcopal church), where John Calhoun stayed as a student at **Tapping Reeve's law school** next door. Across the street is the Oliver Wolcott House, to which, during the Revolutionary War, came Washington, Lafayette, Alexander Hamilton, and the equestrian statue of George III, the latter toppled from its pedestal in Bowling Green, New York City, by the Sons of Liberty, dragged all the way to Litchfield, and melted down into bullets by the women of the town. Farther down South St. is Old South Rd., a righthand fork that takes you to the Ethan Allen House, where the famed Revolutionary War hero and leader of the Green Mountain Boys once lived.

Go back to the green. Here look for a narrow road leading behind the shops on West St. to Cobble Court, a 19th-century cobblestone courtyard ringed by quaint shops. Continue across 202 on 63, now North St., to a number of other historic spots: the home of Benjamin Tallmadge, a Revolutionary War officer, confidential agent, and aide to George Washington; Sheldon's Tavern, another of Washington's many resting places; the site of the birthplace of Henry Ward Beecher and Harriet Beecher Stowe, whose father, the influential clergyman Lyman Beecher, preached at the Congregational church from 1810 to 1826 (the house now here is not the house in which they were born); and the site of Miss Pierce's Academy, the first girls' school in the United States, founded by Sarah Pierce in 1792.

At this point you may wish to continue north on 63 about 6 miles to Goshen, an interesting town not far from some of the sites on the drive in Trip E-2. On your way into town, you pass the Goshen Fairgrounds, home of one of Connecticut's largest agricultural fairs. In the center of town is the **Goshen Historical Society Museum** (203-

491-2665), emphasizing local history and Indian artifacts. About 6 miles west of Goshen, in Mohawk Mountain State Park, is the **Mohawk Mountain Ski Area** (203-672-6464), with excellent facilities for downhill and cross-country skiing.

In Litchfield, at the junction of 63 and 202, go southwest on 202 about two miles to the **White Memorial Foundation** and Bantam Lake. From here, the quickest route back to New York City is to continue south on US-202 and US-7 back to I-84 west to I-684 south.

With its tree-lined streets, gracious homes, and traditional village green, Litchfield appears to have bypassed the 20th century as well as a good part of the 19th. It's a classic New England town of the late 18th century, rich in history, pleasing to the eye, soothing to the harried urban soul. For further information contact the Litchfield Hills Travel Council, P.O. Box 1776, Marbledale, CT 06777 (203-868-2214).

LOURDES IN LITCHFIELD SHRINE, Route 118, Litchfield, CT 06759 (203-567-1041). *Grounds open daily all year. Pilgrimage season May to mid-Oct.; call for schedule of services. Donation. Picnic area, gift shop. Pets discouraged. Grotto, near parking lot, is manageable for wheelchairs.*

At this 35-acre shrine of the Montfort Missionaries, an outdoor chapel faces a replica of the grotto at Lourdes, France, where the Virgin Mary is said to have appeared to Saint Bernadette in 1858. To one side, the Way of the Cross starts up a wooded trail that winds to the top of the hill, ending with a flight of steps up to Calvary. Visitors are welcome to attend mass, vespers, and the outdoor Sunday services held during the pilgrimage season at 3 p.m.

LITCHFIELD HISTORICAL SOCIETY MUSEUM, East & South Sts., Litchfield, CT 06759 (203-567-4501). *Open mid-Mar. to Oct., Tues.–Sat. 10–4, Sun. noon–4; Nov.–Dec., Sat. 10–4, Sun. noon–4; closed holidays, including Tues. after Mon. holiday. Adults $2, children free. Steps into building, parts of interior manageable for wheelchairs.*

Unlike many local museums whose rooms are crammed full of Americana, this one has four spacious galleries where every article on display stands out. The exhibits include early American furniture, locally produced silverware and clocks, a section on Litchfield County history, and a fine collection of paintings by Ralph Earl, among them a portrait of Mariann Wolcott, wife of one of Litchfield's most prominent citizens, Oliver Wolcott, who signed the Declaration of Independence, served in the Continental Congress, and was governor of Connecticut in 1796–97. You'll want time to browse here.

The Tapping Reeve House and Law School
(Photo courtesy of Litchfield Hills Travel Council)

TAPPING REEVE HOUSE AND LAW SCHOOL, South St., Litchfield, CT 06759 (203-567-4501). *Open mid-May to mid-Oct., Tues.–Sat. 10–4, Sun. noon–4; closed July 4th, Labor Day, Mon. holidays. Adults $2, children free. Steps into building, difficult for wheelchairs.*

America's first law school was established in this house in 1774 by Tapping Reeve, lawyer and jurist. He began by holding classes in the parlor, later moving to the school building next door. Reeve was married to Aaron Burr's sister, and Burr was one of his earliest pupils, the first in a long line of distinguished graduates, among them Vice President John C. Calhoun, Horace Mann, three Supreme Court justices, six Cabinet secretaries, and 130 members of Congress. In addition to fine antiques and period furnishings, you can inspect documents relating to the Reeve family, the school's curriculum, and the early history of the legal profession in the United States. The house, the law building, and the attractive gardens are maintained by the Litchfield Historical Society.

WHITE MEMORIAL FOUNDATION, Route 202, Litchfield, CT 06759 (203-567-0857). *Grounds open all year daily; free. Conservation Center (203-567-0015) open all year, Tues.–Sat. 9–5, Sun. 11–5; adults $1, children 50¢. Picnicking, hiking and nature trails, fishing, bridle paths, camping (fees), cross-country skiing. Leashed pets only. Conservation Center* *fully wheelchair-accessible; paved paths and picnic areas manageable for wheelchairs; Braille Trail.*

Connecticut's largest nature sanctuary, on the shores of Connecticut's largest natural lake, offers 4,000 acres of forest, marshlands, ponds, and streams sheltering a diversity of trees, flowers, ferns, mosses, birds, fish, and wildlife. Some 35 miles of trails provide ample opportunity for hiking, horseback riding, birdwatching, nature study, or relaxed contemplation. Beautiful Bantam Lake offers its shores for picnicking and its waters for fishing. The **Conservation Center** is an excellent natural history museum with an extensive library, a children's room, and displays explaining the varied habitats and ecological systems within the sanctuary.

Trip E-6
Laurel Time in
Northwest Connecticut

- **TORRINGTON TO RIVERTON**

DISTANCE: About 120 miles from Columbus Circle to the farthest point.

FOR THE DRIVER: This trip is primarily a scenic drive, so the directions are incorporated with the brief descriptions of attractions along the way, outlined below.

For several weeks in June, lavish displays of mountain laurel burst forth, fully justifying Connecticut's reputation as the Laurel State. Here you can make a loop through one of the prime laurel areas, noting the attractions along the route. The best time for viewing varies with the weather, but the blossoms are usually out by mid-June. For further information, contact the Litchfield Hills Travel Council, P.O. Box 1776, Marbledale, CT 06777 (203-868-2214).

From New York City, take **I-684** north to Brewster. Here pick up **I-84** east to Waterbury and take Exit 19 to **CT-8** north, as you did on Trip E-5. Go north on 8, passing the junction with CT-118 west to Litchfield. About 3 miles beyond this, you'll come to Torrington, birthplace of the abolitionist John Brown and a center of brass manufacture. Before getting down to brass tacks, Torrington was known as "Mast Swamp" because the local pines supplied so many masts for sailing vessels.

At the junction of CT-8 and **CT-4,** take 4 west, but first you might want to make a brief detour to the **Hotchkiss-Fyler House** (203-482-8260) on Main St. in the center of Torrington. A grand Victorian mansion built in 1900, the house features parquet floors, mahogany paneling, hand stenciling, and fine furnishings; local history exhibits are on view in the adjacent museum *(Open Mon.–Fri, 9–4, Sat. 10–3, donation)*. Also on Main St. is the **Warner Theater** (203-489-7180), a former art deco movie palace, now a National Historic Landmark offering a year-round schedule of concerts, as well as performances by the Nutmeg Ballet.

Proceeding through Torrington's business district on 4 west, you'll shortly come to Mountain Rd., where you can turn right to the **Indian Lookout Wildlife Preserve** (203-482-4372). Here, in 1947, Paul Freedman began to clear his 6 acres of mountainside to allow the laurel on it to survive and spread. He and his wife landscaped the area, mingling other plants and trees to provide a natural, balanced setting. The 6 acres became 100, and in 1958 the public was first invited to this fairyland of pink that hangs over the whole mountain like a bank of clouds. Every year since, the preserve has been open for hilly scenic walks during the laurel season. Those unable to walk may drive through late on weekday afternoons; call in advance. *(Open mid- to late June; weekdays 1:30–6, weekends 11–6; donations accepted)*.

Returning to CT-8, continue north about 9 miles to Winsted, hub of the laurel season festivities. The town is also noted for its beautiful ecclesiastical architecture. In Winsted at the junction of **US-44,** take 44 west briefly to **CT-263** west to the corner of Prospect St., where you can visit the **Solomon Rockwell House** (203-379-8433), built in 1813 by a well-to-do iron manufacturer. Sometimes called "Solomon's Temple," the house is of interest today for its Greek Revival architecture and its collection of rare portraits, clocks, chairs, glass-plate negatives, and memorabilia from the Revolutionary and Civil wars. *(Open mid-June to mid-Sept., Thurs.–Sun. 1:30–4, adults $1)*. About 4 miles farther west on 263 in Winchester Center is the quaint **Kerosene Lamp Museum** (203-379-2612), displaying a private collection of 500 hanging and standing lamps used in homes, schools, factories, and railroad cars from 1856 to 1880. *(Open daily, 9:30–4, free)*.

Returning to Winsted on US-44, continue east to New Hartford, passing the **New Hartford Historical Society Museum** (203-379-7235), located in the library in the center of town. Continue east on 44 and turn left at the junction with **CT-219,** heading north to **Lake McDonough** (203-379-3063) for some boating, fishing, picnicking, hiking, or swimming. At the junction of 219 and **CT-318,** turn left on 318,

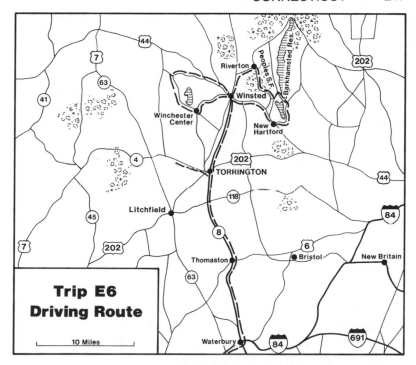

**Trip E6
Driving Route**

10 Miles

crossing the Saville Dam and Spillway of the Barkhamsted Reservoir. Here you may want to stop to take pictures of the superb panorama, a mosaic of hills, lakes, and woodlands forming a backdrop for the cascading white waters of the spillway, particularly beautiful during laurel season.

Continuing west briefly on 318, you'll come to the junction with **CT-181.** Turn left here and go west and south on 318/181 about a mile. Just before a small metal bridge, turn right on a narrow road that winds along the Farmington River through **Peoples State Forest,** a lovely area for picnicking and hiking. Across the river is the **American Legion State Forest,** with ruggedly beautiful terrain for hiking and camping.

The serpentine road through Peoples State Forest takes you north to the junction with **CT-20** in Riverton, where you take a left over the bridge to the **Hitchcock Chair Company Factory Store** (203-379-4826). Riverton was formerly named Hitchcocks-ville. Here in 1826 one Lambert Hitchcock, founder of the village, built a factory for the production of a special kind of chair decorated with fine stenciling that included his name and that of the town. The chairs became famous for quality and style, and today are considered valuable antiques. After the founder's death the factory gradually became inactive. In 1946 a new company was formed to reopen it for the reproduction of chairs and cabinet furniture. Today you can visit the gift shop and look through picture windows into the adjoining factory where maple, oak, and cherry furniture is handcrafted. Near the factory, off CT-20 on River Rd., is the **Hitchcock Museum** (203-379-4826) in the former Old Union Church (1829), housing a superb collection of antique painted and stenciled furniture. *(Open late Mar. to Nov., Wed.–Sun. noon–5, free).*

From Riverton, continue west on CT-20 about 1½ miles to the junction with CT-8, turn left, and retrace your route back to New York.

Trip E-7
Clocks, Locks, and Carousels

- LAKE COMPOUNCE FESTIVAL PARK
- NEW ENGLAND CAROUSEL MUSEUM
- AMERICAN CLOCK AND WATCH MUSEUM
- LOCK MUSEUM OF AMERICA
- STANLEY-WHITMAN HOUSE
- HILL-STEAD MUSEUM

DISTANCE: About 110 miles from Columbus Circle to the farthest point.

FOR THE DRIVER: Take **I-684** north to Brewster. Here pick up **I-84** east past Waterbury to Exit 31, turn left off the ramp, and take **CT-229** north about 3 miles to Lake Compounce Festival Park.

Continue north on 229 and turn left on **CT-72** to the New England Carousel Museum.

Take **CT-69** north to the American Clock and Watch Museum in Bristol. Note that Bristol is the site of Balloons Over Bristol (203-589-4111), a 3-day event held annually on Memorial Day weekend, with hot-air balloonists from all over the country guiding their colorful craft aloft in the skies of Farmington Valley.

Continue north a short distance to **US-6,** turn left, and follow it about 3½ miles to Terryville and the Lock Museum, at 130 Main St. (US-6).

From Terryville, go back through Bristol on 6 and continue east to the junction with **CT-10**. Turn left and go north briefly to Farmington, a picture-perfect New England town of great charm. Watch for the stoplight at Mountain Rd., turn right, and proceed to High St. and the Stanley-Whitman House. A little farther on Mountain Rd., on the left, is a small lane to Hill-Stead.

Returning, go back to CT-10 and continue to the center of Farmington and the junction with **CT-4**. Turn right and go a short way to I-84 west, which heads you back to New York.

This trip takes you from the eastern Litchfield Hills region of Connecticut into the Farmington Valley. For further information about Litchfield Hills, contact the Litchfield Hills Travel Council, P.O. Box 1776, Marbledale, CT 06777 (203-868-2214); for Farmington and points north, contact the Farmington Valley / West Hartford Visitors Bureau, 41 E. Main St., Avon, CT 06001 (203-674-1035).

LAKE COMPOUNCE FESTIVAL PARK, 822 Lake Ave., Bristol, CT 06010 (203-583-6000). *Open daily July and Aug., Tues.–Sun. in June, weekends in May and Sept. Call for current schedule of events and rates. Restrooms and many park facilities are wheelchair-accessible.*

"America's oldest amusement park. *And* its newest." So goes the slogan for the turn-of-the-century theme park at Lake Compounce that has been operating since the late 1800s. It was given a multimillion-dollar facelift and reopened in 1986 with many new rides and shows to add to the traditional fun. Kids will love the Berkshire Rapids flume ride down the mountain and the heart-stopping ups and downs of the Wildcat rollercoaster, while others will enjoy the nostalgic charms of an old miniature steam train, an antique carousel, and the "penny arcade." There are special rides for younger children, a selection of restaurants and eateries, special events in the amphitheater, and a sparkling beach at Lake Compounce. All-in-all, this is a skillful blending of time-tested attractions and modern innovations.

NEW ENGLAND CAROUSEL MUSEUM, 95 Riverside Ave., Bristol, CT 06010 (203-585-5411). *Open June–Aug. Mon.–Fri. 1–5, Sat. 10–5, Sun. noon–5; Sept.–May Tues.–Fri. 1–4, Sat. 10–5, Sun. noon–5. Adults $4, seniors $3.50, children 4–13 $2.50. Partially wheelchair-accessible.*

Here, in a preserved factory building, you can watch as master craftsmen painstakingly restore antique carved horses, chariots, menagerie figures, and other elements of those wondrous merry-go-rounds of yesteryear. Hundreds of prized examples of this nearly-lost art are on display.

AMERICAN CLOCK AND WATCH MUSEUM, 100 Maple St., Bristol, CT 06010 (203-583-6070). *Open March through Nov., daily 10–5. Adults $3, seniors $2.50, children 8–15 $1.50, under 8 free. Steps into building, some exhibits manageable for wheelchairs.*

Bristol has been renowned for its clocks since 1790, when Gideon Roberts began making and selling them locally. It is a fitting home for the American Clock and Watch Museum, where more than 3,000 timepieces, from majestic grandfather clocks to Mickey Mouse watches, are on display in clearly labeled exhibits that unfold the history of American horology. The museum consists of two buildings, the Miles Lewis House (1801), a fine specimen of the post-Revolutionary mansion house, and the Ebenezer Barnes Wing, erected in 1955 using paneling and other materials salvaged from the first permanent residence (1728) in Bristol. In a fireproof vault in the Barnes wing is the Edward Ingraham Library, a comprehensive collection of reference materials on the American clock and watch industries, open to serious researchers by appointment.

LOCK MUSEUM OF AMERICA, 130 Main St., Terryville, CT 06786 (203-589-6359). *Open May through Oct. Tues.–Sun. 1:30–4:30. Adults $2, children under 12 free. Largely wheelchair-accessible.*

If you're ever going to find the key to whatever it is you're looking for, this may be the place. It's a one-of-a-kind collection of more than 22,000 items tracing the American lock industry back to its local beginnings in the early 19th century. There are all kinds of locks and keys for every purpose, from the grim (handcuffs, leg irons) to the utilitarian (trunks, cabinets, safes) to the merely decorative.

STANLEY-WHITMAN HOUSE, 37 High St., Farmington, CT 06032 (203-677-9222). *Open May through Oct. Wed.–Sun. noon–4; Mar.–Apr. and Nov.–Dec. Sun. noon–4; closed major holidays and Jan.–Feb. Adults $3, seniors and children 6–18 $2. A few steps into building; will accommodate wheelchairs.*

This National Historic Landmark is one of the most beautifully restored Colonial houses in the country. The original portion was built around 1663 and is a good example of the "framed overhang" style popular in England and transplanted by the settlers. Many of the furnishings were made by local craftsmen, and the herb and flower gardens have been planted to reflect 17th- and 18th-century horticultural tastes.

HILL-STEAD MUSEUM, 35 Mountain Rd., Farmington, CT 06032 (203-677-4787). *Open Wed.–Sun. noon–5; closed major holidays. Adults $5, children 6–12 $2. Guided tours. Partially wheelchair-accessible; inquire.*

A gracious turn-of-the-century mansion, Hill-Stead was designed by Stanford White for industrialist Alfred A. Pope, an early and prescient connoisseur of Impressionist art. In addition to the fine furnishings, Chinese porcelains, bronzes, and assorted *objets*, Pope's outstanding collection of paintings by Monet, Degas, Manet, Whistler, and other Impressionist artists is on display here, preserved as he left it by his daughter, Theodate. An interesting figure in her own right, Theodate was one of the first women architects in the United States and counted many artists and writers among her acquaintances. During her years at Hill-Stead, her guests included Mary Cassatt, Henry James, Isadora Duncan, and John Masefield.

Trip E-8
Footprints in the Sands of Time

- • WEBB-DEANE-STEVENS MUSEUM
- • OLD ACADEMY MUSEUM
- • BUTTOLPH-WILLIAMS HOUSE
- • DINOSAUR STATE PARK

DISTANCE: About 110 miles from Columbus Circle.

FOR THE DRIVER: Take **I-684** north to Brewster. Here pick up **I-84** east past Waterbury to Exit 27 and the junction with **CT-66** east. Take 66 east about 8 miles to the junction with **I-91.**

Alternative route to I-91: Take the **Hutchinson River Parkway / Merritt Parkway / Wilbur Cross Parkway** north to Exit 67 and the junction with I-91, or take **I-95** north to Exit 47 and the junction with I-91 in New Haven.

Take I-91 north to Exit 26 in Wethersfield. After the ramp turn left on Marsh St. and follow it around to main St., passing Buttolph-Williams House at Marsh and Broad streets. At the corner of Marsh and Main St. is the First Church of Christ, and diagonally across from it (left on Main) is the **Webb-Deane-Stevens** Museum. A little farther down Main, across the street, is the **Old Academy Museum.**

Go back on Main to Marsh. Turn right to Broad St. and the **Buttolph-Williams,** on the right. Before leaving Old Wethersfield, you may want to take a walk and see the many other historic buildings—

116 pre-1840 houses within a dozen blocks, as well as a variety of later 19th-century structures—that make this town so attractive. Note also the Wethersfield is only a few miles south of Hartford (Trip E-9).

Turn right on Broad St., passing the village green, and proceed to Maple St., CT-3. Turn right on Maple briefly to the junction with **CT-99,** at the light. Turn left and go south on 99 past the junction with I-91 to West St. and a sign for the State Veterans' Hospital. Turn right and watch for Dinosaur State park, across the road from the hospital.

For the return trip, continue on West St. briefly to the junction with I-91. Take 91 south to CT-66 and go back the way you came, *or* continue south on 91 to the Wilbur Cross / Merritt parkway / Hutchinson River Parkway south or I-95 south.

You're now in one of Connecticut's oldest settled regions, an early commercial center because of its strategic location on the Connecticut River. For further information about Wethersfield and the nearby towns of Rocky Hill, Glastonbury, and Newington, contact the Olde Town Tourism District, 105 Marsh St., Wethersfield, CT 06190 (203-257-9299).

WEBB-DEANE-STEVENS MUSEUM, 211 Main St., Wethersfield, CT 06109 (203-529-0612). *Open May–Oct., Tues.–Sat. 10–4, Sun. 1–4, last tour at 3. Adults $5, children $2.25. Difficult for wheelchairs.*

Here are three handsome 18th-century houses restored to reflect the lifestyles of their owners—a merchant, a diplomat, and a tradesman. The oldest of them, the **Joseph Webb House** (1752), was the site of a historic meeting between Washington and Rochambeau in 1781, during which the two generals formulated the strategy that led to the British defeat at Yorktown, the concluding battle of the Revolutionary War. Not only did Washington sleep here, but the bedroom boasts the *very same* wallpaper that was hung in his honor on that occasion!

The **Silas Deane House** (1766) was the residence of a diplomat who was instrumental in securing French aid for the Revolutionary cause, and who recruited a number of distinguished foreign military officers (Lafayette, Pulaski, von Steuben, De Kalb) to serve with the Continental Army. During the Revolution, Silas Deane was unjustly accused of profiteering, but his reputation was posthumously cleared. His home, built for entertaining on a grand scale, has many unique structural details and a spaciousness unusual in houses of the period.

The last of the buildings, the **Issac Stevens House** (1788), is the least formal, reflecting the simpler tastes of its owner. In addition to the authentic period furnishings (1640–1840) that adorn all three houses, there is an interesting collection of children's toys and ladies' bonnets here.

OLD ACADEMY MUSEUM, 150 Main St., Wethersfield, CT 06109 (203-529-7656). *Open mid-May to mid-Oct., Mon.–Fri. 1–4, Sat. noon–5, and by appointment. Donation. Largely wheelchair-accessible.*

Built in 1804 by the First School Society, this Federal-style red-brick building had later incarnations as a female seminary, public library, and town hall. Now it is the home of the Wethersfield Historical Society, with changing exhibits on local history and several research libraries. From the museum you have access to the Captain James Francis House (1793), where the furnishings and displays reflect the life of the Francis family over 170 years.

BUTTOLPH-WILLIAMS HOUSE, 249 Broad St., Wethersfield, CT 06109 (203-529-0460 or 247-8996). *Open mid-May to mid-Oct., Tues.–Sun., noon–4. Adults $2, children under 18 $1. Partially accessible for wheelchairs.*

From 1692, when this house was built, to 1752, the date of the Webb House (see above), some radical changes in living occurred. The Buttolph-Williams House is a typical "mansion house" of an earlier and more rugged era, giving you a chance to observe the contrast if you visit both. The house has been carefully restored, and the collections of 17th-century pewter, delft, fabric, and furnishings are outstanding. Of special interest is the kitchen, said to be the best preserved, most fully equipped kitchen of its period in New England.

DINOSAUR STATE PARK, West St., Rocky Hill, CT 06067 (203-529-8423). *Grounds open all year daily, 9–4:30, free. Museum open all year Tues.–Sun. 9–4:30; adults $2, children 6–17 $1, 5 and under free. Picnicking, hiking and nature trails, playing field, cross-country skiing. Leashed pets only, in picnic area only. Picnic area, playing field, museum, and museum restrooms are wheelchair-accessible.*

While excavating a construction site some years ago, a bulldozer operator turned up a stone slab imprinted with curious markings that were soon identified as the three-toes tracks of dinosaurs of the Jurassic Period. Excited paleontologists from the Connecticut Geological Survey and Yale's Peabody Museum (Trip F-10) went to work with their spades, eventually unearthing over 2,000 prints estimated to be 200 million years old. About 500 of the tracks are enclosed under a geodesic dome, and the rest have been electrically sanded and sealed to protect them from weathering. One area of the 60-acre park has been set aside for visitors who wish to make plaster casts of the tracks to take home. In the museum you can inspect a skeletal cast and a life-size model of the creature that left its footprints here, while a greenhouse and a living reptile exhibit suggest something of the lifestyle and period furnishings of this long-extinct race of behemoths.

Trip E-9
A Memorable Day in Hartford

- SCIENCE MUSEUM OF CONNECTICUT
- ELIZABETH PARK
- CONNECTICUT HISTORICAL SOCIETY
- MARK TWAIN AND HARRIET BEECHER STOWE HOUSES
- STATE CAPITOL
- MUSEUM OF CONNECTICUT HISTORY
- WADSWORTH ATHENEUM
- CONSTITUTION PLAZA
- TRAVELERS TOWER
- OLD STATE HOUSE
- BUTLER-McCOOK HOMESTEAD

DISTANCE: About 115 miles from Columbus Circle.

FOR THE DRIVER: Take **I-684** north to Brewster and pick up **I-84** east through Danbury and Waterbury to Exit 43, Park Rd. and West Hartford Center. After ramp, turn right on Park Rd., then left at the next corner, Trout Brook Drive. Go a half-mile on Trout Brook to the **Science Museum,** on the right.

Before leaving West Hartford, abecedarians and admirers of the man who did so much to free American speech and spelling from the King's English may want to visit the **Noah Webster House and Museum** (203-521-5362), birthplace of the author of the groundbreaking *American Dictionary of the English Language* (1828). The Webster House is at 227 South Main St., right near Exit 41 off I-84; it can also be reached by turning left at Park Rd. to Main St. instead of right to Trout Brook Drive and the Science Museum. *(Open daily except Wed.).*

From the Science Museum, turn right and continue on Trout Brook several blocks to Asylum Ave. Turn right on Asylum and watch for **Elizabeth Park** a short distance ahead on the right.

Continue on Asylum Ave. to the end of the park, cross Prospect Ave., and go 3 blocks to Elizabeth St. At this junction, on the right, is the **Connecticut Historical Society,** with a large Hartford fire alarm bell in front.

Go back on Asylum to Prospect Ave. and turn left. Go a couple of blocks to Farmington Ave. (CT-4), turn left, and proceed several blocks to Forest St. Turn right here to **Nook Farm Visitor Center** and **Twain and Stowe Houses.**

Go back to Farmington Ave., turn right, and continue towards downtown Hartford. Just before the entrance to I-84, turn right on Broad St. and proceed to the stoplight at Capitol Ave. Turn left and watch for the distinctive dome of the **State Capitol,** on the left. At this point you may prefer to park in a municipal lot and walk to the next attractions, all within a few blocks of one another and numbered on the map.

Across the street from the Capitol is the **Museum of Connecticut History** and State Library. Behind the Capitol is **Bushnell Park,** the first land in the United States claimed for park purposes under eminent domain, laid out according to a natural landscape design influenced by the ideas of Hartford resident Frederick Law Olmsted. A popular spot for outdoor concerts and special events, the park is also the home of a restored **1914 Carousel,** a real beauty transported here from Canton, Ohio. For fifty cents you can ride one of the 48 brightly-painted hand-carved horses and try for the brass ring.

From the Capitol, continue east on Capitol Ave. several blocks to Main St. Turn left on Main, passing the impressive, highway-spanning Hartford Public Library and the ornate Hartford Municipal Building. Just beyond is the **Wadsworth Atheneum.** Between the Municipal Building and the Wadsworth is Burr Mall, a small park dominated by Alexander Calder's massive steel *Stegosaurus*. A little beyond Wadsworth on Main is **Travelers Tower,** and beyond that is the **Old State House.** Here turn right off Main St. to **Constitution Plaza.**

Go back down Main St. the way you came. On the right, opposite Travelers Tower, is the **Ancient Burying Ground,** final resting place of some of Hartford's early settlers, with headstones dating back to 1640; look for the epitaph of Dr. Thomas Langrell, who "drowned in the glory of his years, and left his mate to drown herself in tears." Beyond the cemetery, opposite the Wadsworth Atheneum, is I. M. Pei's 1969 **Bushnell Tower** and the neighboring **Center Church** (1807), patterned after London's St. Martin's-in-the-Fields, with stained-glass windows by Louis Tiffany. The church stands on the site where the U.S. Constitution was ratified by Connecticut in 1788. Continue on Main to the intersection with Capitol Ave. Here, on the left, is the **Butler-McCook Homestead.**

Note that Hartford is only a few miles north of Wethersfield and the sites on Trip E-8.

PUBLIC TRANSPORTATION: Amtrak provides regular train service to Hartford from New York's Pennsylvania Station, points in New Jersey, New Rochelle, Stamford, Bridgeport, and New Haven. For current schedules call 1-800-USA-RAIL. Most of the sights are within walking distance of the Hartford station; for the rest use local buses or cabs.

Hartford, capital of Connecticut and "Insurance Capital of the World," was established in 1635–36 by Thomas Hooker and a band of discontented Puritan families from Massachusetts. It has a rich historical, cultural, and architectural heritage, and its downtown area is considered one of the country's more successful examples of urban renewal. You can't explore all of the attractions of Hartford in a day, but you could single out a few that especially appeal to you and get a good general introduction to the city. For further information, contact the Greater Hartford Convention and Visitors Bureau, 1 Civic Center Plaza, Hartford, CT 06103 (203-728-6789).

SCIENCE MUSEUM OF CONNECTICUT, 950 Trout Brook Drive, West Hartford, CT 06119 (203-236-2961). *Open all year daily, Mon.–Sat. 10–5, Sun. 1–5; closed Mondays from Jan.–March, Labor Day, Thanksgiving, Christmas, New Year's. Call for schedule of planetarium shows. Adults $6, seniors and children 5–15 $5, under 5 free. Will accommodate wheelchairs; call in advance.*

Formerly the Children's Museum of Hartford, the Science Museum has retained its appeal for young people while greatly expanding its range of exhibits. Outside, a 60-foot cement sperm whale welcomes you, beckoning to the wonders within: a marine aquarium with an 11,000-gallon Caribbean reef tank; a small zoo where you can meet a variety of birds, animals, and reptiles, both native and exotic; a panoply of stars twinkling in the skies of the Gengras Planetarium; a physical science discovery room where you can experiment with the invisible forces that govern the universe; an interactive heart exhibit that shows you how the old ticker works while allowing you to check your pulse and blood pressure; and a hands-on room where you can, among other things, pet the fish. All-in-all, there's something here to engage and enlighten everyone, from the youngest child to the most scientifically retrograde adult.

ELIZABETH PARK, (1), Prospect & Asylum Aves., Hartford, CT 06106 (203-722-6514). *Grounds open all year daily dawn–dusk; greenhouses open all year Mon.–Fri., 8–3. Free. Snack bar, lounge, and auditorium in Pond House. Outdoor displays manageable for wheelchairs.*

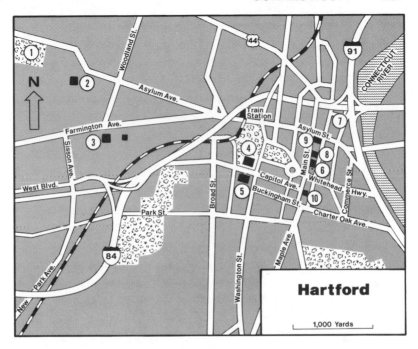

Hartford

1,000 Yards

This city-owned park is famous for its **rose gardens,** with more than 900 varieties blossoming in gorgeous profusion every spring, usually peaking in late June. In addition, there are 14,000 other plants on display during the summer months, and varied vegetation year-round in the greenhouses. The park sponsors a program of outdoor concerts in summer and offers ice skating on the pond in winter.

CONNECTICUT HISTORICAL SOCIETY, (2), 1 Elizabeth St., Hartford, CT 06105 (203-236-5621). *Museum open all year Tues.–Sun. noon–5; library open all year Tues.–Sat. 9–5; both closed Mon. and holidays, also Sat. from Memorial Day to Labor Day. Combined admission: adults $3, children under 18 free. Partially manageable for wheelchairs.*

The leading repository of museum materials on state history, the Connecticut Historical Society has eight galleries of changing exhibits and permanent displays, including two particularly fine furniture collections, the Barbour collection of Connecticut pieces from the Colonial and Federal periods, and the George Dudley Seymour collection of 17th- and 18th-century pieces. You can also see Connecticut-made silver, pewter, toys, glassware, pottery, and stoneware. The art of the tavern sign is well represented by more than 70 specimens, suggesting that a fair number of past Connecticut residents were not customers of the Phoenix Mutual Life Insurance Company, which accepted only teetotalers when it was established in Hartford in 1851. The society also maintains a vast library of almost 2 million historical manuscripts, 100,000 books, 3,500 bound volumes of newspapers and periodicals, extensive genealogical holdings, and assorted maps, prints, and photographs.

MARK TWAIN AND HARRIET BEECHER STOWE HOUSES, (3), Nook Farm, 77 Forest St., Hartford, CT 06105 (203-525-9317). *Open June to Columbus Day and Dec., Mon.–Sat. 9:30–4, Sun. noon–4; Jan. through May, Tues.–Sat. 9:30–4, Sun. noon–4. Closed major holidays. Combined tour: adults $10, children under 16 $4.50. Partially wheelchair-accessible.*

Nook Farm is an old Hartford neighborhood that attracted a remarkable group of 19th-century writers and intellectuals connected by family ties and bonds of friendship. Among the distinguished company that settled here were women's-rights activist Isabella Beecher Hooker, playwright and thespian William Gillette (see Gillette Castle, Trip F-13), Senator Joseph Hawley, and Charles Dudley Warner, editor of the *Hartford Courant* and coauthor with Mark Twain of *The Gilded Age*. Today most of Nook Farm has been torn down, but several of the original buildings remain, including the homes of its most famous residents, Twain and Harriet Beecher Stowe, and the carriage house that now serves as a visitor center.

Twain's house, designed by Edward Tuckerman Potter, is a colorful and idiosyncratic reflection of the author's personality, perhaps best appreciated by those who have read his works and know his humor. The south façade is modeled after a Mississippi River steamboat, the dressing room re-creates a riverboat pilothouse, and the etched windows in the upstairs study, where Twain wrote *The Adventures of Tom Sawyer, The Adventures of Huckleberry Finn,* and five other books, memorialize his great passions in life—smoking, drinking, and billiards. Twain lived at Nook Farm with his wife and three daughters from 1874 to 1891, when financial difficulties forced him to sell the house and take to the lecture circuit.

A stone's throw from the Twain House is the much less flamboyant Victorian "cottage" of Harriet Beecher Stowe, who settled here in 1873 and remained until her death in 1896. This house, too, reflects the personal tastes of its owner: the design of the kitchen follows the specifications set forth in the book Stowe wrote with her sister, *The American Woman's Home;* some of her own paintings hang on the walls; there are mementos of her career as a writer and reformer, and many original items of furniture, including the tiny desk

The Mark Twain House
(Photo courtesy of Mark Twain Memorial, Hartford CT)

at which she penned her most important work, *Uncle Tom's Cabin* (1852), a book that aroused popular sentiment against slavery and sold 300,000 copies within a year—a staggering figure in those days.

STATE CAPITOL, (4), 210 Capitol Ave., Hartford, CT 06106 (203-240-0222). *One-hour tours begin at neighboring Legislative Office Building: year round, Mon.–Fri. first tour at 9:15, last at 1:15; Sat. from Apr. through Oct. 10:15–2:15. Closed state holidays, Thanksgiving through New Year's. Free. Wheelchair-accessible.*

Here is Hartford's most impressive building, seat of Connecticut government since 1879, housing the state executive offices and legislative chambers. A great gold-leaf dome presides over this eclectic architectural concoction by Richard Michell Upjohn. On the tour you'll see statues, murals, and historic displays featuring bullet-riddled flags, Lafayette's camp bed, and other reminders of Connecticut's past, as well as a plaster model of the Genius of Connecticut, which adorned the capitol spire until it was melted down during World War II.

MUSEUM OF CONNECTICUT HISTORY, (5), Connecticut State Library, 231 Capitol Ave., Hartford, CT 06106 (203-566-3056). *Open Mon.–*

Fri. 9–4:45, closed Sat., Sun. and state holidays. Free. Wheelchair-accessible.

This museum in the Connecticut State Library holds a range of exhibits depicting Connecticut history and industrial development. Of particular interest are the Connecticut-made clocks, the Selden auto of 1877, the portrait gallery of leading Connecticut citizens, the **Colt Collection of Firearms,** including a rare Wyatt Earp Buntline Special, and the original **Royal Charter** granted to the Connecticut colonists by Charles II in 1662.

WADSWORTH ATHENEUM, (6), 600 Main St., Hartford, CT 06103 (203-278-2670). *Open all year Tues.–Sun. 11–5; closed Mon. and major holidays. Adults $3, seniors and students $1.50, children under 13 free. Free all day Thurs. and Sat. 11–1. Wheelchair-accessible.*

One of the nation's oldest and best public art museums, the Wadsworth Atheneum has a well-deserved reputation for the excellence and breadth of its collections. More than 45,000 art objects, from ancient Egyptian artifacts to contemporary sculptures, are on display here in spacious galleries occupying five interconnected buildings. There's an extensive selection of paintings representing every major period and style since the 15th century, with some particularly fine works by Monet, Renoir, and other 19th-century French artists. Also noteworthy are the collections of American and English silver, Meissen porcelain, furniture, and period costumes.

CONSTITUTION PLAZA, (7). These 15 acres of elegant high-rises and landscaped promenades show the effects of urban renewal at its best. Completed in 1964 at a cost of $40 million, the plaza combines office space, shopping centers, and parking facilities. Among its features are the boat-shaped elliptical headquarters of Phoenix Mutual Life, one of the few two-sided buildings in the world, and the splashless fountain, designed to resist the fiercest provocations from the plaza winds.

TRAVELERS TOWER, (8). 1 Tower Square, Main St., Hartford, CT 06183-1060 (203-277-2431). *Open for tours June through Aug., Mon.–Fri. 10:30–3:30, every half-hour; May & Sept.–Oct. by reservation with 24-hour notice. Closed weekends and holidays. Free. Not accessible for wheelchairs.*

When this famous tower was built in 1919, only six buildings in America were taller. The highest point in Hartford, it rises 527 feet above sidewalk level, affording a splendid panoramic view of Greater Hartford and the Connecticut River Valley. The tower was built by the Travelers Insurance Company, a venerable Hartford institution that got its start in 1863 by insuring a Captain James Bolter for $5,000 for a

The State Capitol at Hartford
(Photo courtesy of Greater Hartford Convention & Visitors Bureau)

trip from his home to the post office at a premium of two cents. Plenty of other travelers put in their two cents' worth over the years, and the company grew to become one of the giants of the insurance field.

The Travelers Tower stands on a site once occupied by Sanford's Tavern, where in 1687 Sir Edmund Andros, James II's royal governor of New England, demanded the surrender of the original charter granted to the Connecticut colonists by Charles II in 1662. While Andros was engaged in heated debate with the colonists at Sanford's, Captain Joseph Wadsworth took the charter and squirreled it away in the hollow of an ancient white oak, where it remained safely hidden until the colonists succeeded in riding themselves of the autocratic Andros. The Charter Oak, thought to have been more than 1,000 years old, succumbed to a storm in 1856, but the 1662 charter is on display in the Museum of Connecticut History (see above), and the family tree lives on in the white oak on the grounds of the Center Church, across from the Wadsworth Atheneum.

OLD STATE HOUSE, (9), 800 Main St., Hartford, CT 06103 (203-522-6766). *Open all year, Mon.–Sat. 10–5, Sun. noon–5; closed major holidays. Free. Visitor information center, gift shop, changing exhibitions, seasonal events. Partially wheelchair-accessible.*

This elegant Federal structure was the first public commission of Charles Bulfinch (1763–1844), one of America's best early architects. Bulfinch went on to design many other fine buildings, including the statehouse in Boston and the Massachusetts General Hospital, but is perhaps best remembered for bringing the Capitol building in Washington, D.C., to completion in 1830. The Old State House served as Connecticut's state capitol from 1796 to 1878, and as Hartford's city hall from 1879 to 1915. Today it is a National Historic Landmark, museum, and cultural center. A rare Gilbert Stuart full-length portrait of George Washington hangs in the restored senate chamber.

BUTLER-McCOOK HOMESTEAD, (10), 396 Main St., Hartford, CT 06103 (203-247-8996). *Open mid-May to mid-Oct., Tues., Thurs., Sun. noon–4; closed holidays. Adults $2, children under 18 $1. Not wheelchair-accessible.*

This survivor of urban renewal stands in quaint contrast to the glittering office buildings of downtown Hartford. The oldest private home in the city (1782), it has been preserved as a museum of 18th- and 19th-century tastes in furnishings and decorative arts. On display are fine collections of silver, 19th-century American paintings, Chinese bronzes, Egyptian artifacts, toys, and dolls. The annual Victorian Christmas exhibit is a nice way to get into the spirit of the season.

Area F

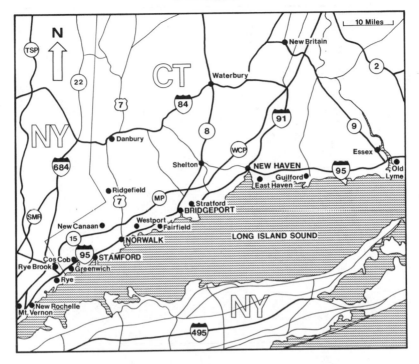

EASTWARD ALONG
CONNECTICUT'S SHORE

Here you can start just over the New York City line and move through parts of Westchester County into southern Connecticut, following the shoreline of Long Island Sound almost to where Rhode Island begins. This is beautiful country for sightseeing or recreation, with many historic port towns and the tang of saltwater and seafaring in the air.

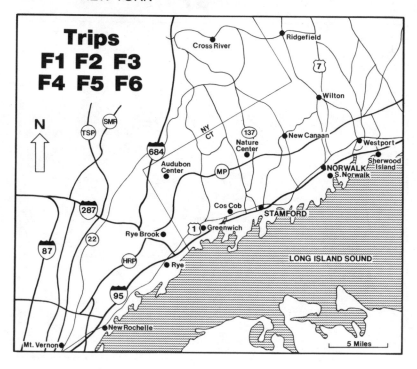

Trip F-1
Fundamental Freedoms
and Common Sense

- **ST. PAUL'S NATIONAL HISTORIC SITE AND BILL OF RIGHTS MUSEUM**
- **HUGUENOT-THOMAS PAINE HISTORICAL ASSOCIATION**
- **SQUARE HOUSE**

DISTANCE: About 25 miles from Columbus Circle to the farthest point.

FOR THE DRIVER: Take **I-95** north to the Conner St. exit, turn left after the ramp, go up one light and make another left. This road crosses US-1 (Boston Post Rd.) and becomes **NY-22,** Columbus Ave., taking you to **St. Paul's National Historic Site,** on the right at 897 S. Columbus.

Go back down 22 to the junction with **US-1,** turn left, and go north about 3 miles to North Ave. Turn left and go a little under 2 miles to the **Thomas Paine Cottage,** at the far end of a lake beyond the statue. Just ahead on North Ave. is the **Huguenot-Paine Historical Association** museum.

Continue on North Ave. to the second light. Turn left on the street after the light to Webster Ave. Turn right on Webster and go to the end, where it merges with the **Hutchinson River Parkway.** Follow this north about 6 miles to the junction with **I-287,** the Cross Westchester Expressway, and take this east to Exit 11, US-1 south to Rye. Follow US-1 south several blocks to the junction with NY-120, Purchase St. Here US-1 bears left and you bear right to the **Square House.**

On this and the next trip, you can visit some sites in Westchester County en route to Connecticut. For further information, contact the Westchester Tourism Council, 148 Martine Ave., White Plains, NY 10601 (914-948-0047).

ST. PAUL'S NATIONAL HISTORIC SITE AND BILL OF RIGHTS MU-SEUM, 897 S. Columbus Ave., Mount Vernon, NY 10550 (914-667-4116). *Grounds open all year daily, daylight hours; site open all year for guided tours by appointment, Wed.–Sun. 9–5, closed legal holidays. Free. Museum is wheelchair-accessible.*

This handsome 1787 church is associated with the events leading to the arrest and trial of John Peter Zenger. A German-born printer, Zenger emigrated to America in 1710 and in 1733 launched his *Weekly Journal,* an opposition paper that attacked the policies of the Colonial government. In an election for Westchester assemblyman held that year on the church green, Quakers were denied the right to vote because they refused to swear an oath on the Bible affirming their status as landowners. Zenger took up their cause in the first issue of his paper, denouncing the corrupt election, and broadening his attacks in subsequent issues. In 1734 he was arrested for seditious libel, a loosely defined legal category that embraced all criticism of the government, whether true or false. At Zenger's trial in 1735, his lawyer, Alexander Hamilton, won his client's acquittal on the grounds that the allegedly libelous material in the *Weekly Journal,* including the article on the 1733 election, was true. This decision, recognizing truth as a defense in cases of libel, was a milestone in establishing freedom of the press, later enshrined in the First Amendment to the U.S. Constitution.

The museum at St. Paul's commemorates these events in a series of dioramas and contains other informative exhibits on the freedoms of speech, press, religion, and assembly. Also here are exhibits on Westchester history, Revolutionary artifacts from the Battle of Pell's Point, and a working replica of Zenger's press. The original church served as a hospital during the Revolution, and the present structure is of considerable historical and architectural interest. The adjoining cemetery contains graves dating back more than three centuries.

HUGUENOT-THOMAS PAINE HISTORICAL ASSOCIATION, 983 North Ave., New Rochelle, NY 10804 (914-632-5376). *Open spring through fall, Fri.–Sun. 2–5 or by appointment. Donation. Not wheelchair-accessible.*

The museum of the Huguenot-Paine Historical Association has an interesting collection of artifacts and documents relating to the early history of New Rochelle, originally home of the Siwanoy Indians, founded as a town by 30 Huguenot families in 1688. The association also maintains the nearby **Thomas Paine Cottage** on Sicard Ave. The great pamphleteer who wrote *Common Sense* and did so much in the cause of American freedom lived here only briefly. His Huguenot neighbors did not welcome his radical views, which had an enormous impact on public opinion during the American Revolution. Today the cottage is furnished much as it was during Paine's lifetime (1737–1809), but there are also some fine Victorian pieces.

SQUARE HOUSE, 1 Purchase St., Rye, NY 10580 (914-967-7588). *Open all year Tues.–Fri. and Sun. 2:30–4:30, and by appointment; closed major holidays. Free. Lectures, films, craft demonstrations, special events. Wheelchair-accessible.*

The Rye Historical Society has its headquarters in this restored 18th-century tavern where George Washington twice stopped in 1789, and which was visited by such notables as John Adams and Lafayette. There are seven rooms with period furnishings and rotating historical exhibits.

Trip F-2
Rye Humor and Other Amusements

- MUSEUM OF CARTOON ART
- PLAYLAND

DISTANCE: About 25 miles from Columbus Circle.

FOR THE DRIVER: Take the **Hutchinson River Parkway** north to Exit 30, marked "King St. to Port Chester." Turn right off the ramp and go south on King St. (NY-120A) about a mile to Comly Ave. Turn left on Comly, then take the first left off Comly onto Magnolia Drive and park here for the **Museum of Cartoon Art.** The museum was formerly in Port Chester; it's still in the same place, but that area of Port Chester was incorporated as the town of Rye Brook in 1982. Don't be dismayed if you can't find Rye Brook on the map—it hasn't made it on all maps yet.

Go back to the Hutchinson River Parkway and take it south to **I-287,** Cross Westchester Expressway. Take I-287 east to Port Chester and pick up **I-95** south to Exit 19, Playland Parkway. This takes you directly to **Playland.**

MUSEUM OF CARTOON ART, Comly Ave., Rye Brook, NY 10573 (914-939-0234). *Open all year Tues.–Fri. 10–4, Sun. 1–5; closed major holidays. Adults $3, ages 12–18 $2, children under 12 $1. Guest demonstrations, films. Not wheelchair-accessible.*

Here, in a fanciful 5-story Victorian castle, are more than 60,000 original works by over 1,000 artists, along with extensive research and archival materials on the history of one of the world's liveliest art forms. The exhibits cover all types of cartoon art and animated films from 1899 to the present, and the greats of the field are enshrined in the Cartoonists' Hall of Fame. There's plenty of humor on display, from the slapstick to the sophisticated, as well as exhibits offering an education in the trenchant art of caricature and the political cartoon. Animated shorts and features are shown on weekdays to groups of 10 or more, and there are occasional guest demonstrations by leading cartoonists.

PLAYLAND, Rye, NY 10580 (914-921-0370). *Open daily May through mid-Sept., noon–11 p.m. Parking, beach, and pool fees. Picnicking,* *hiking, fishing, boat rentals, paddleboat rentals, ice skating, refreshment stand. Leashed pets only. Wheelchair-accessible parking and restrooms.*

This venerable amusement park on Long Island Sound has delighted generations of Westchester children while offering aid and comfort to their parents ("Eat your spinach and I'll take you to Playland"). The 40-acre park features 30 tried-and-true devices for producing exhilaration, plus game arcade, miniature golf, refreshment stands, boardwalk, lake, and Kiddy Land for the younger set. You can swim or sunbathe at the 1,200-foot-long beach, whet your blades at the 3-rink Ice Casino, fish from a rowboat on the lake, or lose yourself in contemplation at the neighboring 170-acre Edith G. Read Natural Park and Wildlife Sanctuary.

Trip F-3
Nature, History,
and Art in Greenwich

- AUDUBON CENTER
- BRUCE MUSEUM
- PUTNAM COTTAGE
- BUSH-HOLLEY HOUSE

DISTANCE: About 40 miles from Columbus Circle to Cos Cob via the Audubon Center.

FOR THE DRIVER: Take the **Hutchinson River Parkway** north into Connecticut, where it becomes the **Merritt Parkway.** Continue to Exit 28, Round Hill Rd. After the ramp, turn left on Round Hill and take it north a little over a mile to John St. Turn left and go about a mile west to the **Audubon Center,** at the corner of John St. and Riversville Rd.

Go south on Riversville Rd. several miles to Glenville. Here turn left on Glenville Rd. and follow it to the end, at a traffic circle. Take the first right off the circle onto Deerfield Drive and follow this to the end at **US-1** (W. Putnam Ave./Boston Post Rd.), passing the Greenwich Library on the left. Turn left on US-1 and proceed to Greenwich Ave. Turn right on Greenwich and go south through the town, passing un-

der the railroad tracks and I-95. Continue on Greenwich, now Steamboat Rd., to the water's edge. Here turn left onto Museum Drive and
watch for the stone pillars of the **Bruce Museum,** driveway on left.

Go back to Steamboat Rd., turn right, and retrace your route until
you can't continue on Greenwich Ave., which is one way in the other
direction. Turn right and go a block to Milbank Ave. Turn left on Milbank and proceed several blocks, continuing through the traffic circle
to the junction with US-1 (E. Putnam Ave.). Turn right and go a short
way to the **Putnam Cottage,** the red building on the left.

From Putnam Cottage, turn left and go north on US-1. Shortly after
the sign for Cos Cob is a major intersection and stoplight at Strickland
Rd. Here a small sign directs you to the right; follow it to River Rd.
and the **Bush-Holley House,** on the right just before the I-95 overpass.

AUDUBON CENTER, 613 Riversville Rd., Greenwich, CT 06831 (203-
869-5272). *Open all year Tues.–Sun. 9–5; closed major holidays. Adults
$2, seniors and children $1, free to members of the Audubon Society.
Self-guided tours, gift and book shop. No picnicking or pets in nature
study areas. Not wheelchair-accessible, but parking area is good for
birdwatching.*

Here's the place to go for information on just about every phase
of nature study. Established in 1942, this 485-acre wildlife sanctuary is
home to about 90 species of birds, many types of small animals, and
a profusion of wildflowers. There are 15 miles of hiking trails through
varied habitats, and the visitor center has many excellent interpretive
exhibits.

BRUCE MUSEUM, One Museum Drive, Greenwich, CT 06830 (203-
869-0376). *Open all year Tues.–Sat. 10–5, Sun. 2–5; closed major holidays. Adults $3, seniors $1.50, children $1. Gift shop. Ramp and step
into building; 1st floor manageable for wheelchairs.*

You might call this the "everything museum," for the range of exhibits here is unusually wide, covering fine arts, history, the natural
sciences, and ethnology. Among other things, you can see wildlife
dioramas, geological specimens, Indian relics, early American tools,
and a nice selection of 19th-century American paintings. At the marine
center you can meet a variety of animals that inhabit Long Island Sound,
and deepen your acquaintance with some of them in the hands-on
aquarium display.

PUTNAM COTTAGE, 243 E. Putnam Ave., Greenwich, CT 06830 (203-
869-9697). *Open all year Wed. & Fri. noon–4; Sun. 1–4; or by appointment. Adults $2, children under 12 free. Steps into building, difficult
for wheelchairs.*

Known as Knapp's Tavern during the Revolutionary War, this small house was built around 1690 and is noteworthy for its rare scalloped shingles and huge fieldstone fireplaces. As a stagecoach station along the Boston Post Road, it was a convenient stopping place for Revolutionary leaders, among them General Israel Putnam. "Old Put" was a guest here in 1779 when he discovered a large number of British troops coming up the Post Road. Hurrying from the house, he urged his horse down the side of the cliff and made his escape. The local D.A.R. chapter, which maintains the house as a museum, is responsible for the fine period furnishings and the lovely garden. There is also a restored barn on the grounds.

BUSH-HOLLEY HOUSE, 39 Strickland Rd., Cos Cob, CT 06807 (203-869-6899). *Open all year Tues.–Fri. noon–4; Sun. 1–4; closed New Year's, Easter, July 4, Thanksgiving, Christmas. Adults $3, seniors $1.50, children 50¢, preschoolers free. Not wheelchair-accessible.*

Originally a Colonial saltbox built around 1685, today the headquarters of the Greenwich Historical Society, this beautiful house shows the architectural accretions and alterations of three centuries. It is furnished with authentic 18th- and 19th-century pieces and has many interesting features, including a room once used as a countinghouse and papered in an unusual design—a tax stamp from the time of King George II. Across from the enormous fireplace in the kitchen, a picture window looks out upon the herb garden. Children will enjoy the antique toy collection.

At the turn of the century, the Bush-Holley House was the residence of Elmer Livingston MacRae, one of the organizers of the historic 1913 Armory Show in New York City, which introduced modern art to the United States. Though outraged critics heaped vituperation on the 1,600 avant-garde paintings on display, denouncing the "degeneracy" of such works as Marcel Duchamp's *Nude Descending a Staircase*, the show helped to win an American public for modern art and revolutionized American painting. During MacRae's time, the Bush-Holley House became a magnet for artists and writers, attracting the likes of Willa Cather, Lincoln Steffens, and John Henry Twachtman. Paintings by MacRae, Twachtman, Childe Hassam, and other American Impressionists adorn the walls of the house. On the grounds is a museum devoted to the works on sculptor John Rogers (1829–1904), who specialized in group studies of slaves, soldiers, and ordinary people. These "Rogers groups" became very popular during the Civil War and remain of interest as vivid records of their period.

Trip F-4
Everything but the Kitchen Sink in Stamford

- WHITNEY MUSEUM OF AMERICAN ART
- HOYT-BARNUM HOUSE
- UNITED HOUSE WRECKING
- STAMFORD MUSEUM & NATURE CENTER
- BARTLETT ARBORETUM

DISTANCE: About 40 miles from Columbus Circle to the farthest point.

FOR THE DRIVER: Take **I-95** north to Exit 8, Atlantic St. After the ramp turn left on Atlantic, going under I-95, and proceed to Tresser Blvd. Turn right here to the Champion garage and parking for the **Whitney Museum.**

Go back on Tresser to Atlantic St. and turn right to the intersection with Broad St. Make a right on Broad and a quick left on Bedford St. Go two blocks to the **Hoyt-Barnum House,** on the corner of Bedford and North Streets.

Go east on North St. and turn left onto Strawberry Hill Ave. Follow this to Colonial Rd., making a right to Hope St. Turn left on Hope and follow it to the **United House Wrecking Co.,** on the right.

Return to Colonial Rd. and go west on it back to Strawberry Hill Ave. Turn north on this and then west on Oaklawn Ave. At the intersection of High Ridge Rd. (CT-137), turn right and follow it north under the Merritt Parkway, passing the Stamford Historical Society Museum (202-329-1183) at 1508 High Ridge. Here turn left on Scofieldtown Rd. to the **Stamford Museum and Nature Center.**

Go back to High Ridge, turn left, and continue north briefly to Brookdale Rd. Turn left here to the **Bartlett Arboretum,** shortly on the right.

To return to New York City, go back down High Ridge to the Merritt Parkway and take it south, *or* go back into Stamford and pick up I-95 south.

Now you're in Stamford, a thriving industrial and research center with a population of 102,000 and a score of Fortune 500 companies, blessed with scenic beauty and an eclectic range of attractions that make it equally inviting as a place to live or visit. For further information, contact the Greater Stamford Convention & Visitors Bureau, One Landmark Sq., Stamford, CT 06901 (203-359-3305).

WHITNEY MUSEUM OF AMERICAN ART, 1 Champion Plaza, Stamford, CT 06921 (203-358-7652). *Open all year Tues.–Sat. 11–5; gallery talks 12:30 Tues., Thurs., Sat. Free admission; free parking in Champion garage. Wheelchair-accessible.*

A varied program of major events awaits you at the Fairfield County branch of the prestigious Whitney Museum in New York City, founded in 1930 by Gertrude Vanderbilt Whitney to foster the development of American art. Carefully researched and beautifully mounted, the exhibits change every two or three months.

HOYT-BARNUM HOUSE, 713 Bedford St., Stamford, CT 06903 (203-323-1183). *Open by appointment only, Tues.–Sat. noon–4. Adults $2, seniors $1, children 50¢. Not wheelchair-accessible.*

The Stamford Historical Society maintains this restored 1699 house, the oldest still standing in Stamford. Originally owned by a blacksmith, the house features four fireplaces, a commanding fieldstone chimney, and period furnishings reflecting life in Stamford over three centuries.

UNITED HOUSE WRECKING CO., 535 Hope St., Stamford, CT 06906 (203-348-5371). *Open all year Mon.–Sat. 9:30–5:30, Sun. noon–5. No admission fee, free parking.*

Here, spread over 30,000 square feet of mostly indoor warehousing, is a mind-boggling, vocabulary-defying collection of whatnots, knick-knacks, doohickeys, and thingamabobs. Need a weathervane, traffic light, church pew, life-size can-can girl, wooden Indian, birdbath, gargoyle, cherub, or New York subway car? On the more practical level, how about some stained or beveled glass or a carved mantel or some antique furniture? Whatever you fancy, chances are you can buy it here, along with thousands of items you'd never have dreamed of looking for, much less finding—a simply unbelievable selection of architectural, agricultural, marine, commercial, and domestic treasures from yesteryear. If America were a great big house and Uncle Sam had decided to clean out the basement and the attic, say, you'd have to imagine that the result would look something like United House Wrecking, "the junkyard with a personality."

STAMFORD MUSEUM & NATURE CENTER, 39 Scofieldtown Rd., Stamford, CT 06903 (203-322-1646). *Open all year daily, Mon.–Sat. &*

holidays 9–5, Sun. 1–5; closed Thanksgiving, Christmas, New Year's. Adults $4, seniors and children 5–13 $3, under 5 free. Planetarium shows Sun. 3:30 (fee). Nature trails, picnicking, gift shop; concerts, lectures, and special events all year. Mostly wheelchair-accessible.

This fabulous mansion that once belonged to Henri Bendel today looks down upon a picturebook Colonial New England farm, a small gem of a lake dotted with waterfowl, a pool of otters, and miles of trails. The working farm has a restored 1750 barn, grazing oxen, sheep, goats, and pigs, and an exhibit on early rural life. In the mansion are three galleries: an art gallery that mounts six to eight major exhibits a year, with a separate space devoted to work by experimental artists; a natural history gallery that shows you how the surrounding Connecticut landscape was formed by millions of years of geological activity; and an Indian gallery that introduces you to the "People of the Dawn." There are regularly scheduled shows at the Edgerton Memorial Planetarium, along with annual events including ice harvesting at Laurel Lake in January, maple sugaring from sap to syrup in March, wool making in May, craft demonstrations in September, and cider making in October.

BARTLETT ARBORETUM, University of Connecticut, 151 Brookdale Rd., Stamford, CT 06903 (203-322-6971). *Grounds open all year daily 8:30–sunset; office and library open all year Mon.–Fri. 9–4. Free. No picnicking, no pets. Difficult for wheelchairs.*

This 63-acre facility of the University of Connecticut College of Agriculture features cultivated gardens surrounded by natural woodlands with several ecology trails and a swamp walk. The arboretum specializes in collections of dwarf conifers, flowering trees and shrubs, and wildflowers. Many more varieties of plants thrive in the greenhouse, and there's a fine horticultural reference library.

Trip F-5
Tradition and Innovation in Small-Town New England

- NEW CANAAN HISTORICAL SOCIETY
- SILVERMINE GUILD ARTS CENTER
- ALDRICH MUSEUM OF CONTEMPORARY ART
- KEELER TAVERN MUSEUM

DISTANCE: About 55 miles from Columbus Circle to the farthest point.

FOR THE DRIVER: Take the **Hutchinson River Parkway** north into Connecticut, where it becomes the **Merritt Parkway.** Proceed to Exit 37 and take **CT-124** (Oenoke Ridge) north about 2½ miles to the **New Canaan Historical Society,** next to St. Michael's Lutheran Church, just beyond God's Acre. A little farther up Oenoke Ridge is the **New Canaan Nature Center** (203-966-9577), 40 acres of woodland with nature trails, seasonal exhibits, a working solar greenhouse, and plants for sale. *(Buildings open Tues.–Sat. 9:30–4:30, Sun. 12:30–4:30, closed holidays. Donation. Wheelchair-accessible).*

Go back down CT-124 to the junction with **CT-106** to Wilton. Turn left and go northeast on 106, which shortly becomes Silvermine Rd. Continue to a three-way stop, where 106 goes left and Silvermine goes right. Stay on Silvermine for about a mile to the **Silvermine Guild Arts Center.**

Continue northeast on 106 to the junction with **CT-33.** Turn sharp left onto 33 and proceed several miles to Ridgefield. In town watch for CT-35 coming in from the left. At this junction, on the right, is the **Keeler Tavern,** and just beyond, also on the right, is the **Aldrich Museum of Contemporary Art.**

Note that Ridgefield is not far from Danbury, Bethel, and the sites on Trip E-3. It is also near the New York line and some of the sites on Trips D-6 and D-7.

To return to New York City from Ridgefield, you can go north a few miles via CT-35 and US-7 to I-84 and take this west to I-684 south, *or* you can go south via CT-33 and US-7 back to the Merritt Parkway south *or* I-95 south.

NEW CANAAN HISTORICAL SOCIETY, 13 Oenoke Ridge, New Canaan, CT 06840 (203-966-1776). *Open all year Tues.–Sat. 9:30–12:30 and 2–4:30; museums open Wed., Thurs., Sun. 2–4; summer hours Tues.–Fri. & Sun. 2–4. Donation. Not wheelchair-accessible.*

Originally known as Canaan Parish, New Canaan was settled in 1731 on the high ridges north of Stamford. Its heritage has been preserved by the New Canaan Historical Society through a series of small, well-organized museums in the old buildings of the historic district. In the original **Town House of Canaan Parish,** you can visit a costume museum, a library of local history and genealogy, and the Cody Drug Store, a restoration of the town's first pharmacy (1845). Also on the grounds are the Georgian-style **Hanford-Silliman House,** a tool museum and print shop with working hand press, the 1799 **Rock Schoolhouse,** and the restored studio of sculptor John Rogers, with examples of his popular "Rogers groups" (see Bush-Holley House, Trip F-3).

SILVERMINE GUILD ARTS CENTER, 1037 Silvermine Rd., New Canaan, CT 06840 (203-966-5617). *Open all year Tues.–Sat. 11–5, Sun. noon–5; closed Mon., Thanksgiving, Christmas, and New Year's. Suggested donation $2. Partially wheelchair-accessible.*

This famous art center has a school and three galleries displaying the works of guild members. The center hosts the annual summer Art of Northeast USA exhibit, one of the nation's oldest juried competitions, and the biennial National Print Show. It also sponsors a summer chamber music festival and a month-long Christmas show and sale featuring an excellent selection of artwork and crafts in all price brackets.

ALDRICH MUSEUM OF CONTEMPORARY ART, 258 Main St., Ridgefield, CT 06877 (203-438-4519). *Sculpture garden open all year daily; free. Museum open in spring and summer: Wed.–Fri. 2:30–4:30, Sat. & Sun. 1–5; in fall and winter: Fri. 2:30–4:30, Sat. & Sun. 1–5; other times by appointment. Adults $3, seniors and children $2. Sculpture garden manageable for wheelchairs, but museum is difficult.*

Here, in the unlikely setting of Ridgefield—settled in 1709 and still preserving the appearance of an 18th-century New England town—is a serious museum of contemporary art, with changing exhibits of modern and avant-garde works. The sculpture garden is an attractively landscaped outdoor installation of large-scale works by leading artists.

KEELER TAVERN MUSEUM, 132 Main St., Ridgefield, CT 06877 (203-438-5485). *Open Wed., Sat., Sun., and holiday Mon. 1–4. Tours every half-hour, last tour at 3:30. Closed Jan. Adults $3, seniors $2, children under 12 $1. Gift shop. Not wheelchair-accessible.*

Considerably more in keeping with Ridgefield's ambience than the Aldrich Museum, this 1733 tavern served as a stagecoach stop and patriot headquarters during the American Revolution and was later converted into a home. During the Battle of Ridgefield in 1777, a British cannonball took up permanent lodging in the wall. Among the subsequent residents was architect Cass Gilbert (1859–1934), designer of the Woolworth Building in New York City, the Supreme Court Building in Washington, D.C., and many other notable structures.

Trip F-6
A Celebration of the Sea
and a Palace at Norwalk

- LOCKWOOD-MATHEWS MANSION
- THE MARITIME CENTER
- NATURE CENTER FOR ENVIRONMENTAL ACTIVITIES
- SHERWOOD ISLAND STATE PARK

DISTANCE: About 45 miles from Columbus Circle.

FOR THE DRIVER: Take **I-95** north to Exit 14 at Norwalk and follow the exit road to West Ave. Turn left on West and go under I-95 to the **Lockwood-Mathews Mansion,** shortly on the right.

Return on West Ave., again going under I-95, and turn left at N. Main St. Make the first left onto Ann St. and park at the municipal lot. Adjacent to this is **The Maritime Center.**

Return to I-95 and continue north to Exit 17 (Westport). Get off here, turn left and go north on **CT-33** to Sylvan Rd. South. Turn left and continue across US-1 (State St.) to where Sylvan Rd. South becomes Sylvan Rd. North. At the fork, Sylvan goes left and you bear right on Stony Brook Rd. to Woodside Lane. Turn left on Woodside and go about a half-mile to the **Nature Center,** on the right.

Go back on Sylvan Rd. to the junction with **US-1.** Turn left and go northeast on 1 across the Saugatuck River to Westport. At the junction with Sherwood Island Connector, turn right and follow it across I-95 into **Sherwood Island State Park.**

PUBLIC TRANSPORTATION: The first two attractions are within walking distance of the Norwalk train station, which has frequent service from New York's Grand Central Terminal. For current schedules call the Metro-North Railroad at 800-638-7646 or 212-532-4900.

LOCKWOOD-MATHEWS MANSION MUSEUM, 295 West Ave., Norwalk, CT 06850 (203-838-1434). *Open Mar. to mid-Dec., Tues.–Fri. 11– 3, Sun. 1–4; 1-hour guided tour, last tour 1 hour before closing. Adults $5, seniors and students $3, children under 12 free. Gift shop. Partially wheelchair-accessible.*

This Victorian palace was built between 1864 and 1868 by financier LeGrand Lockwood, who purchased the finest materials and imported artisans from Europe to create the rich hand-wrought detail found in each of the 50 rooms that surround the octagonal skylit rotunda. After Lockwood's death, the mansion was bought by Charles D. Mathews and remained in his family until 1938, when it was sold to the City of Norwalk. Plans to demolish it and erect a new city hall on the site were squelched by a band of concerned citizens who formed a corporation to undertake a major restoration effort and open the mansion as a National Historic Landmark museum.

THE MARITIME CENTER AT NORWALK, 295 West Ave., Norwalk, CT 06850 (203-838-1434). *Open all year daily 10–6, closing at 5 from Labor Day to Memorial Day. Closed Thanksgiving, Christmas, and New Year's. IMAX theater shows daily; call for schedules. General admission: Adults $7.50, seniors and children $6.50, under 2 free. Combination with IMAX: Adults $11.50, seniors and children $9.50. Snack bar, oyster bar, gift shop. Strollers allowed. No pets allowed. Cruises available in season. Fully wheelchair-accessible.*

Installed in and around a 19th-century factory building on Norwalk's colorful waterfront, The Maritime Center uses the very latest technology to acquaint its visitors with the life of Long Island Sound. An ingenious series of aquariums takes you along a gradual descent from the shallow tidal areas to the depths of the sea. For an unusual sensory experience, you can actually touch some of the living specimens (*not* the 10-foot sharks!). Life in the coastal towns in years past is re-created with replica buildings and boats, and explained by interactive video and computer installations.

Outdoors, an historic sailing vessel is being restored, while the modern age is represented by a futuristic racing catamaran. The IMAX theater uses a curving screen some six stories high and 80 feet wide to surround you with fantastic images.

NATURE CENTER FOR ENVIRONMENTAL ACTIVITIES, 10 Woodside Lane, Westport, CT 06881 (203-227-7253). *Open all year daily, Mon.– Sat. 9–5, Sun. 1–4; closed major holidays. Adults $1, children under 12 50¢. Partially wheelchair-accessible, trails difficult for wheelchairs.*

This 62-acre wildlife sanctuary is an imaginatively designed showcase for natural history exhibits that include live animals of the area, an aquarium, fossils, shells, and some good dioramas. A small garden grows in the center courtyard, and several miles of marked nature trails lead from the building. A gift shop sells books on natural history and related subjects.

SHERWOOD ISLAND STATE PARK, Westport, CT 06880 (203-226-6983). *Open all year daily 8–sunset. Parking fee Memorial Day to Sept., weekdays $4 per car, weekends and holidays $6 per car; off-season free. Picnicking, playing field, fishing, swimming, scuba diving, food concession. No pets. Wheelchair-accessible picnic area, toilets, and telephones.*

This popular 243-acre park includes a one-and-a-half-mile-long beach and two large picnic groves with fine views of neighboring Compo Cove and Long Island Sound. The waters here offer rich opportunities for fishermen and scuba divers, while the sands provide hours of pleasure for sunbathers and castle builders alike.

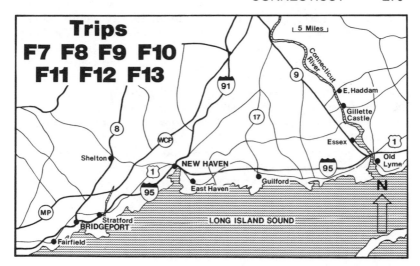

**Trips
F7 F8 F9 F10
F11 F12 F13**

Trip F-7
A Fair Day in Fairfield

- FAIRFIELD HISTORICAL SOCIETY
- BIRDCRAFT MUSEUM AND SANCTUARY
- CONNECTICUT AUDUBON SOCIETY NATURE CEN-
  TER

DISTANCE: About 55 miles from Columbus Circle.

FOR THE DRIVER: Take **I-95** north to Exit 22 and turn right on Beach Rd. After crossing US-1, go a block to Old Post Rd., turn right, and watch for the **Fairfield Historical Society** on the town green, second building on the right. You may want to continue down Old Post Rd. through one of Fairfield's historic districts to Sasco Hill Rd., turn right briefly, and then go left across a bridge onto Harbor Rd. for a look at Southport Harbor.

From the Fairfield Historical Society, go back on Old Post Rd. to Beach Rd., turn left, and go back to **US-1.** Turn left and go south a short way to Unquowa Rd. Turn right here, cross the railroad tracks, and watch for the entrance to the **Birdcraft Museum and Sanctuary,** on the right.

To continue to the **Connecticut Audubon Society Nature Center,** stay on Unquowa Rd. and proceed under I-95 to Mill Plain Rd. Turn right and drive north about 4½ miles on Mill Plain, which becomes Burr St. Proceed past the Merritt Parkway underpass and watch for the sanctuary, shortly on the left.

If you're traveling to Fairfield in mid-May, be sure to attend the **Dogwood Festival** (203-259-5596) at the Greenfield Hills Congregational Church, Old Academy and Bronson roads. For a week or so, this whole area turns into a fairyland of blossoms against the classic New England setting, and you can feast upon the visual delights while nibbling on home-baked goodies or browsing among the many antiques and crafts for sale. The dogwood also produces colorful foliage in the fall, though without the gustatory and acquisitive possibilities of the festival.

For the return trip, go back on Burr St. under the Merritt Parkway and turn left on Congress St. to the entrance for the Merritt back to New York City, *or* continue on Burr St./Mill Plain Rd. back to I-95 south in Fairfield.

FAIRFIELD HISTORICAL SOCIETY, 636 Old Post Rd., Fairfield, CT 06430 (203-259-1598). *Open all year Mon.–Fri. 9:30–4:30, Sun. 1–5; closed Sat. and major holidays. Suggested donation $1 adults, 50¢ seniors and children. Wheelchair-accessible.*

This museum has some fine exhibits, attractively displayed to depict local history since the Great Swamp Fight of 1637, when the Pequot Indians were vanquished by the English in the final battle of the Pequot War. The permanent collections include tools, ornaments, textiles, furniture, ceramics, silverware, paintings, dolls, toys, and maritime memorabilia, along with extensive documentary and genealogical holdings in the research library. The museum is a good place to inquire about sightseeing in Fairfield, which has three historic districts of particular interest: Greenfield Hill, the Old Post Road, and Southport Harbor, a thriving port of entry and shipping center until 1890.

CONNECTICUT AUDUBON SOCIETY BIRDCRAFT MUSEUM AND SANCTUARY, 314 Unquowa Rd., Fairfield, CT 06430 (203-259-0416). *Grounds open all year daily; museum open all year Sat. and Sun. noon– 5. Donation $1. No picnicking, no pets. Steps into building, but exhibits are on one level; trails difficult for wheelchairs.*

The first private songbird refuge in New England (1914), this sanctuary has become a refuge for featherless bipeds as well. From the pleasant walking trails and boardwalk observation area you can spot many different species of birds, along with the occasional government scientist (the sanctuary doubles as a federal banding station). The natural history museum displays dioramas of native and African wildlife, a taxidermy exhibit of animals and birds that died from natural causes and were mounted by one of the museum's early curators, and a set of deceptively lifelike decoys by the legendary Charles "Shang" Wheeler.

CONNECTICUT AUDUBON SOCIETY FAIRFIELD NATURE CENTER AND LARSEN SANCTUARY, 2325 Burr St., Fairfield, CT 06430 (203-259-6305). *Building open all year Tues.–Sat. 9–4:30; free. Sanctuary open all year daily dawn-dusk; trail fee $1 adults, 50¢ children. Building closed on major holidays. No picnicking, no pets. Sensory trail for visually handicapped; gift shop wheelchair-accessible, some trails manageable for wheelchairs on dry days.*

The headquarters of the Connecticut Audubon Society features changing exhibits on state flora and fauna, solar energy applications, and a natural history library. In the adjoining Larsen Sanctuary, six miles of trails wind through 160 acres of woodlands, open fields, and marshes; home to more than 100 species of birds and animals, and an abundance of wildflowers, ferns, and trees. A special delight is the "singing and fragrance walk," designed for the visually handicapped but equally calculated to deepen an appreciation of the senses in those who have all five intact; soft paths with smooth wood handrails brush past prickly, fragrant evergreens across murmuring streams while birdsong fills the air.

Trip F-8
Ships, Circuses,
and Stars in Bridgeport

- CAPTAIN'S COVE MARINA
- THE BARNUM MUSEUM
- THE DISCOVERY MUSEUM
- BEARDSLEY ZOOLOGICAL GARDENS

DISTANCE: About 60 miles from Columbus Circle.

FOR THE DRIVER: Take **I-95** north to Exit 26. After the ramp bear right on Wordin Ave. to Bostwick Ave. and turn left to **Captain's Cove Marina.**

Go back to I-95 and continue briefly to Exit 27. Here take **CT-25** north to Exit 3. Shortly after the ramp, on Main St. across North Ave. (US-1) is **The Barnum Museum.**

Go back on Main to North Ave. Turn right here and go south briefly to Park Ave. Turn right on Park and follow it northwest about 2½ miles to **The Discovery Museum,** in Ninety Acres Park.

Continue northwest on Park Ave. to the **Merritt Parkway** and take it north to Exit 49S. Here take **CT-25** south to Exit 5, Boston Ave. Bear right on Boston after the ramp and go to Noble Ave. Turn left on Noble and go about ¼ mile to the **Beardsley Zoological Gardens,** entrance on the left.

CAPTAIN'S COVE MARINA, 1 Bostwick Ave., Bridgeport, CT 06605 (203-335-1433). *Tours of H.M.S. Rose daily except when not in port; call for current information and fees. Harbor and Long Island Sound cruises offered on other boats. Craft shops, restaurant (Mar.–Oct.), fish market, afternoon band concerts (Sun.), special events. Wheelchair-accessible.*

H.M.S. *Rose* is a replica of the flagship of Captain James Wallace, an officer of the British fleet stationed off the coast of New England in 1775 under the command of Admiral Samuel Graves. Fortunately for the Revolutionary cause, Graves was a singularly inept officer who made poor use of his forces. His half-hearted attempts to intimidate New England's seafaring towns inspired the colonists to take to their whalers and fishing boats and harass the British fleet. From such humble beginnings sprang the fledgling American navy, which had several early successes, including the capture of a tender from the *Rose.* On your tour of the *Rose* replica you will learn more about Colonial naval history and the workings of a British frigate. Afterwards, you'll have an opportunity to take a short cruise of the harbor, visit the craft shops, or dine at the restaurant.

THE BARNUM MUSEUM, 820 Main St., Bridgeport, CT 06604 (203-331-1104). *Open all year, Tues.–Sat. 10–4:30, Sun. noon–4:30. Closed Mon. and major holidays. Adults $5, seniors and students $4, children 4–18 $2, under 4 free. Special exhibitions, gift shop. Wheelchair-accessible.*

You don't have to be one of those suckers born every minute to go for The Barnum Museum, packed with memorabilia of the career of Bridgeport's most famous resident. A master of hype, Phineas Taylor Barnum knew how to turn adjectives into superlatives and curiosity into cash. He spent the better part of the 19th century titillating

Tom Thumb's court suit
(Photo courtesy of The Barnum Museum)

America with such spectacles as the Fiji mermaid (part monkey, part stuffed fish), the Siamese twins Chang and Eng, and Bridgeport native Charles Sherwood Stratton, a.k.a. General Tom Thumb, the 2½-foot midget who entertained kings, queens, presidents, and about 20 million other folks under Barnum's skillful management. In 1850 Barnum promoted the American tour of coloratura soprano Jenny Lind, the "Swedish Nightingale," and made her a tremendous success; in 1871 he opened his famous circus, with Jumbo the African elephant as the major (at 6¼ tons) attraction; and in between he took time out to be mayor of Bridgeport. All this—plus more! more!! more!!!—is recounted in the exhibits at The Barnum Museum. So step right up, ladies and gents, for the Greatest Show on Earth.

THE DISCOVERY MUSEUM, 4450 Park Ave., Bridgeport, CT 06604 (203-372-3521). *Open all year, Tues.–Sat. 10–5, Sun. noon–5; closed Mon. and major holidays. Adults $4.50, seniors and children 4–18 $3.50. Challenger space experience requires advance reservation. Gift shop. Wheelchair-accessible.*

Whether your taste leans towards Indians, antiques, art, stargazing, or space travel, you'll find something of interest here. The Challenger Space Center, where you can experience the space shuttle, is a popular attraction, as are the hands-on science and technology exhibits. The children's museum bustles with activities designed to entertain and inform. The planetarium offers excellent programs suited to all ages from the second grade up, and the adjacent Du Pont-Wheeler Gallery of the Skies has a variety of heavenly displays.

BEARDSLEY ZOOLOGICAL GARDENS, Noble Ave., Bridgeport, CT 06610 (203-576-8082). *Open all year daily 9–4; closed Thanksgiving, Christmas, New Year's. Parking fee $5 per out-of-state car ($3 in-state). Zoo admission: Adults $2, children 3–5 50¢, under 3 free. Picnic area, snack bar, gift shop, pony rides. Wheelchair-accessible.*

More than 200 animals inhabit this 30-acre zoo, Connecticut's largest. Monkeys and birds have the run of a large building, sea lions cavort in an outdoor pool, and farmyard animals mingle with visitors in the children's zoo. Well-tended gardens make Beardsley especially attractive during blooming periods.

Trip F-9
To Stratford on the Housatonic

- **BOOTHE MEMORIAL PARK AND MUSEUM**
- **CAPTAIN DAVID JUDSON HOUSE AND MUSEUM**
- **INDIAN WELL STATE PARK**

DISTANCE: About 70 miles from Columbus Circle to Indian Well.

FOR THE DRIVER: Take the **Hutchinson River Parkway** north into Connecticut, where it becomes the **Merritt Parkway.** Get off at Exit 53S and turn right after the ramp onto **CT-110** towards Stratford. Watch for the first small road on the right, Main St. Turn here and continue briefly to the **Boothe Memorial Park,** on the left.

Continue South on Main St., shortly rejoining CT-110. Proceed to the junction with **CT-113,** bear right, and continue south on 113 (Main St.), crossing US-1 (Barnum Ave.) and passing under railroad tracks and I-95. Several blocks later, just after Broad St., is Academy Hill, a small street on the left. Turn here for the **Judson House and Museum.**

Return to 113 and continue north several miles, crossing CT-8. Soon after that, watch for a road on the right to **Indian Well State Park.**

BOOTHE MEMORIAL PARK, N. Main St., Stratford, CT 06497 (203-375-9895). *Grounds open all year daily 8–dusk; buildings open Memorial Day through Oct., Tues.–Fri. 11–1 and Sat.–Sun. 1–4. Free. Picnic facilities, playground. Leashed pets only. Wheelchair-accessible.*

No one passes this group of strangely constructed buildings for the first time without doing a double-take. Built at random around the turn of the century by two eccentric brothers, the complex includes a renovated windmill, a large redwood structure full of baskets from all over the world, an enormous pipe organ in a building near a sunken garden, a blacksmith shop, a carriage museum, a clock-tower museum, and the old homestead building where the Boothe brothers lived. The park is situated on a hill affording some marvelous views of the whole area. A particular delight for flower fanciers and photographers is the beautiful Jackson and Perkins Trial Rose Garden.

CAPTAIN DAVID JUDSON HOUSE AND MUSEUM, 967 Academy Hill, Stratford, CT 06497 (203-378-0630). *Open mid-Apr. through Oct.; Wed., Sat., & Sun. 11–4, or by appointment. Adults $2, seniors and children $1.50. Not wheelchair-accessible.*

Built around 1750 on a foundation constructed over 100 years earlier, this well-preserved house is filled with typical furnishings from the 18th-century. Of special interest are some of the architectural features—the hand-rived shingles on the east gable end of the house, the graceful curved pediment over the doorway, the traditional center stairway, the original wood paneling. The tour takes you through various rooms steeped in an atmosphere of Colonial living. The cellar holds a lower kitchen once used as a slave quarters, equipped with a huge fireplace and a display of period household implements and tools. Behind the Judson House is the **Catharine Bunnel Mitchell Museum,** with carefully researched exhibits tracing the history of Stratford from the period of Indian settlement to about 1830. Both the house and the museum are maintained by the Stratford Historical Society.

INDIAN WELL STATE PARK, Shelton, CT 06484 (203-735-7108). *Open all year daily 8–sunset. Use fee Memorial Day to Labor Day $2 per car weekdays, $3 weekends and holidays. Picnicking, playing field, hiking trails, swimming, fishing, boating, food concession. Leashed pets only, in picnic areas only. Picnic area, food concession, and restrooms are wheelchair-accessible.*

Here's a lovely 153-acre park on the Housatonic River, perfect for picnicking or more active pursuits. The park takes its name from the Indian legends associated with the splash pool at the bottom of the scenic waterfall near the riverbank.

Trip F-10
Eli for a Day

- ## YALE UNIVERSITY

DISTANCE: About 80 miles from Columbus Circle.

FOR THE DRIVER: Take **I-95** north to Exit 47 and follow Oak St. Connector into downtown New Haven, crossing Church St. and bearing right on N. Frontage Rd. to York St. Turn right here and proceed several blocks north on York to Elm St., turn right two blocks to College St., then right again to the **Phelps Gateway** and the historic **New Haven Green.** The green, dating from 1638, is surrounded by three impressive churches; the games of both football and frisbee were born here, and many delightful events take place here each year.

Parking can be a problem in downtown New Haven, and Yale is best seen on foot in any case, so you may want to park in the commercial lot behind the Center for British Art, which you pass on your way to the green. It's at York and Crown streets, 3 blocks up York after you turn off N. Frontage. The following directions assume you're walking; if you're driving, some of the streets will be one way the wrong way, and you'll have to go around the block.

From Phelps Gateway, continue down College St. to the next corner, Chapel St. Turn right and go past the next corner, High St., to the **Art Gallery,** on the right. Across the street is the **Center for British Art.**

Go back to High St., turn left, and go two blocks to the **Beinecke Library,** at the corner of High and Wall Streets.

Continue up High St. to Grove St., turn right, go 3 blocks to Church St., and turn left. Proceed up Church St., bearing left across the railroad tracks and Trumball St., where Church becomes Whitney Ave. Shortly, Temple St. comes in from the left, and at this junction is a good local history museum, the **New Haven Colony Historical Society** (203-562-4183) *(Open Tues.–Fri. 10–5, Sat. & Sun. 2–5).* On the next corner, Whitney and Sachem St., is the **Peabody Museum.** For the **Collection of Musical Instruments,** turn left on Sachem and go past the museum to tiny Hillhouse Ave., then left again to 15 Hillhouse.

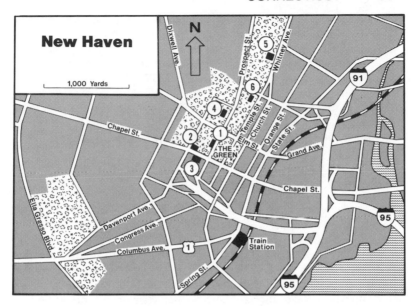

PUBLIC TRANSPORTATION: The New Haven train station is within walking distance of the sights. **Amtrak** provides excellent service from New York's Pennsylvania Station and other communities along the Northeast Corridor (1-800-USA-RAIL); while **Metro-North** offers a frequent slower-but-cheaper commuter train service from New York's Grand Central Terminal, uptown Manhattan, The Bronx, Westchester County, and Connecticut (1-800-638-7646 or 212-532-4900).

On this trip you'll visit New Haven, established by Puritans in 1637–38 under a theocratic form of government that issued strict laws regulating public and private conduct—the original "blue laws," so-named for the colored paper on which they were written. The town developed rapidly as a port of entry and industrial center, contributing many another first to American life, mostly in the field of manufacturing techniques and new products (among them two that would have horrified the promulgators of the blue laws: the corkscrew and the lollipop). Over the years, New Haven has had its fair share of famous citizens, including Noah Webster, Eli Whitney, and Charles Goodyear, not to mention a host of notable temporary residents passing through as students. This trip focuses on New Haven's leading educational and cultural institution, Yale University, but there are many other attractions here besides—Revolutionary War fortifications, historic homes and museums, the renowned Long Wharf Theater and

Yale Repertory Theater, fine municipal parks, cruises on Long Island Sound, and handsome buildings in a variety of architectural styles, from Colonial, Georgian, and Federal to Urban Renewal. For further information, contact the New Haven Convention and Visitors Bureau, 195 Church St., New Haven, CT 06510 (203-777-8550).

YALE UNIVERSITY, New Haven, CT 06520 (203-432-2300). *Campus open all year daily for tours, Mon.–Fri. 10:30 and 2, Sat.–Sun. 1:30; no reservation required, depart from Phelps Gateway. Free. Most of campus is wheelchair-accessible.*

Chartered in 1701, Yale occupied several different locations before settling in New Haven in 1716. It acquired its name in 1718 after a substantial donation from one Elihu Yale, an English merchant who prospered mightily from his somewhat dubious dealings as an official of the British East India Company. One of America's most prestigious universities, Yale became coeducational in 1969 and today has a student population of about 11,000. The tour begins at **Phelps Gateway** (1) on New Haven Green and takes in most of the campus buildings within walking distance, from the historic Old Campus and Connecticut Hall, where Revolutionary hero Nathan Hale once roomed, to the controversial abstract concrete Art and Architecture Building by Paul Rudolph. The attractions described below are numbered and have corresponding numbers on the map.

Yale University Art Gallery (2), 1111 Chapel St., New Haven, CT 06520 (203-432-2600). *Open all year Tues.–Sat. 10–5, Sun. 2–5, also Thurs. until 8 from mid-Sept. to mid-May; closed New Year's, July 4, Thanksgiving, Christmas. Free. Wheelchair-accessible.* The nation's oldest college art museum has impressive collections of pre-Columbian, Oriental, and African art, European paintings from the Middle Ages to the 20th century, American decorative arts from Colonial times to the present, 19th- and 20th-century American paintings, and modern sculpture. The museum has a pleasant, unhurried atmosphere, with enormous picture windows looking out on campus scenes.

Yale Center for British Art (3), 1080 Chapel St., New Haven, CT 06520 (203-432-2800). *Open all year Tues.–Sat. 10–5, Sun. 2–4; closed New Year's, Memorial Day, July 4, Labor Day, Thanksgiving, Christmas. Free. Museum shop. Wheelchair-accessible.* This outstanding public museum was established by Yale graduate Paul Mellon to preserve and display his collection of British art, the largest in the United States. The permanent and changing exhibits of paintings, sculpture, drawings, prints, and rare books trace aesthetic developments from the Elizabethan era to the mid-19th century, with special emphasis on the period between the birth of Hogarth in 1697 and the death of Turner in 1851, often considered the "golden age" of English art. In addition there are 13,000 reference volumes, an extensive photo archive, and a regular program of colloquia, lectures, concerts, and films to enhance your understanding of the artworks and their context. The museum building, a concrete, glass, and steel structure with interiors of travertine marble, white oak, and natural fibers, was the last design of American architect Louis I. Kahn. Fittingly, it stands across the street from his first major commission, the modern wing of the Yale Art Gallery.

Beinecke Rare Book and Manuscript Library (4), 121 Wall St., New Haven, CT 05520 (203-432-2977). *Open all year Mon.–Fri. 8:30–5, Sat. 10–5; closed Sun., major holidays, and Sat. in Aug. Free. Partially wheelchair-accessible.* Some rare treasures await you here, including a Gutenberg Bible, original Audubon prints from *The Birds of America*, medieval illuminated manuscripts, and more-or-less opaque modern manuscripts left by Twain, Hemingway, and other great American writers. The unique windowless building filters light through translucent marble panels that protect the library's collections, if not its visitors, from the ravages of time.

Peabody Museum of Natural History (5), 170 Whitney Ave., New Haven, CT 06511 (203-432-5050). *Open all year daily, Mon.–Sat. 10–5, Sun. and holidays noon–5; closed New Year's, July 4, Thanksgiving, Christmas. Adults $2.50, seniors $2, children 5–15 $1, under 5 free; free to all on weekday afternoons 3–5. Gift shop. Wheelchair-accessible.* The Peabody's admission fee is a small price to pay for a journey through 500 million years of geological and natural history. Here Earth's story unfolds in a series of outstanding exhibits of meteorites, rocks and minerals, invertebrate life, insect specimens, birds, mammals, remains of the ancient cultures of Mexico and Peru, artifacts of the Plains and Connecticut Indians. Perhaps the most dramatic is Dinosaur Hall, where huge fossil skeletons stand frozen against a vivid 110-foot-long mural, Rudolph F. Zallinger's Pulitzer Prize-winning *Age of Reptiles*. The Peabody, New England's largest natural history museum and one of the nation's best, offers a world "big as a Brontosaurus, delicate as a butterfly's wing, varied as human lives."

Yale Collection of Musical Instruments (6), 15 Hillhouse Ave., New Haven, CT 06520 (203-432-0822). *Open Sept.–July, Tues.–Thurs. 1–4; closed Aug. and during university recesses. Free. Not wheelchair-accessible.* Here are 850 beautifully wrought instruments spanning four centuries of musical history, representing the music-making traditions of North and South America, Europe, Africa, and Asia.

Trip F-11
Clang, Clang, Clang
Went the Trolley

- SHORE LINE TROLLEY MUSEUM

DISTANCE: About 80 miles from Columbus Circle.

FOR THE DRIVER: Take **I-95** north to Exit 51, Frontage Rd. (US-1). Proceed to the traffic light at Forbes Place, turn right briefly, then left on Main St. Continue on Main to East Haven Green, then turn right on Hemingway Ave. and left on River St., past the green. Watch for the **Shore Line Trolley Museum,** on the left.

    This trip takes you very close to the sights on Trips F-10 and F-12, and could be combined with some of them.

SHORE LINE TROLLEY MUSEUM, 17 River St., East Haven, CT 06512 (203-467-6927). *Operates Apr. through Nov.: Apr. and Nov., Sun. 11–5; May to Memorial Day and Labor Day through Oct., Sat.–Sun. and holidays 11–5; Memorial Day to Labor Day, daily 11–5. Adults $5, seniors $4, children 2–11 $2, under 2 free; tickets good all day on date of sale. Picnic grove, gift shop. Inquire about schedule and rates for special events and the Santa Claus Special in Dec. Some facilities are wheelchair-accessible.*

    Remember those weather-filled mornings standing on the corner waiting for the trolley? Griping at paying a nickel for the crowded, jouncy ride? Then one day the trolley never came again.

    Today, why not take a long drive to visit some of these creatures from the past? You'll pay about 80 times the old fare, and chances are that you'll love every minute of it. Your ride—a three-mile round trip along the shore—may be on the open "breezer" that once ran to the Yale Bowl, or on one of the other cars so carefully restored by the museum's craftsmen. Afterwards, or between rides (you can take as many as you wish), you'll go on a tour of the car barns and workshops. All told, there are about 100 trolleys, including the world's first electric freight loco, an antique parlor car, and a pioneering rapid-transit car on display, spanning the years between 1878 and 1945. You can deepen your knowledge of trolley history by visiting the Sprague building, named for Frank Julian Sprague, father of electric traction and developer of the first electric street railway (1887).

The Shore Line Trolley Museum is part of the Branford Electric Railway District, a National Historic Site. Apart from its educational value, the ride is a lot of fun, and a cheerful spirit prevails among the patrons, punctuated by an occasional twinge of nostalgia. Children tend to consider the trolleys about a half-step this side of the Conestoga wagon, while their elders wonder, "What happened? Where did they go?"

Trip F-12
Guilford's Historic Houses

- HYLAND HOUSE
- THOMAS GRISWOLD HOUSE
- HENRY WHITFIELD HOUSE

DISTANCE: About 90 miles from Columbus Circle.

FOR THE DRIVER: Take **I-95** north to Exit 58 and turn right on **CT-77** to Guilford Green. Bear around the green to Boston St., turn left on Boston, and proceed a short distance to the **Hyland House.** Continue briefly on Boston St. to the **Griswold House,** on the right at Lovers' Lane. From here ask directions for back roads to the **Whitfield House.**

HYLAND HOUSE, 84 Boston St., Guilford, CT 06437 (203-453-9477). *Open June–Sept., Tues.–Sun. 10–4:30; Labor Day to Columbus Day, Sat.–Sun. 10–4:30. Adults $1.50, seniors $1, children under 12 free. Not wheelchair-accessible.*

Here is a fine example of a Colonial saltbox, built around 1660. The interior features some unusual woodwork, rare early furnishings, and three walk-in fireplaces equipped for 17th-century cooking. Upstairs are sewing rooms, closets filled with period clothing, and wool and flax wheels.

THOMAS GRISWOLD HOUSE, 171 Boston St., Guilford, CT 06437 (203-453-3176). *Open mid-June to mid-Sept., Tues.–Sun. 11–4. Adults $1.50, children 50¢, under 12 free. Not wheelchair-accessible.*

Another excellent example of a Colonial saltbox, this 1774 house was once pictured on a commemorative stamp. It is now the headquarters of the Guilford Keeping Society, serving as a repository for documents, records, pictures, and artifacts dating back to 1735. You'll see the "borning room," the buttery, the "keeping room" where the first was kept burning, a restored working blacksmith shop, a costume exhibit, and some fine local furniture. A barn museum outside holds a collection of antique farm tools.

HENRY WHITFIELD HOUSE, Old Whitfield St., Guilford, CT 06437 (203-453-2457). *Open Apr.–Nov., Wed.–Sun. 10–5; Nov.–Apr., Wed.–Sun. 10–4; closed Thanksgiving, Dec. 15–Jan. 15. Adults $3, seniors and children $1.50. Not wheelchair-accessible.*

This striking edifice, said to be the oldest stone house in New England, belonged to the founder of Guilford, the Reverend Henry Whitfield, who led a group of parishioners from England to America to avoid religious persecution. They arrived in 1639 and promptly set about building a typical English manor house, unaware of the rugged American winters that had taught their Pilgrim predecessors to construct smaller, more easily heated rooms; the Great Hall, 33 feet long and 15 feet wide, required a fireplace at either end and a partition to divide it into two rooms when more space was needed. Apparently the settlers were not unaware of other potential dangers of the New World, for they made the walls about two feet thick. Whitfield and his family lived in this stronghold, which was also used for church meetings. Today it is a museum of 17th- and 18th-century Guilford life.

Trip F-13
Up the Connecticut River

- PRATT HOUSE
- STEAM TRAIN AND RIVERBOAT RIDES
- GILLETTE CASTLE STATE PARK
- FLORENCE GRISWOLD MUSEUM

DISTANCE: About 125 miles from Columbus Circle.

FOR THE DRIVER: Take **I-95** north to Exit 69 at Old Saybrook and pick up **CT-9** north to Exit 3 at Essex. Bear right after the ramp and follow signs to Historic Essex Village and the **Pratt House.** For the **Steam Train and Riverboat,** go straight after the ramp and follow signs.

The next stop, **Gillette Castle,** is on the east bank of the Connecticut River. If you take the combination train and riverboat ride from Essex, you'll see it from the water. If you want to visit it, you have two choices. Return to CT-9, continue north to Exit 6, and take **CT-148** east to Chester, where you can get the Chester-Hadlyme Ferry (Apr.–Nov. daily 7 a.m. to 6:45 p.m., capacity 8 cars), the second-oldest continuously operating ferry in the United States. If the ferry is not operating or you prefer to drive, continue north on CT-9 to Exit 7 and take **CT-82** across the river to East Haddam, where the first building you'll see is the Goodspeed Opera House; continue past it on 82, shortly bear sharp right, and head south a few miles to Gillette Castle State Park, following signs.

Essex and East Haddam are in the southern and eastern portions, respectively, of Middlesex County, a picturesque region stretching north along the Connecticut River. For further information, contact the Connecticut Valley Tourism Commission, 393 Main St., Middletown, CT 06457 (203-347-6924).

From Gillette Castle, continue on CT-82 a few miles to the junction with **CT-156.** Turn right and go south through Hamburg towards Old Lyme. Just before the junction with I-95, turn left on **CT-51** and go past a shopping center to the **Florence Griswold House.**

East of Old Lyme off I-95 are more historic coastal towns that can be reached on a daytrip from New York City, but are better visited when you have more time to spare: **New London** and environs, with an array of historic houses, parks, and beaches, and marine attractions; **Groton,** where the *USS Nautilus,* the world's first nuclear submarine (1954), was built and is now preserved as a memorial and museum; and **Mystic,** with its famous restored seaport and living maritime museum, also a departure point for windjammer cruises on Long Island Sound. For further information about this area of Connecticut, contact the Southeastern Connecticut Tourism District, 27 Masonic St., Post Office Bldg., New London, CT 06320 (203-444-2206 or 1-800-222-6783), and Mystic Seaport, Mystic, CT 06355 (203-572-0711).

PRATT HOUSE, 19 West Ave., Essex, CT 06426 (203-767-1191). *Open June–Labor Day, Sat.–Sun. 1–4. Adults $2, children under 12 free. Not wheelchair-accessible.*

This small center-chimney Colonial house (1732), restored by the Society for the Preservation of New England Antiquities, is filled with furnishings from the 17th, 18th, and 19th centuries. There are fine collections of Connecticut redware and unusual Chinese "courting mirrors."

STEAM TRAIN AND RIVERBOAT, Valley Railroad Company, P.O. Box 452, Essex, CT 06426 (203-767-0103). *Operates May through October on varying days; call for current schedule. Train and boat combination: Adults $12.95, children 2–11 $5.95, under 2 free, 10% discount for seniors. Extra fare for parlor car $2.95. Other plans, group rates, and special events are offered. Will accommodate wheelchairs.*

A vintage steam train uses some 3,000 gallons of water and 3 tons of coal to take you on an hour-long journey into the past, whistling and chugging its way up the scenic Connecticut River from Essex to Deep River Landing. Here you can transfer to a riverboat for an additional hour's voyage farther upriver, passing green hills dotted with fine old houses and landmarks like Gillette Castle (see below) and the Goodspeed Opera House (203-873-8668) in East Haddam, an ornate Victorian theater now devoted exclusively to the presentation and preservation of American musicals.

The train, powered by a classic steam-belching, bell-clanging locomotive, follows the route of the old Valley Railroad, which ran between Hartford and Old Saybrook from 1871 until it was gobbled up by J. P. Morgan's New York, New Haven & Hartford line. This living slice of history is supplemented by the antique cars on display at the Connecticut Valley Railroad Museum, including a rare self-propelled Brill car and a luxurious Pullman with revolving plush seats, rich carpeting, and leaded-glass partitions. Since 1990 the railroad has been using the first brand-new steam locomotive to be ordered by any American railroad in 37 years, built in China where steam is still common.

GILLETTE CASTLE STATE PARK, 67 River Rd., Hadlyme, CT 06439 (203-526-2336). *Grounds open all year daily 8–sunset; free. Castle open Memorial Day to Columbus Day daily 11–5, Columbus Day to the last weekend before Christmas Sat.–Sun. 10–4. Adults $2, children 6–11 $1, 5 and under free. Picnicking, hiking trails, fishing, canoe rentals, food concession. Leashed pets only, in picnic areas only. Wheelchair-accessible picnic shelter; castle not wheelchair-accessible.*

High above the pastoral Connecticut River perches a dream castle built by the great turn-of-the-century actor and portrayer of Sherlock Holmes, William Gillette (1853–1937). A native of Hartford, Gillette chose this site because of the superb view. One of the first actors to hold that a characterization should be based on the performer's own strongest personality traits, he applied the same principle to his castle, which he designed himself and fitted out with many unique mechanical devices of his own invention. He lived here from 1919 to 1937 with a supporting cast of 15 felines to whom he was greatly attached; the 24-room castle contains, among other things, a large collection of cat curios, along with scrapbooks, clippings, and other memorabilia of Gillette's stage career. Today his ivy-covered fieldstone creation in the centerpiece of a beautiful 184-acre state park—a fact that reflects well on Connecticut in light of the stipulation in Gillette's will that his property should under no circumstances pass to "any blithering sap-head who has no conception of where he is or with what sur-rounded."

FLORENCE GRISWOLD MUSEUM, 96 Lyme St., Old Lyme, CT 06371 (203-434-5542). *Open all year: June–Oct. Tues–Sat. 10–5, Sun. 1–5; Nov.–May Wed.–Sun. 1–5. Adults $2, children under 12 free. Wheel-chair-accessible.*

This handsome late Georgian mansion (1817) was the hub of a turn-of-the-century art colony subsidized by Miss Florence Griswold, who lived here and took in such boarders as Childe Hassam, Henry Ward Ranger, and other American Impressionists; when they were short on cash, the boarders did a little painting around the house to pay the rent. Some of their work, including these "house paintings," is on display here, along with New England furnishings, decorative arts, and exhibits on local history. Next door and across the street, Miss Florence's tradition of supporting creativity lives on in the **Lyme Academy of Fine Arts** (203-434-5232), with year-round changing exhibits of paintings and sculpture *(open Mon.–Fri. 9–4:30, free),* and the **Lyme Art Association** (203-434-7802), founded by members of the original Old Lyme art colony, now a noted gallery offering five major shows every summer.

Area G

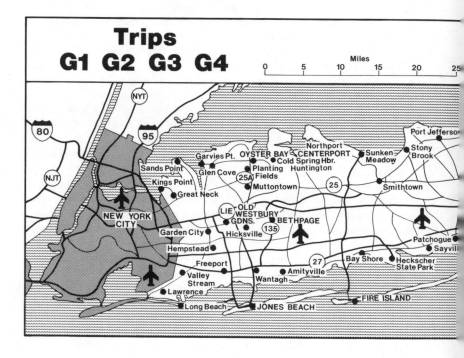

TOURING ON LONG ISLAND

The next trips take you to that famous 120-mile-long fish-shaped piece of glacial deposit called Long Island, with its innumerable bays, coves, and inlets on Long Island Sound to the north and its beautiful ocean beaches to the south—"that slender riotous island which extends itself due east of New York," as F. Scott Fitzgerald called it, "the old island here that flowered once for Dutch sailors' eyes—a fresh, green breast of the new world."

296

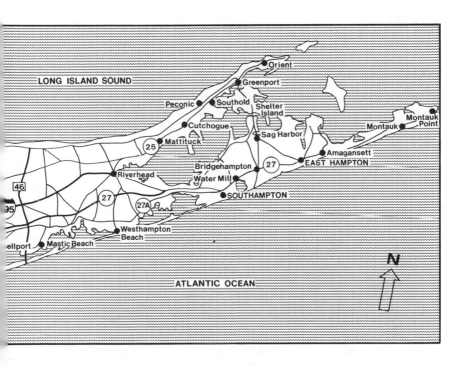

To judge by the way the city empties out and the Long Island Expressway fills up on weekends, many New Yorkers already have their favorite retreats on the island. This section outlines four long drives that take you to all the familiar haunts and suggest some possibilities for exploration off the beaten track. You'll be traveling in a more or less straight line out to the fishtail tip of Long Island, first along the North Shore and North Fork, where historic New England-type towns flourish, then along the South Shore and South Fork, with miles of beaches that apparently come and go at the will of the Atlantic Ocean.

Trip G-1
Gold Coast Mansions and Historic Ports

- ## THE NORTH SHORE

DISTANCE: From Columbus Circle to the farthest point, Riverhead, is about 80 miles.

FOR THE DRIVER: Since this trip is planned mainly for the enjoyment of the drive itself, the directions are incorporated with the brief descriptions of the attractions along the route.

Long Island, occupied on the west by the two New York City boroughs of Brooklyn and Queens, stretches east across Nassau and Suffolk counties, encompassing populous suburbs, thriving seaport towns, quaint villages, and some of the finest beaches to be found anywhere. It is rich in Indian lore and Colonial history, studded with fine architecture, blessed with fertile farmlands and almost limitless recreational opportunities. Most of the island's shore towns have public beaches but require permits or parking stickers for nonresidents; if you're planning a beach outing, check with the nearest municipality first.

For further information about Long Island, contact the Long Island Convention & Visitors Bureau, Nassau Coliseum, Uniondale, NY 11554 (1-800-441-4601).

NORTH SHORE. On this drive, you'll go east on **NY-25A** (Northern Blvd. in Queens), noting the attractions along the route to the north and south.

Just over the Nassau County line from Queens, to the left off 25A in the Great Neck area, is the **U.S. Merchant Marine Academy** (516-773-5000, tour info. 516-773-5527) at Kings Point, where you can visit the Memorial Chapel honoring the service's war dead and see exhibits of shipping history in the American Merchant Marine Museum. On most Saturdays in the spring and fall, regimental reviews are held on the grounds. The academy is very attractively located, and its main administration center, Wiley Hall, was once the country home of automobile magnate Walter P. Chrysler. *(Grounds open year round ex-*

cept July and federal holidays, daily 9–5. Museum Sat.–Sun. 1–4:30. Free.)

Continue east on 25A. North of Manhasset, reached via **NY-101,** is the **Sands Point Park and Preserve** (516-883-1612), former Gold Coast estate of Daniel Guggenheim and his son Harry, founder of *Newsday.* On the grounds are the English Tudor-style Hempstead House, the Irish-influenced Castlegould, and the Normandy-style manor house **Falaise,** which is open for guided tours. *(Apr.–Nov., Sat.–Wed. 10–5, closed Election Day, Veteran's Day, Thanksgiving; no children under 12).* The very, very rich have a knack for picking beautiful spots, and Sands Point is no exception. It has a great view of Long Island Sound and looks across Hempstead Harbor to Glen Cove and Garvies Point, the next stop, reached by returning to 25A, heading east, and turning north on **NY-107.** Here, at the **Garvies Point Museum and Preserve** (516-671-0300), you can see exhibits on the geological formation of the region and its history of Indian settlement as revealed by archaeological finds. You can also follow 5 miles of nature trails through 62 acres of forests, meadows, and high bluffs overlooking boulder-strewn beaches. *(Open daily 9–4:45, closed winter holidays; wheelchair-accessible.)*

Now you're ready to charge up Sagamore Hill for a visit to the beloved summer retreat of America's 26th president, Theodore Roosevelt. The centerpiece of the **Sagamore Hill National Historic Site** (516-922-4447) in Oyster Bay is T.R.'s family home, restored to the period of his presidency (1901–1909). Completed in 1885, this fine old Victorian structure incorporates many of Roosevelt's personal desires, including a large piazza with rocking chairs where the family could sit and watch the setting sun, a bay window with a southern view, and enormous fireplaces. You'll see objects collected on his trips around the world, gifts from the famous, family heirlooms, trophies, and personal mementos such as the "Clara-doll" in the playroom and the Teddy bears named after him. "Nothing," said Roosevelt, "can take the place of family life." Near the house is the **Old Orchard Museum,** offering historical exhibits, documents, photographs, and hourly showings of a stirring documentary on the highlights of T.R.'s life. *(Open daily 9:30–5, closed Thanksgiving, Christmas, New Year's. Wheelchair-accessible.)*

On the way up to Sagamore Hill, you'll pass several other sites well worth visiting. Some of the finest collections of plantings in the East are to be found at the 400-acre **Planting Fields Arboretum** (516-922-9201), with its superb specimens of trees, shrubs, and flowers, particularly lavish displays of rhododendrons and azaleas, and a Synoptic Shrub Collection presenting an A-to-Z sampler of species and varieties best as ornamentals. On the grounds is **Coe Hall,** a 65-room Elizabethan-Tudor mansion, originally the estate of marine insurance magnate William Robertson Coe. *(Arboretum open year round daily 9–5; mansion Apr.–Sept. Mon.–Fri. 1–3:30, closed Christmas. Wheelchair-accessible.)* South of the Planting Fields, just across 25A, is the **Muttontown Nature Center** (516-364-1050) in East Norwich, where you can hike along some lovely nature trails and inspect the displays in the nature study building. *(Trails open daily 9:30–4:30; nature center Mon.–Fri., closed holidays except Memorial Day, July 4, Labor and Columbus days. Free. Wheelchair-accessible.)*

The town of Oyster Bay has several buildings of historic interest. **Raynham Hall** (516-922-6808), 20 W. Main St., is a 1705 clapboard saltbox with a Victorian wing of 1851. Home of the Samuel Townsend family, it served as headquarters for the Queen's Rangers after Long Island was taken by the British during the American Revolution. *(Open Tues.–Sun. 1–5, closed holidays. Not wheelchair-accessible.)* **Wightman House** (516-922-5032), at 20 Summit St., is another Colonial saltbox, built around 1720. It now contains historical exhibits, town memorabilia, and the collection of the Oyster Bay Historical Society. *(Open Sat.–Sun. 1–4, free, partially wheelchair-accessible.)*

On the way to or from Sagamore Hill, you may also want to stop off at the **Theodore Roosevelt Memorial Sanctuary and Trailside Museum** (516-922-3200), 11 acres of woodland maintained by the National Audubon Society as a refuge for wild birds and a tribute to T.R.'s record as an early and ardent conservationist. His grave is in the adjacent cemetery.

Before continuing along the North Shore, you could go south of 25A and west a few miles to **Old Westbury Gardens** (516-333-0048), located on Old Westbury Rd. just below the L.I. Expressway. Now a National Historic Site, the former estate of financier John S. Phipps contains 8 formal gardens; including the Boxwood Garden, with its ancient giant boxwood and reflecting pool; the Walled Garden, with 2 acres of herbaceous borders and brilliant seasonal flower displays; and the charming Cottage Garden, once the playground of the Phipps children, with a small thatched cottage surrounded by a miniature garden and a fairyland of flowering shrubs. Westbury House, a fine Stuart-style mansion built early in this century, contains many priceless antiques and paintings by Gainsborough, Sargent, Reynolds, and other noted English artists. Both the house and grounds are patterned after an English country estate of the 18th century. *(Open May–Oct., Wed.–Sun. & holidays in season, 10–5; wheelchair-accessible.)*

Return to 25A and head east to Cold Spring Harbor, just over the Suffolk County line. As befits an old whaling town, Cold Spring Harbor has a **Whaling Museum** (516-367-3418) with a completely outfitted whaling boat, many tools of the trade, and other artifacts of this by-

Sagamore Hill National Historic Site
(Photo courtesy of L.I. Convention & Visitors Bureau)

gone era, including a scrimshaw collection of over 400 pieces. *(Open June–Aug. daily 11–5, rest of year daily except Mon. & holidays. Largely wheelchair-accessible.)* A considerably less gargantuan fisherman's target is the focus of attention at the 100-year-old **Cold Spring Harbor Fish Hatchery** (516-692-6768), where you can observe trout in various stages of maturation and see exhibits on fish and amphibians native to New York.

The next stop is Huntington, today known chiefly as a commuter suburb and center of precision manufacturing, but a town that still preserves many reminders of its past. The **Huntington Historical Society** (516-427-7045) maintains the **David Conklin Farmhouse** (c. 1750) at New York Ave. & High St., with period furnishings and displays on local history; the **Powell-Jarvis House** (1795), a favorite with antique buffs; and the Huntington Trade School (1905), with local history exhibits and research collections. *(Open Tues.–Fri. & Sun. 1–4, closed major holidays. Not wheelchair-accessible.)* Huntington's Hecksher Park, a popular spot for picnicking and outdoor concerts, contains the noted **Hecksher Museum** (516-351-3250), with a fine permanent collection of paintings and sculpture from the 1500s to the present. *(Open Tues.–Fri. 10–5, weekends 1–5, closed legal holidays. Partially wheelchair-accessible.)*

South of Huntington, on Old Walt Whitman Rd. near West Hills Park, is the **Walt Whitman Birthplace State Historic Site** (516-427-5240), where the "good gray poet" was born in 1819. Whitman spent his boyhood in this small shingled farmhouse, which has been restored as a museum honoring America's first major poet. The lower floor contains period furnishings; upstairs are documents, pictures, some of Whitman's manuscripts, and various exhibits. *(Open Wed.–Fri. 1–4, Sat.–Sun. 10–4, closed holidays. Free. Not wheelchair-accessible.)*

A few miles east of Huntington is Centerport, and here, at the tip of Little Neck Point, is an attraction not to be missed: the **Vanderbilt Museum** (516-262-7880), housed in a mansion built by William K. Vanderbilt II, a great-grandson of the legendary Commodore Cornelius Vanderbilt. Known as the Eagle's Nest, this opulent 24-room Spanish Revival edifice was a simple 6-room country dwelling before it fell under the transforming spell of the Vanderbilt fortune. William K. was an enthusiastic naturalist, sportsman, and collector. Today the exotic art treasures he gathered in his world travels fill the dining room, bedrooms, library, and sitting room. There are several enormous hobby collections and a natural history display of over 17,000 marine and wildlife specimens, many of them quite rare. Outside, you can see panoramic vistas through columns of marble from the ruins of Carthage, Spanish-Moroccan buildings with belltower and bells dating from 1715, courtyards and mosaic-bordered walks, and landscaped gardens overlooking Northport Bay. Also on the grounds is the Vanderbilt Planetarium. *(Open Tues.–Sat. 10–4, Sun. & holidays noon–5, closed Mon., Christmas, Jan. 1, 2. Partially wheelchair-accessible.)*

Continuing east, you come to Northport, settled by English Puritans in 1656 on land purchased from the Matinecock Indians. The town has an excellent harbor, and its rich seafaring past is unfolded in the exhibits at the **Northport Historical Museum** (516-757-9859), located in the Carnegie Library. *(Open Tues.–Sun. 1–4:30, closed holidays. Free.)* On the tip of a spit of land jutting out into Long Island Sound is Eaton's Neck Lighthouse, built in 1798 and still casting its warning beacon almost 18 miles out to sea.

A little east of Northport, just off 25A, is **Sunken Meadow State Park,** with a nice beach for swimming in the generally placid waters of the Sound. Sunken Meadow also has picnicking, hiking trails, fishing, winter sports, and three 9-hole golf courses.

If you continue east on 25A, you'll shortly arrive in Smithtown, where you'll see the famous Bull Statue in a small park in the center of town. The statue commemorates the exploits of one of the early town fathers, Richard Smith, who made a bet with the Indians about how far a man could travel on a bull in a day. Impressed with his demonstration, the Indians granted him all the land he and his mount covered. Researchers are still attempting to determine whether the bull went farther in those days. There are a number of historic buildings in Smithtown, including the Caleb Smith House, where the local historical society makes its headquarters.

Continue on to Stony Brook, an old harbor town where you can easily spend a day. The entire village is a bit of a museum piece, having been restored to the Federal period through the generosity of philanthropist Ward Melville in the early 1940s. It's a pleasant place to shop, dine, stroll, or explore the **Museums at Stony Brook** (516-751-0066), a remarkable historical and cultural complex housing collections of art and artifacts from centuries past. In the History Museum are exhibits of costumes, dolls, toys, textiles, and housewares, and permanent displays of finely crafted decoys and miniature period rooms. The Art Museum offers changing exhibits of 19th-century paintings, with an emphasis on the works of American genre painter William Sydney Mount (1807–1868), a Stony Brook resident and one of the first artists to portray blacks sympathetically, if stereotypically. The Carriage Museum houses over 60 horse-drawn carriages, wagons, and sleighs. There is also a blacksmith shop, a one-room school, and a 1794 barn. *(Open Wed.–Sat. 10–5, Sun. noon–5, closed Thanksgiving, Christmas, New Year's. Partially wheelchair-accessible.)*

Leaving Stony Brook, you can continue east on 25A to Port Jefferson, another attractive harbor town, where the Port Jefferson Ferry (516-473-0286) docks on its four daily round trips to Bridgeport, Connecticut (see Trip F-8), from mid-May to mid-October. Along the way, in Setauket, you'll pass the **Thompson House** (516-941-9444), a Colonial saltbox built around 1700, once the home of Long Island historian Benjamin F. Thompson. It has a good collection of early Long Island furniture and a Colonial herb garden. *(Open June–Oct. Fri.–Sun. 1–5).*

About 15 miles east of Port Jefferson, 25A merges with **NY-25**. From here you can continue east to Riverhead, the last stop on this North Shore drive. Another historic town with fine beaches, boating facilities, and deep-sea fishing, Riverhead is the home of the **Suffolk Historical Museum** (516-727-2881), depicting the history of the county and its people in a series of exhibits highlighting early crafts, transportation, whaling, and the Long Island Indian legacy. *(Open Mon.–Sat. 12:30–4:30, closed holidays. Free.)*

Trip G-2
Fertile Fields, Welcoming Waters

- ## THE NORTH FORK

DISTANCE: From Columbus Circle to the farthest point, Orient Point, is about 105 miles.

FOR THE DRIVER: Road directions for this trip are incorporated into the site descriptions, below.

On this drive, you can pick up where you left off on the North Shore, following NY-25 east. For further information, contact the Long Island Convention and Visitor's Bureau, Nassau Coliseum, Uniondale, NY 11554 (1-800-441-4601). For the specific areas covered on this trip, you might also contact the Greenport-Southold Chamber of Commerce, Box 66, Greenport, NY 11944 (516-477-1383), and the Shelter Island Chamber of Commerce, Box 598, Shelter Island, NY 11964 (516-749-0251). If you visit a municipal beach, remember to inquire about non-resident permits or parking stickers.

NORTH FORK. The drive begins east of Riverhead, and follows **NY-25** through acres of rolling farmland and fields of potato plants, berry vines, vegetables, and fruit trees. Soon you come to Mattituck, with a fine harbor and several buildings of historic interest. You might want to stop at the **Mattituck Hills Winery** (516-298-9150) for a free tour and tastings before pressing on.

About 3 miles east of Mattituck is Cutchogue, where you will find the **Old House,** the **Schoolhouse Museum,** and the **Wickham Farmhouse** (516-734-6532) clustered around the historic village green. The Old House, built in 1649, is a particularly good example of English Tudor architecture and is furnished with authentic period pieces, as is the Wickham Farmhouse, dating from the early 1700s. The Schoolhouse Museum (1840), Cutchogue's first district school, takes you back to the basics of 19th-century education. *(Open May–Oct. Sat.–Mon. 2–5).* Cutchogue is also the home of the **Hargrave Vineyard** (516-734-5111), one of Long Island's oldest and best-known wineries.

Continue east to Southold, passing another fine winery, **Pindar Vineyards** (516-734-6200) in Peconic. Southold, too, is a historic town proud of its past. Its **Archaeological Museum** (516-765-3029) has one

304

of the largest and best collections of Indian artifacts on Long Island. *(Open July–Aug. Fri.–Sun. 1:30–4:30)*. The restored village green complex has some interesting Colonial and Victorian houses that are maintained by the **Southold Historical Society** (516-765-5500) and that may be visited (call for current information). To the north of the village is the **Horton's Point Lighthouse Marine Museum,** facing Long Island Sound. *(Open mid-May to mid-Oct.; Sat., Sun., holidays; 11–4)*.

Not far east of Southold is Greenport, an old whaling town often described as "New England on Long Island." Here in addition to fine beaches, great fishing, and some outstanding seafood restaurants, you'll find the charming **Museum of Childhood** (516-477-0720), with a hand-carved model Swiss village, a miniature Ferris wheel, antique dolls and doll furniture, and an array of other toys. *(Open mid-June to Labor Day, Wed.–Sat. 1–4:30, Sun. 2–5)*.

Greenport is also the docking point for the ferry to **Shelter Island** (516-749-0139), one of Long Island's loveliest and least "touristy" spots. This aptly-named patch of land, 7 miles long and 6 miles wide, was settled in 1652 by New England Quakers fleeing Puritan persecution and is still a peaceful haven today. Situated between the North and South forks, it has a highly irregular coastline pierced by inlets and caressed by coves, with miles of pristine beaches and acres of gently rolling hills. It is also accessible by ferry from Sag Harbor (Trip G-4).

The next stop is Orient, near the eastern tip of the North Fork. Here **Orient Beach State Park** (516-323-2440) spreads over a 357-acre peninsula on Gardiners Bay, offering excellent swimming and fishing. In town, on Village Lane, is the **Oysterponds Museum** (516-323-2480), a complex of 7 museum buildings that have been designated a National Historic District. *(Open June–Sept. Wed.–Thurs., Sat.–Sun., 2–5)*.

From Orient, it's a short hop to Orient Point, which is as far east as you can go on the North Fork unless you want to board the **Orient Point Ferry** (516-323-2525 or 203-443-7394) for a 1½-hour trip to New London, Connecticut. (There's a smallish island east of Orient Point, Plum Island, but it's used by the government for animal disease experiments and is off-limits to the public—no doubt for good reason.) The ferry service operates daily except Christmas and requires advance reservations if you want to take your car along.

Trip G-3
By the Sea, by the Beautiful Sea

- ## THE SOUTH SHORE

DISTANCE: About 85 miles from Columbus Circle to the farthest point, Hampton Bays.

FOR THE DRIVER: Road directions are incorporated into the site descriptions, below.

On this drive you'll use NY-27 and NY-27A as the main routes and reference points. For further information contact the Long Island Convention & Visitors Bureau, Nassau Coliseum, Uniondale, NY 11554 (1-800-441-4601). If you visit a municipal beach, remember to inquire about nonresident permits or parking stickers.

SOUTH SHORE. Cross into Nassau County on **NY-27** (Southern Belt Parkway), which becomes the Sunrise Highway paralleling NY-27A, Montauk Highway, until the two merge. A few miles southwest of Valley Stream, the first major town you come to, is Lawrence, where you can visit **Rock Hall** (516-239-1157), a Georgian Colonial manor filled with artwork and antiques. *(Open Apr.–Nov., Wed.–Sat. & Mon. 10–4, Sun. noon–4, closed holidays; free.)* This is just east of J.F.K. Airport, and can also be reached via Rockaway Blvd. in Queens. From here you may want to continue south across the Atlantic Beach Bridge onto **Long Beach,** a popular resort island with 5 miles of beach, a 3-mile boardwalk, and other recreational facilities.

Continuing east from Valley Stream, you'll shortly come to Lynbrook, and just south of here in Fast Rockaway's Memorial Park is the **Grist Mill Museum** (516-621-1398), with two floors of East Rockaway memorabilia and exhibits on Indian and maritime history. *(Open Memorial Day to Labor Day, Sat.–Sun. 1–5; free.)* North of Lynbrook are several attractions you might want to investigate before proceeding along the shore. In Hempstead, at 110 North Franklin St., you'll find the **African-American Museum** (516-485-0470), with exhibits exploring the history and cultural heritage of Afro-American Long Islanders. *(Open Tues.–Sat. 9–4:45, Sun. 1–4:45; free.)* Also in the Hempstead area are the **Nassau Veterans Memorial Coliseum** (516-422-9222), home of the New York Islanders hockey team, and **Hofstra University** (516-560-

6600), with many sporting events, performances, and galleries open to the public. In Garden City, at Mitchel Field, adjacent to the Nassau Community College, is the **Cradle of Aviation Museum** (516-222-1190), tracing the history of air travel from the Wright Brothers to the Space Age. *(Open May–Oct. Fri.–Sun. noon–5; free)*. Nearby Adelphi University (516-663-1120) offers a range of cultural, theatrical, and sports events.

Back on NY-27, continue east to Freeport, a fishing and boating center with the famous "Nautical Mile" of **Woodcleft Canal,** a great place to dine on seafood, shop for fresh fish, charter a boat, take a canal excursion, or watch the Great Canoe Races held annually in July. Freeport is also the gateway to one of the most popular parks in the Greater New York City area, **Jones Beach State Park** (516-785-1600), a 2,413-acre playground with 5 miles of oceanfront beach, additional swimming at Zach's Bay and in the saltwater and freshwater pools, boat dock and rentals, fishing, nature and bike trails, and a host of other activities. The **Jones Beach Outdoor Theater** (516-221-1000) seats over 10,000 for concerts by name pop, country, and rock entertainers. Jones Beach attracts enormous crowds but by and large knows how to handle them. Getting there is another matter; try to go early on a weekday to avoid the automotive holding pattern on the approach roads on weekends. On the way to Jones Beach from Freeport via Meadowbrook State Parkway, you'll pass a junction with the Loop Parkway, which takes you to several parks and beaches on the east end of Long Beach Island (see above).

A little east of Freeport on 27 is Merrick, settled in 1643 and named for its original inhabitants, the Merokian Indians, commemorated by the town's 18-foot Totem Pole. About 2 miles beyond Merrick is Wantagh, another access point for Jones Beach, via the Wantagh State Parkway. From Wantagh, you might want to detour north several miles to Hicksville to look at the magnificent doors of **Trinity Lutheran Church** (516-931-2225) at 40 West Nichola St., exact replicas of the 15th-century bronze doors executed by the Florentine sculptor Lorenzo Ghiberti for the east portal of the Baptistery of the Duomo of San Giovanni Battista, a milestone of the Italian Renaissance. Ghiberti's fellow Florentines were so impressed with the doors, whose gold-leaf-embellished panels depict scenes from the Old Testament, that they named them the "Gates of Paradise." Also in Hicksville, in the Old Heitz Place courthouse and jail, is the **Hicksville Gregory Museum** (516-822-7505), an outstanding geology museum with over 4,000 rock and mineral specimens, including a fluorescent display, as well as fossils, seashells, Indian and local history artifacts, and a large Lepidoptera collection. *(Open Tues.–Fri. 9:30–4:40, Sat.–Sun. 1–5, closed holidays.)*

Just east of Wantagh, on Washington Ave. in Seaford, is another good place to study natural history, the **Tackapausha Museum and Preserve** (516-785-2802), with exhibits on the flora, fauna, and geological formation of Long Island. Several miles of nature trails wind through the preserve's 80-acre glacial outwash plain, where many species of birds nest. *(Open daily, 10–4:45, closed holidays except Memorial Day, July 4, Labor and Columbus days.)*

From Seaford, it's a short hop north to Bethpage, site of the year-round **Nassau Farmer's Market** (516-931-8400) on Route 107, open Friday and Saturday for shopping in 300 outdoor booths. Nearby, off Bethpage Parkway, is **Bethpage State Park** (516-249-0701), a beautifully groomed facility of almost 1,500 acres, with tennis courts, a regulation baseball diamond, hiking and biking trails, cross-country skiing, and a golfer's paradise of five 18-hole golf courses. North of the park, on Round Swamp Road, is the **Old Bethpage Village Restoration** (516-420-5288), a living history museum with 30 restored pre-Civil War buildings, a working farm, and costumed interpreters reenacting life on rural Long Island from 1830 to 1850, when the Industrial Revolution was beginning to make iteself felt. *(Open Tues.–Sun. 10–5, closing at 4 from Dec.–Feb.; closed holidays except Memorial Day, July 4, Labor and Columbus days, when closed the day after. Largely wheelchair-accessible.)*

Return to NY-27 and continue east through Massapequa across the Suffolk County line to Amityville, with many charming restored homes and antique shops. For an interesting slice of local history, stop in at the Amityville Historical Society's **Lauder Museum** (516-598-1486), where you can inquire about a walking tour of the historic village center. *(Open Tues., Fri., Sun. 2–4, free.)* Just east of Amityville is Lindenhurst, where the local historical society operates two more fine repositories of South Shore history, the **Old Village Hall Museum** (516-957-4385) and the 1901 **Restored Depot and Freight House** (516-226-1254), with railroad memorabilia and an old-time working telegraph system. *(Open July–Aug. Mon.–Fri. 1–3.)*

Continuing east a few miles on 27, you'll come to the Robert Moses Causeway, which takes you across Great South Bay to **Captree State Park** (516-669-0449), on the eastern tip of the same off-shore bar as Jones Beach (see above), and linked to it by Ocean Parkway. Captree is an ideal spot for fishermen, who can try their luck off the piers or rent a fishing boat at the dock.

Proceeding south across Fire Island Inlet on the Robert Moses Causeway, you come to **Robert Moses State Park** (516-669-0449), a 1,000-acre stretch of shore with fine beaches, windswept sand dunes, and excellent swimming and fishing areas. The park occupies the western tip of Fire Island, the famous 32-mile-long barrier beach and resort colony. **Fire Island National Seashore** (516-289-4810) comprises

The Tower at Jones Beach
(Photo courtesy of L.I. Convention & Visitors Bureau)

almost 20,000 acres of the island and has three areas open to the public: Sailors Haven, with marina, swimming beach, snack bar, visitor center, and nature and interpretive activities; Watch Hill, with comparable facilities plus a 26-site campground; and Smith Point West, with visitor center, interpretive activities, and a wheelchair-accessible boardwalk. The extraordinary Sunken Forest, a unique ecosystem trapped in a depression behind the dunes at Sailors Haven, displays many unusual plant adaptations and is shrouded in an air of primeval mystery.

The Robert Moses Causeway is one of only two auto routes to Fire Island; the other is the William Floyd Parkway/Smith Point Bridge at the eastern end. However, no roads run the length of the island, and the only way to reach the points in between is to walk or take one of several passenger ferries that run from the South Shore to various points on the island: **Fire Island Ferry Service** (516-665-3600) from Bay Shore, serving Saltaire, Kismet, Fair Harbor, Dunewood, and Ocean Beach, with charter trips to Sunken Forest; **Sayville Ferry Service** (516-589-0810) from Sayville, serving Fire Island Pines, Cherry Grove, and Barrett Beach; **Sunken Forest Ferry Company** (516-589-8980), also from Sayville, serving Sunken Forest/Sailors Haven; and **Davis Park Ferry Company** (516-475-1665) from Patchogue, serving Davis Park and Watch Hill.

From the Robert Moses Parkway, you can pick up **NY-27A,** Montauk Highway, and continue east to Bay Shore, one of the ferry terminals serving Fire Island. On the way, you'll pass **Sagtikos Manor** (516-665-0093), a Colonial mansion dating from the 1690s, home of an aristocratic family, headquarters of British general Henry Clinton during the Revolutionary War, proud recipient of an overnight stay by George Washington in 1790. *(Open July–Aug. Wed., Thurs., Sun. 1–4; Memorial Day–June & Sept. Sun. noon–4.)* A short way east, in Islip, is **The Grange** (516-472-7016), re-created Long Island farm village complete with a working windmill.

Continuing east briefly on 27A, you'll come to the junction with the Southern State Parkway, which takes you south to **Hecksher State Park** (516-581-2100), some 1,600 scenic acres facing Great South Bay, with 3 miles of waterfront, a nature preserve, and a range of recreational facilities. Just beyond the Southern State junction on 27A is the **Bayard Cutting Arboretum** (516-581-1002), under cultivation since 1887, with a magnificent collection of trees that includes some of the original plantings. The lovely Connetquot River flows by, attracting flocks of aquatic birds, and there are marked nature trails (some of them wheelchair-accessible) through the pinetum, the swamp cypresses, the rhododendron plantings, the wildflower section, and other beautiful areas of this 609-acre horticultural center. *(Open Wed.–Sun., 10–5, closing at 4 during standard time. Free.)* Just north of the arboretum is **Connetquot River State Preserve** (516-581-1005), almost 3,500 acres crisscrossed by hiking trails and bridle paths, with an old gristmill and a fish hatchery on the grounds.

Continue eastbound on 27A to the **Suffolk Marine Museum** (516-567-1733) in West Sayville, where you can see some fascinating exhibits on Long Island maritime history, including a turn-of-the-century boatshop, a 1907 restored oyster cull house, the oyster schooner *Priscilla* (1888) and sloop *Modesty* (1923), and a collection of equipment used in lieu of the poetic gifts of Lewis Carroll's Walrus to pry oysters from their beds. *(Open Mon.–Sat. 10–3, Sun. noon–4, closed Mon. in winter. Largely wheelchair-accessible.)* Nearby Sayville is a terminal for ferries to Fire Island (see above), as is Patchogue, another few miles east on 27A.

Another 3 miles east of Patchogue is a turnoff for Bellport, an interesting Great South Bay village listed on the National Register of Historic Places. Here you'll find the **Bellport-Brookhaven Historical Society Museum** (516-286-0888), a multi-building complex that includes a blacksmith shop, a milk house, the Post Crowell House, the Underhill Studio Museum of Early American Decoration, and the nearby **Barn Museum,** with an eclectic range of exhibits including marine and nautical displays, gyroscopic instruments designed by the noted American inventor Elmer A. Sperry, Indian artifacts, toys, and more. *(Open Memorial Day to Columbus Day, Thurs.–Sat. 1–4:30.)* In the neighboring shore community of Brookhaven, where the Carmans River empties into Bellport Bay, is **Wertheim National Wildlife Refuge** (516-286-0485), established in 1947 to preserve one of the last natural estuarine environments on Long Island. Because of its fragile ecology, the refuge is open to the public only along the Indian Landing Nature Trail, an excellent walk for birdwatchers and naturalists.

Returning to 27A (local road 80), you can continue east a few miles to the turnoff for Mastic Beach, passing the William Floyd Parkway, which leads across Smith Point Bridge to Fire Island (see above). In Mastic Beach, at 244 Park Drive, is the **William Floyd Estate** (516-399-2030), the 250-year-old homestead of Brookhaven-born William Floyd, Long Island's only signer of the Declaration of Independence.

The next stops, about 14 miles east of Mastic Beach, are quaint Quogue and fashionable Westhampton Beach, the former hugging an inlet of Moriches Bay, the latter surrounded by the water, both popular shore resort and recreation areas. In Quogue is the **Old Schoolhouse Museum** (516-653-4111), with artifacts and exhibits on local history. *(Open July–Aug., Mon., Wed., Fri. 2–5, Sat. 10–noon. Free.)*

Another 8 miles farther east on 27A (Montauk Highway, local road 80), where the Shinnecock Canal links Great Peconic Bay and Shinnecock Bay, is the last stop on this South Shore Drive, Hampton Bays, an appealing place for family outings, fishing expeditions, swimming, and sailing.

Trip G-4
Through the Hamptons to Montauk

- ## THE SOUTH FORK

DISTANCE: About 130 miles from Columbus Circle to Montauck Point.

FOR THE DRIVER: Road directions are incorporated into the site descriptions, below.

Here you can continue from the last stop on the South Shore, Hampton Bays, following NY-27/27A, Montauk Highway. For further information contact the Long Island Convention & Visitors Bureau, Nassau Coliseum, Uniondale, NY 11554 (1-800-441-4601). For the specific areas covered on this trip, you might also contact the Southampton Chamber of Commerce, 76 Main St., Southampton, NY 11968 (516-283-0402), the East Hampton Chamber of Commerce, 4 Main St., East Hampton, NY 11937 (516-324-0362), the Sag Harbor Chamber of Commerce, Box 116D, Sag Harbor, NY 11963 (516-725-0011), and Montauk Chamber of Commerce, Box CC, Montauk, NY 11954 (516-668-2428). If you visit a municipal beach, remember to inquire about nonresident permits or parking stickers.

THE SOUTH FORK means the Hamptons, and the Hamptons mean different things to different people. Reams have been written about this string of towns, which have been variously praised as *the* place to be on Long Island and criticized as being too "trendy." Whether your taste runs to celebrity watching or birdwatching, the fact remains that the Hamptons are beautiful and stately old towns, if a bit hectic at times. You may want to be in the thick of the fast-paced social scene, or visit during the week or in the off-season, but whenever you go, you'll soon see why so many of the famous and not-so-famous have succumbed to the Hamptons' charms.

Begin by following **NY-27A** (Montauk Highway, local route 80) across the Shinnecock Canal to Southampton, passing the **Shinnecock Indian Reservation,** site of the colorful Powwow held every year on Labor Day weekend. A prime shopping district, Southampton also offers many cultural and historical attractions. The **Parrish Art Museum** (516-283-2118) in the center of town has a fine permanent collection of paintings and sculptures, including many works by William Merritt

Chase, and sponsors an ambitious program of changing exhibits, concerts, lectures, films, and theatrical productions. *(Open Tues.–Sat.
10–5, Sun. 1–5.)* Southampton was settled in 1640, and its long history
is traced in the Indian, Colonial, and whaling exhibits at the **Southampton Historical Museum** (516-283-2494) on Meeting House Lane, a
lovely, sprawling frame house with restored outbuildings. *(Open mid-
June to mid-Sept., Tues.–Sun. 11–5.)* The **Halsey Homestead** (516-283-
3527) on South Main St. is the oldest saltbox in New York State, and
features period furnishings and a Colonial herb garden. *(Open mid-
June to mid-Sept., Tues.–Sun. 11–5.)*

East of Southampton, shortly after NY-27A merges with NY-27, is
Water Mill, originally 40 acres of land granted by the town of
Southampton to one Edward Howell in 1644, on condition that "sayd
Edward Howell doth promise to build for himself to supply the neces-
sities of the towne, a sufficient mill at Mecoxe." Over the years Howell's mill changed hands many times and provided power for grinding
grain, spinning cloth, and manufacturing paper. Today it has been
restored as the **Water Mill Museum** (516-726-4625) and once again grinds
grain as it did over three centuries ago. Also here are several innova-
tive exhibits on the history of milling and other vanished arts of the
preindustrial era, all designed to encourage visitor participation. *(Open
mid-May to mid-Sept., Thurs.–Sat. 11–5, Sun. 1–5).*

Continuing east on 27, you'll come to Bridgehampton, sometime
hangout of the literati and stop on the social circuit. At the **Bridgehampton Historical Museum** (516-537-1088), you can visit the 1775
Corwith Homestead, a blacksmith shop, and an old engine house.
(Open June–Labor Day, Thurs.– Mon. 10–4). A few miles northwest of
town, near Noyack, is the **Bridgehampton Race Circuit** (516-537-3770),
with auto and motorcycle racing from May to early fall.

From Bridgehamton you can head north on **NY-79,** passing the
Bridgehamton Winery (516-537-3155), open daily 11–6 for guided tours
and tastings. In the picturesque and pleasantly low-key town of Sag
Harbor, once the fourth-largest whaling port in the world, you'll find
many reminders of the Colonial and seafaring past. The **Sag Harbor
Whaling Museum** (516-725-0770), a Greek Revival mansion (1845) with
roof ornamentation of carved blubber spades and harpoons, and a
right whale jawbone arching over the doorway, has several rooms devoted to local history in addition to a large collection of whaling tools
and memorabilia. *(Open mid-May to late Sept., Mon.–Sat. 10–5, Sun.
1–5).* The restored 1787 **Custom House** (516-725-0250) recalls the days
when Sag Harbor was Long Island's principal port of entry. *(Open
Apr.–June Sat.–Sun. & July–Aug. daily, 10:30–4:30).* In the late 19th
century, after the whaling industry declined, Sag Harbor was the site
of a watchcasing factory that employed many Jewish workers. **Temple**

Adas Israel (516-725-1770), a white frame building with striking stained-glass windows, was built in 1898 to serve them and is Long Island's oldest Jewish temple. Above Sag Harbor is North Haven Peninsula, where you can board a ferry (516-749-1200) to Shelter Island (Trip G-2). Across from the peninsula, on a spot of land between Noyack and Little Peconic bays, is the **Elizabeth Morton National Wildlife Refuge** (516-286-0485).

The Sag Harbor-East Hampton Turnpike **(NY-114)** takes you to the next stop, perhaps the most beautiful town on Long Island, as rich in history and architecture as it is in society-page functions and designer labels. East Hampton is best seen on a walking tour, provided you can find a place to park. A good starting point is **Home, Sweet Home** (516-324-0713), inspiration for the 1820s song of that title and boyhood home of its author, actor and playwright John Howard Payne. Built in the late 17th century, it houses fine collections of American furnishings, a gallery with changing exhibits, and Payne memorabilia. The **Pantigo Windmill** (1771) and a period herb garden are on the grounds. *(Open year round, daily 10–4; closed holidays.)* Next door is the **Mulford Farm Museum,** a restored farmhouse built around 1680, now a museum of architectural history maintained by the East Hampton Historical Society. The society has its headquarters at the nearby **Osborn-Jackson House** (516-324-6850), a 1775 Colonial saltbox with later additions, and also maintains the 1784 **Clinton Academy** (516-324-6850), New York's first preparatory school. There's another historic windmill in East Hampton, the handsome and fully equipped **Hook Mill** (516-342-0713), built as a gristmill in 1806 and still up to the old grind. *(Open June–Sept., Mon., Wed.–Fri. 10–5, Sun. 2–5).*

The center of East Hampton cultural life is the **Guild Hall** (516-324-0806), with changing art exhibits and an interesting program of poetry readings and workshops. Guild Hall's **John Drew Theater** (516-324-4050) offers year-round entertainment and a particularly fine summer menu of theatrical productions, concerts, and films. Finally, like the other towns along the South Fork, East Hampton (village and town—note that the town includes East Hampton, Amagansett, and Montauk) offers a full range of facilities for fishing, boating, swimming, and other water sports.

Nearby Amagansett, just east of East Hampton, is a lovely small town with another good museum of local seafaring history, the **Town Marine Museum** (516-267-6544). In addition to whaling exhibits, shipwrecks, and a fascinating installation on underwater archeology, there are several displays on methods of commercial and sport fishing. *(Open June Sat.–Sun. 10–5, July–Aug. daily 10–5).*

The last stop, on the easternmost tip of Long Island far from the madding crowds, is Montauk, justly renowned for its excellent fishing—27 world-record catches have been hauled from its waters—and striking windswept scenery. In the past, Montauk has survived a couple of major development attempts (in one of the few happy results of the Depression, plans to turn it into a northern Miami Beach crashed along with the stock market, though the tower built by the would-be developer still stands rather incongruously in the heart of town), and despite recent encroachments, it remains relatively unscathed by the real-estate boom and social whirl of the Hamptons.

Montauk was settled in 1655 on land purchased from the Montaukett Indians, and danged if the cowboys didn't follow soon after, turning the place into a big ranch whose major social event was the annual cattle drive from Patchogue. There's a lot of wilderness left at several parks in the area, including **Hither Hills State Park** and the starkly beautiful **Montauk Point State Park** (516-668-2461), site of the historic Montauk Point Lighthouse, erected by order of George Washington in 1795.

You don't usually think about cowboys and Indians when you think of New York, much less about eons-old geological processes, but here at Montauk Point, gazing out into the vast gray Atlantic Ocean, you can almost imagine the birth of a continent and the discovery of a New World.

Montauk Point Lighthouse
(Photo courtesy of L.I. Convention & Visitors Bureau)

Index

Special interest attractions are also listed under their category headings.

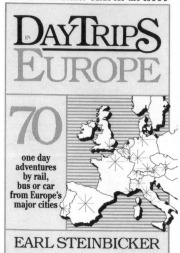

An Earl Steinbicker Guide for the 1990's

DAYTRIPS IN EUROPE

70

one day
adventures
by rail,
bus or car
from Europe's
major cities

EARL STEINBICKER

DAYTRIPS IN EUROPE

Created especially for travelers making the Grand Tour, *Daytrips in Europe* takes a fresh look at 70 of the most enjoyable destinations that can be explored on one-day excursions from London, Paris, Nice, Brussels, Luxembourg City, Amsterdam, Munich, Frankfurt, Vienna, Salzburg, Zürich, Geneva, Rome, Florence, Milan, Madrid, or Lisbon. Each trip description includes:

- A do-it-yourself walking tour
- A detailed town map
- Full travel directions by rail, bus, or car
- Time & weather considerations
- Price-keyed restaurant suggestions
- Photos and background information
- Concise descriptions of all worthwhile sights

92 Maps   97 Photos   432 Pages

• COMING SOON •

DAYTRIPS IN ISRAEL
25 one-day adventures by bus or car from your base in Jerusalem, Tel Aviv, Haifa, or Eilat. Explores the traditional Biblical sites, archaeological digs, natural splendors, ancient towns, modern cities, and places where history is being made today.

DAYTRIPS FROM WASHINGTON, DC
From Philadelphia in the north to Williamsburg in the south, both the famous and the obscure are included in the 50 daytrips described in this book. Walking tours of Washington are also featured.

More

DAYTRIPS

TRAVEL GUIDES BY EARL STEINBICKER

DAYTRIPS/LONDON
Explores the metropolis on 7 one-day walking tours, then describes 23 daytrips to destinations throughout nearby southeastern England. 39 large maps, 58 photos, 240 pages.

DAYTRIPS IN BRITAIN
Takes a close look at 60 of the most exciting destinations for daytrips from London and Edinburgh. 65 maps, 107 photos, 353 pages.

DAYTRIPS IN FRANCE
Describes 45 one-day excursions—including 5 walking tours of Paris, 23 daytrips from the city, 5 in Provence, and 12 along the Riviera. 55 maps, 89 photos. 3rd edition, 336 pages.

DAYTRIPS IN GERMANY
55 of Germany's most enticing destinations can be savored on daytrips from Munich, Frankfurt, Hamburg, and Berlin. Walking tours of the big cities are included. 62 maps, 94 photos. 3rd edition, 336 pages.

DAYTRIPS IN ITALY
Features 40 one-day adventures in and around Rome, Florence, Milan, Venice, and Naples. 45 maps, 69 photos. 2nd edition, 288 pages.

DAYTRIPS IN HOLLAND, BELGIUM AND LUXEMBOURG
Many unusual places are covered on these 40 daytrips, along with all the favorites plus the 3 major cities. 45 maps, 69 photos, 288 pages.

• BY ROBERT D. WOOD •

DAYTRIPS TO ARCHAEOLOGICAL MEXICO
Describes 12 travel routes by car or bus to 100 Pre-Columbian archaeological sites all over Mexico, ranging from the world-famous to the virtually unknown. 23 maps, 6 photos. Revised edition, 176 pages.

"Daytrips" travel guides, written or edited by Earl Steinbicker, describe the easiest and most natural way to travel on your own. Each volume in the growing series contains a balanced selection of enjoyable one-day adventures. Some of these are to famous attractions, while others feature little-known discoveries. For every destination there are historical facts, anecdotes, and a suggested do-it-yourself tour, a local map, travel directions, time and weather considerations, food and lodging recommendations, and concise background material.

SOLD AT LEADING BOOKSTORES EVERYWHERE

Or, if you prefer, by mail direct from the publisher. Use the handy coupon below or just jot your choices on a separate piece of paper.

Hastings House
141 Halstead Avenue
Mamaroneck, NY 10543

Please send the following books:

_____copies   **DAYTRIPS IN LONDON** @ $12.95   _____
(0-8038-9329-9)

_____copies   **DAYTRIPS IN BRITAIN** @ $12.95   _____
(0-8038-9301-9)

_____copies   **DAYTRIPS IN GERMANY** @ $12.95   _____
(0-8038-9327-2)

_____copies   **DAYTRIPS IN FRANCE** @ $12.95   _____
(0-8038-9344-2)

_____copies   **DAYTRIPS IN HOLLAND, BELGIUM**   _____
AND LUXEMBOURG @ $12.95
(0-8038-9310-8)

_____copies   **DAYTRIPS IN ITALY** @ $12.95   _____
(0-8038-9343-4)

_____copies   **DAYTRIPS IN EUROPE** @ $15.95   _____
(0-8038-9330-2)

_____copies   **DAYTRIPS FROM NEW**   _____
YORK @ $12.95
(0-8038-9332-9)

_____copies   **DAYTRIPS TO ARCHAEOLOGICAL**   _____
MEXICO @ $12.95
(0-8038-9336-1)

New York residents add tax: _____

Shipping and handling @ $2.50 per book: _____

Total amount enclosed (check or money order):   _____

Please ship to: _____

_____

_____